THE CLASSICAL ASSOCIATION
THE FIRST CENTURY 1903–2003

John Percival Postgate (1853–1926), whose article in the *Fortnightly Review* of November 1902 led to the founding of the CA just over a year later.

SUPPLEMENT TO **GREECE & ROME**

THE CLASSICAL ASSOCIATION

THE FIRST CENTURY 1903–2003

EDITED BY CHRISTOPHER STRAY

PUBLISHED FOR THE CLASSICAL ASSOCIATION
BY OXFORD UNIVERSITY PRESS 2003

OXFORD

UNIVERSITY PRESS

Oxford New York

Athens Auckland Bangkok Bogotá Bombay Buenos Aires Calcutta
Cape Town Chennai Dar es Salaam Delhi Florence Hong Kong Istanbul
Karachi Kuala Lumpur Madrid Melbourne Mexico City Mumbai
Nairobi Paris São Paulo Taipei Tokyo Toronto Warsaw

Oxford is a registered trade mark of Oxford University Press
in the UK and in certain other countries

ISSN 0017–3835
ISBN 0–19–852874–4

© Classical Association 2003

Typeset by Joshua Associates Ltd., Oxford
Printed in Great Britain
on acid-free paper by
Bell and Bain Ltd., Glasgow

CONTENTS

III Presidential Addresses

IV Appendices

ILLUSTRATIONS

Cover: The Association's logo is based on a coin of Zancle, and was selected by the Council from a number of ideas put forward by members. The dolphin, on an upward trajectory, represents the world of the Mediterranean, where classical culture originated, and the excitement and enjoyment it gives us. The dolphin was described when first introduced as 'cheerfully confident, but not complacent'.

ABBREVIATIONS

AAM	Association of Assistant Mistresses
AIGT	Association for the Improvement of Geometrical Teaching
AMA	Assistant Masters' Association
ARLT	Association for the Reform of Latin Teaching
CA	Classical Association
CAN	*CA News*
CAAS	Classical Association of the Atlantic States
CAMWS	Classical Association of the Middle West and South
CAS	Classical Association of Scotland
CJB	Classical Journals Board
CQ	*Classical Quarterly*
CR	*Classical Review*
CSCP	Cambridge School Classics Project
G&R	*Greece & Rome*
IAAM	Incorporated Association of Assistant Masters in Secondary Schools
ICS	Institute of Classical Studies
JACT	Joint Association of Classical Teachers
JHS	*Journal of Hellenic Studies*
JRS	*Journal of Roman Studies*
LACT	London Association of Classical Teachers
YWCS	*The Year's Work in Classical Studies*

FOREWORD

By ROBERT FOWLER

When the Council of the Association first entertained the idea of a centenary volume, a discussion ensued which readers of the outcome will recognize as typical: several councillors had clear ideas of what the volume should look like, and advanced their views with all the force, clarity, and tricolon'd rhetoric a classical education can impart; others were not so sure; the practical-minded began to think of costs, market-ability, problems of production; everyone bore in mind the varied needs of the CA's many constituencies; views both strong and diffident found expression with the same heedless courtesy, as among friends; all had one eye on the approaching hour for tea, and in the end the matter was referred for further discussion between the Officers and the volume's Editor, though not without a sense of emerging consensus that neither a complete, scholarly history nor a bundle of Presidential addresses was wanted. The volume was to be celebratory, and would have something of the character of a school year book, the year in this case being a century; the main readership, Council acknowledged, would be the CA itself. On the other hand, we had an important story to tell about scholarship, education and cultural history which would be of interest to people outside the Association, while at the same time reminding those within it that no classicist can ever afford to be complacent about the history of the subject. The resulting volume, therefore, is a suitable mix of research, memoirs, aperçus, perspectives, excerpts, and, in the end, a few Presidential Addresses.

Yet, if we cannot afford to be complacent, there is good reason to allow ourselves a moment's celebration. The CA at 100 is healthier than it has ever been. As a new Chair of Council assuming office after the Association's recent transformation, I am in a better position than most to say what an unqualified success the reforms have been. The progress of the change between 1989 and 2003 is eloquently chronicled by Malcolm Schofield within this volume, who gives full and deserved credit to the various players; here I am free to say, as he was not, that he played his full part along with them, bringing good humour, tact and diplomacy to the many delicate negotiations. The growth of the annual conference has been the clearest measure of the CA's success; as I write, here at the centenary meeting half an hour before the conference dinner, it is once again in full, boisterous swing. Membership, finances, publications, and sponsorships are all at healthy, indeed record levels. As has been the case throughout their history, some CA branches are less active than others, but the sum of activity is high. The balance in the Association of schools, universities, and the general public is not as even as it used to be, but the change in the relationship with school members, at least, is accounted for by the creation of the Joint Association of Classical Teachers, with whom the CA works closely. As for the public, though they are not present in large numbers at the annual conference, they are still well represented in the membership, and of course in the great tradition of lay Presidents. This year's President, Peter Jones, who with Jeannie Cohen (member of CA Council) manages the Friends of Classics, can attest that the level of interest in our subject in the country at large is extremely gratifying. It is not matched, I think, in any other country except Greece.

So there is reason to celebrate; but, as in every other year, there is cause for concern. Enrolments in language classes throughout the country have been slipping steadily in the last decade; the rate of decline is slower than in previous decades, but it continues unchecked nonetheless. Recently, however, enrolments have risen in GCSE Greek, for which JACT has produced a much-needed new text (supported by the CA). Barbara Bell's Primary School Latin Project (also supported by the CA) is now in use in over 1,000 schools, producing a bubble of demand which we may expect to rise up through the system. Classical Studies and Ancient History courses are enjoying increased demand at universities. The lone soul who voted against all change at Southampton in 1960 (I have a kind of sneaking admiration for that man, as one admires members of the Flat Earth Society: it takes a special kind of genius to hold out so magnificently against all the evidence) had a point, if in our heart of hearts we think that we would prefer still to be teaching all those hordes their Latin and Greek, and be living in a world where Classics is the established church of education. But whether or not that world was a better one, consider what has happened as a result of the reforms of the 1960s, mirrored in America: the riches of the ancient world have been made available to many more people than ever before; and of those many, a significant number acquire at least some knowledge of the languages. That has to be a good thing.

The CA has faced some grave difficulties in the course of its history, but has always come up trumps. The reason is, without doubt, the dedication of its members. The sense that there is a faith to keep is visible in the earliest documents, in every Presidential Address, and in Council's most recent decisions. As Basil Lanneau Gildersleeve (President of the American Philological Association 1877–78) remarked, classicists' occupation is their avocation. They respond to that call sometimes with religious fervour. Even in 1903 Classics seemed to be fighting a rearguard action against the unbelievers; to counter the threat was the reason for foundation. Conditions in the UK have not changed fundamentally; we still must defend our patch, and cannot take our future for granted. The numbers, of course, are much smaller now, and some might reckon that a failure. But in the face of rampant modernism we have really done rather well. In 2003, the naïve belief in the power of technology to effect progress that caused such damage in the 1960s has become disillusioned, and the jobs-oriented mentality of those who determine the school curriculum is coming under pressure. Popular interest in antiquity is booming; perhaps we may dare to hope that it will be sustained, and have lasting effects in schools, universities, and the world at large.

At the conference dinner (I have finished eating it now) a warmly-welcomed delegation from the APA and the Classical Association of the Atlantic States delivered congratulations and best wishes. The birthday card bore an inscription, adapted from Catullus:

plus uno maneas perenne saeclo.

On past patterns, it is a very realistic hope.

University of Warwick, 13 April 2003

INTRODUCTION

This book, which celebrates the history of the Classical Association, has its own history. When the idea of publishing a celebration of the Association's first century was first mooted, what was thought of was a short booklet providing a historical sketch. The counter-proposal which was accepted was for a collaborative volume which would draw on the experience and interest of CA members to combine a chronological narrative with discussions of different aspects of the Association's activities. This relaxed format has made it possible also to include three samples of that curious genre, the Presidential Address. The plan of the book is as follows. Section I (Chapters 1–5) consists of narrative chapters which describe the CA's foundation and early years, its role in the crisis caused by the abolition of Compulsory Latin in 1960, and its development and revival in the last thirty years. In Section II (Chapters 6–17), four major aspects of the Association's history are surveyed: publications, conferences, branches, and presidents. Section III contains three outstanding Presidential Addresses, with a discussion of the genre by Malcolm Schofield. Finally, Section IV (Appendices 1–4) provides reference material on the history of the CA, officers and on archives, together with an account of the Classical Association of Scotland.

Centuries, like their greater relations the millennia, have an arbitrary but undeniable power to fascinate. In the present context, what is worth noting is that a flurry of foundation activity in one period plants the seeds of centennial retrospection a hundred years later. (Sometimes, indeed, not quite a hundred years – it is not uncommon for societies to get their dates wrong.) The clustered dates of foundation of subject associations in England, discussed in Chapter 1, suggest indeed that a comparative analysis of the phenomenon might be productive. That is not attempted here; nor is a detailed narrative history of the Association's first century. That would have required both more time than has been available (centenaries do not wait), and a systematic cataloguing of the CA's archive. This is rich in evidence for the various aspects of the Association's activities, and when catalogued should provide a fertile basis for a future historian. The archive has however been drawn on in the chapters on the CA's foundation and early years, and on the history of its several publications. What this book loses in the systematic coherence of a single-authored narrative history it gains, I believe, in the variety of the voices to be heard in its sections and chapters – presidents, officers, editors, and members.

Assembling the book has been a complex exercise, but the load has been lightened by the willing co-operation of the contributors. The range of the volume has been extended by Ronald Knox's engaging memoir of the Classical Association of Scotland, which he generously allowed us to include. Clare Morton and her team at OUP have provided advice on format, as has Martin Maw on access to archival material. Pip Sampson kindly combed the Press's journals archive and sent copies of material relating to the history of *Greece & Rome*. My major debt is to Malcolm Schofield and Philip Hooker, who have been unstinting with advice, information and criticism.

Dilys Powell's Presidential Address is reprinted by permission of Ivor B. Powell; Robert Runcie's by permission of Rosalind Runcie. The Address by Carol Handley, and extracts from that of Tony Harrison, are reprinted by permission of the authors.

Christopher Stray
May 2003

CONTRIBUTORS

Gillian Clark is Professor of Ancient History at the University of Bristol.

Barbara Finney has been Honorary Secretary of the CA, with responsibility for branches, since 1997.

Martin Forrest was formerly Senior Lecturer in Education at the University of the West of England.

Robert Fowler is Professor of Greek at the University of Bristol. He has been Chair of the CA Council since 2002.

Carol Handley was formerly Headmistress of Camden School for Girls; she was President of the CA in 1997.

Philip Hooker is a stockbroker with Hoare Govett, London, and has been Treasurer of the CA since 2000.

Ronald Knox is Lecturer in Classics in the Department of Classics, University of Glasgow, and was Secretary of the Classical Association of Scotland from 1995 to 2002.

Ian McAuslan teaches at Eton College, where he was Head of Classics from 1980 to 1992; he has been editor of *Greece & Rome* since 1977 and is now responsible for *New Surveys*.

Jenny March has been editor of *CA News* since its foundation in 1989.

John Muir was formerly Vice-Principal of King's College London.

The late Dilys Powell, a lifelong lover of Greece and a celebrated film critic, was President of the CA in 1967.

Clare Roberts has been Executive Secretary of the CA since 1999.

The late Robert Runcie was Archbishop of Canterbury from 1979 to 1991, and President of the CA in 1992.

Malcolm Schofield is Professor of Ancient Philosophy in the University of Cambridge, and was from 1989 to 2003 Honorary Secretary of the CA.

Christopher Stray is Honorary Research Fellow in the Department of Classics and Ancient History, University of Wales Swansea.

I

Narrative

1

THE FOUNDATION AND ITS CONTEXTS

By CHRISTOPHER STRAY

The Classical Association of England and Wales was formally founded at a public meeting held in the Botanical Theatre of University College London on 19 December 1903. As with other such foundation meetings, we can assume that the programme had been carefully prepared in advance to make sure that all the right proposals were made, and approved. Preparation is also evident in the list of those who convened the meeting: Principal N. Bodington, University of Leeds; Professor R. S. Conway, University of Manchester; Dr J. Gow, headmaster of Westminster School; Miss E. Penrose, principal of Royal Holloway College; Dr J. P. Postgate of Trinity College, Cambridge; Mr A. Sidgwick of Corpus Christi College, Oxford; and Professor E. A. Sonnenschein of the University of Birmingham. This little group reflects in its constitution the range of interests needing to be included: the two ancient universities, the civic universities, the public schools, and women.

The seriousness with which the issue of female membership was treated is clear from the first resolution adopted at the UCL meeting: 'That an Association open to persons of either sex, to be called THE CLASSICAL ASSOCIATION OF ENGLAND AND WALES, be and is hereby constituted'.[1] One could hardly be more up-front with the declaration of equal access.[2] Those who drafted the constitution surely had two considerations in mind. One was that the issue of female access to learned and semi-learned societies had been a contentious one in the previous decades. There had been a running battle within the Royal Geographical Society, for example, where the issues were pointed up by

---

[1] 'Of England and Wales', later deleted, was included in deference to the Classical Association of Scotland, founded in 1902. For the history of the CAS, see Appendix 1.

[2] The constitution agreed in 1904 included as Clause 14, 'Membership of the Association shall be open to all persons of either sex who are in sympathy with its objects.' A defeated amendment would have substituted 'all persons who are in sympathy with the objects of the Association. Women shall be eligible to offices' (a cumbrous attempt, perhaps, to avoid the use of the word 'sex'). The clause was deleted from the constitution in 1971.

invitations to distinguished women speakers, who were nevertheless ineligible for membership because of their sex. The Hellenic Society's rules, issued after its foundation in 1879, had ended with Rule 32, which declared that 'Ladies shall be eligible as Ordinary members of the Society, and when elected shall be entitled to the same privileges as other Ordinary members'. That rule, though its position suggests it was an afterthought, enshrined what was for its day an enlightened policy. By 1903, the controversies on the issue had died down, but were perhaps fresh enough in the founders' memory to prompt them to make the new body's policy explicit. The second consideration was that members were needed – the more the better. UCL itself had opened its classes to women in 1868, not because of a change of heart on matters of principle, but because of a fear that its intake would otherwise be seriously affected by competition from the civic universities, who already accepted women. Emily Penrose, the only woman in the convening group, was as near to the heart of the academic and cultural establishment as a woman could be. Her father Francis Penrose, who had died earlier in 1903, was the nephew of Thomas Arnold's wife. He had had a distinguished career as an architect, studying the temples of the Acropolis and advising on changes at St Paul's. He had served as the first director of the British School at Athens (1886–7), and again in 1890–1. Emily herself belonged to the first generation of women to reach high academic office. At Oxford she had become the first woman to achieve a first in Greats. Her career began was as principal (and soon after, also professor of ancient history) at Bedford College, from which she moved to Royal Holloway in 1898. She later served as principal of Somerville, her old college, and as a member of the 1919 Royal Commission on Oxford.

If there is any one person who could be called the founder of the CA, it is Postgate. He was in 1903 the senior Latinist at Cambridge, and had published extensively on Latin poetry. He also served as Professor of Comparative Philology at University College London from 1880 to 1910, and it is doubtless this link which explains the choice of venue for the foundation meeting. After the aged J. E. B. Mayor's death in 1910, Postgate might have been expected to succeed him; but in the previous year he had moved to a chair at Liverpool, and in case Housman's star was by then in the ascendant.[3] From the beginning of his career at Cambridge

[3] Technically Mayor, Professor of Latin 1872–1910, was the senior Cambridge Latinist in 1903, but his interests had turned to vegetarianism. He had considered retiring from his chair in 1895, but clung to it because the post carried no pension. His famous cheap diet had economic as well as

(he was elected to a Trinity fellowship in 1878), Postgate had shown himself to be an energetic and effective organiser. He had acted as secretary of the Cambridge Philological Society for some years, and had been editor of the *Classical Review* since 1899. His claim to be seen as the CA's founder, however, rests on the article entitled 'Are the Classics to go?' which appeared in the *Fortnightly Review* in November 1902. It was this article which led to a 'large and prolonged correspondence', and eventually to the foundation meeting of December 1903.[4]

Postgate's article is an eloquent and forceful call to arms, and deserves to be quoted. He opened as follows:

The languages and literatures which have had the greatest influence upon the modern world are incontestably three – the Hebrew, the Greek, and the Latin. The first of the three is now hardly more than a study for specialists; and the world is asking already, in Europe at any rate, 'Is this not the doom of the remaining two as well?' On many sides we hear confident assertions, met for the most part by half-hearted and apologetic denials, that the work of Greek and Latin is done – that their day is past. If the extinction of these languages as potent instruments of education is a sacrifice inexorably demanded by the advancement of civilisation, regrets are idle, and we must bow to necessity. But we know from history that not the least of the causes of the fall of great supremacies has been the supineness and shortsightedness of their defenders. It is therefore the duty of those who believe, as I do, that Greek and Latin may continue to confer in the future, as they have done in the past, priceless benefits upon all higher human education, to inquire whether these causes exist, and how they may be at once removed. For if these studies fall, they fall like Lucifer. We can assuredly hope for no second Renaissance.

This admirable exordium has several notable features. The first is Postgate's willingness to point the finger at the half-hearted and the mealy-mouthed: no pretence of the universal virtue for classicists for him. Secondly, he provides a long-term historical context for the current crisis, not only by comparing Latin and Greek with (the fate of) Hebrew, but by invoking both the Renaissance and the myth-history of Christianity. We should remember that the shadow of Anglican faith, and its long association with Classics, still hung over at least the older members of Postgate's audience.[5]

Postgate went on to declare:

---

vegetable roots. See J. Henderson, *Juvenal's Mayor: the Professor who Lived on 2d a day*, PCPS supp. vol. 20 (Cambridge, 1998).

[4] The phrase comes from the *DNB* article on Postgate, written by another of the CA's convening group, R. S. Conway. Postgate's article appeared in the *Fortnightly Review* NS 72 (November 1902), 886–80.

[5] As it did over those who heard the biblical references in A. E. Housman's inaugural lecture seven years later in 1911.

At a time when we appear to be on the eve of extensive reconstructions in the higher educational system of the country, the first duty of those who believe that a due recognition of the claims of Greek and Latin is vital to our intellectual welfare is to know what they want. It is clear that the Classics will not be allowed the lion's share which has been theirs in the past, and the question is, how much must we struggle to retain.

Altogether, a bracing call to arms, and one which combines an affirmation of the author's faith in classics with a realisation that in practical politics, compromises have to be made. The article displays the pragmatic grasp that can also be seen in the note on 'Some friends of the classics' which Postgate had contributed editorially to the *Classical Review* earlier in 1903:

Classics are now being pressed on one side by the advance of science, on the other by that of modern languages. The latter are its more dangerous opponents. They provide to a certain point the same advantages as the classics; their methods are up to date and their teachers alert and enterprising. How then can they be resisted if confronted only by antiquated methods and a defence which is both backward and supine? High aesthetic and intellectual considerations are all very well; but they are of no avail in a squeeze.[6]

Though Postgate's *Fortnightly Review* article was published in November 1902, he states in an appended note that it was written 'some months ago' and that since then there have been 'some signs of an awakening', such as the foundation on 1 March of the Classical Association of Scotland. This suggests that the article was drafted in the run up to the passage of Balfour's Education Act, which passed through parliament at the end of March. Postgate was probably referring to it *inter alia* in his warning of 'extensive reconstructions in the higher educational system'.[7] The 1902 Act abolished the 2,500-odd locally-elected school boards, replacing them with 140 local educational authorities. Many of the tendencies of the Act were in fact conservative – not surprisingly, as it was passed by a Conservative government. In addition, the Board of Education, set up in 1899 to act as a central authority in England and Wales, was staffed in its higher levels by Oxford and Cambridge men, including several who had read Classics. Two of them, J. W. Mackail and J. W. Headlam, feature prominently a little later in this account. Yet Postgate was not the only classicist to sense in these new developments the thin end of a wedge harmful to the subject.

[6] *CR* 17 (1903), 2. Though the phrase 'backward and supine' is not directed explicitly at him, it seems to be aimed at G. G. Ramsay, first president of the CA of Scotland, whose inaugural address Postgate refers to just before the passage quoted above. (It can be read in *Proceedings of the Classical Association of Scotland* (1902–3), 1–33.)

[7] 'Higher' at that time often referred to any level above elementary education. It was so used in the Education Acts of 1902 and 1921. See the note on the term in Board of Education, *The Education of the Adolescent* (London, 1926), 265–6.

To understand why the 1902 Act caused such alarm in some circles – for Postgate was not a lonely voice – we have to remember that English education had up till then been free of state intervention to a degree unparalleled elsewhere in Europe. The centralised mass education system of post-revolutionary France had been copied by Prussia in the early nineteenth century, but in England the first state schools had to wait till after the 1870 Act, which set up a system of state elementary education (not compulsory till 1881). To the public schools and the religious denominations, both of whom had flourished in the absence of effective state control, the 1902 Act clearly represented the tightening of the screw. The leading public schools had been investigated by the Clarendon Commission (1861), but its conclusions on the curriculum were that the amount of time spent on classics might be reduced to three fifths. A subsequent royal commission on endowed grammar schools (Taunton, 1864) had recommended that state control be delegated to regional bodies. The threat of state intervention prompted the foundation of the Headmasters' Conference in 1869, and by 1902 this had become a large and influential body. The official line of the Board of Education (1899) was that it was not to control schools, but merely establish their eligibility for grants. This was however not enough to allay the suspicions of the public schools, whose curriculum was still dominated by classics (Postgate's 'lion's share'). Oxford and Cambridge were also nervous of intervention. The last royal commissions to investigate them, in the 1870s, had made colleges liable to support university funding, and the decline in college funding during the agricultural depression of the 1870s and 1880s had brought the spectre of state funding closer. With state funding came, it was feared, state control. For the arts dons, who were in the majority at both universities, classics was inextricably bound up with this issue, since it was seen as the exemplar of humanistic learning. The long battle over the abolition of Compulsory Greek, which had flared up in 1902 and would do so again two years later, illustrate this entanglement. What was at issue was not just the transcendental value of humanistic learning, symbolised above all by Greek. It was also the right of the universities to decide what they taught, and what requirements they imposed on their students.[8] Fourteen years later, in 1917, a solution

[8] On Compulsory Greek, see C. A. Stray, *Classics Transformed* (Oxford, 1998), 164–6, 265–9; J. Raphaely, 'Nothing but gibberish and shibboleths? The Compulsory Greek debates, 1871–1919', in C. A. Stray (ed.), *Classics in 19ᵗʰ and 20ᵗʰ century Cambridge*, PCPS supp. vol. no 24 (Cambridge, 1999), 71–94.

was found in the establishment of the University Grants Committee, which administered state money but operated at arm's length from government. The gentlemanly consensus which underpinned this arrangement, of course, is now long vanished.

The other development to which Postgate probably referred was a more clear and present danger: the recent changes in London University matriculation requirements. Previously candidates were obliged to sit two papers each in English, maths, Latin and science. Now one paper of Latin only was provided, and candidates could choose between it and a science. The new regulations also removed set books from the Latin paper. In his editorial in *CR* for July 1902, Postgate warned that the changes 'are bound to affect seriously the study of the two classical languages in this country . . . Let classical teachers look to it. The hand has begun to write upon the wall.'[9] Postgate had become editor of the *Review* in October 1898, and had not hesitated to draw his readers' attention to such developments. In 1901 he had printed two letters on classical education by 'G. H. S.', an Oxford graduate and cultured despiser of classics. G. H. S. had been profoundly dissatisfied by his experience of Mods, and concluded that classics was only of interest to specialists: a hackneyed field which he could never fully understand.[10] In April 1902, Postgate welcomed the foundation the previous month of the Classical Association of Scotland, expressing the hope that it 'will be the fore-runner of a Classical Association of England . . .'.[11] In May 1903, the Cambridge Classical Society was founded, at a meeting where 'some of the speakers . . . suggested the further possibility of forming in England a Classical Association on the lines of the Classical Association of Scotland'.[12] By June, Postgate was able to report that steps were being taken to found such an association, and to give the names of the other six members of the group which convened the foundation meeting.[13] The group put out a prospectus in the last week of November with about a hundred names in support; by the end of the month, Postgate claimed, they had between 200 and 300 signatures.[14]

---

[9] *CR* 16 (1902), 289.
[10] 'Classics in education', *CR* 15 (1901), 281–4, 320–2; for Postgate's comments, see ibid., 289–90.
[11] Editorial, *CR* 16 (1902), 145.
[12] *CR* 17 (1903), 268. It is probable that Postgate was one of those speakers.
[13] Ibid., 236.
[14] Ibid., 429. No copy of the prospectus has been found.

The foundation meeting

No record survives of how many attended the foundation meeting on that Saturday afternoon in December 1903, but detailed accounts of the proceedings give a sense of the occasion.[15] The meeting was opened by the major catch of the day, the Master of the Rolls, Sir Richard Henn Collins.[16] Preaching the virtues of a classical training – it 'trained a man to receive other ideas' – he candidly admitted that there had been a reaction against the dominant position of the subject in the public schools: 'they were perhaps not concerned to deny that some of those students who had passed through our public schools had not quite reached the standard of Senior Classics when they came away from school (laughter).' Collins went on to urge that the new body's motto should be 'Defence, not defiance' – echoing the motto of the more conciliatory trades unions. Proposing the foundation of the Association, the Oxford Vice-Chancellor, the Homerist D. B. Monro, drew a parallel with the annual meetings (Philologen-Versammlungen) held in Germany, and hoped that the new body would provide a similar focus for discussion in England.[17]

Next, Postgate stepped forward to deliver an oration in his best pungent style. That 'strong and masterful people the Romans' had bowed to the intellectual superiority of the Greeks. But there was another people (one imagines him moving to *fortissimo* at this point) which possessed a literature comparable only with the literature of Greece. That literature was our own (cheers). But as for the literature of the present day, could they regard it with supreme feelings of contentment? (laughter). There was a tawdriness, a feverishness, a frivolity about it of which they would look for parallels in Greece and Rome. Think of Plato and Rudyard Kipling! (laughter) As for translations, claimed by some to be an adequate substitute for the original texts, what were they? Pickled salmon, tinned salmon!' (laughter). Postgate ended by quoting from Holy Writ: 'Set thine house in order and it shall live' (cheers).

[15] *The Times*, Monday 21 December 1903 (condensed, but reports cheering and laughter); *CR* 18 (1904), 64–9. This latter account was reprinted to mark the Association's coming of age: *Proceedings* 22 (1925), 92–105.

[16] Herbert Asquith sent his regrets, as did the masters of Magdalen College, Oxford (Herbert Warren) and of Trinity College, Cambridge (Montagu Butler), Sir Richard Jebb, T. E. Page and several others.

[17] See Malcolm Schofield's account in Chapter 5 for a later proposal on the same lines with reference to the American Philological Association.

This rousing speech was followed by what appears from the *Times* report to have been a brief word from Emily Penrose. In fact, as the full report of the meeting makes clear, she spoke for several minutes; but her contribution, like that of the other female speaker, the Cambridge-trained Eugénie Strong, was heavily condensed by the *Times*. Penrose stressed the special value of an association for women teachers of classics, who were much less likely to have fellow classicists in their schools than were the masters at boys' public schools. This part of her speech was omitted by the *Times*. Next, the Vice-Chancellor of Cambridge[18] moved a proposal for the objects of the new Association and was seconded. The meeting then descended to details, constitutional and financial (a five-shilling subscription), and ended with an announcement that the membership already stood at 450.[19]

One of the bread-and-butter motions proposed toward the end of the meeting urged that annual meetings should be held in university towns. The proposer was Edward Adolf Sonnenschein, professor of Classics at Birmingham, who was to become as influential as Postgate himself in the running of the CA. He acted as temporary secretary to the Council, and with Postgate was appointed Honorary Secretary to the Association. The two men had much in common. Both had fathers who were experienced campaigners for reform. John Postgate senior had been MP for Birmingham, and had fought a long and eventually successful battle for legislation on food purity.[20] Adolf Sonnenschein, a member of a Moravian Jewish family, had published widely on educational reform, and was a successful mathematics teacher in both schools and colleges (including Bedford College, the London women's college). Edward Sonnenschein's experience of the lack of co-ordination of language teaching as a headmaster in Glasgow had inspired him to campaign for the use of a uniform grammatical terminology; he had also led a campaign at Birmingham for control of the university by academics rather than by local magnates and benefactors.[21]

After the public success of the meeting, the Council it had appointed was left to begin the hard graft of running the new Association. Their very first meeting, on 9 January 1904, had some setbacks to deal with.

[18] F. H. Chase, 8th classic 1878; Norrisian Professor of Divinity and president of Queens' College; later Bishop of Ely.

[19] By the following July, it had reached 720. (Council minutes, 9 July 1904). In October 1906 it stood at 1140; 1250 in October 1907; 1350 in October 1908. (Council minutes, 9 October 1908).

[20] Postgate's 'pickled salmon' metaphor perhaps echoes this concern. Cf. his article on 'To "eat" and to "drink" in Latin', *CR* 16 (1902), 110–15.

[21] Both men are in *DNB*. For Sonnenschein's campaigns, see a booklet by his son: E. J. Somerset *The Birth of a University. A Passage in the Life of E. A. Sonnenschein* (Oxford, 1934).

Emily Penrose had been elected one of their number, presumably with her consent, but on the day before the meeting sent in a letter of resignation.[22] Walter Leaf, appointed treasurer at the December meeting, had already made it clear that he would not serve, and J. W. Mackail agreed to take his place *pro tem.*[23] More damaging than either resignation was the letter of complaint sent by the Cambridge Vice-Chancellor. He was ex-officio chairman of a syndicate recently set up by the university to examine its curriculum, and having heard an attack on the syndicate by Postgate, felt that his official position might be compromised if he remained a member of the CA. Would the new Association take up 'militant' positions in public on such matters? If it might do so, he thought it best to resign. Sonnenschein assured him in his reply that the CA had no intention of doing anything which would commit it to a 'controversial attitude' on such questions.[24]

The issue was clearly one which lay at the heart of the CA's strategy. It had been founded to defend classics from its enemies, and as we have seen, Postgate, in his usual trenchant way, had been ready to identify at least some of them. Monro, in his speech to the foundation meeting, had been more diplomatic:

They were not there in any narrow spirit of intolerance of other studies . . . there was no department of intellectual effort which the classic did not look upon with sympathy . . . The study of classics trained a man to receive other ideas, to prove and assimilate them . . .[25]

The dilemma was plain: the CA was confronted by a choice between warfare and diplomacy, each with its benefits and disadvantages. In practice, as with most such organisations, the choice was refused. The public voice of the Association preached a dignified message of defence, reaching out to potential allies and building bridges wherever it could. In private, the scientists, the modern linguists, the government and philistine parents were denounced. The overall policy was dictated by the situation of Classics in public schools and universities as a dominant force whose dominance was declining, and would clearly continue to do so. Its defenders were obliged to make obeisance both to the transcendental virtues of mental training and cultural value they ascribed to it, and

[22] This was because of her other commitments. Sonnenschein having urged on her that it was 'impolitic' for one of the original signatories to withdraw from the Council, she agreed to stay, although she would only be able to attend one of four proposed meetings. (Council minutes, 13 February 1904.)

[23] Leaf was the obvious candidate, being both an accomplished classical scholar and a banker. He acted as treasurer of the British School at Athens.

[24] Council minute book, meeting of 9 January 1904.

[25] *Proceedings* 22 (1925), 94, quoted from the third-person account which was then conventional.

to the English sense of fair play appealed to by their opponents. In short, they needed to manage what Gilbert Murray called 'an orderly retreat', while forging alliances with as many as possible of their potential rivals for time in school and university curricula. And to appear 'orderly', they had to avoid internal divisions, while promoting discussion of questions of policy, curriculum and teaching method.

Friends and rivals

The new association entered an arena already populated with special interest bodies of various kinds. Its restriction to England and Wales was dictated by the founding of the Classical Association of Scotland in the previous year. At the end of 1905 W. R. Hardie, president of the CAS, wrote to Henry Butcher, the CA president, suggesting that 'some kind of combination or alliance . . . seems desirable – perhaps a merely financial arrangement'. He went on to propose a combined subscription system in which part of a subscription would be transferred between the two bodies.[26] We don't know what the Council thought of this, since the minutes tell us only that the Finance Committee stated their opinion, and that Butcher undertook to communicate it to Hardie. The implication is that it was negative.[27] Later on, we hear that informal negotiations took place between the two bodies on the proposed removal of the phrase 'of England and Wales' from the CA's title. The Council were in favour of this, apparently because it would make it easier to bring overseas bodies into association. The phrase was dropped from the CA's title in 1906, no objection being raised from north of the border.[28]

Ireland was a different matter – it had no organised association of classicists (and was of course at this point still part of the Union). Miss M. C. Dawes, a member from Weybridge, wrote to suggest that Ireland be included in the Association's title, but Professors Tyrrell and Purser of Trinity College Dublin, consulted by Sonnenschein, advised against the move. Few members would be gained, they thought, and in any case there was nothing to stop Irish residents from joining.[29] Their discoura-

---

[26] The two men knew each other well, and it is possible that the letter was agreed between them beforehand. Hardie had been Professor of Humanity (i.e. Latin) at Edinburgh since 1895; Butcher was appointed to the Greek chair there in 1882 and had only recently resigned it.

[27] Council minutes, 3 February and 3 March, 1906. For later attempts at combination, see Ronald Knox's account of the history of the CAS in Appendix 1.

[28] Council minutes, 21 October 1905.

[29] Council minutes, 12 March 1904.

ging response was followed, however, by a vigorously supportive letter from Henry Browne, professor of Greek at TCD's Catholic neighbour, University College.[30] He had consulted his UCD colleagues and some of the classical fellows of TCD, including the Professor of Greek, John Beare, and had found general support for the extension of the CA's remit to Ireland. Two later letters display a gradual abandonment of hope: '. . . things here are at a standstill, and nothing further can be done. To me it is most disappointing, especially as the difficulties are most trivial . . .' [31] The source of the 'trivial difficulties' can only be guessed at – so let me offer but two guesses: (1) there was disagreement between TCD and its younger Catholic counterpart. The relationship, in this context, might be compared with that between Cambridge and Oxford – the older, more classically dominated institution being more reluctant to act; (2) there was a split between the supporters of membership of the CA and those who wanted to establish an Irish counterpart. The Classical Association of Ireland was in fact founded in 1908, prompted by the establishment of the National University of Ireland by the Irish University Act in that year.[32] John Beare was eventually appointed local representative of the CA for Dublin, thus maintaining a (tenuous) link with Ireland.[33]

Subsequent letters from Henry Browne suggest that Beare's sphere of action was confined to Trinity College. In 1906, Sonnenschein asked Browne to act as local representative for the Royal University of Ireland (to which UCD belonged). Browne replied in May of that year, offering to do what he could, but warning that 'the Catholic colleges, which are really secondary schools', would not act unless the universities took a lead. Presumably Sonnenschein expressed his bafflement at the state of Irish education, for a week later, Browne wrote again:

Academical arrangements are so mixed here that I do not wonder your Council find it difficult to understand them. The Royal University . . . is strictly undenominational in theory, but practically acts for Presbyterians and Catholics about equally – while the Church people go to Trinity. . . . I agree with you there would be great danger of wrecking the whole thing, if any thing like religious sections were recognised by the

[30] Browne was an energetic reformer, some of whose opinions can be recovered from his *Our Renaissance: Essays on the Reform and Revival of Classical Studies* (London, 1917). The Classical Museum he set up there, and for which he acquired coins and other antiquities, flourishes to this day.

[31] Browne to Sonnenschein, 22 May 1904 (Council minutes, 27 May 1904).

[32] The Association published proceedings from 1908 until 1920, but went into abeyance in the 1920's, leaving a gap which was not filled until the founding of the Association of Classical Teachers in 1958. In 1993 the ACT relaunched itself as the Classical Association of Ireland.

[33] Council minutes, 11 November 1905. The appointment of such representatives is discussed further below.

Classical Association, and for this reason I do not think the proposal to have different local correspondents for different local churches a good one. If the Council are of opinion that on account of the backwardness of Trinity College, it is unwise to recognise the Royal University as a separate sphere of action at present, it would be much better to leave the whole matter in abeyance . . . [34]

Beyond Classics itself, there were other subject associations, which might be seen variously as potential allies, rivals or opponents: the Modern Language Association (1892), the Geographical Association (1893), the Mathematical Association (1897) and the Association of Public School Science Masters (1901). By the outbreak of war in 1914, these had been joined by the Historical Association (1906), the English Association (1907) and the Association of Women Science Teachers (1912). Most of these organisations represented the teachers of subjects which were relatively new to the formal curriculum of the public schools and universities. English, for example, had entered the Oxford syllabus only in the 1890s, and would not be formally recognised in Cambridge until 1917. One of the bases for their foundation or development was the recognition of specialist subjects, first in the post-1870 elementary schools, and then in the municipal secondary schools set up after the 1902 Act. In some cases – this is most evident in science – differences of interest and self-image were evident between the largely male teachers in the public schools and the often female staff of the new secondary schools. The histories of the two science associations, the APSSM and AWST, provide a striking case study.[35] (The opposed resonances of the terms 'master' and 'teacher' symbolised the separate but overlapping gaps of status and gender.)[36] The AWST began life as the Association of Science Teachers, but changed its name in 1922. Meanwhile the APSSM had extended its membership to secondary school teachers in 1919, changing its name to the Science Masters' Association. For 41 years, the AWST and SMA worked separately but in parallel, until in 1963 they merged as the Association for Science Education: now a body with over 20,000 members. One of the bases for this unique long-term separation lay in the distribution of teachers among different school subjects. The men dominated the 'hard' science subject like physics and chemistry, whereas teachers of biology and botany were almost all

---

[34] Browne to Sonnenschein, 23 and 30 May 1906. (Council minutes, 23 June 1906).

[35] For the history of the ASE and its predecessors, see David Layton, *Interpreters of Science* (London, 1984).

[36] I can remember being addressed by a subtly rebellious pupil in the fifth form of a London direct grant school in 1968 as 'teacher'. The word was meant, however gently, to wound the ego of the master.

female. The Historical Association derived from an initiative by two women teachers, one of whom brought in her old professor. Its foundation meeting was held, like the CA's, at University College London.[37] The English Association was founded by a schoolmaster, E. S. Valentine of Dundee High School.[38] The Mathematical Association was a special case. It was founded in 1897, but was in effect a broadening in focus and membership of the Association for the Improvement of Geometrical Teaching (AIGT), an anti-Euclidean pressure-group founded in 1871.[39] All these bodies combined a concern to support specialist teachers with a mission to bring in lay members with amateur interests. The two imperatives did not always run in parallel, and the CA, like the other bodies, was at times faced with difficult decisions in providing events and publications which kept all its members happy.

A different kind of context for the CA was provided by the associations which catered for groups of teachers irrespective of subject. The Association of Assistant Mistresses (1884) and Assistant Masters' Association (1891) represented at first those working in endowed schools for girls and the boys' public schools.[40] By the 1920s, they had set up subject committees, whose membership overlapped heavily with those of subject associations. The early work of the AMA and AAM must, at the very least, have suggested the possibility of joint action by teachers of single subjects.[41] The National Union of Teachers had been founded in 1870, the year of the act which established state elementary schooling in England and Wales. The word 'elementary' was considered degrading, and in 1888 the executive proposed to change the title while retaining the acronym by changing 'Elementary' to 'English';

[37] [G. Stretton] 'The Historical Association 1906–1956', in *The Historical Association 1906–1956* (London, 1957), 5–54.

[38] N. Smith, *The Origin and History of the Association* (London, 1942).

[39] See M. H. Price, *Mathematics for the Multitude? A History of the Mathematical Association* (Leicester, 1994). Understandably, antiquity being prized, the history of the AIGT is told here as the beginning of the MA's history.

[40] They merged in 1978 as the Assistant Masters' and Mistresses' Association, and in 1993 became the Association of Teachers and Lecturers

[41] The (US) Classical Association of the Atlantic States (CAAS) was founded in 1907 largely in response to a proposal emanating from the 1904 'classical conference' of the Association of Colleges and Preparatory School of the Middle States and Maryland. W. Donlan, 'A brief history of the Classical Association of the Atlantic States and *The Classical World*: 1907–1980', www.caas-cw.org/history.pdf. Its original name was the CA of the Middle States and Maryland, but was changed, presumably to avoid confusion with the CA of the Middle West and South (1905). For this latter, see H. W. Benario, *The Classical Association of the Middle West and South: the First Eighty Years* (Greenville SC, 1989). The CAAS was followed by associations for the Pacific North West (1911) and for the Pacific States (1915).

after heated protests by Welsh teachers, in 1889 the current title was adopted.[42] The CA had little to do with the NUT, most of its members feeling much more at home with (and often belonging to) the AMA or AAM.

Yet another kind of context was constituted by other classical bodies. The oldest of these was the Society for the Promotion of Hellenic Studies (1879). Its foundation was largely the work of the young George Macmillan, who was inspired by a visit to Greece in 1877 and by the example of the French Association pour l'encouragement des études grecques to found an English body. Macmillan drew up a list of 120 names, and finding that most of them were enthusiastic, organised a foundation meeting at the Freemasons' Tavern in London, a popular venue for such events. The Hellenic Society was originally intended for 'those who have been in Greece', and its concern was to report and publish monuments and inscriptions. It thus formed part of the widening of the classical curriculum – in universities at least – from texts to history and archaeology.[43] Richard Jebb, then Professor of Greek at Glasgow, hoped that the Society would act as a springboard for the foundation of a British archaeological school in Athens. Finding insufficient support in the Society's council, he mounted an independent campaign, and in 1883 a foundation meeting was held which starred the Prince of Wales and the Bishop of Durham.[44] Not until the turn of the century was support assembled for similar initiatives on the Roman front. The campaign for a school at Rome was almost derailed by the Boer War campaign, which made it impolitic to ask for financial support for merely academic causes, but the School was finally set up in 1900.[45] The Roman Society emerged only in 1910, after a proposal to extend the purview of the Hellenic Society to Roman topics was rejected. Its foundation meeting was a relatively low-key event, and it had a lower profile than its elder sister, which 'appealed to a wider and better-to-do and even somewhat fashionable public'.[46]

These bodies clearly operated in different spheres – schools, uni-

---

[42] A. Tropp, *The School Teachers* (London, 1977), 108–59.

[43] G. A. Macmillan, *An Outline of the History of the Society for the Promotion of Hellenic Studies, 1879–1904* (London, 1904); P. T Stevens, *The Society for the Promotion of Hellenic Studies 1879–1979. A Historical Sketch* (London, 1979).

[44] H. Waterhouse, *The British School at Athens: the first hundred years* (London, 1986).

[45] T. P Wiseman, *A Short History of the British School at Rome* (London, 1990); A. Wallace-Hadrill, *The British School at Rome. One Hundred Years* (London, 2001).

[46] M. V. Taylor 'The Society for the Promotion of Roman Studies, 1910–60', *JRS* 50 (1960), 129–34. This short sketch remains the only treatment of the Society's history; a centenary account is currently under consideration.

versities, abroad, high culture – and so to a degree could be separately engaged with. Within classics, the CA emerged as the central body and the most convenient arena for bringing the others together. It was general in its terms of reference, and its range extended from culture through scholarship to pedagogy. Within its own membership, the CA contained a variety of positions and opinions. Here the potential for embarrassment which had exercised Chase certainly existed. In reporting the foundation of the CA's first local branch, in Manchester in 1904, the *Manchester Guardian* remarked that

On the questions which vex the educational world – 'compulsory Greek', archaeology versus the study of texts, or, again, the philological ideal versus that of literary culture – the Classical Association has so far avoided taking sides. Men [sic] of all views have so far been welcome within its ranks, and it has been a parliament rather than a party machine to press specific views upon the country. Doubt may be felt as to the possibility of continuing this indefinitely . . . the defence of the classical studies . . . necessitates sooner or later a policy on the disputed points to which we have referred.[47]

In the early days, when the priority was to gain members and establish the Association on firm ground, the avoidance of controversy was a priority. This accounts, perhaps, for a string of cryptic entries in the Council Minutes of 1904 and 1905, recording simply that the motions or proposals brought forward by one Council member or another were withdrawn, or 'would not be put upon the agenda'.

For the most part, then, differences were glossed over, or controversial ground avoided. At times, however, they can still be glimpsed through the discreet patina of institutional historiography. The point can be illustrated by looking at the role of W. H. D. Rouse, headmaster of the Perse School in Cambridge from 1902 to 1928.[48] Rouse was a competent scholar, who had published a large book on Greek religion.[49] In 1911 he became, with his friend T. E. Page, one of the founding editors of the Loeb Classical Library; a post he held until his death in 1950. A vigorous organiser, an ex-secretary of the AMA and a member of the Headmasters' Conference, he was a useful man to have; and he was co-opted onto the CA Council after the foundation meeting. But Rouse was also a man with a mission: the reformation of classical

---

[47] 'The teaching of the classics. A Manchester branch association', *Manchester Guardian*, 19 November 1904. The author may well have been one of the two men who were elected to membership of the CA on 10 March 1905, and who gave their address as 'Guardian Office, Manchester'. (Council minutes, 18 March 1905.)

[48] For Rouse, see in general C. A. Stray, *The Living Word: W. H. D. Rouse and the Crisis of Classics in Edwardian England* (Bristol, 1992).

[49] *Greek Votive Offerings: an Essay in the History of Greek Religion* (Cambridge, 1902).

teaching in England through the direct method (teaching in Latin or Greek). The zeal with which he pursued this mission led to some embarrassing disagreements, and it was probably the unwillingness of his CA colleagues to be recruited to his cause which led him and a few sympathisers to run direct method summer schools in 1911 and 1912, and at the third school, in 1913, to found the Association for the Reform of Latin Teaching. By this time Rouse had been the editor of the CA's *The Year's Work in Classical Studies* for several years (plugging the direct method in the sections on pedagogy, which he wrote himself), and was also co-editor of the *Classical Review*. Here too disagreements arose over editorial policy, and eventually Rouse was replaced.[50]

The difficult relationship between the CA and the ARLT began when the former was invited to endorse the latter's advocacy of direct method; its refusal to do so initiated a period of mutual avoidance. One consequence was that the CA tried to keep clear of discussions of pedagogic method, and this left the field open to the ARLT, whose members provided discussions of classical teaching for manuals and encyclopedias. Another avoidance was so complete that it hardly appears in the record: the debate on Compulsory Greek at Oxford and Cambridge. This had begun in 1870, when the Endowed Schools Commissioners had asked the Vice-Chancellors of Oxford, Cambridge and London to consider changing their regulations so that they did not discriminate against school leavers who had not learned Greek. The debate had erupted every few years since then (a notable late outbreak took place in 1905), and it had divided classicists in schools, colleges and universities. The issue had non-classical ramifications, since Compulsory Greek became a symbol of the universities' autonomy from the state; but within the classical community it was so divisive that to take a position, or even to encourage debate, might well have been fatal to the CA. Chase's threatened withdrawal was not the only warning the Council was sent; in February 1904 Sonnenschein received a letter from Henry Jackson of Trinity College Cambridge, a leading opponent of Compulsory Greek, stating that if the Association intended to support its maintenance, he would not join.[51]

---

[50] For the journals, see the account in Chapter 6.

[51] Council minutes, 13 February 1904. Jackson was the leading teacher of ancient philosophy in Cambridge; in 1906 he succeeded Richard Jebb as Regius Professor of Greek. On Jackson, see R. B. Todd, 'One of the great English worthies and his "professional hobby": Henry Jackson reassessed', in C. A. Stray (ed.), *The Owl of Minerva* (Cambridge, 2004).

'A certain phrase which at present distracts this University'

The nearest approach to a discussion of Compulsory Greek came in a reference by J. W. Mackail at the Association's first General Meeting, at Oxford in May 1904. In what would now in some quarters be termed a keynote address 'On the place of Greek and Latin in human life', he remarked that

The President of Magdalen [Herbert Warren], with tears in his voice, implored me not to utter even in a whisper a certain phrase which at present distracts this University; and in any case I should not have been much inclined to pursue what seems to me a curiously confused issue. A controversy as to compulsory bread as an article of diet might conceivably be carried on with equal heat and pertinacity, were the supply of bread, and let us say of potatoes, in the hands of two bodies of highly educated persons representing enormous interests, and if the question were further complicated by one section of the disputants insisting that bread was not beef, while potatoes were, and another, that what was true of bread must be true of wine also.[52]

Mackail spoke with confidence as well as with rhetorical brilliance, for two reasons. First of all, he was now in a sense above the fray, having been a civil servant since 1884, when he joined what was then the Education Office; he was now, in 1904, a senior official of the Board of Education, in charge of the Secondary Branch. But in addition, he was an Oxford man, one of that stream of talented Scots who had come to Balliol as Snell Exhibitioners, and well enough regarded, it was rumoured, to have been offered the Mastership of Balliol.[53]

The Oxford meeting was important not only because it was the first general meeting of the new Association, but because it was designed to bring Oxford into the fold. Here we come to another kind of internal politics, where again the public rhetoric of alliance and mutual congratulation veiled differences of interest. The initial impetus to found the CA had come from Cambridge, and this reflected a more general tendency. In the nineteenth century, not only did Oxford maintain a higher public profile than Cambridge; classics held the central place in its curriculum which in Cambridge was occupied by mathematics.[54] Yet most of the institutional initiatives in classics in the period originated in Cambridge. This is true both of journals (*Museum Criticum, Philological Museum,*

---

[52] *Proceedings* (1904), 19.

[53] According to his grandson Lance Thirkell (in conversation), the offer was turned down because his wife Margaret Burne-Jones (daughter of the artist) refused to leave London.

[54] In the second half of the century, this situation was complicated by the foundation of new courses in law, history and natural science in both universities.

Journal of Classical and Sacred Philology, Journal of Philology) and of
societies (the Cambridge Philological Society may have been founded
later than its Oxford equivalent, but seems to have been more vigorous
in publishing). The Hellenic Society is difficult to classify in these terms,
as it was the brainchild of George Macmillan, who went straight from
Eton to the family firm; but a Cambridge branch was set up early on and
flourished, while Oxford had no branch.[55] Oxford was thus both the
primary home of classics in England, and a *pays de mission* for those who
wanted to organise classicists. The paradox is only apparent – primacy
brought with it complacency.

The Oxford meeting of May 1904, like the foundation meeting of
six months before, was carefully set up and stage-managed. The first
day's programme consisted of an evening Conversazione. The Reception Committee which greeted attenders consisted of a long list of
university dignitaries, including the Vice-Chancellor, the Proctors and
fifteen heads of houses. Members could then go on to inspect an
exhibition of papyri, prints, photography and lantern slides, with
experts in attendance to explain them. The second day's proceedings
centred on addresses by two senior members of the Board of
Education, J. W. Mackail and J. W. Headlam. The division of
labour is clear: Mackail's task was to deliver an inspirational address,
his subordinate Headlam's was to provoke discussion on the reform of
classics teaching. Mackail's high-flown rhetoric fitted the bill perfectly,
especially in his encomium on the virtues of Greek and Latin, whose
separateness he emphasised:

The place of Rome, of the Latin temper and civilisation, the Latin achievement in the
conquest of life, is definite and assured. It represents all the constructive and conservative forces which make life into an organic structure. . . . Greece represents the dissolving
influence of analysis and the creative force of pure intelligence. The return to Greece, it
has been said, is the return to nature; it has to be made again and again, always with a
fresh access of insight, a fresh impulse of vitality . . . While Rome has laid down for us a
realised standard of human conduct, Greece rears aloft, wavering and glittering before
us, an unrealisable ideal of superhuman intelligence.[56]

Mackail's speech was perhaps not intended to provoke discussion. In the
event only two responses were made. The first came from Admiral Sir

[55] Macmillan's ally in organising the foundation of the Hellenic Society was A. H. Sayce of
Oxford, to whom he was introduced in Dublin by their mutual friend J. P. Mahaffy.

[56] *Proceedings* (1904), 14–15, 17. Postgate described the speech as 'the remarkable discourse
with which Mr Mackail alternately dazzled, enchanted, and tantalized his audience for three
quarters of an hour': *CR* 18 (1904), 239. For a discussion of Mackail, Headlam and their addresses,
see Stray, *Classics Transformed*, 240–6.

Cyprian Bridge, who told the meeting of an incident from early in his naval career. As captain of a ship which had intercepted a vessel suspected of carrying contraband, he had boarded it with a young officer whose classical training enabled him to translate a relevant document written in Latin. When the ancient mariner had ceased diverting the assembled audience, Herbert Warren, Master of Magdalen, rose to respond gracefully to Mackail's teasing reference to Compulsory Greek.[57]

Headlam's address however, given after tea time, provoked extensive comment. He began by contrasting his experience with Mackail's. His superior was familiar with classical teaching in the great public schools, but his own experience was with 'schools where the subjects they were accustomed to call classics hardly existed at all'.[58] From this worm's-eye perspective, he painted a fairly gloomy picture of the realities of classical teaching. While listening to Mackail's address, he said, he had been thinking of a very different scene: 'the fourth form of a grammar school, where unwilling boys were being driven by a sleepy and worn and weary teacher'. Thinking of this, he wondered 'whether all the labour which they had to go through really did succeed in bringing them to the end which Mr Mackail had so eloquently placed before them'.[59] At this point one might wonder if Headlam's brutal realism was intended to hint at a criticism of his superior's rhetorical portrait of classics. But he proceeded to urge an approach to teaching which would help learners to come nearer to the ideal ends Mackail had sketched out, by singling out for criticism 'the predominance of the tendency towards perfection of style, analysis of language, grammar, and stylistic criticism'. This clinging to purely linguistic concerns he identified as 'The great weakness of the classical system'.[60] In Headlam's opinion, the ossified system of fifty years before, in which a pupil learnt the whole Latin grammar in Latin and understood very little of it, was not entirely dead. His analysis was offered to his audience with a double authority, for not only did Headlam have extensive experience of classical teaching in schools, he had achieved first-class honours at Cambridge in both the language-dominated Part I and the ancient history section of Part II of the Tripos; he had subsequently held a fellowship at King's College, and

---

[57] *Proceedings* (1904), 22–6.

[58] Headlam was a member of the Secondary Education Branch of the Board of Education; since 1893 he had been inspecting schools for the Board and for its predecessor the Office of Education.

[59] *Proceedings* (1904), 35.

[60] Ibid., 37.

his prize essay on *Election by Lot at Athens* had been published in 1893.[61] The discussion he provoked was contributed to by eleven speakers (including one woman, Miss Gavin, headmistress of Notting Hill High School, who began by complaining that the five minutes allotted her were not enough to explain the very different problems of girls' schools). The final speaker, R. S. Conway of the University of Manchester, reinforced Headlam's main point by urging that the ideals of a classical education should be kept in mind when organising its details. 'They should not pick out the least interesting books, nor waste time on triflers like Ovid or empty rhetoric like the Pro Milone'.[62]

---

[61] It was reprinted twice in the twentieth century. Headlam (later Headlam-Morley) became a distinguished diplomatic historian. He was knighted in 1929, the year of his death.

[62] *Proceedings* (1904), 53. His choice of books to ban may have occasioned some rumblings in the audience, but if so, they do not appear in the printed record. But by now it was 6.30, the session was closing and doubtless a pre-prandial sherry beckoned.

2

GETTING UNDER WAY:
CHALLENGE AND RESPONSE, 1904–22

By CHRISTOPHER STRAY

With the Oxford meeting successfully accomplished, the Council began to plan the more mundane but vital tasks of gaining members, keeping afloat financially, publicising the Association, collecting information and establishing policy in disputed areas. The minute books make it plain that while Postgate had taken the original initiative, his co-secretary Sonnenschein bore the brunt of running the Association. Indeed, it may be that the dual office was conceived as a way of reconciling the (senior) founder to the assumption of effective control by his junior partner. In any event, Postgate announced in June 1905 that he would be obliged to resign his post that Christmas, and that so far he had no suggestions for a replacement.[1]

Three committees were formally appointed by Council on 18 March 1905.[2] Their remits were as follows:

1 To consider and report on the best methods of introducing a uniform pronunciation of Latin (and Greek). Convener: Prof. S. H. Butcher.
2 To consider by what methods those employed in Classical Teaching can be helped to keep in touch with the most recent results of discovery and investigation. Convener: Prof. E. A. Gardner.
3 To consider in what respect the present school curriculum in Latin and Greek can be lightened and the means of instruction improved. Convener: Prof. E. A. Sonnenschein.

---

[1] Council minutes, 1 July 1905. An inefficiently deleted note in the minutes gives the intriguing information that Francis Cornford, then a young don at Trinity College, Cambridge, was suggested as a successor – probably because he had been the prime mover of the Cambridge Classical Society, founded in 1903. His name does not recur in this connection; eventually another young fellow of Trinity, Ernest Harrison, was appointed to succeed Postgate.

[2] Committees on finance and on spelling had been set up in the previous year; the latter is discussed below.

The Pronunciation of Latin

The pronunciation of Latin (less so, of Greek – as the parenthesis suggests) had been a matter of continual dispute in England since about 1870. In that year, the newly-formed Philological Societies of Oxford and Cambridge had issued a joint pamphlet proposing the use of a 'restored' pronunciation. This was designed to imitate the pronunciation of late republican and early imperial Rome, and to replace the longstanding English pronunciation. This latter was notable for its use of English vowels, and for using a hard V for Roman V: thus 'vigeat' was pronounced 'VY-GEE-AT' (G being pronounced as J). The 'restored' version, by contrast, was 'WI-GAY-AT'. The proposals prompted a storm of protest and discussion; the sounding of V as W, especially, brought denunciation of its 'Weediness'. In Cambridge, the new pronunciation was pioneered by the Professor of Latin, Hugh Munro, whose younger colleague Richard Jebb employed modern Greek pronunciation as Public Orator in introducing a Greek Orthodox archbishop for an honorary degree. The interested reader will find accounts of this campaign elsewhere,[3] but it may be pertinent to cite additional, unpublished evidence here: in 1883, Jebb's friend Thomas Escott, editor of the *Fortnightly Review*, asked him about the current state of the question. Jebb replied that he did not think the reform campaign could be called a success. Munro and his successor as Professor of Latin, John Mayor, had used it, and so had the liberal reformer and comparative philologist John Peile. But the university registrary Henry Luard, a leading Tory, refused to do so. He himself, as Public Orator, had had to give it up, since it was not understood by the majority of members of the university senate. As for Postgate's detailed proposals, they really would not work: 'weni widi wici, kikero, willa – repulsive!' [4] Jebb was not alone in his aesthetic shuddering, and it is clear from the committee's Preamble that they felt a vigorous blow was needed to defeat a powerful and entrenched opponent:

... there was little hope of founding any general agreement upon a uniform system if its basis were sought in what has been known as 'the English pronunciation' ... where the standard or London pronunciation is most carefully inculcated, there the result is, in

---

[3] For the campaigns, see Stray, *Classics Transformed*, 126–30; cf H. Copeman, *Singing in Latin*, second edition (Oxford, 1996), 199–202, 283–4. There is some useful material in P. G. Naiditch, 'A. E. Housman's pronunciation of Latin', *Housman Society Journal*, 27 (November 2001), 36–45.
[4] British Library, Add. Ms. 58783, ff. 54–8: R. C. Jebb to T. H. S. Escott, 28 October 1883.

fact, furthest from the true Latin sounds . . . The Committee see no reason why the degraded vowel sounds peculiar to modern English should be allowed to remain in the teaching of Greek any longer than in Latin.[5]

The committee proposed that a schedule of approved pronunciation be drawn up for Latin, but that before publication it should be agreed at a meeting with the Oxford and Cambridge Philological Societies and the CA of Scotland.[6] In May 1906 the committee announced to Council the happy discovery that the scheme proposed by the two Philological Societies was 'practically that of the Pronunciation Committee in a shorter form'.[7] Not since the Septuagint had such a fated convergence been witnessed! The Committee's report was issued in October 1906. The last two of its twenty pages were devoted to Greek; the rest presented the restored pronunciation of Latin, with a Preamble which closed with this stirring appeal:

The Committee venture to hope that all friends of classical studies will loyally support the Classical Association in its attempt to free the study of Greek and Latin from the entanglements of an irrational, though time-honoured usage which have at length become a serious burden.[8]

The members of the AMA certainly appear to have been generally supportive of the CA's proposals, as appears from a letter to *The Times* from S. E. Winbolt, headmaster of Christ's Hospital:[9]

By June, 1901, a short scheme, the basis of which was, of course, the pamphlet of the Cambridge Philological Society, had been drawn up by our educational subcommittee and issued to all members. To this 35 replies were received, but 11 of these were from branch secretaries, and therefore represented the opinion of a very large body of members. Of these 35, 31 were definitely in favour of the reformed pronunciation; two dissented, but acknowledged that 'all scientific reasons are, course, in favour of a restored pronunciation'. Out of 264 members in 5 branches, only one dissented. The majority accepted the scheme without alteration; a few making minor suggestions.[10]

This is not the place to follow the subsequent history of Latin pronunciation in this country. Suffice it to say that the restored pronunciation gained ground quickly in Cambridge, less so in Oxford;

---

[5] Draft preamble. (Council minutes, 12 May 1906.)

[6] Council minutes, 21 October 1905. In approving the proposal, Council deleted this last body from the list.

[7] Council minutes, 12 May 1906.

[8] Report, 13.

[9] On Winbolt, see E. J. Kenney's article in R. B. Todd (ed.), *Dictionary of British Classicists, 1500–1960* (Bristol, 2004).

[10] *The Times*, 16 January, 1905, 7d. Winbolt wrote the letter because, much to his annoyance, he had not been able to give his information at the CA meeting held a week before.

quite fast in public school sixth forms, but much less so in the teaching of lower forms and in prep. schools; and that the lawcourts and Inns of Court formed the last redoubt of this 'irrational usage', as of so many others.[11]

Investigations

The committee set up 'to consider by what methods those employed in Classical Teaching can be helped to keep in touch with the most recent results of discovery and investigation' was informally known as the 'investigations committee'. Its convener, Ernest Gardner, was Yates Professor of Classical Archaeology at UCL, and with his brother Percy (Lincoln Professor of the subject at Oxford) a keen campaigner for the increased use of archaeological evidence in school Classics teaching (the two brothers combined forces to provide vacation courses in archaeology for schoolteachers). Gardner had been the first student enrolled at the British School at Athens, and went on to direct the School from 1887 to 1895; he was elected to the Yates chair in 1896.

The investigations committee's report was submitted to Council at its meeting on 1 July 1905. Its recommendations were straightforward: 'the best way to carry out the object for which the Committee is appointed would be the publication of an annual Account of the progress of Classical Studies in all branches . . . This account to be confined to such matters as are likely to be useful to classical teachers in Schools'. The proposed volume, they thought, should be offered to CA members at 2*s* and to non-members at 3*s*, and should appear in early autumn each year. The report was referred to yet another committee, the Finance Committee of Council. Their conclusion was that if 1,000 copies of a 100-page annual volume were published, a small loss could be predicted; but that the exercise would be a worthwhile use of the Association's money, and could be halted if it failed.[12] This was the genesis of *The Year's Work in Classical Studies*, which first appeared in 1907, and whose final volume was issued in 1948. (Its history is discussed in Chapter 6.)

---

[11] See for more detail the sources cited in note 3 above. Either the AMA members Winbolt referred to were thicker on the ground in the more 'enlightened' sectors of the education system, or a lot of backsliding went on.

[12] Council minutes, 21 October 1905.

Curricula

This committee, set up 'to consider in what respect the present school curriculum in Latin and Greek can be lightened and the means of instruction improved', was the largest of the three. While the other two committees had seven members each, this had twenty.[13] Its secretary, Christopher Cookson, previously a classical master at St Paul's, was then a Mods tutor at Magdalen College, Oxford; other members included Rouse, his friend T. E. Page, and Gilbert Murray, who had just become a fellow of New College. One reason for its size, and an indicator of the importance of its role, was that it included representatives of the Headmasters' Conference, the Headmasters' Association, the Head Mistresses' Association, the AMA and the AAM. Its convener was Sonnenschein, an experienced campaigner for curricular reform and uniform provision and teaching across different subjects, who had briefly been a headmaster himself before becoming Professor of Classics at Birmingham. Soon after his appointment there, he had founded the Grammatical Society, a group of dons and teachers who worked to secure the use of uniform grammatical terminology across the curriculum. The curricula committee functioned, among other things, as a basis for the Joint Committee on Uniform Grammatical Terminology, launched at the CA meeting on his home ground of Birmingham in 1908, and which lapsed with his death in 1929.[14]

The committee began by writing to all members of the Headmasters' Conference, as well as 'the Head Mistresses of certain girls' schools', to collect information on the place of classics in the curriculum. They received replies from 37 headmasters and 19 headmistresses.[15] The picture built up from replies was this: out of an average teaching week of about 27 hours, boys in the larger public schools spent 12 hours on classics at age 13, rising to 15 hours at age 17. The figures for the smaller schools were 8 and 13.5 hours respectively. The girls' schools showed more variation, since some of them had morning sessions only; the day schools offered from 2 to 4 hours at age 13, from 4 to 7 hours at age 17. The boarding schools provided 'more than twice as much time'

---

[13] The pronunciation committee subsequently co-opted three additional members – Robinson Ellis (Oxford), R. S. Conway (Manchester) and Rouse; and John Baker-Penoyre, secretary of the Hellenic Society, was added to the investigations committee.

[14] For Sonnenschein and his campaigns, see Stray, *Classics Transformed*, 227–9, 261–4.

[15] At this point there were just over 100 schools in the HMC. It is not clear how many headmistresses were written to.

as the lower levels just cited. The committee's main concern was with the 'average boy': they felt that 'The system of Classical teaching in most schools seems to be directed towards the ultimate production of a certain number of finished scholars both in Latin and in Greek, educated for the most part on what may be called linguistic lines, *i.e.*, with special attention to Grammar and Composition'.[16] This was all very well for the minority of high flyers, but the average pupils needed something else. In particular, the committee thought, they should be introduced to Greek literature rather than to grammar and composition.[17] Where these latter were taught, rare and abnormal forms should be avoided, and the teaching oriented to the forms commonly found in literature. In the girls' schools 'the teaching seems to be directed towards acquiring facility in translation'.[18] The committee approved.

Spelling

A committee on 'the spelling and printing of Latin texts for school and college use' was set up by resolution of Council on 28 May 1904. Postgate was in the chair, and given his interest in the matter, it is likely that the initiative was his.[19] The other members were Rouse, Winbolt and A. E. Housman (not normally a man to join committees, and presumably co-opted by Postgate).[20] This was an early example of collaboration with other organisations, since the remit of the committee directed it to confer with the AMA on the subject. Its recommendations were *inter alia* that long vowels should be marked except where they were 'long by position'; that u and v should be printed as such only in beginners' books; and that better-attested spellings should be universally adopted. The background to the formation of this committee, apart from Postgate's own interest, includes both the expansion in the publication of school series of classical texts, and the development of a historicist philology which insisted on distinguishing between the

---

[16] Interim report of the Curricula Committee, pp. 6–7.

[17] This concern for the average boy was widespread in educational circles in the 1900s. In 1912 a lengthy correspondence in *The Times* and in its new *Educational Supplement* (1910) led to the publication of selected letters under the title *Classics and the Average Boy* (1912). See Stray, *Classics Transformed*, 259–60.

[18] Interim report, 7.

[19] He had complained of the confused state of argument on the question in *CR* 13 (1899), 145–6.

[20] This is the opinion of P. G Naiditch, *A. E. Housman at University College, London: the Election of 1892* (Leiden, 1988), 86.

spelling (and pronunciation) of Latin and Greek of different periods –
hence Postgate's concern to avoid some spellings seen as either archaic
or post-classical.

Branching out

Any new organisation which, like the CA, intended to achieve some kind
of national coverage, inevitably had to consider local or regional
representation. An early precursor of this principle was the American
Institute of Archaeology, founded in Boston in 1879, which soon
established branches elsewhere on the East Coast, and after 1884
became a national body.[21] The CA proceeded along two parallel
paths. First of all, the Council decided in May 1905 to establish a list
of local correspondents, whose task was to gather members, publicise
the Association's activities and organise local meetings.[22] By June 1906,
28 such correspondents had been elected. They included several women
– Jane Harrison for Newnham, Kitty Jex-Blake for Girton, Hilda
Lorimer for Somerville and 'Miss A. M. A. Rogers for women at
Oxford'. Several other correspondents were in effect representatives of
particular schools or colleges, including Eton, Winchester, Royal Holloway and Cheltenham Ladies' College. Ireland was represented by John
Beare at TCD, and Professor Exon at Galway; Henry Browne of UCD
does not appear. Overseas correspondents covered Canada, Burma
(listed under the heading 'India') and the USA.[23] There were also
contacts with, and enquiries from, foreign associations. The first was
in May 1904, when Wilhem Knös of Uppsala, of the Swedish Classical
Association, wrote asking for a copy of the CA's rules.[24]

Secondly, a series of local branches were established. On 9 July 1904,
Council agreed that a Local Organisation committee should be established, and that local branches should be encouraged. They also agreed
that if local branches collected CA subscriptions, they would be given 20
per cent of the total for their own use. The first branch was set up at
Manchester, the leading light being R. S. Conway, Professor of Classics

[21] S. L. Dyson, *Ancient Marbles to American Shores: Classical Archaeology in the United States* (Philadelphia, 1998), 42.

[22] Council minutes, 5 May 1905.

[23] By 1908, the number of correspondents had risen to 49: *Proceedings* 6 (1908), 69.

[24] The title is as given by Knös; the Swedish title is Svenska Humanistika Forbunder. The association was founded in 1906, and despite its more general title, was then primarily concerned with the defence and promotion of classics. My thanks to Gunhold Vidén for information.

at the Victoria University. Conway's energy and commitment appear in the Council minutes of this period in a series of motions and proposals (many of which were denied or deferred).[25] The branch was constituted at a meeting of the university Classical Society on 18 November 1904, and almost immediately announced a president (Augustus Wilkins, Professor of Latin), eight vice-presidents (mostly local worthies, including the Bishop of Manchester), and a committee of seven. In the following February, the new branch appointed an Excavations Committee to promote the investigation of local remains of the Roman occupation. By 1911, it had published four excavation reports. The second branch to be established, in October 1905, was in Birmingham, where Sonnenschein took the lead. As with Manchester, a printed copy of draft rules was sent to Council for approval and amendment.[26] The two branches showed their mettle by putting on two general meetings, both organised on a large and lavish scale: Manchester in 1906, and Birmingham in 1908 (complete with a special performance of the *Hippolytus* in Gilbert Murray's translation, which Murray spent nine days rehearsing).[27] The foundation dates of later branches are given in Barbara Finney's account below.[28]

In a letter to Council of December 1904, Gilbert Norwood, secretary of the Manchester branch, referred to it as 'the Manchester Classical Association'.[29] The phrase was not commented on, but implicitly it raised the question of the status of branches in relation to the CA. The question did not lie dormant for long, since it became contentious in the foundation of the third local branch, that at Liverpool. Here the Classical Association of Liverpool had been founded on 13 December 1907 by senior members of the University, its committee being packed, as at Manchester and Birmingham, with local dignitaries – a bishop, several headmasters and headmistresses. The Lord Mayor consented to become its first president. At its first annual meeting, a discussion was held on 'The place of classical studies in a modern city'.[30] In March, its secretary wrote to the CA Council asking that the Association be affiliated with the CA; he was told that 'the Council finds a real practical difficulty in recognising as a branch an institution that bears the title of

---

[25] His leading role in the early stages is indicated by his being one of the three men Postgate asked the readers of *CR* to contact to express their support for the founding of the Association; the others being Sonnenschein and Postgate himself. (*CR* 17 (1903), 237.)

[26] Council minutes, 21 October 1905 (foundation), 11 November 1905 (draft rules).

[27] *Proceedings* 6 (1908), 96.

[28] See Chapter 11.

[29] Letter of 13 December 1904: (Council minutes, 19 December 1904).

[30] *Proceedings* 6 (1908), 186–7.

an independent Association'. The pill was sweetened by the suggestion that 'the Council has no objection whatever to the title of 'The Liverpool Classical Association' being employed for popular use in reports of your meetings in the local press . . . a similar popular use . . . is already current both at Birmingham and at Manchester and creates no difficulty. The only point is that the *official* title must include the word 'branch' if affiliation is to be effected'.[31]

The Liverpool Association responded by voting to change its official title to 'the Liverpool and District Branch of the Classical Association'; but it also changed Rule 2 of its constitution to read 'The name of the Association for local purposes shall be the Liverpool Classical Association'. The Council then asked that the official title should stand at the head of its printed rules. Meanwhile Sonnenschein had suggested that if the name was not changed, the Liverpool Association could only affiliate to the CA as the newly-founded Classical Association of Ireland had done; in which case, he pointed out, Liverpool would lose the financial advantage of being a CA branch. By the end of 1908, local pride seems to have been satisfied and the issue had died down.[32] The sensitivities of Council on this point may have abated in later years, since the Northumberland and Durham Classical Association (*sic*) published three records of its work between 1922 and 1936 under that title, referring to the CA as 'the (Central) Classical Association'.[33]

The recognition of later branches was more straightforward, even in the case of the Cardiff branch (1914). This had begun life in 1898/9 as 'The Frogs', a university society whose name suggests a concern with productions of ancient drama. There was, however, no suggestion of rebellion against affiliation beyond a mild lament in a student newspaper. For the details and activities of the branches, the reader is referred to Barbara Finney's account in Chapter 11, below. But a word should be said about one of the most exotic of the branches, that in Bombay.

The first mention of Bombay occurs in January 1909, when a letter from Mrs Agnes Haigh was read out to Council proposing the formation of a Bombay Classical Association. She sent in several CA subscriptions,

[31] E. A. Sonnenschein to J. M. McGregor, 24 March 1908. (Council minutes, 2 May 1908.)

[32] But in the account of the new branch in *Proceedings* (note 78 above), it was at one point referred to as 'the Society'.

[33] B. Anderton, *The First Ten Years' Work of the Northumberland and Durham Classical Association*, (Newcastle-upon-Tyne, [1923?]); id., *A Second Record of Classical Activities, being vignettes of meetings during seven years, from October, 1922, to July, 1929* (Newcastle, 1929); id., *A Third Record (1929–36) of the Proceedings* (Newcastle, 1936). Basil Anderton was City Librarian of Newcastle and the author of several local bibliographies.

but added that a separate body would be able to attract considerable local support, 'mainly, no doubt, from the Civil Service'.[34] This was referred to the committee which considered the claims of overseas associations to be 'affederated'; which decided that the proposed body should be not an Association but a branch. In a second letter, Mrs Haigh herself agreed, since 'there is no purely scholastic or academic life here'; but she stressed that there were classically-trained residents who were keen to keep up with the news of classical work and discovery.[35] Later in the year she was in England, and discussed the project with Henry Butcher, then president of the CA, who seems to have been supportive. Before returning to India, Mrs Haigh wrote again going into more detail. She proposed a branch subscription of 6 rupees (about 8s), rather than the normal 2s 6d, to cover the higher costs of correspondence and the distribution of Proceedings. She also had a plan of meetings worked out: mostly in the winter months, since 'Government assembles in Bombay about the middle of November and goes to the hills early in March'.[36] In February 1910, Council heard that the branch had been founded, and at the same meeting, elected thirteen Bombay residents to membership.[37] Most were members of the Indian Civil Service, but two who were not deserve a mention. One of these was F. T. Rickards, whom we know from other sources to have been the local Agent for the Bombay and Peninsular Railway, and a keen practitioner and collector of Latin and Greek compositions.[38] The other was Father Albert Ailinger, Professor of Latin at St. Xavier's College. Ailinger revealed himself in a letter to Postgate advocating the use of Latin as an international language, which was read to the Council in June 1911. 'I am one of those wicked Germans and, worse still, belong to that iniquitous body of men, called Jesuits!'[39]

Ailinger was equally revealing about the Bombay branch in a letter to J. H. Sleeman, who was now one of the CA's secretaries:

And how is our Branch getting on? Well, I am going to give you some confidential information. The Branch is doing well and is growing slowly but steadily, not in the way

---

[34] Mrs Agnes Haigh to E. A. Sonnenschein, 11 December 1908 (Council minutes, 30 January 1909).

[35] Mrs Haigh to Sonnenschein, 12 February 1909. Ibid.

[36] Mrs Haigh to Sonnenschein, 10 October 1909 (Council minutes, 30 October 1909). This letter was written from Alfreton Vicarage; Mrs Haigh was probably the wife of Rev. Henry Haigh (1853–1917), missionary in Bombay and author of *Some Leading Ideas of Hinduism* (1903).

[37] Council minutes, 5 February 1910.

[38] For Rickards see Stray, *Classics Transformed*, 125–6. On 9 March 1911 he read a paper to the Branch on 'Classical scholarship, past and present': *Proceedings* 9 (1912), 200.

[39] Ailinger to Postgate, 27 April 1911 (Council minutes, 10 June 1911). Ailinger's paper on this subject was read to the 1913 general meeting by Postgate: *Proceedings* 10 (1913), 109–23.

it grew in the first year of its existence. When Mrs Haigh, the founder, left Bombay, I was elected Secretary. What was my surprise when I found out the real feeling among quite a number of our members! They told me quite openly that they had joined only to oblige, or not to disappoint, 'the lady'. One I. C. S., in a good position, told me we ought to have given up the thing when Mrs Haigh left. When I replied it would have been a disgrace to our sex if we gave up a work so well begun by a lady, he said everybody would have understood the reason. . . . another member told me quite plainly it was all a humbug. To my question why he had accepted the office, he answered: 'I didn't want to offend the lady'.[40]

Mrs Haigh was evidently either very attractive or very forceful, or both. Without her fragrant presence, the branch would have withered but for Ailinger's energy. The 1915 report announced that he had 'withdrawn . . . due to the War'. (Perhaps the Jesuit Order had transferred him to avoid his internment as an enemy alien.) The reports for 1916 and 1917 listed officers, but stated that the branch was 'in a state of suspended animation'. And that is the last we hear of the Bombay branch.[41]

The differences of interest and expectation which one would expect to find between local branches and the governing elite of the Association also emerged into the light, on occasion, at conferences and in correspondence with the Council. An example from the conference of May 1919 gives a hint of the kind of disquiet in the ranks which probably existed more widely in an unverbalised form. At the end of a Friday afternoon discussion of the Report on Greek Curricula, 'a lady' suggested (in vain) that a vote should be postponed, since so few schoolteachers had been able to attend the session. On Saturday afternoon, Miss Purdie, headmistress of a London girls' school, rose to ask:

Would it be possible to democratise the Association a little more? There is a feeling among many schoolmasters and schoolmistresses that everything is done over their heads, and it is a common remark that the Classical Association needs fresh blood. As an instance I would mention the drawing up of the timetable of this meeting. The most vital question regarding Greek was put down for a day when very few teachers could be present, whilst the academic discussion was arranged for Saturday, when teachers could be present. . . . Might not the Association be brought into touch with the humble men and women, especially in municipal schools, who want to work for the classics in their schools?[42]

---

[40] Ailinger to Sleeman, 7 December 1911 (Council minutes, 8 January 1912).

[41] *Proceedings* 13 (1916),103; 14 (1917), 262; 15 (1918), 146. Ailinger seems to have survived his removal or internment, since his pamphlet *Three Messages of Gladness* was published in 1940 by the Catholic Truth Society.

[42] *Proceedings* 16 (1919), 58. Miss Purdie was probably the 'lady' who had spoken up on the previous day.

No response to Miss Purdie's plea is recorded, and the impression one gains is that of an organisation run largely by male academics which had lost touch with its rank and file.

An earlier plea, also from a woman, gives a vivid sense of the problems faced by teachers isolated from fellow-classicists and from libraries. In 1905, Hilda Lorimer of Somerville College, Oxford wrote to Edward Sonnenschein to propose the setting up of a lending library for teachers. She painted a picture of the average women teacher:

There is generally only one classical mistress to each school, and in the absence of encouragement and external stimulus her interest in her own subject is apt to wane. She may improve in the mechanical accuracy with which she teaches a few familiar texts; but at the end of a few years the range of her knowledge is narrower and her grasp of the subject weaker than when she left the university.

Lorimer emphasised that though her own direct knowledge was of women teachers, she had 'heard from several quarters that men teaching in schools other than the larger public schools labour under the same disadvantages'.[43] Her proposal was that a classical lending library should be financed by an addition of 2s 6d to the existing 5s subscription, so it is not surprising that the Council felt unable to act on her suggestion. Lorimer's letter is valuable not only for her proposal, but for the picture she paints of the isolated teacher whose grasp of his or her subject gradually withers away. University teachers like Lorimer had an interest in this, since such a decline in skills resulted in their being sent inferior pupils. As Lorimer wrote in her letter, 'It is impossible not to regard lack of scholarliness in the teacher as one of the causes of that unsoundness in the very elements of classics which is the chief difficulty encountered by those who have to direct women's work at the universities.'

The Association in Wartime

The outbreak of war in 1914 disrupted activity in education as in so many other areas. In Oxford and Cambridge, it froze the ongoing debates on Compulsory Greek, because there were soon so few dons left to debate that by tacit agreement, serious academic issues were allowed to hang over till hostilities ended. More generally, the war brought about a crisis of legitimacy for Classics, since Britain's relative lack of scientific and technical training, exposed in the harsh light of

---

[43] Letter inserted in Council minutes, 1 July 1905.

conflict, was widely ascribed to the dominance of humanistic, and especially classical, education.

On 2 February 1916 the Committee on the Neglect of Science, including such vociferous propagandists as Ray Lankester and H. G. Wells, published a manifesto in *The Times*. Looking back on this episode in 1921 in his Presidential Address, Walter Leaf, classical scholar and banker, commented that

> The depression in the popular estimate of Classics reached its nadir undoubtedly early in the war, at a meeting in Burlington House, of which I will merely say that a good many people who ought to have known better made a good many rather foolish statements of which we hope they are now repenting. That meeting was a conspicuous example of what we have taken to calling the 'herd instinct'. At that moment it seemed that nothing could win the war except pure science: no education that did not lead directly to the invention of a new poison gas was worth the attention of rational people. . . . There was a jeer at some statesman who did not know the origin of glycerine, and it was inferred that no one could lead the people in war if he had not been trained in the chemistry of fats.[44]

At the Council meeting on 26 February, it was agreed to ask R. W. Livingstone to draft a humanist counter-manifesto.[45] This was circulated to gain wider support, and was finally published in *The Times* on 4 May. Once battle had been joined, the forces of moderation on both sides organised a meeting of scientific and humanistic bodies, chaired by Frederic Kenyon, whose position as Director of the British Museum enabled him to play a mediating role. A Council on Humanistic Studies was set up, representing the arts subjects, and meetings between its members and the scientists' representatives eventually produced a joint declaration in 1917.[46] This was debated at length at the Association's 1917 General Meeting; the discussion was continued at the Meeting of the following year.[47]

Meanwhile, in 1917 the continuing pressure for science education led the CA to send a deputation to Herbert Fisher, the new Minister of

---

[44] *Proceedings* 18 (1921), 22–3. The notion of the 'herd instinct' was popularised by William Trotter's book *The Instincts of the Herd in Peace and War* (1916). In the previous year, Gilbert Murray had published an article on 'Herd instinct and the war' (*Atlantic Monthly* 115 (1915), 830–39).

[45] In 1940 the then Joint Secretary, J. J. R. Bridge, wrote a leaflet on 'The Classical Association and the War of 1914–18' in which he looked back on these developments. He erroneously assigned the Council's initiative to the previous meeting, of 7 January; but it must be said that the minutes for this period are written in a messy hand.

[46] Kenyon's daughter Kathleen inherited the Council's minute book, and later gave it to the CA, in whose archives it is now held. For more detail on this episode, see Stray, *Classics Transformed*, 264–5.

[47] 'Education Report' and 'Debate on the Education Report', *Proceedings* 14 (1917), 40–87; 'Debate on the Education Report', *Proceedings* 15 (1918), 99–117.

Education. The deputation was led by his old friend James Bryce (now Viscount Bryce). He and his colleagues spoke their pieces, and were rewarded by a supportive response from Fisher. This was in part a propaganda exercise, an elaborate piece of theatre conducted by the members of a classically-educated elite. Bryce's eminence made this an important occasion for the CA, and the speeches were reprinted in full in *Proceedings*.[48]

The public debates provoked by the Committee on the Neglect of Science in 1916 led to the appointment of two Prime Minister's Committees, on Natural Science and on Modern Languages; both reported in 1918. Their reports in turn prompted further debate, especially as it was becoming clear that educational reform could be expected as part of postwar reconstruction. If the sciences and modern languages could have their committees, reports and, subsequently, claims to timetable time based on these, why not other subjects? As a result, committees were appointed in 1919 to investigate the position of classics and of English;[49] both reports were published in 1921. English had been something of a Cinderella subject, and without the wartime surge of patriotic feeling might not have had a committee of its own.[50]

The End of an Era

The Classics Report (*The Classics in Education*) provided a survey of the nature and extent of the provision of classics in schools and universities, a historical outline, a discussion of the justifications for teaching the subject, and statistical appendices: it remains a mine of information for the historian of Classics. The Prime Minister's Committee's findings were debated at the CA General Meeting held in Cambridge in August that year.[51] This was an unusual meeting, in that it included a strong non-English presence which gave its discussions additional perspectives. The conference opened with an address by Charles Forster Smith of the University of Wisconsin, and continued with a message from Andrew

[48] 'Report of deputation from the Classical Association to the President of the Board of Education', *Proceedings* 15 (1908), 5–40.

[49] The English Committee was not a Prime Minister's Committee, since its remit was confined to England, rather than to the United Kingdom, as with the other committees. For the work of the Classics Committee, see Stray, *Classics Transformed*, 265–9.

[50] It should be remembered that Oxford had only begun teaching English in the 1890s, and the Cambridge English Tripos dated only from 1917. The Cambridge chair of English had been established in 1911; its first incumbent, who died the following year, was the classicist A. W. Verrall.

[51] *Proceedings* 18 (1921), 43–67, 119–32.

West of Princeton, on behalf of the American Classical League.[52] The debate in which the Classics Committee's Report was discussed was entitled 'The best method of strengthening the position of the classics in English and American education', and was opened by a Scot: John Harrower, Professor of Greek at Aberdeen. The situation disclosed by the Report was encouraging in some ways, since Latin was clearly embedded in a large number of schools. The position of Greek, however, was precarious. The returns from 612 boys' schools showed that about 44 per cent of the pupils were learning Latin, but less than five per cent were learning Greek. The comparable figures from 343 girls' schools were 27.5 per cent learning Latin, 0.4 per cent Greek.[53] These figures, taken together with the recent abolition of compulsory Greek requirements by Oxford and Cambridge, made it clear that English Classics had moved out of the world of Victorian Hellenism. The mainstay of Classics henceforth was to be the teaching and learning of Latin.

With the appearance and discussion of the Classics Report, the reconstruction of both Classics and the secondary school curriculum was essentially complete. Radical change by the state was ruled out by the serious financial problems faced by the government after the war, when the 'Geddes Axe' fell on many plans for central funding. In 1922, the Board of Education issued a circular tabulating the timetabling proposals made by the four Committees. The total, predictably enough, came to well over 100 percent, and the Board indicated that it did not propose to intervene. Four years later, the Board formally indicated its withdrawal from curricular prescription. In future, supply and demand for subjects would be allowed to establish levels of provision in schools.[54] The end of an era of challenge and defence was reflected in *Proceedings*, whose contents were now for the most part devoted to the routine round of conference papers and speeches.

[52] This was also the meeting at which A. E. Housman gave his well-known paper 'The application of thought to textual criticism'; it was printed in *Proceedings* 18 (1921), 67–84.
[53] *The Classics in Education* (London, 1921), 43–6.
[54] For details see Stray, *Classics Transformed*, 271–2.

3

A LULL BETWEEN TWO STORMS:
FROM THE 1920S TO THE 1950S

By CHRISTOPHER STRAY

The history of the Association between the mid 1920s and mid 1950s contains, as my title suggests, no events as striking as those described in the previous two chapters. The Second World War was, of course, even longer and more devastating than its predecessor. Yet it did not give rise, either in wartime or afterwards, to the kind of public ideological dogfighting which took place after 1914. The main reason for this, as far as Classics was concerned, was undoubtedly that the perceived 'lion's share' the subject held in the 1910s had by the 1940s been relinquished. Though Latin was firmly embedded in the curriculum of the grammar schools, science, modern languages and – especially since the early 1920s – English had assumed what we now take to be their proper place beside it. World War II itself, as has been suggested, did not figure largely in the CA's history. It should be mentioned, however, that a spirit of wartime co-operation did lead to collaborative postwar ventures. In September 1943 a Classical Teachers' Conference was held at Cheltenham Ladies' College with the general aim of re-enthusing teachers for their subject. From this came both the reconciliation of the CA and the ARLT, and the Triennial Conferences (Hellenic and Roman Societies and the CA). These conferences were for long the largest regular events in the British classical calendar, though they are now rivalled by the CA's annual meetings.

The character of stability referred to above – one could call it a state of truce, or of dullness, depending on one's point of view – reflected that of English education as a whole. Between the alarums of the First World War and of the 1960s, there were few public debates on school curricula. Three major educational reports were issued. The first of these, the Hadow Report (1926), was important in extending the notion of 'secondary education' beyond the grammar schools to other kinds of schools – what were to become technical and modern schools. Drawing on the work of educational psychologists, it identified adolescence as a developmental stage whose needs were emotional as well as intellectual. The report brought into the centre of educational planning the notion of pupil interest, and thus reinforced the erosion of the ideology of mental discipline to which so many classical teachers clung. In 1938 appeared the Spens Report, which established the tripartite system of grammar, technical and modern schools. The Consultative Committee of the Board of Education, which issued the report, had been instructed to consider secondary education in general, with special reference to grammar and technical schools. The Association sent it a memorandum in which, while mention was made of non-classical languages and of classical civilisation, the major emphasis was on 'training in exactness and self-discipline and in distinguishing between right and wrong, between mastery and half-knowledge'.[1] This emphasis was firmly rejected in the Committee's Report:

> We have no intention of depreciating the value of linguistic study, but we believe that the traditional methods of this study are fundamentally wrong. In the emphasis which its exponents lay on formal and abstract grammar, they are apt to lose sight of the fact that language is not a series of formulae, but a living function of the mind whereby it expresses living ideas; and hence they are apt to destroy the pupil's interest both in the ideas, and in the method of expressing them.

They went on to recommend that Latin should be taught in relation to English, and that a much wider range of Latin authors than the traditional pedagogic canon should be covered.[2]

The Report was discussed at the CA's next general meeting, in April 1939, in what seems to have been a rather desultory way. J. J. R. Bridge, one of the Honorary Secretaries, concluded his comments on the Report by remarking that

> these recommendations were not new. They were to be found in reports of the Curricular Committee of the Association published over thirty years ago. One wondered whether it was teaching or examining methods that had been so conservative that the recommendations had come to nothing and now had to be made all over again.[3]

The third major report which deserves mention is the Norwood Report (1943).[4] This was named after its chairman Sir Cyril Norwood,

---

[1] 'Memorandum from the Classical Association to the Consultative Committee of the Board of Education', reprinted in *Greece & Rome* 4 (1934), 114–18. The quotation is on p. 116.

[2] Board of Education, *Secondary Education, with Special Reference to Grammar Schools and Technical High Schools* (London, 1938), 230. The section on Latin (230–4) is followed by a brief comment on Greek (234–5).

[3] *Proceedings* 36 (1939), 48. The reader will doubtless be able to think of similar examples from his or her own experience.

[4] Basic information about all three reports, together with extracts from their texts, can be found in S. Maclure, *Educational Documents. England and Wales, 1816–1963* (London, 1965).

an experienced public school headmaster who had been something of a radical as a young man, but who was by now conservative in his views. The secretary of the committee which produced the report was R. H. Barrow, Staff HMI for Classics and moving spirit behind the foundation of *Greece & Rome*.[5] The effect of the Norwood Report was to confirm the supremacy of the grammar school in a tripartite system. The Labour government elected after the Second World War took over this doctrine, thus making possible a kind of Indian summer for Classics in the 1950s. As secondary school enrolments rose, so too did those for Latin, though in relative terms its recruitment was shrinking. But by the end of the decade, the Cold War and its associated alarms about the lack of scientific training in schools and universities had transformed the curricular debate. The result was the abolition of Compulsory Latin by Oxford and Cambridge in 1960; a critical blow to Classics whose consequences are explored by Martin Forrest in the next chapter.[6]

As is often the case, it is more difficult to recover information about those who worked for the CA in this period than it is for earlier times. We catch only occasional glimpses in memoirs. For example, G. C. Richards of Oriel College, Oxford (later Professor of Greek at Durham), recalled his tenure as Secretary (1920–6), and his long and 'ideal' friendship with A. C. Pearson of Cambridge, his colleague in the Secretaryship from 1920 to 1923. Richards dealt with general business, while Pearson looked after publications. As Richards points out, Pearson's experience in business made him an ideal organiser. Remarkably, as it now seems, when Pearson was 'obliged to leave [his teaching post at] Dulwich, by business demands on his time, he devoted himself to completing Jebb's *Sophocles* by an exhaustive treatment of the Fragments, which appeared in 1917 in three volumes'.[7] Richards was particularly proud of the successful founding of several branches. The Oxford branch had John Myres as a leading figure, but Myres fell out with a retired headmaster who had been appointed treasurer. Luckily, the latter soon resigned, and all was well. In those days the Oxford Philological Society did not accept women as members, and Richards clearly saw the CA branch as a forum in which women were able to join in discussions on classical topics.[8]

---

[5] See Chapter 6.

[6] For a more detailed discussion of the period 1920–60, see Stray, *Classics Transformed*, 271–97.

[7] G. C. Richards, *An Oxonian Looks Back* (Washington DC, 1960), 20. Richards kept Pearson's letters to him and hoped they might be preserved after his own death; so far they have not been located.

[8] Ibid.

Of later officers, the outstanding figures were L. J. D. Richardson of Cardiff and Tommy Melluish of London, both of whom acted as Secretary for twenty years (1943–63 and 1948–68 respectively).[9] Richardson inaugurated a period in which the CA seemed to some to be run by an academic Welsh 'Taffia'. His successors in the 1960s and '70s included Bryn Rees and Chris Collard, while L. A. Moritz acted as Treasurer – all holders of chairs in the University of Wales. Melluish was a versatile schoolmaster who was adept at translation and composition.[10] He wrote constantly to the *Spectator* and other papers, and also wrote to new Classics graduates urging them to join the CA. Beyond the Association, he actively supported the Orbilian Society and its *Acta Diurna*, a newspaper full of teaching material. Melluish also held office in the Association for the Reform of Latin Teaching. Indeed he had fingers in so many pies that when JACT was emerging in the late 1950s, his conservative views constituted a major obstacle to change.[11] At this point, the reformers of the 1940s had become stuck in their prewar ways; so it was not perhaps surprising that the discussions which led to the publication of *Re-appraisal* in 1962 seem to us now remarkably complacent.[12] The subscription remained, as it had always been, five shillings, and expenses were expected to be low. Before the war, Miss Gedge (Secretary 1927–34) had her gardener produce address labels when these were needed. In the 1960s, L. A. Moritz's purchase of an electric typewriter was considered by some distinctly extravagant. The financial situation was rescued by grants from the University of Cambridge and from John Spedan Lewis, founder of the department store chain. But the inflation of the 1970s made it imperative to increase the by then absurdly small subscription, and forced the improved financial planning which is now firmly in place.

[9] Richardson's photograph formed the frontispiece of *Proceedings* 60 (1963); Melhuish's, that of *Proceedings* 65 (1968).

[10] These skills were displayed in his response to a greetings card sent to him by sixty CA members when it was learned that he was too ill to attend the 1970 Conference. This was a poem in seven stanzas, stress-scanned and rhymed, which included a Latinised versions of all sixty names. It was printed in *Proceedings* 67 (1970), 40–1, with a key at p. 75.

[11] See Martin Forrest's account in the next chapter.

[12] The reader is referred to the next chapter for a detailed account. It might be noted (as Philip Hooker does in Chapter 12) that the Presidents of the 1950s tended to be over 70.

4

THE ABOLITION OF COMPULSORY LATIN AND ITS CONSEQUENCES

By MARTIN FORREST

School Classics in the Post-War Period

The 1950s represent the last full decade of the twentieth century in which the teaching of Latin in secondary schools was dominated by university requirements. In 1960 the Universities of Oxford and Cambridge ceased to require a pass in Ordinary Level Latin as an entry qualification for undergraduate students. This was to have deep and far-reaching consequences for the teaching of Latin and Classics in schools.

During the decade and a half that followed World War II, Classics departments in the more prestigious grammar schools and in the independent sector continued the ascendancy which they had hitherto enjoyed, although there was the constant pressure from other subjects to reduce the amount of timetabled allocation. Some study of Latin was generally *de rigueur* at least in the early stages of a grammar and public school education, with the more linguistically able youngsters expected to study Latin at least to Ordinary Level and sometimes to Advanced and Scholarship Level. The Norwood Report (1943) with its emphasis upon a traditional curriculum had been publicly hailed by one leading member of the Classical Association, T. W. (Tommy) Melluish as 'a rainbow in the sky'.[1] Following the Butler Education Act (1944) pupils in the maintained sector were to be taught according to 'age, ability and aptitude' in three different kinds of school. With a rigorous selective system in place, Classics Departments in the post-war years were given the confidence to continue their work of producing, as in earlier days, a steady flow of potential university students, with a thorough sixth-form grounding in Latin, Greek and Ancient History. The numerous grammar schools which did not have a separate Classical Sixth, and in

---

[1] *G & R* 13(1944), 59.

which the teaching of Greek was rare or non-existent, ensured that all potential university candidates were at least given the opportunity to pass Latin at Ordinary level. Those who showed special ability in the subject could continue it to Advanced level along with other subjects available in the Sixth Form such as history, English and French.

The Classical Association itself provided some support for the teaching of Classics in schools by sponsoring annual reading competitions for schools, the first of these being held in 1943. Local branches were encouraged to provide lectures by university scholars for school pupils to attend. In addition, an Education Sub-committee had been formed in 1944.

There was, however, another side to this story. During the 1950s, there was growing disaffection among a minority of classicists whose daily business was with and inside secondary schools. The principal cause for concern was the large number of 'dropouts' from Latin courses in such schools. Pupils who struggled with accidence and syntax in their early years of studying Latin, and who failed to reach a point where they could apply their grammatical studies in the reading of original Latin, became disillusioned and asked to withdraw. Such a concern, already publicly acknowledged in the 1938 Spens Report ('In no other subject has the end been placed at so great a distance and the realisation of its value emerged so late'),[2] had been swept under the carpet in the drive to consolidate the post-war secondary school Classics curriculum. However some classicists began to ask serious questions about the appropriateness of the traditional Latin course for all who embarked upon it. Alternative courses were promoted under the *aegis* of *Latin Teaching*, organ of the Association for the Reform of Latin Teaching and edited by a grammar school headmaster, C. W. E (Cyril) Peckett of the Priory School, Shrewsbury. It was argued that all pupils in the Grammar School should be introduced to the classical world through the medium of English, irrespective of whether or not they went on to study Latin.

Dora Pym, who had responsibility for the training of Classics teachers at Bristol University, organised two conferences in 1954 at which the whole place and purpose of Classics in the school curriculum was placed under critical examination. Pym's motives are revealed in a memorandum which she wrote to her Professor: 'The teaching of Classics in all but a few schools is hampered, not as it appears on the surface, *only* by

---

[2] *The Spens Report* (1938), 176.

examination requirements and deep controversy about 'methods', but also by unexamined assumptions as to the place and contribution of the Classics in contemporary schools.' [3]

The vast majority of students who at this time were educated outside the Grammar and Independent Schools rarely came into contact with a teacher of Classics, let alone had the opportunity to begin Latin. However, the needs of these pupils were not entirely forgotten. Francis Kinchin Smith, who trained Classics teachers at the University of London Institute of Education, had in 1949 organised a conference entitled 'Classical background in emergency training colleges and modern schools'. He subsequently raised the issue with the Classical Association.[4] Although the conference was attended by thirty representatives from the colleges, it is difficult to know how far any impact was made. The IAAM handbook on the teaching of Classics first published in 1953 and edited by Tommy Melluish contains one chapter entitled 'Classics in the Secondary Modern School'. This contains a variety of suggestions including Greek and Roman stories, the Greek theatre, art and architecture and ancient sport.

The other cause of disaffection among some Classics teachers which bubbled under the surface during the 1950s was the Ordinary Level Latin syllabus itself. By the end of the 1950s the O-level examination comprised formal grammar questions, English into Latin translation and Latin into English translation (either from unprepared passages of prose and verse or from set books). Questions on the 'background' to Latin were few and carried a small number of marks. Understanding of the literature read as set books was mainly tested by requiring the candidates to translate selected passages into English, rather than by the use of carefully structured questions.

The Abolition of Compulsory Latin and its Impact

By the time that the Association held its Annual Meeting at Southampton in April 1960, moves were already well advanced for the removal of the entrance requirement of an O-level pass in a classical language at the Universities of Oxford and Cambridge. Cambridge, followed by Oxford, in fact agreed the relevant changes to their statutes in May of that year. The debate on the future of Latin teaching which

[3] Dora Pym Papers/Memorandum, 21 April 1954.
[4] Council minutes, 2 July 1949.

took place at the Southampton meeting was the first occasion when the minds of classicists collectively concentrated upon the consequences of these decisions for the future of their subject.

The lead was taken by C. O. (Charles) Brink, Kennedy Professor of Latin at the University of Cambridge. Brink challenged the whole nature and purpose of the existing O-level Latin syllabus and examination. The fact that a relatively small number of candidates subsequently proceeded to A-level Latin suggested that the content of O level should no longer be regarded as an introduction to more advanced studies but as an entity in itself. If this were the case, a number of further questions needed to be asked. Did the subject, as it was at that time, justify its existence? Did pupils make the best use of their time? What should be taught in an O-level Latin course of two or three years' duration? Was the content satisfactory for older students who did not intend to continue with Latin beyond O level? Referring to what he regarded as the deplorably low standard of translation from Latin into English achieved by O-level candidates, Brink proposed that there be a reduction in the time spent in future on English into Latin composition and that there should be a shift of emphasis towards unseen translation.[5]

The discussion which followed Brink's clarion call appears to have been substantial and not without controversy. However, a resolution formulated by Brink himself was carried by 200 votes with only one person dissenting. The text read as follows: 'That this meeting recommends a general reconsideration of the aims and syllabus of the Ordinary level Latin examination with special reference to the requirements of non-specialists'.[6] Brink's speech to the Association's annual meeting in the spring of 1960 must be seen as a landmark in the history of twentieth-century Classics teaching, and events at Southampton were to provide the backdrop to three developments which took place in the succeeding years. One of these developments, however, proved in the long run to have more far-reaching consequences than the others.

The first of these developments was a direct consequence of the resolution passed at Southampton. A preliminary letter together with a memorandum was sent to the Examining Boards under the signature of Professor L. J. D. Richardson, one of the Joint Secretaries, informing them of the decision of the Annual General Meeting:

The existing course seems to aim primarily at providing for the needs of future classical scholars, who in fact represent only a small proportion of those taking Latin. The

[5] *Proceedings* (1960), 22.   [6] *Reappraisal* (Supplement to *G&R* NS 9), 8.

problem that has to be faced is that of constructing a course in Latin to Ordinary level which shall be of intrinsic value to those who are not likely to continue the formal study of Latin. At the same time, in order to meet the needs of potential classical scholars, and of others who will take Latin to Advanced level or beyond, a high standard of accuracy must be demanded in basic grammatical knowledge.[7]

The accompanying memorandum included the following:

. . . the Classical Association regards the oral and written manipulation of Latin as a most valuable ancillary exercise towards the understanding of the language but does not think that, for most pupils, a paper with an undue concentration on details of syntax should weigh as heavily as one which tests the pupils' reading knowledge of Latin. [8]

The Classical Association's Education Sub-committee, under the chairmanship of Professor T. B. L. Webster since 1959, was asked to conduct a survey of the Association's branches. A copy of the letter and memorandum sent to the Boards was prepared for circulation to the branches, together with a series of questions aimed at promoting discussion. The questions were framed with a view to inviting branches to consider ways in which the existing O-level Latin course might be reshaped. The questionnaire conducted on behalf of the Association by the Education Sub-committee during the summer of 1960 was sent to 28 regional branches. Letters were sent out to all branches inviting them to put the matter before their members.

The second development was the offer made by the Editorial Board of *Greece & Rome* to publish a 46-page supplement devoted entirely to the problems and opportunities of the teacher of Classics in school. The Editor was to be Melluish, himself a schoolmaster and one of the Association's Joint Secretaries as well as a leading figure in other spheres of classical activity.

The third development was the initiative to bring together the Classical Association, the Association for the Reform of Latin Teaching and the Orbilian Society under a single umbrella.[9] The case for having one organisation to speak for Classics teachers at such a critical time seemed to be of the utmost importance for the future of Classics in schools. Of the developments which followed the Southampton Annual Meeting, this last was to prove by far the most significant. The Joint Association of Classical Teachers, which was to emerge in 1962, in due course provided a range of initiatives to support Classics teachers as they faced the impact of change in their schools, and it was the new

---

[7] CA, letter to Examining Boards, 1960. [8] Ibid.
[9] Membership of the Orbilian Society was by invitation. The Society published the Latin newspaper *Acta Diurna* and other materials to support the teaching of Latin in grammar schools.

organisation that was to press forward the urgent case for research into the teaching of Latin to O level.

The first two developments on the other hand, whilst being in themselves useful exercises which were welcome at the time, had outcomes which scarcely provided Classics teachers with the practical means to cope with imminent change in their schools. In retrospect, the outcomes of the questionnaire in the form in which they were communicated both to the Council and to the wider membership appear remarkably complacent. The subsequent memorandum, sent to the Examining Boards almost a year later, after taking account of responses from the branches, appears with hindsight to be deeply conservative, whilst maintaining the semblance of openness to experimentation. The responses from the branches, many of which had held general meetings for the purpose, were summarised by D. G. (Donald) Bentliff, a close associate of Melluish and also a schoolmaster member of the Education Sub-committee. Melluish himself reported on the findings of the survey to the Classical Association's Council at two stages. His reports, whilst implying some criticism of the existing O-level syllabus, in no way echo the apparent overwhelming dissatisfaction with the existing examination which had been registered by those who voted for Brink's Southampton resolution. In fact the Council claimed to have found the response from large numbers of people in the branches 'heartening'.

The Council in this second memorandum to the Examination Boards emphasised three points:

- 'O' Level Latin should be primarily an examination in language.
- the examination should be as simple as possible with minimum prescription, but standards of accuracy should be high.
- there should be a maximum number of alternative syllabuses with maximum freedom for teachers to develop what they thought to be most desirable.[10]

The Council was at pains to stress that the primary and essential purpose of O-level Latin was to test the ability to understand Latin and to translate into English; but to ensure that basic grammar and syntax were known, the examination should also test the ability to translate English into Latin. Members of Council went on to call for a strict marking scheme which would encourage concentration on the elements of syntax, grammar and usage, although there was some

[10] CA, letter to Examining Boards, April 1961.

recognition that alternative syllabuses should be available experimentally for those who would discontinue Latin after O level. As Melluish in summarising the responses put it:

> One gathers that there is a solid hump of resistance, doggedly reiterating 'First things first: Latin is a language and ours is primarily a linguistic task'. Perhaps there is more than verbal niggling in the purists' objection that this background knowledge, eminently desirable though it may be, cannot be described as Latin.[11]

A survey carried out among its members by the ARLT produced responses which broadly matched those recorded in the Classical Association branches, although only ten per cent of the membership returned the tear-off pro forma which was printed in *Latin Teaching*.

The supplement published by *Greece & Rome* in 1962, entitled *Re-appraisal*, provided an opportunity for Professor Brink to elaborate upon his plea for change to the GCE O-level Latin syllabus and examination. Brink again emphasised the need to offer something more worthwhile to the pupil who takes Latin to Ordinary level and no further: '. . . whether it is English into Latin, or Latin into English, I suggest that it should be *chiefly* a one-way road. The sophisticated dual carriage-way of the classical tradition asks too much of the small Latinist, and offers him too little.'[12]

The publication of *Re-appraisal* came too early to register the impact felt in schools as a result of the Oxbridge decisions on university admission. In fact, the Staff Inspector for Classics in schools, C. W. (Charles) Baty, sounded remarkably upbeat in his statement that 'There is, in fact, every sign that the change in those requirements is having little or no effect in schools.'[13] On the other hand, Brink and Baty in their respective contributions both emphasised the large wastage through pupils dropping out, the outdated nature of textbooks and the inappropriateness of the existing examination rubric. There was a need to switch the emphasis to reading Latin literature. A number of chapters of *Re-appraisal*, by different authors, contributed to the debate about what, if anything, should replace the existing Latin syllabus and what other alternative syllabuses should be developed as a support for the Classics teacher in school.

Contributions included a proposal that dictionaries might be used in combination with harder passages for unseen translation, suggestions for an improved Latin O-level course aimed at enhancing reading and comprehension skills, an innovative approach aimed at producing a

---

[11] *Re-appraisal*, 46.   [12] Ibid, 9.   [13] Ibid, 12.

worthwhile course for the two-year Latinist who did not continue to GCE level, and a plea for the reading of Latin aloud to be taken more seriously. Conspicuous by its absence is any reference to the possibility of courses in classical civilisation, although a course in classical civilisation for non-specialists was originally mooted.[14] The prevailing view among some leading activists in the Association in the post-war years had been that courses based upon life, society and history, whilst appropriate for those who abandoned Latin, were a very poor second best. Those who suggested that there should be a cultural element as background to linguistic study were traditionally seen as 'specious', or even 'dangerous'.[15] The decision to appoint Melluish as Editor of *Re-appraisal* ensured that this volume dealt mainly with those areas of traditional Classics teaching with which he felt most comfortable.

The articles by Brink and Baty established an agenda for a major reconsideration of the way that Latin was taught, but such reform could not take place overnight. The two articles are however crucial to an understanding of the developments which led to the establishment of a curriculum development project and the large-scale reform of Latin teaching that took place in the late 1960s. These two articles represent the most important contributions to *Re-appraisal.*

The Origins of JACT

By the summer of 1962 a new organisation, the Joint Association of Classical Teachers, had come into being, which brought together under a single umbrella the Classical Association, the Association for the Reform of Latin Teaching and the Orbilian Society. The emergence of this new organisation, however, did not come about without considerable birth pangs. That it came into being at all was largely due to the energy, persistence and political skill of J. E. (John) Sharwood Smith, who had relatively recently been appointed to succeed Kinchin Smith as trainer of Classics teachers at the London Institute of Education.

Sharwood Smith recognised the urgency for concerted action by classicists in the wake of the 1960 decisions at Oxford and Cambridge. He recognised that without such action, prospects for Classics in secondary schools would be bleak. Following his appointment to the

---

[14] CA Education Sub-committee minutes, 24 February 1962.
[15] *G&R* 15 (1946), 114–15.

Classical Association's Council, he had observed the efforts made by a fellow teacher-trainer, W. B. (William) Thompson of Leeds University, to persuade the Council to broaden its scope. Thompson's concern had been to metamorphose the Classical Association into a 'service bureau' along the lines of that provided for teachers by the American Classical League. His intention was that teachers of Classics in school would be offered among other things an advisory service, a range of teaching materials, including audio-visual aids, and syllabuses. Refresher courses would be provided on a regional basis. The Association should be publishing a range of periodicals as well as occasional publications concerned with the teaching of Classics. In order to achieve this, there should be an initial grant as well as an annual subsidy.[16] It was inevitable that an organisation which had retained an annual membership fee of five shillings since its inauguration in 1903 would baulk at such an ambitious change of function with its implied dramatic increase in financial out-goings. Thompson's proposals foundered when Council finally agreed to keep the fee as it was.[17] Sharwood Smith later commented on moves to increase the subscription: 'A major reason given for the defeat was that the proposal went against one of the principles of the CA, namely that it should cater for the needs of retired and impoverished classically-educated clergymen who wished to solace their retirement by refreshing their classical learning.'[18] Furthermore, there was a clear division of opinion even among those who had the closest involvement with schools as to the urgency of the situation and the need for change.

In 1961 there was also an unsuccessful attempt at persuading the ARLT to change its name and to undertake a much wider range of activities than hitherto. Whilst some favoured widening the Association's activities and changing its name, some of the longest-standing members, whose memories went back to the days of their revered founding father, Dr W. H. D. Rouse, strongly opposed these changes. A proposal to set out the arguments for and against changing the Association's name and to canvass the views of members in the next issue of *Latin Teaching* failed when the President, Tommy Melluish, who was chairing the meeting, abruptly brought the discussion to an end.[19]

[16] Thompson Collection/Personal notes for CA Council, 31 October 1959.

[17] Council minutes, 9 July 1960.

[18] *JACT Review* (Summer 2000), 1.

[19] The reason for the sudden closure of the debate was that Cyril Peckett announced that he and his school would not remain in or support the Association if the name were changed. It is worth noting that Peckett had himself triggered an attempt to change the Association's name ten years earlier, but had changed his mind on the subject when it became clear in a ballot that a hard core of the membership was opposed to any change.

It did not take Sharwood Smith very long to realise the difficulties involved in attempting to make the existing organisations more effective – a fresh organisation was the only realistic solution. It was clear to him that such an organisation was needed to keep teachers in touch with developments and provide them with support in the face of changing circumstances. There was a particular need of support for the solitary classicist, and there were very many of them. Approaches were made to individuals whom Sharwood Smith thought likely to be sympathetic. In explaining the need for a new organisation he identified three particular areas of concern: relaxation of Oxford and Cambridge entry requirements, the spread of comprehensive schooling and possibly Leicestershire-type schools[20] with their break at 14-plus and thirdly the 'future invasion' of technology into the classroom (tape recorders, television, and perhaps the language laboratory or even teaching machines). There was the additional need to have an organisation which could conduct systematic research and experiment in relation to examination syllabuses.[21]

Writing a decade later of the moves to establish a new organisation, John Sharwood Smith, under the pseudonym *Extispex*, recorded his reflections in *Didaskalos*. It was only after two cliff-hanging conferences, nine months of intensive work by a committee of four, chaired by Professor Brink, and a change of proposed name from Federated to Joint Association of Classical Teachers, that the new organisation could be brought into existence. [22]

Sharwood Smith recognised that there was likely to be considerable opposition to his efforts in some quarters and that he first needed to build a bridgehead of support within each of the existing classical organisations. His initial overtures were to Cyril Peckett and A. R. (Arthur) Munday, leading members of the ARLT, both headmasters and joint authors of the Latin course book *Principia*.[23] The three of them were due to meet at Munday's Grammar School in Solihull (Tudor Grange), but in the event, Peckett missed his bus.[24] Nonetheless it was agreed between them that a conference should be called but the

---

[20] The Director of Education for Leicestershire had introduced a two-tier comprehensive plan for his County's secondary schools involving the creation of 11–14 and 14–18 high schools.

[21] Sharwood Smith papers, documents on the foundation of JACT.

[22] *Didaskalos* 4. 2 (1973), 260.

[23] At that time they were also collaborating on a Greek course subsequently known as *Thrasymachus*.

[24] Strictly speaking, Peckett did not miss his bus but failed to catch it having realised that the timetable of his itinerary would allow him just ten minutes or so before he had to leave and get back to Shrewsbury.

numbers would be kept to modest proportions with 12–14 attending. Invitations would be sent out to individuals who were known to be eager for change as well as to representatives of the existing organisations. The meeting would take place in late September 1961, and it was agreed that Sharwood Smith would draft as a basis for discussion a few possible schemes whereby the ARLT and the Orbilian Society might join together with the Classical Association without losing their respective identities.

Within the ARLT, additional support was forthcoming from W. L. Rowe, editor of its journal, *Latin Teaching*, and from the secretary, Margaret Drury, who was herself a practising teacher in a London grammar school. Approaches were made to the current President and Vice-President, W. E. Rees and F. R. Dale, both of whom had retired from teaching. Whereas the former expressed concern about his Association losing its identity, he appears to have been open to persuasion. Dale on the other hand was not wholly convinced of the value of a new organisation. However, he was fully in support of the concern for the lone Classics teacher and supported Sharwood Smith's initiative in seeking to keep Classics in schools alive. [25] An approach to the Orbilian Society was warmly received. The Society's then President G. M. Lyne, based at Blackpool Grammar School, welcomed Sharwood Smith's overtures and nominated the editor of the Latin newspaper, *Acta Diurna*, D. W. (Dennis) Blandford, also a practising Classics master, to represent the organisation at the proposed conference. [26]

Securing the necessary support from the Classical Association was far more difficult. Two leading members of the Association's Education Sub-committee, Melluish and Bentliff, who both taught in schools, were close associates and could be truly said to represent the 'chalk face'; and they were deeply sceptical about the need for a new organisation. Their opposition to moves which would change the nature of the Classical Association or establish what they saw as an unnecessary new organisation was fierce and sustained from the outset. As in the case of earlier proposals to expand the work of the Association, financial concerns about any proposed new organisation were never far away, nor were claims that support would not be forthcoming from grass-roots teachers. These arguments, deployed by those who opposed change, could always be guaranteed to find support within the Association. Melluish was a dominant figure at the time, being Joint

[25] Notes of interview with J. E. Sharwood Smith, 30 September 1986.   [26] Ibid.

Secretary of the Classical Association and a leading member of the Education Sub-committee, who had also concurrently held office as Vice-President of the ARLT and of the Orbilian Society. He had been the Editor of *Re-appraisal* and also Editor of the IAAM Handbook on the teaching of Classics.

There was however some support within the Education Sub-committee. Professor Webster, the Committee's Chairman, and Thompson were eager for an umbrella organisation. Sharwood Smith himself was of course also a member of the committee. None of these however was a practising teacher of Classics in secondary schools. Further efforts were therefore directed at recruiting others who could speak in support of the proposed new organisation from the school perspective. Two heads, M. M. Black (Bradford Girls' Grammar School) and B. M. Forrest (Southgate County Grammar School) were invited to attend the conference. The latter was invited to chair the proceedings. The conference was also attended by the Staff HMI for Classics, Charles Baty.

Members of the ARLT Committee had previously expressed some anxiety about the proposals, and those officers who had been invited to the conference were urged by their colleagues to act as individuals and not to speak on behalf of the Association.[27] Other constituencies with a direct or indirect interest in the teaching of Classics in schools were the University Departments of Education and the Departments of Classics. Energetic support was forthcoming from Departments of Education at the Universities of Cambridge, Nottingham and Birmingham as well as the London Institute and Leeds University.[28] The only representative of a University Classics Department was Professor Webster. Others who had been approached were, for various reasons, unable to attend the September conference.

The conference passed three resolutions. There was unanimous agreement on the need for some new means of enabling teachers to help one another to meet the challenge of changing circumstances. There was also general agreement on the need to establish an information service bureau for the assistance of all Classics teachers. The proposal to establish a 'federated association' of Classical teachers achieved considerable but not unanimous support, there being two

---

[27] ARLT Committee Minutes, 29 August 1961.

[28] At this time Classics teachers were trained in a large number of university Education departments. The first annual conference of lecturers in the teaching of Classics was convened by William Thompson in September 1959.

votes recorded against the proposal. In some quarters, the term 'Federation' aroused suspicions of a take-over bid, a concept from the world of business that was very much in the public eye at that time. A delaying tactic aimed at 'investigating the possibilities of establishing' a new association only attracted five votes. It was agreed to convene a second conference with an expanded membership in January 1962.

Although there is no official record of this second conference, at which the decision to go ahead was taken, two unofficial sets of notes from the meeting make it possible to establish the main arguments put forward for the new organisation and to identify the main sources of opposition to the venture.[29] On this occasion the Chair was taken by D. M. (David) Balme, Reader in Classics at Queen Mary College London. The proposals for a new organisation that would represent all teachers was widely endorsed. Support for the Federation was also forthcoming from the Heads present and from many of the University teachers, including representatives from Departments of Education. In the closing stages of the meeting, eloquent pleas were made by Professors Brink and Webster. The vote in favour of establishing the new organisation in principle was finally carried by 27 votes to four. In an attempt to mollify the bitterest opponents of the new organisation, two concessions were made before the meeting closed. The name was agreed as 'The Joint Association of Classical Teachers', and the organisation would only come into effective existence once the three constituent organisations had accepted the proposed arrangements.

A further argument advanced by the minority who opposed the setting up of a new organisation had been that a rift would be caused between school teachers and university teachers. Brink assured the conference that far from creating a schism, the new association could do much to strengthen the ties between them and that furthermore University teachers would be awakened to the problems facing schools. Webster felt that, from the evidence of candidates he had interviewed, the impact of the Classical Association across the country was 'patchy'. He wanted University teachers to be able to provide the necessary help to schools. The Education Sub-committee's work would come to an end. In some respects they were unable to help. Hence the need for a bureau and information service.

In the event, the agreement of the Classical Association to the proposed new organisation was not achieved without considerable

---

[29] Sharwood Smith Papers, ibid.

argument among Council members. The final battle was a close run thing. That there was, in the end, a positive outcome was said to be due to the warm and powerful support from a few personalities within the existing organisations and to the immense skill of the Chairman, Professor Webster.

Once the three societies had accepted JACT, they collaborated well from the outset and provided generous support, both financial and organisational. One of the most valuable offers of help came from the Classical Association itself, in the form of a temporary loan of its modestly proportioned room in the Institute of Classical Studies in which the headquarters were established and from which the Inquiry Bureau could operate.

One immediate effect of creating a new association which embraced the three existing organisations, and which enabled teachers to belong to all four organisations through the payment of a single annual fee of two guineas, was a boost in numbers for the Classical Association. Surveys conducted by the University Department of Education lecturers showed that there was a fresh reservoir of support among newly qualified and qualifying teachers. Furthermore concern expressed by opponents of reform that public school teachers were 'content to do their own thing' and were unlikely to give their support to the new organisation, led to redoubled efforts to recruit teachers in the independent and voluntary sectors.[30]

The Joint Association of Classical Teachers

The new Joint Association was soon perceived to be 'joint' not only in terms of facilitating reciprocal membership of the various classical organisations but in terms of the collaboration between university teachers and teachers in schools. Universities had a direct interest in what went on in schools and practical opportunities for them to be involved in school Classics were now more obviously possible. John Murrell, a former Executive Secretary of JACT, has reflected in recent correspondence upon the high level of cooperation that has been made possible over the years between universities and schools. The JACT Greek Project must surely rank as one of the most successful achievements of JACT, not least as an example of cooperation between school

[30] Ibid.

and university. Advanced-level syllabuses in Ancient History and Classical Civilisation, annual summer schools and the regular publication of *Omnibus* are other living examples.

Early JACT initiatives included the establishment of panels of scholars who provided detailed advice for schools, for example on the teaching of Ancient History, a termly bulletin published for all members and a yearly journal, *Didaskalos*. One memorable feature of the new journal was the early series of articles devoted to theoretical discussion of what might constitute a 'classical education'. At local level, branches of JACT were, in due course, set up with the express intention of supporting school teachers, many of whom were lone classicists in maintained grammar schools. Especially significant was the establishment in 1966 of the London Association of Classical Teachers (LACT), whose influence was to spread far beyond the capital. It was the first local branch to be set up and, as in the case of JACT and for similar reasons, initially met with opposition from the London Branch of the Classical Association. Its founding Secretary, M. R. F. (Michael) Gunningham, recalls a meeting attended by close on 300 Classics teachers, convened at a large South London comprehensive school the previous autumn with a view to debating the merits of establishing a new body specifically aimed at serving the interests of Classics teachers in the London area. He found himself sitting quite fortuitously next to Tommy Melluish, whom he had not met before. The chance encounter with Melluish was to prove useful the following year when Gunningham was asked by Sharwood Smith to put the case for setting up LACT to the London Branch of the Classical Association. The Committee was persuaded that the work of the new organisation would in no way encroach upon that of the London Branch as their aims were entirely different. Seminal conferences were held by LACT which generated publications (for example, Classical Studies in CSE and Classics at Advanced Level) and helped to establish courses in classical civilisation at different stages of the secondary school. London Association of Classical Teachers Original Records (LACTORS), which were launched by Christopher Stray, have become a widely known and respected range of translated texts for use in sixth forms and in university courses.

The need for the JACT Committee to initiate research into the teaching of Latin became even more urgent as the implications of comprehensive reorganisation gradually began to sink in. It was not until the fifth meeting of the Committee, held in April 1964, that detailed consideration was given to ways in which Classics teachers might respond. By this date some Local Education Authorities were actively considering comprehensive reorganisation plans. Furthermore, opinion polls suggested that the next general election might result in the election of a Labour government committed to abolishing the 11-plus examination. The Leicestershire Plan proposals appeared to present the most serious challenge to existing Classics courses, since there was to be a break in schooling at 14-plus, although the concept of 'all-in' comprehensive schools in which Latin was seen as a subject for a small minority of pupils was challenging enough! It is recorded in the minutes that 'a good deal of alarm was felt and some despondency'. The editorial of the fourth Bulletin published by JACT reads as follows:

JACT is not inclined to campaign for more Latin among weaker pupils; but its policy is to insist that a proper Latin course contributes to general education and does not merely aim at overcoming ever lowered examination hurdles by means of rushed courses.[31]

An internal memorandum drafted by Sharwood Smith a month earlier provides more detail of the policy being formulated:

However sound the arguments may be against the Leicestershire Plan, it would be a mistake for JACT to campaign against it. To do so would be to reinforce the popular identification of classics with reaction and to consolidate progressive opinion in favour of the Plan; we have not enough influence seriously to affect the issue and we could only damage any attempt to get Latin and Greek taught in Leicestershire-type schools . . . JACT should oppose Latin in the middle school, except in very favourable circumstances . . . It is important that there should be an opportunity for kindling an interest in Greco-Roman civilisation at this stage, so that a pupil may opt for Latin as soon as he reaches the Upper School. [32]

An immediate response to discussion within the JACT Committee was the organisation of a conference to consider the 'Leicestershire Plan' and its effect on classical teaching in June 1964. At this conference, held in Hughes Hall, Cambridge, there was much discussion of the type of course that might be developed in the Junior High Schools to precede the study of Latin in the post-14 High Schools. A major difficulty was the conservatism of the teachers from Leicestershire who were present at the conference and who were at the 'sharp end' of these developments; as Baty remarked to a former HMI colleague, the Leicestershire teachers felt prevented from doing their real job, which was to impart North and Hillard and Hillard and Botting to their pupils.[33] Arising from the conference a pamphlet was published by JACT setting out

[31] JACT *Bulletin* 4.
[32] JACT records, Leicestershire Plan file: internal memorandum, 26 March 1964.
[33] Ibid., letter from C. W. Baty to a former HMI colleague.

various possible forms of comprehensive reorganisation and the ways in which Latin in particular might feature within them. The pamphlet was not published until 1965, but in the meantime there had been several other developments.[34]

The Classical Association, prior to the establishment of JACT, had by tradition been the custodian of the Classics teachers' interests. Now that JACT had been formed, with its substantial overlap in membership with the Classical Association, it was inevitable that JACT rather than the Association would be seen as speaking on behalf of Classics in schools. The transition however did not prove easy, nor did the proposal to disband the Education Sub-committee. Melluish continued to argue that the Classical Association had the necessary authority, membership and standing in the country to be able to give Directors of Education a stick with which to beat their 'politically obsessed Education Commi-tees'.[35] As one of the Joint Secretaries of the Classical Association, Melluish, although now a member of the JACT Committee, does not appear to have associated himself publicly with any of the new organ-isation's initiatives; instead he chose to take action himself by adopting in public, as well as in private, a more confrontational approach. He proposed a resolution which was unanimously adopted at the Council's meeting on 4th July 1964 and which read as follows: 'That the Classical Association is gravely concerned at the prospect that new schemes for the reorganisation of secondary education may make it extremely difficult, even impossible, for pupils to take Latin and Greek.'[36]

A copy of the resolution, under the signature of the President, Sir Basil Blackwell, was sent to the main newspapers and to the Secretary of State for Education and Science, Mr Quintin Hogg. Although the resolution had received unanimous support, the Joint Secretary's action was seen by some as being at the very least unhelpful. At worst, the Association appeared to align itself with the forces of reaction and this was bound to damage the cause of Classics.

Research into the Teaching of Classics

A central figure in all the early developments which took place under the aegis of JACT was the organisation's first Secretary General,

---

[34] *Secondary Reorganisation and the Classics*, ed. D. J. Morton (JACT Pamphlet 2).
[35] JACT records, CA File. Letter from T. W. Melluish to C. W. Baty, 20 September 1964.
[36] Council minutes, 4 July 1964.

Charles Baty, who had retired from HM Inspectorate in 1962. In July 1964, soon after the Leicestershire Plan Conference, the first of a series of secret meetings took place with the Nuffield Foundation; Baty was the key figure. He clearly relished his role as a tireless diplomat, drawing upon his long experience in HM Inspectorate. These meetings were to lead in due course to the setting up of the Cambridge School Classics Project (CSCP). Those who were close to developments at the time suggest that there was an air of conspiracy about the whole affair. In recent years it has emerged that the idea of funding for a curriculum development project in Classics had first been mooted by R. W. (Robert) Morris, a senior HMI who had been seconded to work for the Curriculum Study Group established by Sir David Eccles, during his time as Education Secretary. Morris held regular meetings with R. A. (Tony) Becher of the Nuffield Foundation with a view to promoting projects which might benefit from Nuffield Foundation funding. Financial grants had already been provided for curriculum projects in Science, Mathematics and Modern Foreign Languages. Morris, himself a mathematician, had a high regard for Classics. An approach was made to K. G. (Kenneth) Todd, Baty's successor as Staff Inspector for Classics, and it was not long before a small group consisting of Morris, Becher, Baty and Todd were holding regular meetings to establish the framework for a Classics Project. Two conferences held at Nuffield Lodge and a meeting held in Professor Brink's rooms at Gonville and Caius College in Cambridge led, after one potentially serious 'blip', to a joint proposal from the Faculty Board of Classics and the University's Department of Education to the Nuffield Foundation.[37]

The Cambridge School Classics Project (CSCP) first came into being on 1st January 1966 with a grant from Nuffield of £34,500. Under its energetic first Director, D. J. (David) Morton, who had been seconded from his post at the University of Nottingham, the Project team set about the following tasks:

1. To investigate ways of improving the teaching of Latin at the early stage, ie. up to O Level, with special reference to the task of improving reading fluency.
2. To investigate a course of a non-linguistic kind for pupils who lack the ability or opportunity to take a linguistic course. We shall also devise

---

[37] For a detailed account of the origins and early history of the Cambridge School Classics Project, see M. Forrest, *Modernising the Classics* (Exeter, 1996).

non-linguistic foundation courses to precede, in some cases, the language-based course.[38]

The team insisted that the emphasis in their new Latin course would from the outset be upon reading. Whilst this did not preclude composition activities, they insisted that composition was a means and not an end in itself.

After extensive trialling in schools and following considerable internal difficulties within the Project, the new Latin Course emerged as *The Cambridge Latin Course* (*CLC*), published by the Cambridge University Press from 1970 onwards. The course in its early stages was divided up into units, each of which was presented to the pupils as a series of pamplets. Each unit had its distinctive colour coding. From the outset, the Project engaged the services of Dr J. B. (John) Wilkins of Queen Mary College, London. His thinking was powerfully influenced by the contemporary schools of grammatical analysis of Noam Chomsky in the USA and of M. A. K. Halliday in England and at that time he was researching new approaches to the teaching of Latin. The objective of the new course was defined as reading skill, thus distinguishing it from traditional courses whose objectives included composition as well as reading. The heavy burden of grammar that was formerly handled openly with the pupils had not vanished completely, but overt grammatical drilling had been replaced by a 'programmed grammatical experience' in the reading passages. In the view of the Linguistic Consultant, the Latin sentence was seen as 'the most valid analytical entity'.[39] Sentence patterns were compared with one another and all other parts of the language were treated with reference to their typical place in the sentence structure. One important result of this was that formal paradigms and sets of inflexions, both of which featured strongly in traditional courses, received what was regarded as a more realistic assessment.

The other innovative feature of the new Latin course was the emphasis upon systematic study of aspects of Roman civilisation. What had previously been referred to by Classics teachers as 'background' was now promoted to being 'paralinguistic' material, to be studied *alongside* the language work, as an English account of aspects of Roman culture. More importantly, the Latin passages themselves were designed to highlight these cultural aspects. C. (Clary) Greig and J. A. (John) Jones worked as an imaginative and effective team creating the language

---

[38] Forrest, *Modernising*, 50.   [39] Ibid., 66.

material around the linguistic formulations of John Wilkins. At the same time they drew upon other scholarly expertise in locating their stories in Pompeii, Britain and Alexandria during the time of the Flavian Emperors. The Project once again sought to break new ground by engaging a professional husband and wife team as illustrators and by arranging for new photographic material to be created on Italy and Roman Britain. The new course was well supported by slide sets and audio tapes.

Early overtures to the media made by the CSCP and JACT resulted in widespread coverage of the new Latin course. Geoffrey Fallows, at that time Classics Master at Crown Woods Comprehensive School, Eltham, suggested that the new material put greater responsibility on the teacher to ensure that the grammar was being understood, but 'He finds that children who under the selective system would have gone to secondary modern schools are learning to read – and enjoy – Latin authors'.[40] Another striking feature of the new course was the engagement of pupils with the stories and with the people who featured in them. Reports in the press refer to one class of schoolgirls who wept through two Latin lessons following the destruction of Pompeii and with it the deaths of their favourite characters.[41]

In parallel with the Cambridge Course and hard on its heels, the Scottish Teachers Group produced their own course, *Ecce Romani* (Oliver and Boyd 1971). This also had aims similar to those of the Cambridge Latin Course, although the structure and presentation were more cautious than the approach adopted by Cambridge. Many schools stubbornly adhered to the traditional courses such as those by Paterson and Macnaughton, or even the much earlier North and Hillard. Some, understandably, were adopting a 'wait and see' approach. Others had little alternative but to opt for the new streamlined courses if the subject was to survive at all in their schools. The availability of both new courses, with their emphasis upon reading and the study of Roman civilisation, meant that the way was now open to schools in England and Wales to choose a course which reflected the realities of school life in the maintained sector of the mid-twentieth century.

The second important development within the CSCP was the attention paid to the creation of 'non-linguistic' courses aimed at pupils below sixth form level. Because of the urgent need to help those grammar schools facing reorganisation by the late 1960s, the development of a classical foundation course for 11- to 13-year olds was

---

[40] *The Guardian*, 25 May 1971, 7.   [41] Ibid.

deemed to be the priority. Even in the independent sector the traditional order of things appeared to be changing. Not only was there often a desire for updating the teaching of Classics in ways which reflected the post-1960 climate, but the Labour Government appeared to have its sights on the independent sector as well as the maintained schools as targets for its comprehensive reform of secondary education. Some independent schools, among them a number of Direct Grant Grammar Schools, had been attracted to the new Latin course, for which the Southern Universities Board had been willing to provide an examination. For example, Malcolm Ricketts, Senior Classics Master at Manchester Grammar School, was quoted as believing his pupils finished at O-level standard with a greater ability to read and understand Latin than they did under the traditional method.[42] There was some interest here too in the development of non-linguistic courses given the possibility that these schools too seemed likely to change in character. Additional funding from the Schools Council enabled the CSCP to appoint Martin Forrest, who was given the task of building upon experimental work in classical civilisation already being undertaken in various parts of the country. This included work pioneered in the West Riding of Yorkshire by William Thompson and the early initiatives undertaken by LACT. The CSCP was soon in the business of producing course guidelines and resource packs which would enable schools to introduce programmes based on myths, legends and historical story material from ancient Greece. These materials, trialled in schools like their linguistic counterparts, were first published in 1972. Some of those trial schools which had recently become comprehensive were given wide publicity as they linked classical civilisation with film making, drama, puppetry, music and movement and other forms of creative activity. These developments were followed up by a later set of Roman materials in the 1970s.[43]

The Mid-Seventies

The late 1960s and the early part of the 1970s were a period of great turbulence for many maintained secondary schools as comprehensive reorganisation got under way across the country. The Donnison

---

[42] Ibid.

[43] 'The Roman World', largely the brainchild of M. J. (Mike) Hughes, was an evidence-based approach, introducing young students to Gallo-Roman Lugdunum through some of the epigraphic evidence and through a wide range of visual sources and translated texts. A short set of texts aimed at 13 to 16-year olds enabled the approach to be continued to GCSE level.

Committee which had recommended integration of the Direct Grant Schools and Independent Schools within the comprehensive system came and went. In 1970 a change of government meant that the public schools now felt more secure. Here the teaching of Classics continued to flourish, with some take-up of the new approaches to teaching Latin and Classics. Some erosion of classical teaching was evident in many Preparatory Schools, but most of the former Direct Grant Grammar Schools had opted for complete independence and here Classics prospered, often reinforced by the adoption of new methods of teaching. But as far as the maintained sector was concerned, large numbers of Local Education Authorities were already in the throes of reorganisation by 1970 and there could be no turning back.

The HMI survey of the new comprehensive schools undertaken in 1973 presented a picture which was generally encouraging.[44] In those reorganised schools which resulted from mergers that included grammar schools with strong Classics departments, there was evidence to show that the teaching of Latin had been able to hold its own. There was in some schools evidence of substantial growth as other forms of classical course had developed alongside the languages. Those who were pre- pared to take up the challenge were generally rewarded with a huge expansion in take-up of classical civilisation courses and an assured future for their language programmes in the school. As Nigel Slater, a former Head of Classics promoted to Head of Humanities, puts it: 'Comprehensive reorganisation was an amazing opportunity to deliver Classics to a much wider and, dare I say it, more appreciative audience'. Writing in *JACT Bulletin* 33 in 1973, John Sharwood Smith expressed astonishment at the way in which so many Classics teachers had radically altered their outlook and practices. A survey undertaken by the Schools Council in the 1970s showed that the CSCP had enjoyed a higher level of take-up than any other curriculum development project. As many as 55% of teachers who responded were using the CSCP's materials and a further 16% claimed to have been influenced by the Project's thinking. The pressure which Classics teachers felt was undoubtedly a factor. From 1970 onwards, JACT and also the Schools Council that had put further resources into the Cambridge Project were major disseminators of the Project's work. HMI were helpful too, although officially they had to maintain their neutrality. The continuing existence of the Project itself was a crucial factor in the dissemination of

---

[44] Dept. of Education and Science, *Classics in Comprehensive Schools: a Survey by HMI* (London, 1977).

the new materials and methods. However, the Classical Association and its local branches contributed to the dissemination of new thinking, by sponsoring, often in collaboration with others, conferences at which new developments could be presented and discussed.

There were examples of school Classics departments being closed down (some of them widely publicised); many classicists left the profession or voluntarily went for diversification outside the classical field; opportunities were lost. What was especially disappointing about the new comprehensive system, though perhaps this was hardly surprising, was the fact that non-linguistic Classics courses were taught in less than a quarter of the schools surveyed in the HMI sample. Although examples could be identified of classical studies, and later Latin, being introduced into reorganised schools, where no previous tradition of classical teaching existed, such schools were very much the exception and furthermore such innovation often proved to be vulnerable. Christopher Stray, in his study of a Welsh LEA in which the decision was taken to implement the CSCP's Latin and classical studies courses in all its reorganised secondary schools, has provided insights into the responses of teachers in these changed circumstances.[45] Stray's work supports evidence from elsewhere that many Classics teachers at that time, by virtue of their training, saw themselves primarily as linguists and felt ill at ease in the role of humanities teacher. Those teachers who were not classical specialists but who were recruited to assist in the teaching of classical studies included some who felt no long-term commitment to the subject and would feel no alarm at the subject's disappearance.[46]

In 1976 the CSCP conducted a large-scale evaluation study as a preliminary to preparing a revised edition of its Latin course. The results confirmed earlier soundings that the new course was popular both with the pupils and with many teachers. The overall impression gained from the abundant data gathered was that teachers were not keen to compromise the principles and spirit of the course. They were, however, anxious to receive more help with the grammatical content of the course and to be provided with additional linguistic exercises. E. P. (Pat) Story, who directed the Project from 1987, reflected that the Project's early handbooks had been very good at suggesting to teachers how they might

---

[45] C. A. Stray, 'Classics in crisis: the changing forms and current decline of Classics as exemplary knowledge, with reference to the experience of Classics teachers in South Wales' (MSc thesis, University College of Swansea, 1977).

[46] Stray, 'Classics in crisis', 207.

introduce language features but very bad at consolidation. The revised course published in its second edition between 1982 and 1990 under its Revision Editor, R. M. (Robin) Griffin, himself an experienced teacher of the course and former full-time member of the Project team, remained faithful to the original spirit of the course, whilst enhancing the amount of linguistic support that teachers had sought and writing more material to reduce the gradient of difficulty.[47]

Looking back over more than three decades upon the reforms that were introduced in the 1960s, John Sharwood Smith reflects:

> . . . one could look upon JACT and the CSCP as two parallel initiatives to preserve the study of Greece and Rome in school and university education, both inspired by the thought that as it was being taught in 1960, it scarcely deserved preserving (except perhaps as specialist interests at postgraduate level. . .). What we wanted classicists to be able to say (with the character in Addison's *Cato*) . . . was, ' 'Tis not in mortals to command success. We'll do more. We'll deserve it'.[48]

In the 1970s the reformers consistently urged schools in England and Wales to adopt the *CLC* and to introduce courses in classical civilisation at different stages in the secondary school curriculum. If they did not adopt the *CLC*, many schools were persuaded to purchase the Scottish Teachers' alternative inductive approach to Latin teaching, *Ecce Romani*. By the mid-1980s the *Oxford Latin Course*, aimed at combining the best of traditional and progressive methodologies, tempted many of those who had been reluctant to commit themselves to the *CLC* in its earlier form to change their ways. Classical civilisation courses have in recent years become a major growth subject in schools, with opportunities opening up at sixth-form level. The concept of all children in the maintained sector learning something about the classical world through the medium of English has now been accepted and this principle, since the arrival of a National Curriculum, has been enshrined in the primary school curriculum.[49]

Thus both battles to change the nature of traditional Classics courses in schools may be said to have been won. Correspondingly, moves to expand traditional courses in Universities to include classical

---

[47] The Cambridge School Classics Project has continued to extend and develop its pioneering work of the 1960's and 1970's and has a just claim to be the longest surviving curriculum development project of this period. The British edition of the Cambridge Latin Course now follows the example of its North American version and is published by Cambridge University Press in full colour. An important initiative to offer Latin 'on-line' is currently under way.

[48] Communication from John Sharwood Smith.

[49] In a further recent development, the CSCP's Iliad Project is making available on CDs a storytelling of Homer's epic together with resources which can be used by all primary schools as part of their 'Literacy Hour'.

civilisation were well under way by the early 1970s, and these early initiatives were met with enthusiastic responses by university students. By the end of that decade, university courses had also undergone an irreversible shift with these new courses forming a major part of the degree programmes.

Assistance with the preparation of this chapter is gratefullly acknowledged from Geoffrey Fallows, Robin Griffin, Michael Gunningham, Dr Alison Henshaw, James Morwood, John Murrell, John Sharwood Smith, Nigel Slater, Pat Story and William Thompson.

5

THE RECENT HISTORY OF THE CA

By MALCOLM SCHOFIELD

Introduction

In 1989 the Classical Association's membership was estimated by the Treasurer at 3,400. In 2002 the figures supplied by the CA's Secretary showed it standing at 3,500. Anyone who looked at just those overall totals might think that nothing much had changed in the intervening years. In fact they conceal a dramatic story. Something can already be deduced from a breakdown of the global figures. Back in 1989 there were around 1,550 members paying a joint subscription through JACT, 750 paying an annual subscription to the CA direct, and 800 CA life members, together with 300 institutions. Life members were still thought to number 800 in 2002.[1] But the institutional subscription had been phased out (it had been little more than a device for obtaining the Association's journals at the member's rate), JACT members were down to 1,150, and there were now over 1,550 paying the CA direct.

The most striking difference between 1989 and 2002 is in the number of members paying an annual subscription direct to the CA. In a little over ten years this figure more than doubled, while the number of those subscribing to JACT and the CA jointly had been dropping – presumably in part because of dwindling numbers of Classics teachers in the UK school system. Since the CA element in the joint subscription has always constituted a relatively small proportion of the whole, it seems fair to infer that in 1989 the Association was being propped up to a significant extent by members whose primary allegiance was to JACT. In 2002 their support remained important, but they were now well outnumbered by others paying direct who had been attracted – one must assume – simply because of what the CA itself had to offer.

One might venture a further guess. It is likely that in 1989 a majority

---

[1] The figure for life subscriptions is inevitably less secure than other figures: the Association may have no particulars except those subscribers supplied when they first took out their membership, and it is seldom notified of deaths of persons in this category.

of the 750 paying the CA direct were over 50, having taken out their subscriptions before the foundation of JACT in 1962.[2] In 2002, on the other hand, the great majority of JACT members were probably thirteen years older, whereas the recruits paying to the CA direct will mostly have been relatively young, drawn in by the Association's revival in the 1990s. I use the word 'recruits' advisedly, since that revival involved among other things two serious recruitment drives. The first started in 1989 (hence my choice of that year for comparison with 2002), and took the form of wide distribution of the first ever CA publicity leaflet. Efforts were redoubled from 1996, when Jenny March became the Association's first Publicity Officer, and throughout the duration of her tenure (which lasted until 2002) regularly reported significant success in signing up students in particular.[3] Her initiatives included preparation of a new publicity leaflet, identification of CA contacts in university departments of Classics, and efforts to interest particularly part-time students taking Open University courses.

What is not guesswork is the subject of this chapter: the phenomenon of revival itself. In the last twenty years or so, John Percival has said,[4] 'the Association has undergone the most radical transformation in its history, most obviously in respect of the organisation of its finances, the format and conduct of its annual conference, and the overall administration of its affairs'. The various sections of the chapter look at these aspects in turn: first the reinvention of the conference (with a digression on the invention of *CA News*); then the associated system of student bursaries, which itself proved a powerful engine of change; next finance, and particularly the dynamism achieved by more active financial management of the Association's scholarly journals; lastly the introduction of arrangements for governance and administration appropriate to a medium-sized educational charity obliged to operate in the regulated professional environment of the early 21st century.[5] In the early 1980s the CA was arguably 'a largely traditional, inward-looking organisation', to quote John Percival again. Nobody will question that it has now recaptured a central role in fostering the study of Classics in the UK, even if its founders' interconnected ambitions of penetrating the school

[2] So Richard Wallace (Treasurer 1985–1999) recalls (email to the author of 18 November 2002).

[3] Students took out a year's free membership, and it is unfortunately not possible to track the pattern of their subsequent conversion or non-conversion into regular paying members.

[4] Letter to the author, 5 December 2002; John Percival served as Secretary to the Council of the Association from 1979 to 1989 and as its Chairman from 1990 to 1995.

[5] The final section of the chapter ('The view from HQ') is the work of Clare Roberts, the Association's first full-time administrator.

curriculum on one side and influencing public policy on the other have been almost wholly abandoned.[6]

Conference: the Problem

To oversimplify: the recent history of the CA is above all the history of its annual conference.[7]

1982 is a good place to start. On Saturday 17 April of that year the Association's Council reported to the annual business meeting that it 'has become increasingly aware in recent years of a fall in the numbers attending the Association's Annual Meeting, and is anxious to discover the reasons for this. At the moment there are no proposals for any radical changes in the Meeting's format . . .' Those present had been renewing their experience of the customary format. The three days just past had been shaped by it. The pattern was the one usual (with variations) for some decades: a sequence of six plenary one hour lectures by invited speakers, together with the Presidential Address and (on this occasion) a choice on the second evening between the presentation by Peter Jones and Keith Sidwell of an embryonic plan for *Reading Latin* and videos first of a student Plautus production and then of 'Greek papyri: the rediscovery of the Ancient World'. I need scarcely add that there were receptions and excursions.

The next year Council's Report returned to the 1982 theme: 'Council continues to enjoy the privilege of conducting its business against a background of stable finances and a steady membership of something over 4,000. It is, however, still concerned at the drop in the numbers attending the Annual Meeting in recent years, and proposes to consider this in more detail during the coming year, together with possible ways of establishing a closer relationship between the central organisation and the branches.' In 1984 Council was still stuck. True, it told the AGM that it was considering sympathetically the proposals of the working party it had appointed to conduct a review. The main concrete outcome, however, did not concern the annual meeting at all. It was a decision on

---

[6] The main sources for this chapter are: annual reports in *Proceedings*; Council minutes and associated papers; correspondence and other papers in my files as Secretary to Council from 1989 to 2003. I am grateful to Clare Roberts, Chris Stray, Richard Wallace and especially John Percival for information and comments on my draft.

[7] It is in the 1990 edition of *Proceedings* that the conference is there first described as the conference: until then it had always been 'the annual meeting', with the expression 'annual general meeting' creeping in from time to time.

Council's recommendation by the AGM that year to raise the annual subscription to £3. Council noted that it saw this 'very much as an enabling measure and as part of a wider and more long-term programme'. It went on at once to say: 'There are at the moment no radical proposals for changing the format of the Annual Meeting.' The working party's report had contained a few cosmetic suggestions for enhancing its appeal. But the issue of the annual meeting had evidently been pushed down the agenda, whether due to its intractability or because any sense of urgency had dissipated or been smothered. Here the working party took their cue from the Council, as is confirmed by the minute of what was evidently the key discussion at its meeting of 26 November 1983.

Next year (1985) a minor change in format was agreed for the 1987 meeting (to be held in Reading). The same academic content was to occupy two days, not three, with no provision for a long excursion or an evening entertainment. It will come as no surprise by now that in its Report to the AGM that year Council was silent on the matter of the Annual Meeting. Yet as basis for the crucial discussion of 26 November 1983, only 16 months before, Council had received from its Secretary, John Percival (who chaired the subsequent working party), a paper stating in no uncertain terms that the Annual Meeting 'provokes more criticism and comment than any other of our activities'. 'In the 1960's it was usual for 200–250 people to attend', John Percival observed, whereas 'nowadays we think ourselves lucky to get more than 100' – who would be unlikely to include many '*young* Classicists, either 'amateur' or 'professional''. Indeed, numbers at the 1985 Annual Meeting itself (held in Bangor) were down to 103. At the first Annual Meeting I attended (Sheffield, in 1989) I was one of just 101 participants, probably the lowest peace-time figure ever recorded. It snowed on the afternoon devoted to excursions.

In 2002 the CA held its annual conference in Edinburgh in conjunction with the CA of Scotland, at its invitation and in celebration of its centenary. Conditions were a little misty the first afternoon and evening, but for the next two days the Athens of the North basked in unbroken sunshine under clear blue skies. According to the official tally there were 373 participants and – in addition to the opening lecture and Philip Howard's Presidential Address in the magnificent Playfair Library – 145 short papers, distributed between six parallel sessions. An exceptional event. Yet numbers of papers and participants had for a decade been moving in the Edinburgh direction. At Oxford in 1992 nearly 300 participants had a choice of 72 shorter papers (many others were offered but could not be accommodated within the timetable), as well as the Presidential Address and plenary lectures at the beginning and to close proceedings. At St Andrews in 1995 (another conference held jointly with the CA of Scotland) the choice for around 300 participants had grown to 115 shorter papers, together with the Presidential Address and two plenary lectures. And since 1997 (at Royal Holloway) the papers on offer have consistently numbered a few more or less than 100, while attendance has regularly totalled 300 or more, even in a venue as remote as Lampeter, where 311 were registered for the 1998 conference.

Conference: the Debate and the Revolution

The catalyst for 'radical change' was a paper submitted to CA Council for its meeting in November 1988, i.e. five years on from John Percival's abortive attempt to stir the Association from its slumbers. Its author was Richard Wallace, who as its Treasurer since autumn 1985 had had the opportunity to observe the CA and its workings from the closest possible range, and now felt moved to speak his mind about what he saw. The opening paragraphs of the paper set out trenchantly and succinctly a diagnosis of what was wrong and a proposed remedy. As its title 'Structural changes – some proposals' already indicates, Richard Wallace thought that what was crippling the CA's efforts to move forward was the structure of its governance:

When I took over the office of treasurer three years ago, the Association, it seemed to me, had put itself in a position which offered exciting opportunities for new developments. Thanks to the care and good management of my predecessor, our financial affairs were in exceptionally good order; a substantial increase in the level of subscriptions had been agreed, which allowed a very comfortable margin to fund innovations, and made it possible to adopt a less cautious approach than had been necessary in the past; papers had been put before Council proposing the inception of a policy of encouraging new projects and ideas. At the same time, Classics was under pressure at every level, and there was a clear need for the sort of new initiatives which had become possible.

It has to be said frankly that we have responded adequately neither to the opportunity nor to the need. Although some things have been achieved, we have not been able to use the resources available to us as effectively as we should. New ideas have not been coming forward. Our structures do not allow us to respond quickly enough to a changing situation, nor do they encourage innovation. Two Council meetings a year (which have to be kept short, and in any case must deal with a lot of routine but essential business) simply do not offer sufficient opportunity to do much in the way of strategic thinking, and any proposal which requires discussion and the exchange of ideas proceeds with painful slowness. The Council's normal response to this situation is to give the officers executive powers, but that is not a very satisfactory solution. It is not so much that the officers are overworked already (although they are), nor that it is bad in principle for the governing body of any association to hand over its responsibilities to a couple of individuals (although it is). The real problem is that there is a limit to the number of ideas that a small group of people can generate, and a limit to the number of projects they can handle effectively. We need help, and for that reason I am proposing a radical revision of our structures.

I am frequently distressed (and sometimes a little offended) when members of the Council tell me that the Classical Association doesn't *do* anything'. In fact the Association does a great many things, but not all of them are the immediate concern of the Council. Some learned bodies exist for the sole purpose of producing a single journal; we produce *three* (and very good ones too), *plus* an excellent series of monographs (the *Greece and Rome* Supplements). The Reading Competitions and the Tape Library are both very successful operations. None of these things happens by accident. They are the result of the hard work of Classical Association members appointed to take on these responsibilities by the Council. These are the areas where we have been most successful, and what they have in common is that earlier Councils had the sense to delegate the management of these enterprises to small groups or individuals, who are then allowed to get on with the job, reporting to the Council annually, but only coming to the Council for decisions in the unusual situation where something goes wrong, or some change of substance is proposed.

My suggestion is that we should learn the lesson of our successes, and devolve most of our activities to small working parties. The Council can then give its attention to questions of general strategy, to the broad supervision of our activities, and to feeding in new ideas, and generating proposals for new projects. I would hope that such a structure would enable members of the Council to get a more balanced view of the activities of the Association.

Richard Wallace then went on to identify what areas of activity might be particularly suitable for the treatment he advocated.

Council welcomed the initiative. 'The Officers were authorised to set up groups, of three persons in each case plus the Officers themselves, to deal with Membership and Publicity, Branches, and the AGM. A further group, on Classics in Schools, was desirable, but its formation was postponed until the outcome of the discussions referred to in Minute 738 below was known.' So Minute 735; Minute 738 dealt with discussions which were to lead to the creation of the national Co-ordinating Committee for Classics, and to the appointment of Peter Jones as the subject's national spokesman.

The Membership and Publicity group was the first to be constituted and start work. Its membership was confirmed at the Council meeting of

6 April 1989. Jenny March (then much involved in the publishing of the Institute of Classical Studies' monograph series) and Richard Stoneman (publisher with Routledge), both outgoing members of Council, were appointed, and also Rosemary Wright (then at University College Aberystwyth, and Director of the highly successful Aberystwyth Summer Workshop), a current member of Council. They were joined by Richard Wallace and myself, newly appointed as Secretary to Council. The group met on four occasions in the spring and summer of 1989.[8] Their first achievement was a publicity leaflet, sponsored by Routledge and published later that year in a print run of 10,000, and subsequently several times republished in revised versions. The major innovation they proposed was the launching of a twice-yearly CA newsletter, 'designed to keep members informed of academic and educational developments, and to provide a forum for discussion of classical matters'. At its next meeting on 2 December 1989 Council was presented not merely with the proposal but with proofs of the first number of *CA News*, edited by Jenny March, who was duly confirmed by Council as its first and (at the time of writing) only Editor.

CA News has gone on to establish itself as the Association's major vehicle for communication with the membership. Indeed from 2000 onwards *Proceedings* (whose presentation, status and future had been under intermittent review for the best part of twenty years) were discontinued, the core formal matter they contained being included as a four-page insert in *CA News*. The new journal has turned out to be more of a magazine than a newsletter, with its staple diet of feature articles, Greek and Latin verses, cartoons, reminiscences and competitions, although from time to time there has been vigorous correspondence on key educational issues, and *CA News* now reports annually on the conference and regularly profiles incoming Presidents and other classicists in the news. Some members enjoy it greatly, others never read a word, but nobody has ever complained that it lacks any distinctive style. It may well appeal most to a generation of classicists brought up on a diet of prose and verse composition which has all but disappeared in today's educational system. But if the conference has become more 'academic', Council has been keenly aware of an obligation to offer members of the Association at large something different. *CA News* and its Editor are supported by a management committee consisting of Barbara Goward, Philip Howard, Richard Wallace, David

---

[8] There was a subsequent meeting early in 1990, at which the group generated some proposals relating to *Proceedings* which found little favour with Council.

West, and the current Treasurer Philip Hooker. It was David West who in 1995 suggested that the Presidential Address should be removed from *Proceedings* and issued as a separate publication. Since then the Presidential Address has appeared as an attractive independent booklet, produced to a high standard appreciated by all sectors of the membership, with the Editor of *CA News* overseeing production.

But I rush ahead of myself: back to the AGM group, which like the Membership and Publicity group was appointed at the Council meeting of 6 April 1989. The membership as proposed by Richard Wallace on behalf of the officers was: William Duggan (Warwick School), Richard Seaford (University of Exeter), both newly elected members of Council, and Stan Ireland (University of Warwick), who was to be organiser of the 1991 conference. The officers on the group were again Richard Wallace himself and Malcolm Schofield. At the AGM just past the Association had found itself without a Branches Secretary; it was envisaged that the new Branches Secretary once appointed would also join the group, and very soon Marion Baldock (then Head of Sixth Form at Haberdashers' Aske's School for Girls; now Marion Gibbs, Headmistress of James Allen's Girls School, and currently Chair of JACT Council) duly became a member too.

The group held its first meeting on Wednesday 29 November 1989 in Stan Ireland's room at the University of Warwick. Marion Baldock and William Duggan sent apologies. Those present had in front of them a letter dated 7 April 1989 from David West (Professor of Latin at Newcastle, Chairman of the Board of Management for *Greece & Rome*), a long-standing supporter of the CA and gadfly of its officers, who had been heavily involved in the deliberations of Council for some years – indeed he had been a member of the 1984 working party. Marion Baldock had sent in a side of A4 under the heading: 'Thoughts on AGM and response to David West's comments'.

David West's letter began characteristically with the proposition: 'The Association needs young members. This is obvious and vital.' After some thoughts on conference bursaries, he continued: 'At the moment we are too few (perhaps 80 paying members at Sheffield), and too old. We have about seven lectures, each one on a different area of classical scholarship – something, one thing, for everybody and nobody comes. These are harsh words but they are true in the sense that hardly a scholar attends now unless he is on the committee or has some non-scholarly reason for attending.' His solution? He proposed that each year a particular topic should be selected – e.g. Greek Tragedy, Virgil,

Thucydides, Augustus – which would be the subject of six lectures to be given by six of the best scholars in the country, with the seventh session devoted to presentations by handpicked postgraduates followed by a half hour discussion. His final words: 'We must not worry about making the Association too intellectual. If we do not stand for the intellectual vitality of classical studies, what do we stand for? If we don't stand for this, how shall we recruit our successors?'[9]

The AGM group found themselves entirely in accord with David West's concluding sentiments. But the formula for thoroughgoing change they were to advocate would differ from his – he was essentially advocating new wine (and a better vintage) in old bottles – in virtually every particular. Marion Baldock for her part apologised for posing more questions than answers. 'WHO is the AGM intended to attract and stimulate?' was her first. On the occasions when she had attended it she had found the intellectual fare on offer too often too familiar and too superficial ('and I am not really a scholar' she added, after a crack about 'very elderly retired Classics dons and people who were having a sort of mini-break and visiting friends in the area'). 'Why does the AGM last 4 days?' (i.e. from the afternoon of day 1 to lunch on day 4) was her next question. Her comments here about the 'very leisurely pace' and 'afternoon excursions and evenings spent listening to chamber music or Scottish dancing' struck a definite chord with Stan Ireland. 'The timing is very difficult for teachers', she continued, with only two weeks holiday at Easter in the state sector, and school party trips to Greece or Italy to fit in too. The working group acknowledged the point, but in the end – 'with misgivings', and *faute de mieux* – stuck with the traditional date.

The key player present at the meeting on 29 November 1989 was Richard Seaford. Things *could* be very different, he argued. At the moment there was a gaping hole in the intellectual life of UK Classicists: they had no single occasion when the whole profession (not its specialist sub-communities), including younger scholars, could talk seriously to itself. He appealed to the model of the APA. As the working group's report to Council dated 10 March 1990 was to put the point:

The annual three day convention of the American Philological Association regularly attracts a high percentage of all the academics in the subject in U.S. and Canadian universities (not just young hopefuls in pursuit of a job). Most papers are short and

---

[9] But a note of anxiety had been struck earlier in the letter: 'This change need not alienate any of our members. We could urge our speakers not to be too technical. Of course some of them will get it wrong. But then we do at the moment, don't we?'

volunteered, not invited; extensive use is made of parallel sessions, often devoted to specific areas or themes handled by a 'panel' of speakers. The programme is packed, but there is plenty of socialising, both with and without an intellectual focus.

Why should not the CA AGM serve the same sort of function in the same sort of style in this country? Why should it not be *the* central classical event of the year?[10]

I recorded Richard Seaford's blueprint for a new form of CA conference in my note of the 29 November meeting as follows:

There should be no more than 2 hour-long lectures (+ Presidential address); otherwise there should be a lot of shorter papers scheduled for 30 minutes + 30 minutes discussion. The majority of papers should not as at present be invited. The CA should rather issue a widely advertised call for papers (placed e.g. in the major journals, in other CA advertising literature and member mailshots, and sent to University Classical Departments), inviting abstracts up to 500 words, and indicating that selection will be made by a scrutiny committee. The resulting programme should cater for as many simultaneous alternative choices of paper as is consistent with the accommodation available. Subsidy for travel/bursaries (additional to the current student bursaries) should be made available not for all paper readers but only for those who are students or unemployed. The opportunity thus presented might be especially attractive to research students.

The other members of the group present were strongly attracted by the idea of 'intellectualising and democratising' the annual meeting. Stan Ireland, in particular, was keen to try it out at the Warwick conference in 1991; and in due course the working group reported that they had encouraged him in this, 'to the extent of issuing without further ado a call for papers as proposed, and subject to the views of Council in both April and December 1990 on detailed planning of the programme.'

The working group met a second time, again at Warwick, on 27 January 1990, with a view to agreeing on firm proposals for the next meeting of Council. This time Marion Baldock and William Duggan were able to be present (Richard Seaford, however, was not). David West had responded with some concern in a letter of 4 December 1989 to a brief oral report on the group's initial ideas that had been presented to the Council meeting of 2 December:

Clearly we must be very careful not to *seem* to be reducing the social pleasures of the AGM. Our job is not to present a research entrepot. This is what the Roman and Hellenic Societies are for. Our main job is to present things Classical to teachers and to the wider public.

[10] This final sentence is as much Richard Wallace as Richard Seaford. In a letter to me dated 5 October 1989, he had written: 'Our long term aim should be to increase attendance substantially and to make the AGM of the Classical Association the one conference which everyone attends every year (which is what it should be)'.

And again (letter of 9 January 1990), following receipt of the notes on the first meeting of the group:

We are on a tightrope. If we leave the AGM as it is, it will wither away. If we make it too specialised and intense we will endanger the tradition of friendship and enjoyment and alienate our faithful members.[11]

His views were reported to the working group.

Marion Baldock and William Duggan were clear that the old pattern of annual meeting had had its day. Marion argued in favour of the Seaford model. She saw it as giving the conference a much more flexible structure which could accommodate treatments of specific *and* more general topics, and one better suited to the Association's ambition to be a Broad Church meeting the needs of professional and lay members alike. At the same time she urged the importance of publicising the conference better, particularly by exploiting its potential as a classical event taking place in the local community. William Duggan endorsed Marion's views. He asked particularly for more sophistication in communicating with the potential clientele. He was in no doubt that the Association should set a premium on attracting young academics.

The group asked itself whether a stronger orientation towards research would (as David West seemed to fear) let down the Association's school teacher constituency. Marion Baldock in particular argued again to the contrary, and in fact the group thought a new style of conference on the Seaford model might fill another hole in the market:

School teachers are relatively well supplied with conference opportunities relating to pedagogic problems and developments, and can also get to hear general lectures on classical subjects in various gatherings, particularly if they live near London or other major cities. It is much harder for them to find opportunities to hear academic speakers talking about the way their own or others' research is affecting approaches to central topics such as the Roman Forum or Roman religion or Greek tragedy; or again about specialist techniques and expertise whose applications concern many others besides specialists, e.g. numismatics, papyrology, epigraphy or 'post-structuralism'.

Why should not such opportunities be created within the framework of the CA AGM? But not only there: there is a case for proposing that the CA organise one-day conferences in major centres, in recognition of the fact that the place and timing of the 3-day AGM in a given year are likely not to suit many teachers who would otherwise be interested in this sort of fare.[12]

---

[11] And indeed the old style of annual meeting was friendly. I recall that my wife, a professional Prehellenic archaeologist without a UK institutional attachment, thoroughly enjoyed her first experience of a CA conference (Canterbury in 1990) not least for that very reason. But the new-style conference has not abandoned the tradition.

[12] The idea of one-day conferences was cautiously received by Council. The working group subsequently agreed on an approach to one 'major centre', but nothing came of it.

At the Council meeting of 9 April 1990 there was agreement that the working group's proposals for restructuring the annual meeting should be tried out, initially at the Warwick AGM, and reviewed in the light of that experience. The group had been clear that: 'A much fuller programme will require the 3 days the AGM has usually occupied. So no reduction in length is proposed.' However there was debate at Council on the issue, leading to a straw vote to test feeling: 4 were for a reduction in length, 8 for the status quo. Not everyone liked the prospect of simultaneous sessions, and some doubted whether it would be possible to construct a successful programme by asking for papers to be volunteered. On the other hand members stressed the need to encourage post-graduate students to offer papers.

The working group held two more meetings, in July and September 1990, mostly to assist Stan Ireland in planning the Warwick conference and to act as the 'scrutiny committee' in paper selection. The existing membership was reinforced by Robin Osborne, representing the committee planning the Oxford conference of 1992, and John Percival, now Chairman of Council. Bernard Gredley (Secretary of the Council of University Classical Departments) also attended the July meeting, to discuss the possibility of including CUCD sessions in the CA conference programme: an ingredient which was to continue throughout the 1990s (but not beyond). The working group was especially keen to encourage panels, and these have become a popular feature of the conferences, often provocative and often of high scholarly quality. The group wanted more discussion of papers than had been usual at the annual meeting, and settled on the formula of a half-hour slot for this purpose at the end of each session.

In the end just over fifty short papers, mostly half an hour each, were arranged as a programme of nine sessions (one – including the CUCD meeting – set against the excursion), in some cases three in parallel, in others just two. Roughly two thirds of them were volunteered, with the rest secured by invitations of one kind or another from Stan Ireland. Although the working group had been prepared to exclude submissions if the quantity was too great or the quality questionable, this proved unnecessary. There was no plenary lecture other than George Kerferd's Presidential Address. 175 participants were recorded on the official list of those attending, up 70 on the last old-style annual meeting of the previous year (at Canterbury).

Council held its usual end-of-conference meeting on 11 April 1991. Attendance was thin: those present were Philip Howard (who had been doubling as correspondent for *The Times*, of course: his reporting has been one of the constants in the recent history of the Association), George Kerferd, Jenny March (re-elected the previous year), Robin Osborne, Jean Read and David West, together with the four officers (John Percival in the chair, Marion Baldock, Richard Wallace and myself). Minute 832 of that meeting reads as follows:

A questionnaire on the Warwick Conference had been distributed to those attending. 62 had been returned completed. Dr Schofield summarised the results as follows:

1) 60 agreed that the concept of multiple concurrent lecture sessions was a good one.

2) A very large majority had found the papers informative, stimulating, and on a good range of subjects.

3) Most thought that a format in which the great majority of papers lasted no longer than half an hour was right. There was virtually no enthusiasm for returning to a system in which all papers lasted an hour.

4) About two thirds of the respondents indicated that they had attended previous CA conferences, and of these about 40% said without qualification that the Warwick Conference was better than previous conferences; others said it was better from the intellectual point of view, while indicating reservations on other aspects.

5) Many suggestions were made about 'fine tuning' of the basic Warwick format.

6) Almost all respondents said that they would attend the CA Conference again.

Dr Schofield undertook to forward copies of the returns to the organisers of the Oxford and Durham Conferences. There was general agreement that the basic pattern of the Warwick Conference was the appropriate model for the future.

In my brief informal report on the conference in the 1991 *Proceedings* I wrote: 'Regulars – from all age-groups and all sectors of the classical world – as well as newcomers found the experience an exhilarating one, and the papers were voted stimulating and informative, particularly perhaps those presented by graduate students', of which there were perhaps ten or a dozen: the proportion was to rise dramatically over the next few years. It is not hard to spot among the offerings preparatory studies for some important and indeed path-breaking contributions to scholarship, e.g. Chris Stray's *Classics Transformed* (his talk was entitled: 'On first looking into Kennedy's *Latin Primer*') or James Davidson's *Courtesans and Fishcakes* (he spoke on 'Buying fish for a tyranny: sea-perch and revolution in classical Athens'), both of them enjoyably accessible to a wide readership. And the three days ended with a bang, as my report informed the membership of the Association: 'A notable event was the panel on the last morning, which provoked an electrifying discussion focused on gender issues.' This was in fact the only panel conceived as such, other than in the CUCD session. Its topic was 'Obscenity in Roman Literature'. Susanna Braund (then like Richard Seaford at Exeter University) had put together a team consisting of Adrian Gratwick (St Andrews), Marilyn Skinner (University of Northern Illinois, an American feminist voice deliberately introduced into what was still a mostly indigenous gathering),[13] John Henderson (Cambridge, in magnificently witty form, attacking the very idea of a specific vocabulary of obscenity), and herself. I ran into David West a few minutes after it was over: he described the occasion as the most intellectually exciting event in which he had ever participated at a CA conference.

So change had been effected. Different individuals and groups of people made decisive contributions to the process at different points for different reasons. In a sense there was no inevitability about it. Nonetheless it is hard to doubt that it came about because there was a general will to change on the part of a good number of classicists who cared about the Association or about the role it could potentially play in the future of the subject. Not the least significant thing to emerge from the Warwick conference questionnaire is point (6), particularly if it tends to be the dissatisfied rather than the satisfied (according to conventional wisdom) who answer questionnaires: virtually all respondents saw themselves as ready to attend another CA conference. As is also clear from the questionnaire return, there were many aspects of the conference that were not to everyone's liking, a reaction probably aggravated by the absence of any dedicated CA social space – we were rather swamped by larger conferences being held concurrently with ours. But it is true of many people that habits once established are not quickly or lightly abandoned, and the Association's often elderly 'faithful members' continued coming to the conference regularly in the years that followed. What they cared about above all else, as it seemed to me, was the future of Classics. They wanted for a new generation the pleasure and enrichment they felt they had been lucky enough to have had themselves; and they were prepared to give their support to a new style of conference if it seemed the best way of promoting that objective.

If the revolution was not already irreversible, it became so with the Oxford conference of 1992, announced in the call for papers as 'a *special*

---

[13] The presence of visitors from many parts of the world, and particularly from the USA, has since become a regular feature of the conferences. During Christopher Rowe's period as Chair of Council (1995–2002), and thanks largely to his initiative in the matter, efforts were made to establish formal representation from the CA and the APA at each others' annual meetings. These eventually came to nothing, but it is partly thanks to them that American colleagues – some every year – now participate in greater numbers in the CA Conference.

event in celebration of the reunification of Europe and the quincentenary of Greek teaching in Britain', and conceived on a grand scale. The 1992 *Proceedings* reported on it as follows:

The most memorable event of the Oxford Conference was undoubtedly the Presidential address, delivered by Lord Runcie on a glorious spring afternoon to a huge audience packed into the vast East School. Readers of *Proceedings* can enjoy the wit, learning, profundity of thought and passionate commitment to the values of a liberal education rooted in the Classics which moved those present: impossible to recapture is the sense of occasion. But there were other splendid occasions too, notably receptions in the Ashmolean Museum and in Blackwell's: and the riches of a packed programme of exhibitions and parallel papers and panels are indicated in later pages. . . . The scale of the logistics of the operation was unparalleled in the recent history of the CA. . . . The new format for the Conference is clearly proving popular, particular among younger Classicists. These included not only the graduate students who read many of the papers (or came to hear their friends do so), but as in former years, undergraduates and some PGCE students supported by Association Bursaries.

Bursaries and Graduate Students

At a Council meeting on 4 April 1994 I was asked whether graduate students were eligible under the terms of the conference bursary scheme. I replied (Minute 926) that 'while formally speaking they were not, some Heads of Department had recently nominated graduates, in some cases explicitly commenting on the greater interest in the Conference shown by them; some bursaries had accordingly been awarded to graduates in the current year'. It was agreed to write to University Departments inviting comments on the scheme.

In fact I was mistaken. On 29 November 1986 Council had agreed that 'a number of bursaries might be made available to enable students (both undergraduate and postgraduate, and including students in Departments of Education) to attend the Annual General Meeting'. But the mistake was understandable: for the first few years of the operation of the scheme, those applying for bursaries included few if any graduates. So in effect it *had* been an undergraduate affair (except for the occasional PGCE student), and as such the single most significant – and indeed almost the only – innovation of the 1980s in the annual meeting, both because of the impact of a student presence on morale and because of the subsequent developments to which it was gradually to lead. Initially provision for 20 full bursaries was approved, although in the first three years the take-up fell short of that figure.

Nonetheless in 1989 (for example) the 18 student bursars accounted for something approaching 20% of the total attendance of 101.[14]

1990 was the year when the full complement of 20 was achieved: demand for places, Council was informed, had outstripped supply by a substantial margin. For the first time PGCE and Open University students were among the bursars. Since then demand has always been fairly heavy, and over the years Council has responded by approving a sequence of increases in bursaries available: to 25 in 1992,[15] 30 in 1995, 40 in 1996,[16] and 50 – the current figure – in 1998. It was scarcely an accident that the question about the eligibility of graduates was raised at a Council meeting held during the 1994 Conference (in Exeter). As well as a rich fruitcake of a Presidential Address from Colin Haycraft, legendary Duckworth publisher,[17] a plenary lecture on orientalism and Greek art by Nigel Spivey, a student performance of Catullus 63, and a debate on Roman religion between Peter Wiseman and Mary Beard, there were 80 shorter papers, a record at the time, 'with graduate students' (as my report in *Proceedings* recorded) 'again very much to the fore, and growing in confidence and presentation skills'. It was not only that the proportion of talks given by graduate students was rising, but that their absolute number was for the first time itself stamping its impression on the character of the conference.

So it came as no surprise that there was general support in Departments of Classics for the 'extension' of the bursary scheme to graduate students. At its meeting of 26 November 1994 Council agreed to their eligibility, noting that current selection procedures would not disadvantage undergraduate applicants, and that since graduate students could often obtain funding from other sources there was a case for offering more part-bursaries (a practice initiated the previous year). At the same meeting Michael Whitby, principal organiser of the 1995 conference at St Andrews, announced that he had raised a loan from the University to provide for a subvention of £25 a head to defray expenses of any graduate student reading a paper – this in response to concerns

---

[14] It would be interesting to know where the first bursars are now. In the class of 1987 (Reading) I spot the names of Rhiannon Ash and Vanda Zajko, now lecturers respectively at University College London and the University of Bristol. Littini Newcombe – a lively bursarial presence at Bristol (1988) and Sheffield (1989), and subsequently a member of Council – teaches in a tertiary college in Cumbria.

[15] Three of the five new bursaries were to go preferentially to PGCE students.

[16] But this rise was mainly accounted for by the extension of the scheme to school teachers – in an attempt to stimulate rather than meet demand: the ten new bursaries were to be awarded preferentially to applicants in this category. This is discussed further below.

[17] I was to represent the Association at his funeral the following September.

expressed at a previous Council meeting that travel costs might be seen by some potential participants as prohibitive. By the 1996 conference graduate bursars were outnumbering undergraduate. There are now very few applications from undergraduates; Heads of Department occasionally ask whether they are actually eligible. The development of the part-bursary system has meant that very large numbers of students – mostly graduates – now attend the conference with bursary support (e.g. for Bristol in 2000 64 individual awards were made, for Manchester in 2001 52, and for Edinburgh in 2002 59), mirroring their now major if not dominant position in its academic programme. Whatever else it has become, the CA Conference is now a focal event in the UK graduate student calendar.

In expanding its conference bursary scheme, Council tried not to neglect the interests of constituencies other than undergraduate or postgraduate students. In April 1991 ways of encouraging PGCE students to apply were discussed, and it was agreed to earmark three extra bursaries specifically for students in this category, without excluding them from consideration for those available in the general scheme. But take-up over the years has been patchy (and there has been none since 2000). For example, in 1995 two PGCE students applied and were awarded bursaries, but in the event did not make it to the conference. Everybody redoubled their efforts, and at the 1996 conference in Nottingham a record number of eight PGCE bursars were present. Meanwhile David West (who had delivered the 1995 Presidential Address) wrote to Council urging reconsideration of various aspects of the bursary scheme. He was particularly concerned at the low representation of school teachers among those attending the 1995 conference. Council noted that semesterisation in universities would make it increasingly difficult to schedule the timing of the conference to coincide with the school Easter holidays in England (which in 1995 were over by the time of the conference) – although in the event this has not proved so much of a problem as was feared. It subsequently agreed to earmark ten bursaries for teachers – including provision for part-bursaries in the case of those unable to attend the whole conference. In 1999 Council designated one of these the G. B. Kerferd Bursary, in memory of its Chairman from 1977 to 1990.[18] This scheme also has to date not attracted substantial numbers of applicants, and generally speaking no more than a couple of teacher bursaries have been awarded in any one year.

[18] Through the generosity of his son George Kerferd this award has now been endowed in perpetuity.

The view expressed by the AGM working group of 1989–90 that there should be considerable potential in the new conference format for attracting teachers has not been borne out as they hoped. At the last old-style conference (Canterbury in 1990), teachers active or retired represented around a quarter of the total number of persons attending. At Edinburgh in 2002 there were almost four times as many participants overall, but the number of present or former teachers present was probably at most three fifths the Canterbury number, scarcely a 'critical mass'. Every year teachers answer the call for papers; the talk which Mick Morris (twice G. B. Kerferd Bursar) delivered in Edinburgh on Edmund Law Lushington, Apostle, brother in law to Tennyson, and Professor of Greek at Glasgow from 1838 to 1875, is still bright in my memory. Teachers who do attend have often been enthusiastic about the intellectual stimulation they have got from it. But as more academics participate and give talks in ever greater numbers, it is no doubt harder for teachers to feel ownership of the conference; the Easter holiday remains an awkward time for many of them; and other bodies or institutions mount residential conferences or colloquia which function *inter alia* as academic refresher courses targeted specifically at teachers, such as the annual conference of the Association for Latin Teaching (ARLT), held at the start of the summer holiday, and the annual Cambridge teachers' colloquium, held at the end of it, and themed rather as David West had suggested the CA conference might be.

The irruption of substantial numbers of graduate student papers into conference programmes has not been altogether frictionless. There have been repeated suggestions that relative to the programme as a whole they are too many, or too specialised, or too poorly presented (organisers have for some years issued explicit instructions on what to do and what not to do in preparing and delivering a twenty-minute talk). Sometimes – inevitably – content has been disappointing; one Cambridge graduate student of some seniority once confessed to me that the UK graduate community felt it was not all that difficult to have a paper accepted for the CA conference. Sometimes members of the audience have not been reticent in expressing their reactions. I recall one graduate speaker gabbling at speed through a weak paper far longer than it should have been for the 25 minutes or so available. After one or two polite questions a senior ex-teacher took him to task, above all for failing to imagine the needs of his audience, and suggested he think harder about that before delivering any more talks. The speaker looked shell-shocked – but it was what he deserved and needed to hear. Intellectual approaches have also been subject to vigorous comment: one colleague tells me that when in more junior days she was savaged by a distinguished Latinist in a CA panel session, she thought her academic career was over. On the other hand, the two grisliest occasions I recall in the last decade were one-hour plenary lectures by senior scholars with substantial international reputations. A Council minute of 29 November 1997 perhaps hits the right note: 'It was agreed that a better balance between senior and junior speakers in parallel sessions than had been apparent on some occasions would be a better way [viz. than more plenary sessions addressed by established scholars] to ensure that all tastes were properly catered for. Members commented on the vitality younger speakers often communicated.'

Subscriptions and Donations

Another way into the recent history of the CA is the story of its finances.

The Council which reported to the 1984 annual business meeting may not have been able to achieve a successful rethinking of the CA conference. But it did formulate and to some degree implement a coherent strategy for the Association's future, based on a reconsideration of the CA's financial situation. More particularly, 1984 marks the beginning of a process which has today put the CA in a position to spend £45,000 in the financial year 2002 on grant-giving activity. The first phase of this development was initiated by a decision to raise subscriptions, prompted by the paper John Percival put to the Council meeting of 26 November 1983.

The last page of his paper dealt with the topic of finances as follows:

The most obvious point that emerges from the Association's Income and Expenditure Account is that we spend almost the whole of our annual income on *Proceedings* plus the general administration of the Association's affairs. The figures (in very simplified form) are as follows:

Income		Expenditure	
Subscriptions	£3,000	Administrative expenses	£5,000
Investment income	£4,000	*Proceedings* (printing)	£2,500
Legacies, profits on minor publications, occasional profits on *Greece & Rome*	£1,000		
	£8,000		£7,500

In fact, as will be seen from these figures, we *depend* on legacies, occasional profits, etc. to keep ourselves afloat. There is virtually no money available, in this account, for worthy causes and projects: these have to be financed entirely from the Jubilee Fund, which has about £300 per annum available for expenditure.

It is hard to avoid the criticism that the Association is too inward-looking, and too constrained by its finances to be an effective force. It is not simply that we cannot adequately support existing causes and projects: we cannot *initiate* anything useful, because we have no spare money to spend.

John Percival then sketched a number of possible solutions 'in ascending order of radicalism': (i) reduce the size of *Proceedings*; (ii) raise the subscription to such a level that subscription income would pay for administrative costs and *Proceedings*, leaving the whole of the investment income available for causes and project; (iii) start spending the Association's capital (currently £35,000) – 'an extreme suggestion', he commented, 'but those who favour it would argue that Classics is facing an extreme crisis.'

No punches had been pulled, and the blows struck home. It was clearly this section of its Secretary's paper which concentrated the Council's mind.[19] As we saw above, in April 1984 Council accepted its working party's proposal of an increase in the subscription to £3 per annum, 'with appropriate adjustment of Life Membership subscription'. The scope of the 'wider and more long-term programme' it hoped this change would enable is indicated in the final paragraph of the working party's report. The report recommended:

That greater stress be placed by the Association on positive action to further the cause of Classics, (a) by making funds available to assist individuals or groups with projects such as specialist conferences, schools conferences, performance of classical plays, etc., (b) by more active recruitment of members, particularly among university students and those training as classical teachers, and (c) by greater contact with the media, educational bodies, government departments etc, perhaps in the first instance by the publication of a booklet making the case for Classics in the 80's and 90's.

The Working Party feels that in the present climate the Association has a duty to be more outward-looking and more aggressive in the pursuit of the aims for which it was founded. Its proposals have two main aims: first, to give the Association a secure financial base; and second, to increase the scale and range of the Association's activities. The two are clearly inseparable.

Not much was achieved with regard to item (c) on this agenda until the formation of the Co-ordinating Committee for Classics in 1988–9 (in which the CA participated but was not prime mover), and the

---

[19] The reception given to its material on the annual meeting has been described above.

associated appointment of Peter Jones as national spokesman. The CA collaborated with JACT throughout the rest of the 1980s – chiefly through John Percival's membership of JACT's Working Party on Examinations and Curriculum – on various issues relating to developments in this area, initially the introduction of GCSE in particular. It was by mutual consent JACT which took the lead in this area, as it was later to do e.g. in securing a meeting with Kenneth Baker, when Secretary of State for Education, as plans for the National Curriculum were developed, or in establishing and maintaining communication with Nick Tate in the later 1990s during his period as Chief Executive of the Schools Curriculum and Assessment Authority in efforts to mitigate the damage done to the subject by the Baker curriculum. And it was to be the Council of University Classical Departments which in 1989 commissioned the research which led to publication the following year of the booklet – entitled *Classics in the Market Place* – which the CA's Working Party had visualised.

Rather little appears even to have been attempted in the way of 'more active recruitment of members' (b) during the 1980s. In fact comprehensive *in*activity prompted an outburst from Richard Wallace in his 1988 memorandum:

I think that I have raised the question of membership at every meeting of the Council since I took office. The present situation is absurd. Apart from the statements on the covers of our journals, the only way an interested individual can get to know even of the existence of the Classical Association is by casual word of mouth. How can any organisation which runs its affairs on this basis hope to survive? . . . Whatever decision is made about these proposals in general, I very much hope that the Council will agree to take some urgent action over the question of membership.

The formation of a Membership and Publicity working group in spring 1989 (as described above) was at least a first step.

There was only one element in the 'long-term programme' of 1984 – (a), the generation of funds available for grants 'to further the cause of Classics' – which could be directly achieved (at any rate if one assumes otherwise stable income and sound financial management) by doing what the Association actually did that year, i.e. by raising subscriptions and taking action to reduce costs. The impact of this change on the CA's finances could be expected to be registered for the first time in the accounts for the financial year 1985–6. With this in mind Council resumed discussion of future projects at its meetings in November 1985 and April 1986. On the second occasion it received and approved after amendment a set of principles, priorities and procedures prepared by

John Percival as Secretary. Council reported on these to the AGM as follows:

Council is anxious that help should be given to projects which might otherwise be at risk or in some cases not available at all, rather than to activities which are already flourishing. There will be an emphasis on the needs of teachers and pupils in schools, and in this context particularly Council will wish to work closely with JACT and with the parallel activities of the Hellenic and Roman Societies.

Continued support of the JACT Summer Schools was identified as the first priority, followed by funding for in-service training for teachers, and then for 'conferences, day-schools, workshops etc.'. Other eligible activities were ranked lower. The existing subsidies to branch reading and project competitions were to continue as a ring-fenced activity not included in the general grants and projects budget.

In a note he had written for the Council meeting of November 1985 John Percival had repeated the suggestion that a figure 'perhaps of the order of £3,000 *per annum*' might be possible for this purpose. In the event Richard Wallace was able to recommend that '£6,000 should be made available to be spent on grants, donations, and projects in the next financial year', i.e. in 1986–7 (Treasurer's Report presented at the November 1986 Council). For the financial year 1985–6 a surplus of £15,827 had been recorded, a different order of magnitude from any previously registered. The Treasurer noted as the principal ingredients in the increase (up more than £10,000 on the previous year): the increase in subscription income (£2,254); administrative expenses down by £2,483 and the costs of *Proceedings*, from 1985 on produced from camera-ready copy, by £1,230, in each case a saving of one third; a substantial increase in donations, including a substantial legacy (up by £3,070); and – in retrospect very significantly – a healthy surplus on *Greece & Rome* (up by £3,437).

The acceptance of the Treasurer's proposal represented a momentous change of gear for the Association. Consider by contrast the financial year 1976–7. The only grants Council made in that year were for branch reading prizes (£130) and – from the Jubilee Fund – for the JACT Greek Summer School (£75). Five years later (1981–2) the position was not much changed: £132.25 for branch reading prizes, £35 for the Virgil reading and essay prizes, and from the Jubilee Fund £125 each to the JACT Greek and Latin Summer Schools. By 1985–6 the Association was supporting a few more activities (including now the Aberystwyth Summer Workshop), and the sum available for reading prizes had risen to £350, but the total disbursed for other purposes was still only £855. It proved too much to expect that in 1986–7 Council would actually spend sevenfold that sum: it would take a little longer for its horizons to shift as far as Richard Wallace was trying to encourage. But the figure did treble. Council managed to get through £2,625 of the £6,000 available. The largest single sum (£950) was accounted for by a new venture not envisaged by the 1985–6 Council. For it was at the November 1986 meeting that Council had responded positively to a suggestion that it should fund bursaries to enable students to attend the annual meeting.[20] The other £1,675 went to summer schools and to a variety of schools conferences and publications (and Latin classes were funded in Northumberland and Durham).

Over the next few years the volume of grants expenditure showed rapid growth, but its general pattern remained very similar. For example, in 1993 Council reported record disbursements amounting to £9,339 in all. Just over a third of this total was used to fund conference bursaries for students, and just under a third went to support summer schools, now including the ARLT and JACT Classical Civilisation summer schools. A quarter was paid in grants to conferences and festivals, including funding for an event named 'The Leeds Classical Experience', support for the London Festival of Greek Drama (already assisted by the CA on a regular basis), and a subvention of £1,500 enabling scholars from Russia, Bulgaria, Czechoslovakia, Hungary, Rumania and Serbia to attend the 1992 Symposium Platonicum, held in Bristol.[21] Finally, there was assistance as always for the branches (London, Manchester, Leeds, Cambridge, Exeter, Guildford, Gloucestershire and Southampton in 1991–2), and for schools classics days in Northamptonshire, the East Midlands, and Leeds and Sheffield. Every alternate year the British School at Athens mounted a course for teachers over the Easter break, and the CA has regularly enabled individuals to attend. Other causes supported from time to time during the 1990s included PGCE tuition at Exeter, sustained by Ron Impey of Exeter School, the work of the JACT 5–13 Committee and various other initiatives designed to foster Classics in schools, the

---

[20] The relevant minute goes on to record: 'It was agreed that the bursaries might be of the order of £50 each, and that a total sum of £1,000 should be provisionally set aside for this purpose.' In the end the decisions taken by the 1983–4 Council *did* after all help to initiate a development which, as we have already seen, was to be a significant factor in the eventual reshaping of the conference.

[21] Council was particularly keen to promote contact with Eastern Europe. The previous year there had been support for Eastern European visitors attending the Triennial Conference in Cambridge.

Library of the Institute of Classical Studies, and the Association's own extensive Tape Library, run singlehanded by Wilf O'Neill in Leeds.

The Association's increased resources enabled it to undertake a number of publishing projects which would have been impossible in previous years. The birth of *CA News* in 1989 has been described above. In the same year wall maps of Greece and Italy were published by Routledge with financial assistance from the CA and editorial input from Richard Wallace in particular. The maps can now be found adorning the walls of lecture rooms in University Departments of Classics up and down the country. Three more were to follow in the autumn of 1991: the Roman Empire, Alexander's Empire, and the Ancient Near East (Bible Lands). Also in 1989 (and triennially ever since) the Association published a new edition of the directory *Classics Departments in British Universities*, still widely known as 'the CUCD booklet', even though it has been an exclusively CA production from that year on. There is now a web version too, and it has been renamed *Classicists in British Universities*. The following year (1990) saw the appearance of *Virgil*, the first in a sequence of volumes of selected articles from *Greece & Rome* entitled Greece & Rome Studies.[22]

Journals and Surpluses

A rise in the level of the subscriptions was the key move that enabled the Association to begin supporting classical 'projects and other positive activities' (Report of the Council, 1986) on a larger scale. But the CA's ability to sustain and increase the level of available funding in subsequent years (up to £10,000 from £6,000 in 1990–1, then to £15,000 in 1995–6, £30,000 in 1997–8, £40,000 in 1999–2000, £45,000 in 2002) had very little to do with subscription income. Indeed, although subscriptions and investment income continued for some years to exceed expenditure on administration, *Proceedings* and (from 1989–90) *CA News*, 1992–3 saw the first deficit in this equation (of £5,603), and that has been the pattern every year since (in 2001 the figure had risen as high as £12,780). To maintain and enhance its grants and projects budget in these circumstances the Association has not been raiding its piggy bank: total assets at 31 December 2001 stood at

---

[22] Last and least, 1989 also marked the introduction of the CA logo: 'to a design based on a coin of Zancle which shows a cheerfully confident, but not complacent, dolphin', as Council informed the membership in its annual Report.

£441,979, compared with £203,591 at 30 September 1993; and there have been small overall deficits on the annual accounts only twice since 1992–3 (in 1995–6 and 1999–2000). What has powered the CA's finances for the past fifteen years has been the profitability of its journals – initially *Greece & Rome*, in more recent years *Classical Quarterly* and *Classical Review* as well.

The surplus on *Greece & Rome* in the financial year 1985–6 itself (i.e. the year crucial for Council's decision to allocate a substantial annual sum for grants and donations) contributed significantly to the overall surplus in the accounts of £15,827. It stood at £8,032, a sum on its own in excess of the £6,000 approved for expenditure on grants and projects in the following year. It was supplemented by a transfer of £962 from the *Greece & Rome* reserve fund, which was to be held at £5,000. There was an element of the one-off about the 1985–6 figure (OUP had received payment of a large outstanding bill), and the following year the surplus was down to £4,509. Thereafter, however, it rose steadily to £5,693 in 1989–90, and then leaped to £10,183 in 1990–1. From 1993–4 onwards the accounts regularly showed a five-figure number, usually in the region of £15,000 to £17,000, although latterly £25,000 to £30,000. With the accounts overall generally showing modest surpluses throughout this period, it was hardly surprising that Council agreed the increases it did in expenditure on grants and donations in 1990–1 and 1995–6. In his November 1983 assessment of the Association's finances, John Percival had argued that 'we *depend* on legacies, occasional profits, etc. to keep ourselves afloat'. By the late 1980s the profits were no longer in the least occasional; and dependence on their not being so had in effect become policy.

It was not until the 1996–7 financial year that surpluses from the Classical Journals Board Fund (which existed to support *Classical Quarterly* and *Classical Review*) were regularly transferred to the Association's General Fund, giving the CA an ability to make grants and donations to classical causes on a different scale from ever before: the second major change of gear in its recent financial history. Why this development occurred so late in the twentieth century is part of the general story of the journals and of relations between the CA and the CJB, told elsewhere in this volume. *How* it eventually came about is a rather tangled tale, drawn out over a full decade.

A significant moment was the presentation of the accounts in *Proceedings* for 1989. This was the first occasion on which assets held in the CJB Fund were not only published in the balance sheet (that had happened the previous year), but incorporated in a consolidated figure for the Association as a whole. The change had a dramatic effect on the impression it gave of the CA's financial position. *Proceedings* for 1987 showed total assets less current liabilities at £52,892, with an additional £3,488 in the Jubilee Fund (as at 30 September 1986). They were silent – as they always had been – about the existence of the CJB Fund. In *Proceedings* for 1989, by contrast, the membership learned that the Association's total assets stood at £196,259 as at 30 September 1988, £118,972 of that sum being held in the CJB Fund. Readers who did not look at the fine print might have assumed that the Association had over a couple of years become nearly four times richer.

What prompted the change of practice regarding the Classical Journals Board's accounts and balance sheet was a ruling by the Association's Auditor in April 1987. Her intervention was the faintly improbable outcome of a sequence of exchanges between the Officers and the Journals Board originally triggered by something which was little more than a passing thought. The Board had wanted to fund from their surplus a competition for computer applications in the field of Classical studies. However Council agreed at its November 1986 meeting that such a project fell outside the limits of the Board's current terms of reference, and that 'without prejudice to any final decision on the proposal now being considered, discussions should take place between the Officers and the Journals Board with a view to providing new and more flexible terms of reference for the use of its accumulated surplus'.

To have achieved a change with that effect would obviously not have required a general revision of the terms of reference, but the Board had agreed in May 1986 to ask its Secretary (Chris Collard) to attempt the broader exercise of defining its 'relation with the Association as it affected the control of its monies' – and in the event he took on a wholesale recasting of the document. In this context the matter of audit became a bone of particularly serious contention throughout much of 1987. Paradoxically, in the meantime Council decided that after all the production of the computer software envisaged in the Board's original suggestion of a competition was at any rate 'not contrary to the spirit of the Terms of Reference laid down in 1909', and withdrew its objection (Minute 673, 8 April 1987).

Although the framework for the Board's operation drawn up in 1909 required that it 'keep accounts separate from those of the Classical Association to be audited and confirmed by the Council of the Classical Association', Chris Collard drafted a substitute clause in line with practice stating that the CJB's accounts 'are approved annually and . . . are subject to general comment in the Board's Annual Report to the Council of the Classical Association'. This and the other changes mooted set in train a long, bulky and at times tortuous correspondence between the Board's officers (mostly its Secretary) and the CA Treasurer.[23] By September 1987 the recast document was in its fourth revised draft. Some ground had been ceded by the Board. In particular, after the substitute clause the Board's officers proposed a significant addition: 'an audited statement of accounts shall form part of the Board's Annual Report'. But this proved still too weak to satisfy the Association's Auditor. At its November 1987 meeting Council was informed that she 'had been unwilling to issue the appropriate certificate [i.e. for the audit of the Association's annual statement and balance sheet] until the accounts of the Journals Board had been fully integrated with the Accounts of the Association'. The relevant provision in the new Terms of Reference eventually agreed stated: '*That* the Board of Management shall maintain full financial records separate from those of the Classical Association, and shall make them available to the Treasurer of the Classical Association for the preparation and audit of the Classical Association's Annual Accounts.'

Once the CJB reserve started to appear in the Association's balance sheet, the classicist in the street began to ask why the organisation kept such a large sum of money sitting idle in the bank when financial support for maintaining or initiating worthwhile classical activities was hard to secure.[24] The perception of the CA as incorrigibly dozy seemed to be being confirmed. In a letter dated 7 March 1991 to the Secretary of the CJB, I referred to 'the embarrassment of the Officers and members of Council over suggestions that the CA is mismanaging its resources in holding a surplus of this magnitude.' I went on: 'We have tried saying that it is not our money, but the Board's. This cuts little ice, since the sum (quite properly) appears in the Accounts of the Association and is formally approved by Council.'

The Board for its part had been anxious to do its best for subscribers in its pricing policy for the journals. The growth in the size of its reserve

---

[23] Something of the flavour of some of the discussion may be conveyed by a brief extract from a letter from Richard Wallace (Treasurer) to John Percival (Secretary of Council) dated 30 March 1987: 'I haven't done a point by point working over of his letter. He is just wrong, and that's that. I am, believe it or not, trying to be conciliatory (but I'm afraid it goes against all my instincts).'

[24] I recall one particular conversation along these lines with Lorna Kellett, a Norwich teacher who had served as Executive Secretary of JACT and was subsequently to become a stalwart of the Madingley Hall Latin programme.

had been largely accidental. A decision to increase prices in the early 1980s had been followed by a favourable change in the exchange rate with the US dollar, and by a period of stable costs and high interest rates in the UK. It was against this background that, as Chris Collard explained at the November 1991 meeting of Council, the reserves

had been used to increase the size of the journals without a commensurate increase in subscriptions, thus protecting the interests of the subscribers as the persons who had in the event funded the surplus in the first place. The increase in size had helped to promote the standing and quality of the journals; both now held an enviable international reputation, and the *Classical Review* was probably the most distinguished review journal for Classics in existence.

Council too was proud of the journals. But at this point they were being run at a loss; a steep rise in subscriptions of 16.66% had recently had to be approved; and the new figure still fell some way short of covering the true cost of production, which was itself rising with inflation. There was concern that if current policy continued unchanged the reserves would quickly become exhausted. Both the Board and the Council took professional advice (from different sources) in the autumn of 1991, and the experts proved unanimous in their view that the reserves should not be used to finance trading losses of the journals – which were projected for the next two or three years – on a systematic basis. The Board had earlier responded to Council's representations about the size of the reserves by agreeing in May 1991 to transfer a sum of £25,000 to the Association, to be used at the Association's discretion. But by November 1991 the issue of a policy on the handling of reserves had in Council's eyes been overtaken by the need for a business plan, as John Percival (speaking as its Chairman) confirmed at a special meeting of the Board summoned on 1 February 1992.

Council wanted to see the Board's current account in surplus by 1995, and the total deficit for the whole period between 1992 and 1995 held below £40,000. After the Association's Treasurer had provided the Board with alternative projections for achieving this outcome, a strategy based on incremental rises in subscriptions together with reductions in costs of production and distribution was formally agreed at the Board's regular meeting in May 1992. Council was relieved that a satisfactory conclusion to the matter had been secured, and its appreciation of the role played by James Diggle[25] as Chairman of the Board was minuted (Minute 847, 6 April 1992). In November 1994 the Treasurer was able

[25] Editor of Euripides and Fellow of Queens' College, Cambridge, where he was University Orator at the time.

to report to Council that the Board had brought the journals back into profitability ahead of the date projected in its business plan.

In April of that same year Council had noted that the CJB would shortly be returning to questions relating to the transfer of reserves to the Association. But it was not until November 1995 that Council once more turned its mind to the subject, when a vigilant recently-elected member (Colin Sydenham, London solicitor and leading light of the Horatian Society)[26] queried a line in the accounts: why had not the CJB surplus for the year (£14,807) been credited to the Association's General Fund? Council members were then regaled with an epitome of the history of the relationship between the Council and the Board, and of the Board's financial position. The key sentence in the minute recording the discussion reads as follows (Minute 984):

Current policy agreed by Council with the Board was that the journals should be so priced as to cover their costs; that nonetheless a reserve should be held equivalent to the production and distribution costs of one issue of each of the journals; and that at some stage the issue of formal transfer of funds held by the Board to the CA, delayed by complications with VAT registration, should be resolved.

Council duly asked its officers to establish whether the reserves (which now stood at £92,203) were above the agreed level, and to seek to make progress on the issue of transfer.

The end of the saga was in sight. In April 1996 Council agreed to put to the Board the proposal – 'with a view to immediate implementation' – that the fund administered by the Board should not exceed one year's costs for the journals, and that any sum accruing in excess of that should be transferred to the Association's General Fund. And in the November following Richard Wallace was able to report that the CJB had ratified Council's decision on the management of its surplus. He was authorised to sign a supplement to the contract with OUP reflecting the changed situation, according the Association 'complete control over any surpluses'. At the same meeting, in noting a deficit of £3,558 on the General Fund, he stressed that 'the Association's finances were fundamentally healthy, although they depended heavily on journal profits'. He predicted a large transfer from the CJB in the following year. Correctly as things transpired: the figure was £23,891, and its buoyancy was what made the difference to the Association's financial outcome for 1996–7 –

---

[26] Colin Sydenham was to be principal draftsman of the new constitution of the Association which from April 1997 replaced the original (but often amended) Rules. The change had been prompted by Council's consideration of the Charities Act 1992, although the opportunity was taken to carry through a more far-reaching review.

an overall surplus of £20,454. There is a hint of triumph in Minute 1062 of the Council meeting of 29 November 1997:[27]

In view mainly of the impact on the Association's finances likely to be made by the projected annual transfers from the Classical Journals Board surpluses, the Treasurer recommended that the grants budget for 1997–8 be set at £30,000. He noted that while some increases in recurrent grants and some additional permanent commitments might be desirable, these would not absorb a significant proportion of the extra money available if Council accepted the recommendation, and suggested that there was an opportunity for Council to identify some new projects deserving of support. Council accepted the recommendation, and it was agreed that members should consider ways in which the Association might best use the opportunity indicated by the Treasurer.

As Richard Wallace indicated, with a much enhanced disposable income the Association was in a position to be more ambitious in its grant-giving activity. It now supports more summer schools than ever before. The London Summer School in Classics has been added to the annual list, as has one run by the University of Newcastle and the Palatine Association of Classical Teachers; and in the last three years the Association has also been helping to fund a new style of summer school, running on the American model for six weeks and designed with the needs of graduate students in mind, at the University of Cork. Lifelong learning is an area in which Council would like to do more. At present activity is mostly confined to annual provision of funds enabling Madingley Hall to offer bursaries to mature students on Greek language courses.[28] Two major ventures have been regarded as appropriate new projects for support. One is the Primary Latin Project. The CA helped with the initial funding for the production of *Minimus*, Barbara Bell's immensely successful Latin course for primary school children. Subsequently the Primary Latin Project Grant Fund was established to provide financial assistance to schools (many in the state sector) wishing to purchase copies of *Minimus* and the associated teacher's manual. Council has contributed periodic injections of cash into the Fund, now totalling £14,000. A second enterprise which appealed to Council's imagination was the New Greek Lexicon Project, devoted to producing a modern dictionary accessible to less advanced students of Greek, and being prepared by a small editorial team in Cambridge led by Anne

---

[27] Coincidentally Chris Collard, who as Secretary of the Board had fought valiantly for its continued control over the reserves, crowned his service to the journals and the CJB by undertaking in his retirement the Editorship of *Classical Quarterly* (for a while without a co-Editor) from 1997–2002.

[28] Among other bodies supported by the CA I would mention several grants to the travelling theatre company Actors of Dionysus, which performs Greek drama mostly in school venues all over the country.

Thompson. The largest grant in the Association's history – £45,000 in three annual instalments – was approved for this purpose in 1999, followed by a further grant agreed in 2002 of £50,000 in five annual instalments.

Governance and Administration

Richard Wallace's November 1988 call for change proved highly effective. But it did not produce the reform of governance structures he had advocated. The working groups Council established at his suggestion met, did some work, and then lapsed. They did not become permanent features of the scene. Toward the end of his Treasurership he was to make another proposal for a change in governance of a rather different kind, however, which shows every sign of being irreversible.

In his report to Council in November 1997 the Treasurer urged the establishment of a finance committee charged with management of the finances of *Classical Quarterly*, *Classical Review* and *Greece & Rome*, including decisions on prices. What triggered the proposal at this particular moment will be obvious from the scope of the business Richard Wallace envisaged the new committee undertaking. If Council was now taking responsibility for managing the surpluses not only on *Greece & Rome* but also (since the settlement with the CJB) on *Classical Quarterly* and *Classical Review*, it made sense for it to take over management of journal finances in their entirety, especially the crucial decisions about pricing on which they depended. To carry out this function a standing committee would obviously be required.

Council accepted the principle of a finance committee at once. As long ago as November 1991, when discussing management of the CJB surplus, members of Council had commented on the 'danger of Board and Association policies and objectives drifting apart' so long as both Council and the CJB retained separate responsibilities with regard to the journal surpluses. Moreover the membership of the Board was generally appointed with an eye principally to its advisory role on editorial matters, not to financial expertise. So once the suggestion of a finance committee had been made, its acceptance was only to be expected.

However the first properly constituted meeting of the new committee did not take place until over a year and a half later, in July 1999, although a precursor group met twelve months before that. There were two reasons for the delay. First was a concern that the extent of the governance restructuring suggested in the proposal was not thorough-going enough. The proposal had been discussed at both the CJB and the *Greece & Rome* Board at their spring 1998 meetings. Minute 1097 of the Council meeting of 28 November 1998 takes up the story:

At both Boards it had been commented that a structure of two Boards, a Finance Committee charged principally with their financial management, and a Council threatened to be unwieldy. It had been suggested at both meetings that consideration should be given to the possibility of combining the two Boards. Council discussed the suggestion further. There was general support for the principle of a merger, and it was agreed to ask the Officers to bring back to April Council a draft proposal for a combined Board, covering membership (which would need to be appropriately broad) and terms of reference, after further consultation with the two Boards.

The outcome was agreement in spring 1999 by all three bodies concerned – Council, the CJB and the *Greece & Rome* Board – on a combined editorial advisory board. Thus came to an end with remark-ably little disagreement or emotion two long and distinctive histories, epitomised by contrasted styles of meetings: the Classical Journals Board preceding its deliberations with long and elegant lunches in the private dining rooms of Oxbridge colleges, the *Greece & Rome* Board getting the business done in the morning before adjourning to comparatively rumbustious eating and drinking in the rather more demotic setting of the Italian restaurants of the Charlotte Street district of Bloomsbury. Each of the two Boards met for the last time in spring 2000, and since September 2000 a new Classical Association Journals Board has had responsibility for the three journals.[29] Like its predecessor bodies it operates at arm's length from Council, though the Chair and Secretary of Council as well as the Treasurer are ex officio members, and unlike either of its predecessors it forwards its minutes to Council.

The second issue was the scope of the Finance Committee's remit. Richard Wallace's original proposal in November 1997 restricted it to management of journal finances. But that restriction was no sooner mooted than queried. Given the central place of journal prices and surpluses in the Association's financial affairs, and given also enhanced expectations of transparency and strategic management of resources on the part of the Charity Commissioners, Council agreed in the event to have the Finance Committee advise it on matters of financial policy generally. The Committee at its first meeting the following July took as a main item of business a far-reaching paper from the new Treasurer

[29] It meets in the morning in Senate House, and eats a sumptuous sandwich lunch.

(Kevin Rix) on a general reserves policy, covering the whole of the Association's assets. It has subsequently approved a new investment policy and a risk management strategy, both duly ratified by Council. Journals business is always a major agenda item, and three of the Committee's seven members are Classical Association Journals Board representatives, including the Chair of CAJB *ex officio* – currently Richard Hunter, Regius Professor of Greek at Cambridge.

These changes in governance arrangements coincided with a more fundamental transformation in the Association's affairs. After being run almost exclusively on volunteer labour for nearly a century, in spring 1999 the CA's administration became the responsibility of a salaried secretary. This development was precipitated by Richard Wallace's decision that the 1998 AGM would be the last at which he would accept nomination as Treasurer, bringing to an end thirteen and a half years of service. Along with Bron Morris, the Classics departmental secretary at Keele, over that period he had delivered all the Association's key member services as well as managing its finances: subscriptions, journal orders, purchases of *Greece & Rome* New Surveys, and (with student help) the January mailing of *Proceedings*, *CA News* and the annual order form, not to mention fielding enquiries of every kind. A large cellar in the Department basement housed most of the stock of CA publications. When the other officers asked for an estimate of the hours the Treasurer personally devoted to the job, they were told two hours a day on average – but had no doubt this was a sizeable underestimate.

By the time Council met in November 1998, the officers had formed a clear view of the shape the future must take, as Minute 1096 records:

The Chair, introducing discussion, explained that the starting-point for the Officers' consideration of the issues had been the premiss that Mr Wallace as Treasurer was irreplaceable in many senses. In particular, it was clear that it was no longer feasible for the Association's administrative systems to depend on the spare time voluntarily given up by someone in full-time professional employment. The time had come for the Association to employ an Office Administrator who would carry the responsibility for the day-to-day administration of its affairs, financial and otherwise (with the exception of CA member subscriptions to the journals and much of the *New Surveys* business, which would be managed by OUP), leaving a greatly reduced workload for the Hon. Treasurer, who would retain overall financial responsibility. Discussions with JACT Officers had indicated that JACT would like to move in the same direction, and to cooperate with the CA in a shared venture.

The Officers were therefore proposing to Council that a full-time position of Office Administrator be established (to be remunerated on the London Administrative Officer Grade 1 scale), the post-holder to be responsible jointly to CA and JACT, and to operate from the JACT/CA office in the Senate House. A paper had been circulated setting out in some detail the duties proposed for the post. Mr Murrell confirmed that JACT Council had for its part agreed in principle the basic proposal of a shared Office Administrator.

Council approved these proposals. Members observed that there would be the opportunity for considerable benefits to the Association from sharing office space with JACT in a location adjacent to the Hellenic and Roman Society offices, e.g. in co-ordinating grant-giving activity. It was noted that arrangements for the management of the Administrator's post were still to be determined, and the Officers were asked to pursue early discussions with the JACT Officers in this regard. It was envisaged, subject to confirmation from JACT, that CA would initially bear two-thirds of the costs of the post, JACT one-third.

Council also approved a draft form of advertisement for the Office of Treasurer, subject to the addition of reference to the Association's links with other classical organisations nationally and internationally. It was noted that the position would now become comparable with the Treasurerships of the Hellenic and Roman Societies.

The Association had a lot of luck. It was fortunate that two years earlier the Institute of Classical Studies had moved from Gordon Square to more spacious premises in Senate House. It was fortunate that following its settlement with the CJB Council had recently secured for the Association the kind of financial base which was necessary if it was to employ a professional administrator. It was fortunate that the key JACT officers (Geoffrey Williams as Chair of Council, John Murrell as Consultant Secretary) had made a similar assessment of their own administrative needs, and were committed to practical steps towards closer collaboration between all the national Classical bodies and with the CA in particular. Last but very far from least, the Association had in Christopher Rowe a Chair of Council with exceptional vision, drive and determination, who steered to a conclusion the complex sequence of negotiations and decisions involved in putting the new arrangements in place, and undertook the trouble-shooting necessary when teething problems occurred.[30] Even so, the plan might still have gone awry if the two associations had been unable to recruit an administrator with guts, ability and dedication to the cause.

That went right, too. So I leave Clare Roberts – who was appointed from 30 April 1999 and since November 2000 has been designated Secretary to the Association – with the last word.

---

[30] In the winter of 1999–2000 the unexpected resignation of the new Treasurer meant that he also had to assume overall responsibility for managing the finances and the preparation of the accounts, albeit with indispensable support from Clare Roberts and the Auditor.

The View from HQ

CLARE ROBERTS

The CA has been closely connected with the University of London's Institute of Classical Studies since the foundation of the ICS in the early 1950s. Professor T. B. L. Webster of UCL was one of the founding fathers of the ICS and the first Director – and his strong support of the CA (he was President 1959–1960) ensured that a home for the CA's administration would always be available to the Association. At the ICS's former Gordon Square premises the CA office was used almost exclusively by JACT (Dr Jenny March had a typewriter on call in the Office – but there was little other physical presence of the CA). Following the ICS's transition to the University's Senate House building in summer 1997 to join other School of Advanced Study institutes on the 3rd Floor, the JACT/CA office space expanded, and now a usefully sized administrative office replaced the cubby-hole some members will remember from Gordon Square days. With the retirement of Richard Wallace as CA Hon. Treasurer, the CA activities (a huge accumulation of papers, records, and a myriad of boxes of magazines) based at the University of Keele needed a new home from the 1998–1999 session and as explained above, this change was the catalyst for the administrator appointment for the Senate House office jointly employed by JACT. So on 30 April 1999, the ICS at Senate House became the CA's official HQ, and I became the first ever full-time secretarial employee for the CA and JACT.

The new appointment was certainly a baptism of fire: concurrent with a number of boxes arriving from Keele (with one file urgently marked 'read this first'), the failure of the hard drive on the existing computer and the collapse of an ageing table when too many papers were placed upon it. But as always in such situations, order began to adhere to what at first seemed chaos, and great progress was made in computerising databases and financial records and providing the Association with the modern procedures and systems to tackle the 21st century. Of course, some questions remain unanswered: why on earth was the Classical Association bequeathed a legacy of detailed cricketing memoirs unearthed amongst old files and papers? And some quirks became immediately apparent: I was instructed that under no circumstances should I destroy the now very moth-eaten and mouldy pair of curtains found on the dusty top shelf of the Office or JACT would fall out with the CA. (I now know the full story: Mrs Edna M. Hooker, a long-standing officer and devotee of the CA, had them made for the JACT/CA office at Gordon Square – indeed specially designed at Heal's with a Grecian pot pattern. This slice of bijou history was preserved when I took a rash and unilateral decision to cut out the frayed and mouldy edgings and turned the patterned material into a table cover for use at conferences for CA book displays.)

But despite the complexities of sorting out the past, the HQ move to the ICS has led to increased and valuable collaboration with other classical organisations (Roman Society, Hellenic Society, JACT, British School at Athens, etc.). On a serious level, this ensures that we are all working in the right direction to achieve our shared goals in supporting Classics, often with the sharing of information and systems, and also the sharing of costs (such as software for direct debit payments and credit cards). This collaborative approach has allowed the CA to clarify its position on grant giving and initiatives. It also provides a great deal of moral support when you are the only employee of an organisation. On a less serious level, this of course enables the sharing of essential gossip with regular lunches, to make sure that we all know exactly what's going on (often hosted, one notes, in the office of the Hellenic Society Secretary . . .). Another sharing that can be found throughout the CA's history is the almost incestuous exchange of executive officers amongst the Classical organisations: in the most recent period there has been much cross-over with the Hellenic Society – examples are the ex-Chair of the CA Council also being the ex-President of the Hellenic Society; the Hon. Secretary of the Hellenic Society being the President of JACT; the current Chair of the CA Council being the Editor of JHS; the ex-Editor of JHS being the Chair of the CA Journals Board.

Members will be most aware of the office activities which directly concern their subscription: the maintenance of databases, dealing with all types of queries, taking and chasing subscriptions, arranging mailings . . . But collecting the subs is only the start of quite a complex financial process for a charity and association as large and varied as the CA. I remember preparing for the first audit with our new Auditors – and quaking in my boots as the auditor randomly pointed to some financial transaction which occurred before I had even started to work for the CA, and demanded to be shown the necessary paper trail to validate this. Often all I could do was to point to a box on the top shelf marked 'MISC' saying, 'Well it might be in there . . .'.

The governance of the CA involves a regular cycle of annual meetings, with all the attendant paperwork and fall-out: two Finance Committees, one Journals Board, one AGM, three Council meetings, one Officers Committee, and of course one Conference. (The Conference is my main opportunity to meet the many and varied CA membership.) And people tend to forget that because the CA is a registered charity, this involves annual returns, risk assessment, policies on reserves, grants, overseeing the paying of any trustees, strict accounting regulations, data protection . . . Important recent developments include the tenth on-line and print versions of the essential guide *Classicists in British Universities* (always a harrowingly complex job getting academics to tell you what their specialist interests are in a mere short phrase, and getting some even to respond to your several emails and letters at all), and the introduction of the CA's own website.[1]

So in 2002–2003 the HQ Office is in good heart, and has equipped itself to face a future of supporting Classics for the next 100 years. (And out of interest my wish list includes: office fridge/mini-bar, nearby sauna facilities for Association staff, and an all-singing-all-dancing membership system whereby members can update their own records . . .)

[1] www.sas.ac.uk/icls/ClassAss/

II

Perspectives

6

THE CA'S PUBLICATIONS

By CHRISTOPHER STRAY

It might be said that the history of the CA is largely the history of its publications. Certainly they have been, especially for members who could not attend the annual general meetings, the main point of contact with the CA. In this chapter the various publications of the Association are surveyed in chronological order.[1] It is followed by a memoir of Robert Sewter, editor of *Greece & Rome* from 1946 to 1971, by his pupil and colleague John Muir, and a survey of the presence (or absence) of women in the journal by Gillian Clark. These are followed by an account of its newest production, *CA News*, by its first and so far only editor, Jenny March.

Proceedings

At its second meeting, in February 1904, the Council set up a small publications sub-committee with James Gow, headmaster of Westminster, as convener. Their task was 'to consider the best means of printing and circulating the proceedings of the Association'.[2] Gow presented their report at the next Council meeting but one, in May 1904. He began by declaring that 'the best form of Journal to be issued by the Association does not appear to be urgent' – for the simple reason that the CA did not have enough money to print more than a report of the Oxford meeting. What could be done in the future would depend on the subscription rate. After comparing the costs of monthly, quarterly and annual journals, he pointed out that advertisements might be used to recoup expenses. The obvious existing journal for comparison was the *Proceedings of the Classical Association of Scotland*: but though this was a small volume, the Scottish Association had been compelled in March 1904, in order to cover its costs, to raise its subscription from 5s to 7s 6d.

---

[1] The *Classical Review* predates the CA, having first appeared in 1887.
[2] Council minutes, 13 February 1904.

Of the other subject associations, 'the Modern Language Association, having 520 members, spends 5s 6d per Member, about £140, on its so-called quarterly, which appears only 3 times per year'. Another plan would be to ask David Nutt, publisher of the *Classical Review*, to provide the journal for members. But he could hardly be expected to do so at 5s (the CA's annual subscription) a head, when about half of the CA's membership were already subscribing to the journal at 13s 6d.[3]

At the same meeting, Sonnenschein produced a letter from S. G. Owen of Christ Church, Oxford, in which he warned that 'The *Classical Review* is in low water financially – The same is also the state of the Oxford Philological Society, which has recently subscribed towards Greek excavations'. Owen went on to declare that *CR* was doing a good job and deserved to be helped; he asked that the CA should discuss what it could do to help. At the next Council meeting, Gow reported that since it was impossible to link up with *CR*, and since the CA had about £90 in the bank, the best course of action was to produce a pamphlet of about 80 pages, which would cost £45 for 1000 copies. The Council approved the plan, and instructed Gow's committee to find a publisher willing to produce the pamphlet.[4] At the next meeting, they reported that after comparing quotations from several publishers and printers, they had chosen John Murray as publisher, and Hazell Watson and Viney as printers, of the CA's 1904 Proceedings. Murray had urged that their proposed cover price of 2s 6d was too high, so they had reduced it to 2s. They had also acceded to his proposal that advertisements be allowed at both front and back of the volume.

The 1904 *Proceedings* appeared in October – a handsomely-printed volume of 87 pages, with discreet advertisements from publishers at front (Macmillan, Ginn, OUP, CUP) and back (Murray). The bulk of the volume was taken up by a detailed account of the Oxford meeting; this was followed by a list of officers, the Association's rules, and the names and addresses of members. This format was followed until 1940 with minor variations: topographical lists of members were soon added, and reports of the activities of branches as these were funded. Though these early volumes are technically 'paperbacks', their look and feel bespeak another era: the paper is thick, the type imprint heavy, the lettering on the covers raised.[5] The practice of printing verbatim

---

[3] Council minutes, 7 May 1904.

[4] Council minutes, 27 May 1904.

[5] Even more so in my own copy of *Proceedings* 1904–6, formerly owned by the Earl of Cromer (Evelyn Baring), president in 1910 – bound together in three-quarter leather, with raised bands and austere gold lettering on the spine.

accounts of discussions at meetings continued into the 1920s, and makes the early volumes of *Proceedings* an invaluable source for the history of the CA. From its initial 87 pages it quickly climbed to 200, reaching a peak of 266 pages in 1911.[6] Thereafter it hovered around the 200-page mark until the early 1930s, when it began a slow decline in size, ending up at just under 80 pp in 1971. In the next year, a rise of nearly 40 per cent in printing and distribution costs led Council to cancel the CA's longstanding contract with John Murray, who since 1904 had produced *Proceedings* by letterpress. In future it was to be published by the Association itself, and printed by offset litho. From 1985 onwards, perfect binding disappeared, to be replaced by the indignity of staples; and in 2000 *Proceedings* was discontinued. As Malcolm Schofield has explained (p. 73 above), by that time a newsletter, *CA News*, had been published twice yearly since 1990, carrying when necessary the formal announcements which had previously appeared in *Proceedings*.[7]

Pamphlets

During its first century, the CA has published a variety of pamphlets. The largest group consists of presidential addresses. The first to be published in pamphlet form seems to have been that by Sir William Osler (*The Old Humanities and the New Science*, 1919); the second, J. W. Mackail's 1923 address (*The Classics*). In the 1940s and '50s, the addresses were issued in a stylish small square format. Later their publication was confined to *Proceedings*; but a few years after this lapsed, in 1988, separate publication was resumed with Sir Anthony Cleaver's *From Homer to Harwell* (1993). Other addresses were published as 'Occasional Publications', a series which began with D. Slater's *Ovid in the* Metamorphoses (1913), and came to an end with No. 7, F. B. Jevons's *Masks and Acting* (1916).[8] Five reports on Latin and Greek teaching were issued between 1905 and 1909, and then published together as *Recommendations of the Classical Association on the Teaching of Latin and Greek* (1912). Later pamphlets, apart from the presidential

---

[6] In part because of the lengthy discussion on uniform grammatical terminology in that year.

[7] See Chapter 5; and cf. Jenny March's account of editing *CA News* in Chapter 10.

[8] These pamphlets were printed by Cambridge University Press. Slater's is undated, but is referred to in *Proceedings* 11 (January 1914) as having been issued, so almost certainly belongs to 1913. After the publication of No. 7, the CA decided that it could not afford to produce any more, and dissolved the editorial board which had published the series.

addresses, were few and far between, and were usually designed to spread the word of the value of Classics to a doubting world. An example is *The Testimony of the Nations to the Value of Classical Studies* edited by Frederic Kenyon, which appeared in 1925. This collected together testimony from the Marquess of Crewe (chairman of the Prime Minister's Committee on Classics, 1919–21); Viscount Finlay (Scotland), Léon Berard of France, Giovanni Gentile (Italy) and the President of the USA, Calvin Coolidge. *Re-appraisal* (1962), issued as a supplement to *Greece & Rome*, followed in this sub-genre; the present volume follows the same format.

Classical Review and *Classical Quarterly*

It is surely one of the CA's main claims to fame that it publishes two of the leading English-language classical journals. *CR* and *CQ* are now so much part of the scholarly landscape that it is easy to forget that they were once struggling youngsters whose very survival was in doubt. In 1887, when *CR* was founded, only two classical journals had been established in this country which survive today: the *Journal of Hellenic Studies* (1880) and the *Proceedings of the Cambridge Philological Society* (1882). Earlier journals had foundered after a few years, usually either because their editors had received ecclesiastical preferment or because the support of contributors or subscribers had fallen away. When no journal was in existence, as in the 1860s, scholars were at times obliged to publish their findings in pamphlets.[9] The *Journal of Philology* (1868–1920) is an interesting case: it survived in its early years because the Cambridge Philological Society bought it *en bloc* and supplied it to its members. Rising production costs during and after World War I forced its publisher, Macmillan, to raise the cover price; the Society cancelled its subscription; and the Journal closed. But by that time, both *CR* and *CQ* were providing competition, and unlike *JP*, appeared on time.

The *Classical Review* was published by David Nutt, a long-established firm of publishers and booksellers. The *Review* had been founded in 1886 by Joseph Mayor, Professor of Classics at King's College London.[10] He not only built up a large group of British contributors, but also arranged US distribution and the involvement

---

[9] An example was recalled by D. B. Monro during the first general meeting: *Proceedings* (1904), 5. He was referring to H. W. Chandler's *Miscellaneous Emendations & Suggestions* (1866).

[10] Not to be confused with his elder brother John, Professor of Latin at Cambridge and editor of Juvenal.

of American scholars in contributing to and editing the journal. In 1906, Nutt set up the *Classical Quarterly*, which was designed to take over longer articles, while *CR* was to publish shorter pieces and general articles and to appeal to schoolteachers. This was a risky move, since as we have seen above, the finances of *CR* were not in a very satisfactory state.[11] At the end of 1908, Conway reported to Council on this, asking if a grant in aid could be provided. Council were unhappy at the idea, since the journals were beyond their control; but the discussion led to the decision to offer to buy the journals. In 1909 the CA, in conjunction with the Oxford and Cambridge Philological Societies, established that Nutt was willing to sell the two journals, and in 1910 the Association set up a Classical Journals Board to manage them; soon afterwards the *Year's Work in Classical Studies* (which is considered separately below) was transferred to the care of the Board.[12] There was considerable resistance to the duplication of journals, some feeling that a single large journal would be a better option, and that *CR* was now too small to take the material offered it; but the objectors were soothed by the editors.

The CA council felt it had gained a considerable financial bargain, and it was even suggested that it might soon take over the *Journal of Philology* as well. The negotiations with Nutt had in fact become extremely difficult, since it appears that Alfred Nutt soon regretted the price agreed in July 1909. At least that is the obvious interpretation of Conway's remark that 'We have paid the former proprietor of the Journals a sum which he himself in the first instance gladly accepted'.[13] In the same discussion, Gilbert Murray referred to Conway's able handling of a 'new, delicate, troublesome negotiation'.[14] Nutt's resentment later led him to demand £200 for the back issues of the journals – for which the Council was prepared to offer £50 at most – and to refuse to hand over copies of unreviewed books.[15] The project of taking over *JP* was abandoned, but during 1910 the Journals Board drew up a plan to publish 'a journal of Roman studies'. The cost would not exceed £400 a year, they thought; the journal would be offered to CA members

---

[11] The next volume of *CR* was noticeably thinner than the 1906 volume – little more than half the size. This will have reduced costs, but may have been a result of the appearance of *CQ*.

[12] The price asked was £500. The CA provided £150, the two societies £100 each; the rest was raised by an appeal to members and benefactors.

[13] *Proceedings* 7 (1910), 23.

[14] Ibid., 29.

[15] In his Jubilee history (p.23), Richardson quotes a CA report as saying that the final transfer from Nutt was achieved 'not without the able and spirited help of the firm of solicitors acting for the Classical Association'. The solicitors' bill of £40 suggests that a lot of work was needed.

at a reduced price. All subscribers would have the right to use the Hellenic Society's library, and in return the CA would subsidise the purchase of 'Latin books' for the library. This expansive plan came to nothing, presumably because of the establishment of its own journal (*JRS*) by the newly-founded Society for the Promotion of Roman Studies. (The CA's relations with the infant Roman Society are dealt with on p. 16 above.)

The two journals presented different faces to the reader. *CR* retained its previous layout, with double columns and rather small type; *CQ*, on the other hand, had dignified pages of single-column type of a larger size. The message was plain: one journal was aiming to be grander and more 'serious', the other to be informative and useful. Council discussion of the period show a concern to spread the Association's message, and information about books and events, to a wider audience than professional scholars. The remit of *CR* was now to fulfil this aim, and to this end the editors appealed for general cultural articles; but largely in vain. In 1925 we still find the editors agreeing to look for such articles, but warning that nobody seemed to want to supply them.[16] The ground was being laid for the foundation of *Greece & Rome* (on which, see below).

The history of the two journals from the late 1920s is in a sense separate from that of the Association. The Classical Journals Board operated semi-autonomously, and references to the parent body are uncommon in its minutes.[17] Instead, they are full of the matter of any academic journal: submissions, rejections, print run and subscriptions. Occasionally a ragged cry of protest breaks the smoothness of this mundane flow. On one occasion, an eminent Greek scholar wrote to protest that a recent work of his had been roughly handled in a review in *CR*. He wanted to know why the task had been given to a young scholar of whom he had never heard. The editors explained that several leading scholars had been invited to review the book but had refused the task (a statement which in itself might have given the complaining author pause!); but he was little mollified. On another occasion, in 1931, A. E. Housman offered *CQ* an article entitled 'Praefanda', which discussed aspects of Latin erotic poetry and was written in Latin. The editor, J. D. Denniston, was inclined to refuse it, but referred the matter to the Board, who eventually voted by four to three to approve his decision.[18]

[16] Letter from W. M. Calder, CJB minutes.
[17] This comfortable situation was to be rudely disturbed: see Malcolm Schofield's account of the CA's recent history in Chap. 5.
[18] CJB minutes, 7 March 1931. The article was subsequently published in *Hermes* 66 (1931), 402–412. A translation by James Jayo appeared in *Arion* (3rd series) 9 (2001), 180–200.

Increasing production costs led in the late 1930s to a financial crisis. John Murray were willing to keep charges as low as possible, but even this was not enough, and in 1938 the journals were in effect rescued by the Clarendon Press, which took over production in that year.[19] The format of both journals continued unchanged until 1951, when each began a new series. In 1976, increased production costs led to an experiment with unjustified typesetting, but the traditional layout was restored in 1980. An earlier casualty of the financial crisis was the section of short articles at the front of *CR*. An editorial note announced in 1974 that 'Rising costs have compelled the Classical Journals Board to reduce the size of the volume and to ask the editors to refrain from accepting original articles and notes in the meantime'.[20] The 'meantime' became a permanent state, and the *Review* is now completely devoted to reviews: a final farewell to the late-Victorian aspiration to belong to a world of literary Reviews, already long abandoned.

The Year's Work in Classical Studies

In his jubilee sketch of the CA's first half century, L. J. D. Richardson remarked, 'I do not think that any of our publications reflected so truly the aims and ideals of the Classical Association as did *The Year's Work*'.[21] The first annual number of *YWCS* appeared in 1907, the editor, W. H. D. Rouse, having been left insufficient time to meet the agreed deadline the previous year; later numbers appeared in the early autumn of each year. From 1907 to 1910, Rouse contributed an initial chapter on classical teaching in schools, in which a survey of recent literature was combined with the exposition of his own support for direct method teaching and his objections to the university entrance scholarship system.[22] His chapter was followed in the 1906 volume by nineteen others, covering an impressive range: from prehistoric archaeology to numismatics; from the Greek warship to Latin inscriptions. Some of the authors were well known (Francis Haverfield, William Warde Fowler). The names of others are either forgotten (Louise Matthaei, whose German connections led to her being forced out of

---

[19] See *Proceedings* 36 (1939), 44.

[20] *CR* NS 24 (1974), 320.

[21] L. J. D. Richardson, 'The Classical Association – the first fifty years', in *Jubilee Addresses* (London, 1954), 26.

[22] As Richardson diplomatically put it in his historical sketch, 'Dr Rouse himself contributed to each volume a characteristic and valuable chapter . . .': 'The Classical Association', 24.

Cambridge several years later) or were changed (M. O. B. Caspari became Max Cary, and did not advertise the fact that his middle initials stood for 'Otto Bismarck'). The 1907 volume contained eighteen chapters, covering a comparable range but with some changes: the survey of Latin inscriptions continued, but chapters were inserted on the New Testament and on Greek sculpture. This pattern continued, with a substantial core of regular articles and a rotating fringe of other pieces. A browse through these early volumes has many incidental benefits. Not only do they offer useful sidelights on contemporary scholarly discussions; there are often comments which have an idiosyncratic charm. Thus Sonnenschein, in his survey of Grammar in 1907, complains that 'I should . . . have liked to see a discussion of my suggestion . . . that *quin* with the imperative is really interrogative'; and J. E. Sandys, treating Literature in 1908, reveals that the spelling 'Vergil' in his and M. R. James's chapters in the *Cambridge Bibliography of English Literature* is due to an editorial decision: 'neither of these contributors is responsible for this departure from the true English tradition'.[23]

YWCS was from the first a heavy drain on the CA's financial resources. The first issue was offered to members at a reduced price (1*s* 6*d* instead of 2*s* 6*d*), but only about a fifth of the membership subscribed. In 1908 it was decided to send it free to all members, in the hope that this might produce an increase in membership. They had only to pay the postage, but even this was made free in 1912. Clearly the Council was convinced that it was a worthwhile project on which to spend money; and they must have realised that it gave members something for their money. As the costs rose, their response was to encourage the recruiting of new members. Eventually, however, the costs became disproportionate when printing and paper charges rose steeply after the First World War. The Treasurer's report of May 1919 was a gloomy one: the costs associated with *YWCS* took up nearly half the CA's income (£167 out of £350), and 'the actual cost of publications amounts to 4s 7d per member, leaving only 5d for expenses!'[24] No separate 1919 volume of *YWCS* was issued, a temporary measure which helped to balance the books, but as was pointed out at the time, weakened the value of the publication: its regular annual publication. In 1920 it was agreed to begin charging members, the price being fixed at 2*s* 6*d* (3*s* 6*d* for non-members).

The later history of *YWCS* can be briefly told. The appearance of the

[23] Sonnenschein, *YWCS* (1907), 96; Sandys, *YWCS* (1908), 142.
[24] *Proceedings* 16 (1919), 61.

first volume of Marouzeau's *L'Année philologique* in 1924 caused some to wonder if the CA's annual survey was now redundant, but the majority opinion was that for schoolteachers, the convenient summary discussions in *YWCS* were invaluable. This opinion was reinforced during a later crisis of conscience, in 1933, when foreign scholars, including Jerôme Carcopino, Gaetano De Sanctis and Tenney Frank, wrote in to support its continued publication. It was clear from their letters that *YWCS* was valued for its clarity of organisation, its prompt and regular appearance and what Carcopino called the 'sharpness of its contributors' comments'.[25] The death early in 1940 of the longstanding editor S. G. Owen (he had edited *YWCS* since 1926) delayed publication till later that year, and wartime shortages and the sheer difficulty of gaining access to foreign publications made publication impossible for several years. Eventually, in 1948, a volume appeared covering the war years, and in 1950 a final volume dealing with 1945–7.[26] The costs of production were the main cause of the final cancellation of *YWCS*, but the defence offered in 1933 was now fatally weakened by the existence of another CA publication, *Greece & Rome*.

Greece & Rome

By the mid-1920s, *CQ* and *CR* were firmly established, but increasing printing costs were making their financial situation precarious. At the same time, protests reached Council from several quarters (including J. W. Mackail and the Association's Sussex branch) that both journals were losing touch with non-university members of the CA because of the lack of 'general' articles and reviews of schoolbooks.[27] As the Classical Journals Board minutes summarised the message, 'the view was expressed that neither the Review nor the Quarterly appealed to most teachers, who wanted information as to new knowledge and ideas in scholarship, and would appreciate articles and correspondence on methods of study and teaching'. The Board was firmly against the option of starting a new publication, and so R. S. Conway agreed to

[25] Richardson, 'First fifty years', 25.

[26] A compendious survey of the previous half-century's scholarship was issued in the CA's jubilee, edited by Maurice Platnauer, who had edited the final volume of *YWCS*: *Fifty Years of Classical Scholarship* (Oxford, 1954). Platnauer followed this in 1968 with *Fifty Years (and Twelve) of Classical Scholarship*. The current series of New Surveys in a sense follows on from this tradition of expository digest.

[27] The CA had expressed an interest in supporting a popular journal called *Discovery*, launched in 1920, but the connection seems not to have persisted.

draft a report on the possibilities for making changes in *CR* to make it 'more attractive'.[28] His report concluded that a third journal was unlikely to be self-supporting and would probably 'injure the circulation of the existing journals'. *CR* should therefore be changed by including more articles and reviews of interest to schoolteachers; he also suggested that an Occasional Paper of this kind should be produced each year as an extra number.[29] Little was achieved in this direction, however, and in 1929 the Board was told that the Council's standing committee proposed to consider the case for starting a new journal.

By 1930, detailed proposals were being discussed for what became *Greece & Rome*, but might also have been called *The School Classical Journal* (a title which was wisely rejected). The committee appointed by Council to make recommendations concluded that 'The object of the new journal should be to make accessible, in a form having special regard to use in schools, new or important aspects of Classical knowledge, but not to publish papers definitely devoted to original research.' The journal should appear three times a year, and before it was first published, subscriptions should be sought from schools as well as from CA members.[30]

In May a small group had met to plan the policy of the new journal. Something of their thinking can be learned from an OUP memo by A. P. Norrington of 19 May.[31] Norrington had been visited by Norman Gardiner, an Oxford don who was also one of the CA's Secretaries, to sound him out on the prospects of the Press's publishing *Greece & Rome*. The memo notes that

The Journal will be for Schoolmasters primarily, and especially the Schoolmasters in Secondary Schools. *The Classical Review* and *The Classical Quarterly* have grown much too highbrow and specialist for *this* public, and yet this public does want to know of the latest theories and discoveries . . . Gardiner quoted *Discovery* and *The School Science Review* as two comparable Journals . . . Barrow and Macnaughton of the Board of Education, both, I understand, HMIs, are very keen on the scheme and prepared to push it. . . . The question of a Publisher was brought up, and Gardiner suggested that we should be approached . . . Gardiner told me that Bells have already been nosing after it.[32]

---

[28] CJB minutes, 14 November 1925.

[29] The report is inserted in the minutes of the meeting of 11 December 1925.

[30] Council minutes, 12 July 1930.

[31] Norrington, then an employee of the Clarendon Press, later became Master of Trinity College. The basement room of Blackwell's Broad St bookshop, which runs under the Trinity quad, is named after him.

[32] Memo, PP. 2032/AN, 19 May 1930: © Oxford University Press. This memo and that referred to in note 34 below are reproduced by permission of the Secretary to the Delegates of Oxford University Press.

Clearly the large number of teachers (many of them female, though that fact had apparently not penetrated some male-dominated enclaves) in the municipal schools were by now perceived as a distinct market. The vital role of the first Staff HMI for Classics, D. A. Macnaughton, and his colleague and eventual successor R. H. Barrow, can be glimpsed in Norrington's summary. In 1929, Macnaughton had conducted a survey of classical teaching in grant-aided schools, finding that much of it was very weak, and that some teachers were interested only in the mental discipline imputed to grammar learning.[33]

The first issue of *Greece & Rome* appeared in October 1931, under the editorship of two London schoolmasters: C. J. Ellingham of City of London School and A. G. Russell of St Olave's Grammar School. It was handsomely produced by the Clarendon Press, with a cover design printed from a woodblock specially commissioned from Eric Gill. The first item in the issue was an address to its readers by Cyril Bailey. Bailey is now remembered largely as the editor of Lucretius, but he was an influential and approachable Oxford don whose ability to mediate betweens scholars and schoolteachers was widely recognised; he chaired an annual meeting of 'dons and beaks' – a good choice, then, to introduce the new journal. Bailey's welcoming statement is reproduced below; and it is worth noticing that his use of 'technical', which one might expect to refer to scholarship, in fact refers to the techniques of pedagogy. He may have been gently making the point that discussion of classroom technique could be as off-putting to some as accounts of, say, manuscript transmission were to others. (The reader will note that Bailey's first and last sentences both include Greek.)

AD LECTORES

When a new journal makes its bow to the public, it is expected to submit to a δοκιμασία and to explain the reasons for its existence. Greece and Rome is a classical journal, or, as its claim might be stated more modestly, a journal for readers of the classics. It has many elder sisters, the Classical Quarterly, the Classical Review, the journals of Hellenic and of Roman Studies, to which it would be an impertinence to appear as a rival. But Greece and Rome has no intention of rivalling these grave and reverend seniors; its function is rather to be a supplement. For all of these, though many of their articles have a wide appeal, are in fact the journals of the professors and the learned dons, whose business is in the deep waters of the minutiae of classical scholarship, and of the latest developments in its many branches. But there is another public, less learned perhaps but not less keen,

---

[33] Board of Education, *Memorandum on the Present Position of Latin and Greek in the Grant-Aided Schools of the United Kingdom* (London, 1929). The message was repeated, with variations, by Barrow in the Board's *Suggestions for the Teaching of Classics* (London, 1939). See Stray, *Classics Transformed*, 278–9.

the classical schoolmasters and schoolmistresses, who, though their occupations do not permit them to keep abreast with details, are yet eager to know the general trend of recent criticism and to hear of important new discoveries in archaeology or to learn the gist of a striking new theory. There are many too, as the list of the members of the Classical Association makes clear, whose avocations lie in quite different fields, but who maintain their study of the classics and their love of all connected with the ancient world. It is for such as these that Greece and Rome hopes to cater. It will be its endeavour to provide interesting and attractive articles on general topics connected with the study of the classics as well as to give an efficient record of work that is being done. Nor does it wish merely to provide for readers, but also for writers. There must be many who, though they would not claim to have conducted research and so to have a right to ask for space from the editors of the senior journals, yet feel that they have something to say on classical literature or art which will be of interest to others. From such writers the editors of Greece and Rome will be glad to consider contributions: they will welcome, too, the raising of questions which might be discussed in its columns.

The contents of this first number will serve to illustrate the scope and range of the journal. Literature is represented by Mr. Ellingham's article on the Georgics, history by Mr. Wheeler's account of Roman Africa, ancient life by Mr Barton's provocative paper on Greek art and Mr Hett's contribution on Greek games. The more technical aspect of Greek and Latin studies has its share in the valuable information supplied by Mr Symonds on Aids to Classical Teaching and Miss Beames's description of a new method in instruction. Finally there are reviews of books of the kind which school librarians will wish to consider as possible additions to their shelves.

It will surely be generally agreed that there is room for a new journal on these lines. It need not – it is to be hoped that it will not – entice a single subscriber away from the older journals. To many of these subscribers it will be a welcome addition, and at the same time it will gather round it a new clientele of those who will find in it the *pabulum* which they have hitherto lacked. I should like then in the name of many other well-wishers, as I feel assured, to applaud the first appearance of Greece and Rome and to say to it, in the words of the Aristophanic choruses, ἀλλ᾽ ἴθι ... ἔμον.

Cyril Bailey

Norrington had originally hoped that someone with a higher public profile could be found to launch the first issue: 'I was rather sorry to see that you had not secured any 'celebrity' to give the Journal a send off; I think a short message of goodwill from His Grace of York or Gilbert Murray or Mackail would have helped very much. . . . I think the contents of the first number will strike people as honest and interesting, but not arresting.'[34]

By May 1932, the new journal's board of management was able to report satisfactory sales: about 1,250 subscriptions, as well as 200 sales of single copies of the first number.[35] But though schoolteachers read it, they seem to have been reluctant to contribute, a fact bemoaned in an

---

[34] Norrington to H. A. Ormerod, 11 June 1931. OUP Journals dept. records, P.9213/AN.
[35] *Proceedings* 28 (1932), 54–5.

editorial of February 1933: 'The editors have received much and kindly help from many quarters, but not much yet from that body for whom more than any other *Greece and Rome* is intended. Schoolmasters and schoolmistresses are very loath to write.'[36] Barrow resigned as chairman of the Board of Management in March 1952; when the Board put on record its gratitude for 'the long and skilful fostering of the Journal which owes its inception to him'.[37] Ellingham continued in office till 1953 when he resigned, to be replaced by G. T. W. Hooker. The new editorial era was marked by the commissioning of a new cover, and the inception of a new series of the journal; the first issue appeared in February 1954.

Something of the thinking behind the beginning of the new series can be discerned by a memorandum circulated in August 1953 by its new editor, Geoffrey Hooker.[38] He began by emphasising that *Greece & Rome* 'as a non-technical journal . . . should not attempt the tasks of a learned or pedagogical journal', and went on discuss its resources:

It appears that at present G & R can make ends meet. But no payment is made for contributions or for many of the plates, so that in fact it depends for its existence on charity. This is an unsatisfactory position, not least because its effect is to deprive the editor of initiative in the running of the journal: he has to take what happens to be offered, which may not be what is wanted.

Hooker went on to discuss the journal's reputation:

My own opinion has for some time been that G & R was rather dull, giving the impression at times that classical studies were moribund, and that it was all too often left unread. The outer cover, insipid in colour and crowded with print, makes little appeal to the eye. Among the articles there have been too many small subjects, too many that are obscure and out-of-the-way; too often it seems that they ought to have appeared in one of the learned journals but for one reason or another have not found a place there.

Art, architecture, landscape and seascape – indeed, the whole visual side of classical civilization – are mostly left untouched (the supplementary Plates apart), and there is little about interesting recent and current developments . . . some reviews are too painstakingly highbrow, and at times deal with the wrong books – especially the more specialised foreign works. What is the point (to take an extreme example) of reviewing in G & R Hemburg's *Die Kabiren*, published in Uppsala? Who but specialists would read that, and yet what specialist would look to G & R for a review of it?

An elderly scholar, who might be expected to have fairly austere tastes, has roundly told me that G & R 'has for several years been getting duller and duller – without really becoming any better to compensate for the dullness'. I have also circulated a

---

[36] *G&R* 2 (1933), 123.
[37] Board of Management minutes, 1 March 1952.
[38] On Hooker's editorship, as on other aspects of the journal, see also Ian McAuslan's contribution (Chapter 7).

questionnaire and collected the opinions of several Classics teachers, nearly all of them masters in scholarship-winning schools. One or two seem fairly satisfied with *G & R* as it is, but the rest generally agree that *G & R* is too specialised and 'strays too much down the byways', and urge that it must have a wider appeal and 'get down to the level of the schools' – in particular, the level of the sixth forms. 'Their specific suggestions include: general articles on the stock authors; historical and biographical essays; articles on the Hellenistic age, and on women,[39] armies, navies, architecture, sculpture and the like; articles explaining the content and context of important, and possibly difficult, new books, . . . or discussing the significance of key words such as (in Latin) ratio, auctoritas or fides.

After this strategic invocation of the views of the market, Hooker concluded that

> *G & R* should remember not only the teacher but also the general reader, and that its task is not only Sustenance but also Popularisation: to make the ancient world known and appreciated as widely as possible; to serve as a link between the Classical Association and the general public – or rather, that portion of it which may be prepared to take an interest in things classical. This will of course be only a minority of the Public, but the success of the Penguin Classics suggests that it is not a negligible one. In doing this *G & R* must maintain a high standard of scholarship – the aim must be to satisfy those who know while at the same time attracting those who are merely interested.[40]

Hooker ended his memo by urging that articles should be commissioned, perhaps to commemorate specific events (like the bimillenary of Caesar's death in March 1957), rather than simply taking what was offered. (The point might have been extended to reviews: one might guess that *Die Kabiren* had been reviewed simply because a review copy had been sent in.)[41]

Two years later, *Greece & Rome* celebrated its jubilee, with a foreword by Cyril Bailey in which he declared that the initial promise had been maintained: the world had changed, but readership was steady at about 1,200, and a wide variety of useful and stimulating articles had been published.[42] In an appended note, the editors announced the publication of an index to the 66 numbers of the first Series, prepared by C. J. Nash,

[39] See Gillian Clark's survey of *G & R*'s coverage of this topic in Chapter 9.

[40] G. T. W. Hooker, 'Greece and Rome', memo of 17 August 1953; copy in OUP Journals dept records. The Penguin Classics, launched by Allen Lane at the end of the war under the editorship of E. V. Rieu, had included Rieu's translations of the *Odyssey* (1945) and the *Iliad* (1950). The first of these became the best-selling of all Penguins (3 million copies in all), being overtaken only by *Lady Chatterley's Lover* and eventually by *Animal Farm*.

[41] The book had been reviewed by 'J. R. T. P.' in vol. 22 (1953), 45. The volume also contained another Scandinavian piece: Per Krarup's article on 'Greek culture in Danish schools' (11–17). Otherwise, it was something of an *omnium gatherum*; the opening article was a discussion of 'Ancient groceries' by Sir John Myres, which the author disarmingly declared had originally been delivered to the 'grocers' assistants and apprentices of Liverpool' in 1910.

[42] *Greece and Rome* NS 3 (1956), 97–8.

who dedicated it to his old teacher, the founding editor C. J. Ellingham. Ellingham had occupied the editorial seat for 22 years, but Russell's successor E. R. A. Sewter had an even longer run, from 1946 to 1971, and is remembered below by an ex-pupil and colleague.

7

GREECE & ROME

By IAN MCAUSLAN

Looking back in 1981 over the first half-century of the journal, Peter Walcot wrote: '*Greece & Rome* has become, in the opinion of many and to the distress of some, an international academic publication . . . concentrating hopefully on what is of central interest rather than on the esoteric or excessively technical'.[1] It had begun in 1931 as a journal aiming 'to make accessible new or important aspects of classical knowledge in a form having especial regard to use in colleges and schools and which will also appeal to all interested in classical learning'[2] – an initiative by the Classical Association to cater, largely, for British schools and schoolteachers as they then were. The teaching of Latin was a recurrent issue: for some years the back cover of the journal carried an advertisement for *Latin for Today*, a reading-based course which had originated in America; and articles in the journal discussed and reviewed the 'Mason Gray method' which it embodied, and the 'Direct Method'.[3] The focus on language and the knowledge of it was also regularly exemplified in Latin and Greek versions of English poetry (e.g. Maurice Bowra's Greek lyrics after Swinburne's *Atalanta in Calydon*)[4] and by Latin and Greek crosswords set by T.W.M. (Tommy Melluish).[5] And it is now somewhat chastening to find (unannounced on the Contents page – a 'space-filler')[6] a rather good Theophrastian pastiche by 'The VI Form at St. Olave's'.

At the same time, there were articles with titles that one might

---

[1] *G&R* 28 (1981), 2. This article gives an excellent conspectus of the first fifty years of *Greece & Rome*; in it, Walcot notes ironically the recurring problems which editors confront in trying to produce a journal and keep it fresh.

[2] OUP leaflet (1931) – the second part of this a blatant puff.

[3] E.g., for the Mason Gray method, 4 (1934), 35–9; 6 (1937), 111–15. For the Direct Method, see 6 (1937), 11–17.

[4] 5 (1935), 53–6.

[5] E.g. the Aeschylean crossword in 4 (1934), 122: the clue to 8 down reads 'Porson's unerring account of the defeat to Atossa' (7 letters).

[6] 4 (1934), 23.

(almost) meet today: 'Plot and Character in Sophocles',[7] 'Plato's Commonwealth',[8] 'Aeneas and History'.[9] Cosier pieces, too: 'Roman Board Games', 'Pets in Classical Times', 'Down the High Street' (the Latin roots of 'tailor', 'stationer', 'confectioner', etc.); though 'Roman Education', with its exclusive reference to boys – and in general the use of the masculine pronoun – may have raised fewer hackles then than it would now.[10] The attempt was there, certainly, to appeal to 'the schoolteacher on Sunday, the parson on Monday', and the original editors, the Revd. C. J. Ellingham of City of London School and A. G. Russell of St Olave's Grammar School, kept the show on the road throughout the thirties and the Second World War, until Russell retired in 1946. He, as well as contributing the occasional article,[11] had been responsible for the Book Reviews. In a typical issue, fewer than twenty books might be reviewed, mostly (anonymously) by Russell himself, some substantially, some briefly; others bore the initials of other reviewers (e.g., H.H.S., F.W.W., L.P.W., T.B.L.W.).[12]

Russell was succeeded by E. R. A. Sewter, Senior Classical Master at St Bartholomew's Grammar School, Newbury. His work on the 'Brief Reviews' section was formidable: in his valedictory note[13] he was able to claim: 'All unsigned reviews, from 1946 onwards, together with those to which my initials or name will be found appended, are my responsibility – *sola culpa mea.* The rest are the work of scholars who volunteered or consented to express their opinions.' He would himself review some hundred books each year, on all aspects of the classical world; and it was said that, when he retired, his house in Newbury was crammed from floor to ceiling with *G&R* review copies of books.[14]

As Walcot noted,[15] the appointment of G. T. W. Hooker, of the University of Birmingham, to replace Ellingham in 1953 foreshadowed a shift in the nature of the journal. The Second Series was initiated with a new cover design in 1954;[16] an editorial in the June issue [17] sounded a

---

[7] Ibid., 13–23.   [8] Ibid., 92–108.   [9] 6 (1937), 70–7.
[10] 4 (1937), 24–34 and 76–82; ibid., 109–113; 6 (1937), 51–5; 4 (1937), 1–12.
[11] E.g. 'Euripides and the New Comedy', 6 (1937), 103–10.
[12] For those who don't recognise them, the quoted initials belong to Scullard, Walbank, Wilkinson and Webster.
[13] NS 18 (1971), 237.
[14] See the warm tribute to Sewter after his death in 1977 by 'J.V.M.' in NS 25 (1978), 69; and John Muir's memoir of Sewter, below.
[15] Art. cit., n. 1, 5.
[16] The plain buff of the First Series gave way to red on a grey background, but the 'ear of corn' motif (suggesting nourishment and vitality?) was retained – as it was to be when the Jubilee Edition initiated a new orange cover in 1981.
[17] NS 1 (1954), 49.

somewhat beleaguered note: 'How, in this age of science and technology, the Classics have been dethroned is a familiar story . . .', though the final sentence spoke of the 'challenge of the new half-century'. As part of an answer to this challenge, the issue carried an article on 'Philosophy and History among the Greeks' by Karl Reinhardt,[18] which, together with articles in the October issue from university lecturers in New Zealand, Jamaica, Copenhagen and South Africa, suggested both a re-affirmation of the commonwealth of scholarship after the War and an indication that the journal was perhaps exploring a rather wider readership. There were to be fewer 'versions' and puzzles; there were to be more articles. To this era belong also the special issues on Julius Caesar and Alexander the Great,[19] and the supplements entitled *Re-appraisal: some new thoughts on the teaching of Classics* and *Parthenos and Parthenon*.[20] The former suggest not only a marking of anniversaries and a proper scholarly re-evaluation but also, possibly, some astute marketing, and perhaps an anxiety about 'great men' in the aftermath of the great dictatorships and with the Sixties looming; the latter pair cannot be corralled together. *Re-appraisal* foreshadows the crucial thinking about the teaching of Classics that was to come with the foundation of the Joint Association of Classical Teachers (JACT) and the publication of the journal *Didaskalos*;[21] it is harder to see what prompted *Parthenos and Parthenon*, though one may note that the Athens Gallery of the Royal Ontario Museum, with its new models of the Parthenon and of the chryselephantine statue of Athena Parthenos had recently opened.[22]

Change was in the air, and in fact a new editor had taken over from Hooker in 1964. This was J. V. Muir, who had been a pupil of Sewter in Newbury, had himself been a classical schoolmaster, and was by this time a lecturer in education at King's College, London. Responsible as he was for the training of new teachers, Muir was well placed to see and respond to the altered world of classics teaching; and his own major initiative was a new series of annual supplements to the journal, jointly sponsored by the CA and JACT and designed to be accessible to schoolteachers and their pupils. The series was to recruit scholars to

[18] Ibid., 82–90.
[19] NS 4 (1957), 1–77; NS 12 (1965), 113–228.
[20] 1962, 1963. For *Re-appraisal*, see pp. 48 and 53 above.
[21] *Didaskalos* was produced annually between 1963 and 1977; it was succeeded by the smaller and slimmer *Hesperiam* (6 volumes, 1978–83).
[22] And one might also note, though without wishing to make too much of it, that 1960 had seen the production of Jules Dassin's film, *Never on Sunday*, starring Melina Mercouri as the 'whore with a heart of gold', who later, as Greek Minister of Culture, was to be eloquent in reclaiming the Elgin Marbles for Greece.

produce a short, authoritative review of the state of play within their own area of expertise, and most of the early volumes were devoted to a single classical author. R. D. Williams got the series – New Surveys in the Classics – off to an impressive start with his *Virgil* (1967); other early pamphlets (they then ran to some forty-five pages) surveyed Cicero, Homer, Tacitus and Greek Tragedy.[23]

In 1970 Muir was succeeded as editor by Peter Walcot of what was then University College, Cardiff, and a year later Sewter laid down his reviewer's pen and retired as 'school' editor, to be replaced by Anthony Verity, then Head of Classics at Bristol Grammar School. The next few years saw two principal developments: Walcot, who had taken over responsibility for the Reviews section, restructured it into (essentially) its present form, with separate sections on Greek and Roman Literature and History, Archaeology and Art, Philosophy, School Books, a catch-all section of General Books, and Reprints. Walcot himself, in addition to editing all reviews, ran the last two sections himself while farming out the rest to a shifting team of specialist subject reviewers. Verity, as well as looking after New Surveys, initiated an occasional series of Critical Appreciations in the journal, in which two critics were invited to write about the same passage of Greek or Latin literature. This was the era of M. G. Balme and M. S. Warman's *Aestimanda* and the various books which it inspired, including Verity's own *Latin as Literature*.[24] Literary criticism of classical texts was now firmly on the agenda, and this was the journal's appropriate response.[25]

Verity became Headmaster of Leeds Grammar School in 1976, and was succeeded as 'school' editor by the present writer, then Head of Classics at King Edward VI School, Southampton and subsequently Head of Classics at Eton College. A long and stable period of joint editorship with Walcot ensued, lasting until 2001. During this time, the journal celebrated its golden jubilee,[26] acquired a new cover[27] and marked the birth of the EU with a 'European Volume', featuring articles

---

[23] *Cicero*, by A. E. Douglas (1968); *Homer*, by J. B. Hainsworth (1969); *Tacitus*, by F. R. D. Goodyear (1970); *Greek Tragedy*, by T. B. L. Webster (1971).

[24] *Aestimanda* (Oxford, 1965); D. G. Fratter, *Aere Perennius* (London, 1968); *Latin as Literature* (Basingstoke and London, 1971); C. Stace and P. V. Jones, *Stilus Artifex* (Cambridge, 1972).

[25] 'Critical Appreciations I' on Propertius 3.10, NS 20 (1973), 38–48, with a follow-up piece by J. C. Bramble, ibid., 155–61; II on Virgil, *Aeneid* 12.843–86, NS 21 (1974), 165–77; III on Tacitus, *Histories* 3.38–9, NS 25 (1978), 70–80; IV on Ovid, *Amores*, NS 10, ibid., 125–40; V on Addison's *Pax Gulielmi Auspiciis Europae Reddita, 1697*, NS 27 (1980), 48–59; and VI on Homer, *Iliad* 1.1–52, NS 29 (1982), 126–42.

[26] See n. 1 above.

[27] See n. 15 above.

by a wide range of distinguished scholars.[28] There were no other 'special issues';[29] but one major new initiative was the series Greece & Rome Studies. It had been observed that other journals were issuing collections of their past articles on a given topic, and it was rightly felt that *Greece & Rome* had the scope to do likewise. Four volumes were produced between 1990 and 1998;[30] in each case the original author of an article was invited, if still alive and traceable, to provide a brief update. The first two volumes were prefaced by brief editorial notes; in the other two, a scholar currently working in the field was invited to provide an introduction, setting the chosen articles in context.[31] Also during this period 'Brief Reviews' were renamed 'Subject Reviews' (the Reviews section was expanding, as publishers sent more books to a journal which had the reputation of reviewing very soon after publication;[32] and some reviewers were now by no means brief).[33] An Index to Reviews became a regular feature from 1992 onwards; a Volume Index followed in 1997.

The transformation to an 'international academic publication' was by now complete. Statistics from Oxford University Press showed that the typical subscriber was no longer a British schoolmaster or school library, but a North American university or college library. The Board of Management which had overseen the journal since its inception, origin-ally chaired by R. H. Barrow, schoolmaster and HMI, and containing representatives of the Head Masters' and Head Mistresses', Assistant

---

[28] NS 39 (1992). The invited contributors were de Romilly (Paris), Hansen (Copenhagen), Versnel (The Netherlands), Simon (Germany), Sifakis (Greece), Blazquez (Spain), Dillon (Eire) and Bremmer (The Netherlands).

[29] Walcot had been eloquent on the trouble that these can cause an editor in his 1981 review article.

[30] *Virgil* (1990); *Greek Tragedy* (1993); *Women in Antiquity* (1996); and *Homer* (1998).

[31] Further volumes, on history and on comedy, were discussed; but there was some doubt as to whether the journal had amassed a sufficient number of good articles on each topic, and the amount of extra work caused to the editors by the existing four volumes was also somewhat debilitating – not least the *Women* volume. The original selection of articles, which showed very clearly how discussion of the subject had developed over the years, had to be modified as two (strongly feminist) readers for the Press objected to the inclusion of two of the earliest articles. Gillian Clark showed great forbearance in revising her introduction to the volume to take account of the changes demanded. (See her own take on this in Ch. 9 below.)

[32] *Most* publishers, that is; following a (justifiably!) severe review by the present writer, for which the editors refused to print an apology, one rather flamboyant publisher declined to send books to the journal for some years. Walcot managed to re-open lines of communication with a junior member of the firm, and the flow of books resumed.

[33] By the 1990s the journal was typically reviewing some 250 books each year. The Roman Literature reviews of the late Don Fowler, published between 1986 and 1993, became famous for their length, wit and ideological importance. Reviewers typically served for some five years, but mention should be made of Brian Sparkes, an utterly reliable and sprightly Archaeology and Art reviewer from 1974 to 1994. Walcot himself almost came to out-Sewter Sewter; by the end of his term as editor, he was (often briefly) reviewing some eighty General books and Reprints each year.

Masters' and Assistant Mistresses' Associations, was now chaired by a professor and contained four representatives of the CA, and representatives of the Classical Journals Board and the Council of University Classical Departments. One representative of the Joint Association of Classical Teachers remained; but when in 2000 the *Greece & Rome* Board of Management was dissolved and the journal became the responsibility of a new Classical Journals Board, JACT was no longer specifically represented.[34]

JACT had, in fact, withdrawn from its interest in New Surveys in the Classics in the 1980s, and the Board of Management had encouraged an expansion of the series. Single authors increasingly gave way to topics,[35] and with the publication of *Greek Art* (1991),[36] the Surveys began to increase in length and substance. Recent volumes have been of book length (100–150 pages); it has been seen as one purpose of the series to revisit authors and topics dealt with earlier;[37] and new scholarly concerns are represented.[38] The series, which has attracted a lot of praise, has been most fortunate in its authors, and with *Greek Historians* (2001) acquired its first transatlantic contributor;[39] the collaboration between author and editor was an entirely easy and pleasant one, and was managed almost exclusively by e-mail.

In 2001 a twenty-five year editorial partnership came to an end with the sudden resignation of Peter Walcot.[40] He had served the journal loyally and efficiently for over thirty years, had shown robust judgement about what worked well in terms of articles and series, and had developed the Reviews section into a substantial and lively first port of call for those wanting crisp and authoritative views of recent classical

[34] Lest the Board should sound too faceless and impersonal from this description, it should be noted that from 1986, when David West took over as its chairman, the business of the annual meeting continued over a lively lunch in Goodge Street, and many good ideas were generated which were unerringly remembered by the Chairman (little notes would be sent out afterwards with reminders of action to be taken). This pleasant and useful practice continued under his successor, Christopher Rowe, until the dissolution of the Board in 2000.

[35] *The Early Principate* (1982), *The Athenian Empire* (1985), *Slavery* (1987), *Women in the Ancient World* (1989).

[36] The first fully illustrated Survey. Illustrations have been a feature of the journal since its early days.

[37] Philip Hardie's *Virgil* (1998) replaces R. D. Williams's Survey (1967); R. B. Rutherford's *Homer* (1996) replaces the Survey by J. B. Hainsworth (1969).

[38] *The Invention of Prose*, by Simon Goldhill (2002); *Reception Studies*, by Lorna Hardwick (2003); *The Second Sophistic*, to be written by Tim Whitmarsh (due in 2005).

[39] John Marincola, of New York University.

[40] The wording of a review published in the journal had given offence to some readers in the Far East. Walcot felt strongly, as a matter of principle, that no editorial apology should appear (cf. n. 32 above); the Board felt otherwise. Walcot resigned, with immediate effect.

publications. The journal's continued success owed much to him. Fortunately, the Classical Journals Board was quickly able to appoint two new editors to take charge of the journal.[41] At the time of writing, *Greece & Rome* and its associated New Surveys Series seem in good health, well able to survive and innovate further in the new millennium.

[41] Dr Katherine Clarke, Fellow of St Hilda's College, Oxford, and Dr Christopher Burnand, Head of Classics at Abingdon School. They have quickly settled into the job and have restructured the Reviews section, by allocating more books, including all reprints, to individual Subject Reviewers and slimming down the General Books section. I remain as Senior Editor of the journal in an advisory capacity, but effectively my exclusive concern now is with the New Surveys series, which I continue to edit.

8

ROBERT SEWTER – A PERSONAL REMINISCENCE

By JOHN MUIR

E. R. A. Sewter, for twenty-five years joint editor of *Greece & Rome,* was an extraordinarily modest man of rather extraordinary gifts. I first met him when I was a boy at St. Bartholomew's Grammar School, Newbury – an old-established school which owed much of its modern success to the inspired headship of Mr. Sharwood Smith (the father of someone not unknown to members of JACT and the CA). Robert Sewter had then returned from the Second World War (in which he served in the characteristically modest rank of Quartermaster Sergeant) and, in taking up the Classics department, he showed unmistakeably that the disciplinary skills of the Army could be effectively applied to the learning of elementary Latin and could produce consistently excellent results. He was never brutal or sarcastic or unfair or disliked, but the high standards he demanded and his capacity for squashing the mildest signs of adolescent revolt produced a slightly alarmed awe and respect in all his classes. This situation changed quite amazingly for those lucky enough to join his Classical Sixth; I shall always remember his kindly welcome to me on my first day, calling me by my Christian name. The home of the Classical Sixth was the quiet, friendly School Library and, though academic standards were never relaxed, we were treated with the utmost courtesy and more as undergraduates than schoolboys; it was as civilised and pleasant a company as you could wish. There was already quite a tradition of scholarship success (before our time D. L. Page had been one of the school's students), and there was the unspoken expectation that we would try our best to maintain it – though there was no trace of an unhealthy, hothouse atmosphere or exclusive competition. 'Alfie', as Robert was mysteriously and quite affectionately known, taught nearly everything classical; he had been one of Tommy Higham's students at Trinity College, Oxford and had inherited from him a delight in the cultivation of style, especially in prose-writing, but his main enthusiasm was ancient history which he taught with a fine sense of perspective allied to a marvellous attention to detail – a bit of a fox and a bit of a hedgehog. Curiously, the full extent of his historical interests was never revealed to us – I don't ever recall the Byzantine world being mentioned – and it came as quite a shock to discover later that our dedicated classical mentor was also a highly-respected Byzantine scholar at a time when Byzantine and Late Antique studies were much less popular than they are now. Robert's Penguin translations of Anna Comnena and Michael Psellus are distinguished works of scholarship and still standard works.

We *were* aware that he was known to the outside world as one of the editors of *Greece & Rome*, and on occasional trips with him on the bus to Oxford to the Ashmolean or the theatre we were intrigued by the carpet-bags full of books which he was taking to Blackwells. Again, the full picture only emerged later. As the sole reviews editor, he undertook for many years a truly colossal task, and, had his modest semi in Rectory Close allowed, he could have amassed a library worth a king's ransom today. At that time publishers were generous with review copies of even the most expensive books, and *Greece & Rome* provided a short and pretty up-to-date descriptive review of most of what was being published – a useful service when the longer critical reviews in the more learned journals took two years or more to appear. The astonishing thing is that Robert did it all himself – literature, philosophy, history, archaeology, epigraphy, numismatics, art history – the lot; he rarely consulted elsewhere and a glance at one of his review sections shows the scale of what he undertook. He did have the odd tetchy letter claiming misrepresentation or misunderstanding (which editor does not?), but on the whole he kept up a very high standard across a field of scholarship which no-one today would dare to cover. When he retired in 1971, it was literally impossible to replace him and the reviews had to be sectionalized.

Robert Sewter never sought and never received any kind of limelight. Few of his teaching colleagues and none of his neighbours had any inkling that he was more than a quiet, unassuming schoolmaster who was also an enthusiastic cricket coach. Towards the end of his career he was invited to spend a year as a visiting professor at the University of Nebraska, and that must have surprised most of his colleagues as much as it delighted him. He was certainly always regarded as a stalwart member of the school staff; his pupils, though, had other debts, and so did the world of Byzantine scholarship, and so did hundreds of authors and thousands of readers of *Greece & Rome* all over the world. History sometimes makes amends, and it is perhaps appropriate for the Classical Association at its centenary to remember one of its more remarkable, retiring and dedicated servants.

(On the first page of *Greece & Rome* 16 (1970), Robert Sewter cried *Vale!* to John Muir, who had resigned his editorship after six years' work. Recognising the insistent calls of family life – Muir now had 'three fine sons' – Sewter praised his colleague for his 'scholarly approach and modesty'. Like teacher, like pupil. *Ed.*)

9

SILENCE AND WOMEN IN *GREECE & ROME*

By GILLIAN CLARK

In 1992 (I think!) Ian McAuslan and Peter Walcot invited me to write an introduction for the papers they had selected as *Greece & Rome Studies 3: Women in Antiquity*. 'Women' and 'antiquity' were already contested terms, but interest in the topic was widespread in the early 1990s. The papers originally chosen reflected half a century in which conditions of life for women, at least for women in the western world, changed faster than ever before. Social change, as always, was evident in scholarship: in the subjects that scholars found interesting, the way they wrote, and the kind of people who were scholars. The history of women in *Greece & Rome* is quite instructive.

Greece & Rome was founded in 1931, with the modest intention of being useful to persons, not necessarily professional scholars or teachers, who were interested in the Classics. The first article concerned with women appeared in 1942, in the austerity wartime format, among the soberly phrased suggestions that members of the Armed Forces might welcome books, preferably general books, on the Classics. It was a solidly political account of 'The Women of the Caesars' by H. G. Mullens. Nothing was said about their experience as women: the article discussed women of the imperial family as factors in Roman political history.

This article did not qualify for *Studies 3*. The first paper in the original selection came out as the war in Europe ended, in 1945. It is an elegant and optimistic survey of 'Women in Roman Life and Letters', by the distinguished F. E. Adcock. 'Life and Letters', a phrase often used in popular scholarship of the time, assumes that letters, i.e. literature, report life. Adcock accepted the perspective of his literary sources. Bad women commit murder, adultery or fraud; good women are virtuous, and Adcock particularly admires the homely virtues, the 'domestic happiness of humble folk'. Even Campanian tomb-paintings show women 'spruce, dignified and house-proud'. (How did he know?) Roman women might be unequal in law and without public status, but they were loved and respected at home. Meanwhile in Britain, the slow return of the armed forces began, and women who had served in the forces and driven ambulances and fire-watched in the Blitz were heading back to domesticity. The 1946 issue of *Greece & Rome* included 'My Lady's Toilet', an attempt to answer the queries of the 'modern miss' about Roman makeup. It was not selected.

Silence again prevailed on the subject of women, and Classics, as reflected in *Greece & Rome*, continued to interest itself in the teaching of metre and Latin prose, in modestly perceptive literary criticism, and in new perspectives on political history. The new series began in 1954, and in 1955 came Charles Seltman's affirmation, taken from the preface of his *Women in Antiquity*, that the Athenians shared his own well-attested liking for the company of women:

'Women'. There is no need to attempt a definition. We are always with them, and they with us. Fortunately.

No need to ask who 'we' are. Seltman wanted readers to question the received idea that Athenian women were kept in 'Oriental seclusion' and held in contempt. He used vase-paintings to illustrate 'happy women, wives and mothers, seeing their men off to the wars . . . wide-open doors admitting visitors.' He also 'outed' Athenian male homosexuality and the kind of erotic vase-painting that was once kept in museum cupboards. These paintings, he argued, showed Athenian enjoyment of heterosexual activity; but he did not ask who used the pottery and in what context. Adcock and Seltman do not appear in *Studies 3*, for one of OUP's readers was outraged at the thought of their appalling sexism made available to a wider audience. I have met *Greece & Rome* readers for whom Seltman, read in a school library in the 1950s, was liberation. Like the editors, I thought that OUP's reader lacked historical awareness: but it was the early 1990s.

After Seltman, silence falls again, this time for twenty years. The next article on women, and the first in *Studies 3*, was published in 1975 and comes from another world. North American scholars date the recognition of 'women in antiquity' as a field of scholarship to a very different journal, *Arethusa* 1973, the publication of a New York conference. 1975 saw Sarah Pomeroy's *Goddesses, Whores, Wives and Slaves*, a pioneering survey with a consciously shocking title: she argued that classical scholarship had ignored women and classical culture was to blame for downgrading them. The *Greece & Rome* 1975 paper, by Anthony Marshall, did a very professional job on (surprise) women and Roman imperial politics. He was aware of new work by women scholars on the status of Roman women, but thought them lacking in historical awareness; and they did not write articles for *Greece & Rome*.

1980 is a *Greece & Rome* watershed: the first article on women by a woman scholar, Averil Cameron, and the first that challenged generalisations about 'women', or Roman women, or Christian women, made without regard to social, cultural and economic status. From the mid-1980s to the early 1990s there were few issues that lacked a paper on women, and many were by women. But the editors, perceptive as always, had recognised the Women Moment in *Greece & Rome*. The paper that appropriately concludes *Studies 3* is H. S. Versnel, April 1992, on the Bona Dea and the Thesmophoria: women in the political centres of Rome and Athens. (And what do they do there? Something religious, what else?) After that, there are Walter Scheidel's two papers (1995–6) on the *most* silent women of Greece and Rome, and Joan Burton (1998) on women's commensality. Otherwise (have I missed something?) silence. Perhaps everyone is now so alert to gender questions that they do not need, or want, to write articles on the history and representation of women. But what will future editors include in *Greece & Rome Studies x: the Crisis of Masculinity?*

10

CA NEWS: A PERSONAL VIEW FROM
THE EDITOR

By JENNY MARCH

It has been a great pleasure to look back over 27 issues of *CA News* in order to set on record its history, and something of its typical content, over the thirteen and a half years of its existence. Since I have been its only Editor until the time of writing, this will necessarily be a very personal overview – my own brief history of *CAN* – for which I have selected some short extracts from the magazine over the years, in an attempt to give something of its essential flavour.

Malcolm Schofield has written in Chapter 5 of the reasons behind *CAN*'s inauguration. This story begins at the moment in 1989 when I was asked if I would like to produce an experimental newsletter for the CA. Fired with enthusiasm by the idea, I accepted gladly, and very soon had a clear idea of what I aimed to create.

First, the name: this was to be a newsletter, so *CA News* seemed the obvious choice. Then the content: as a newsletter, it had to include 'news' of CA matters and of any developments on the wider classical front. But I wanted more than that. CA members are a varied breed, so I aimed first of all to cover as wide a range of classical topics as possible, in the hope that every reader would find something of interest in each issue. Here, too, CA members would have a forum in which to air their opinions and to write about their own particular classical concerns. I also very much wanted to give readers, however isolated or far-flung, the sense of belonging to a community (and whenever I put together an issue, I always feel that I am writing to friends). And of course I hoped to promote Classics – to do what I could to keep the torch alight and Classics alive and flourishing for the future.

So these were all serious concerns, to be tackled seriously; and yet I also wanted to mix all this with an element of lightheartedness. I wrote in issue 11 (December 1994): 'My concern is to show how vital, in every sense of the word, our subject is: how many kinds of areas it invades, how it is an integral part of our lives, how it affects our ways of thinking, in frivolous matters as well as serious. Classics can be tremendous fun, as well as a deep and abiding delight.'

This, then, was the spirit in which I set about creating that first issue. It appeared in December 1989 and included several articles on Roman Britain, Richard Hawley writing on women's studies in Classics, and Oliver Taplin on Greek drama. There were sections on museum news (Susan Walker on the new Etruscan and Roman galleries at the British Museum), classical sites abroad (Jeremy Paterson on the Roman Forum), travellers' tips, and people in the news (Peter Parsons, recently appointed Regius Professor of Greek at Oxford, Ana Healey, retiring after 18 years as Librarian of the Classics Library in Gordon Square, and Patricia Gilbert, retiring after 29 years as Secretary of the Roman Society). Peter Jones wrote on the newly-formed Co-ordinating Committee for Classics, and Chris Emlyn-Jones on the new Classical Studies course at the Open University, *Fifth-Century Athens: Democracy and City-State*. There were several poems by Patrick Hunt, news of forthcoming events, and a competition section with what has since proved an ever-popular item, the Caption Competition. There was less humour in this first issue than later, but humour is not always something easily acquired to order – and obviously most of the content of this first issue had had to be commissioned from classical friends and colleagues. The intention always was that once the magazine was established, most of its content would generate itself as spontaneous offerings from CA members.

This turned out to be the case, and I have long been in the privileged editorial position of always having a rich store of excellent material to draw on. The first issue ran to 16 pages. In June 1995 this was increased to 20 pages, and in December 1999 there came the first 24-page issue. *CAN* has now settled to a steady 24 pages, with the central four pages devoted to the 'business' matters once published in *Proceedings*.

After five issues had been produced, *CAN* was no longer seen as an experiment but as a proven success, so it then became an official publication of the Classical Association and a small committee was formed to give editorial back-up. We are currently six: Barbara Goward, David West and Richard Wallace have been stalwarts from the beginning; they were soon joined by Philip Howard, and lately by Philip Hooker. CANAPE meetings – '*CA News* Advisory Panel *Extraordinaire*', so named by David West – take place twice a year, and (like the Philologen-Versammlungen meetings in Germany – see Philip Hooker's chapter on Conferences, p. 169) they always include a very considerable convivial element. This without doubt helps to make *CAN* the kind of magazine it is.

...and don't forget... "beware the ideas of March..."

In 1997 we launched a competition to choose a *CAN* motto. I printed a selection of entries in issue 18 and asked readers to vote on them. These included *aliquid usus, aliquid lusus* (Alan Beale), Carry the *CAN* (John Smalman-Smith), *semper possumus* (Betty Halifax), and three suggestions from John Foley, who wrote as follows:

(1) It is widely rumoured that since the advent of that Girl from Naupactus [on this, see below] the Archbishop of Canterbury has asked for his copy of *CA News* to be sent in a plain brown envelope. So: *cave canews*?

OK, just joking. I'm sure Aristophanes would be delighted.

(2) I read my *CA News* in the shade of a rather splendid olive tree, which I have named Horace. I called it that because I had the firm intention of spending my summer leisure sitting in its shade reading the *Odes*. However, in practice, once I had got myself there over a certain amount of terrain carrying text, crib, Nisbet and Hubbard, pen and paper, folding chair, bottle and corkscrew, accompanied by *perusta solibus pernicis uxor* (she's Spanish, you see) only to find I had to make another journey because the uxor had forgotten to bring the *OLD*, I began to see the advantages of reading something that involved fewer impedimenta. *CA News* goes well with a bottle of wine; in fact, the humour goes up as the bottle goes down. So: *nunc est ridendum*?

(3) Not quite, perhaps, but I think this is the right direction. In fact, *CA News* entertains with wit and erudition. I think Apuleius got it exactly right and you could do no better than borrow his line: *lector intende: laetaberis*.

This last suggestion was the one that readers chose as our most suitable motto, and it has ever since accompanied the CA dolphin on the magazine's title page. So too has the *CA News* logo, brilliantly designed at about this same time by sixth-form student Adam Tuck. He based it on Canova's lovely statue of Cupid and Psyche, so it is coincidentally another link with Apuleius.

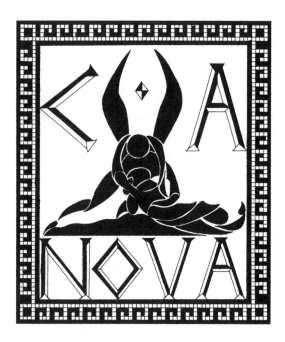

Down the years the Classical Association News of our title has largely comprised news of Presidents and conferences. Profiles (with photographs) of Presidents have added substance to the circulated booklets of the annual Presidential Address, and often they themselves have written for *CAN*. Conferences have been advertised and later reported on – by academics, by students, and in recent years by our incomparable 'Argus'. The pseudonym may suggest a wish for anonymity, but I shall be giving nothing away if I say that Argus is one of our Presidents, as careful readers of their Presidential Addresses will already have realised. Long may he continue to report us!

On the wider classical front, *CAN* has included lively correspondence on key educational issues, such as the falling PGCE numbers of young people training to be teachers (from issue 5) and educational standards (from issue 18). Countless pieces over the years have reported on experiences in teaching and learning Classics. A series of articles has analysed the state of Classics in various countries abroad. The Open

University has kept us up to date on their Classical Studies courses, and we have celebrated the inauguration of Friends of Classics (issue 5) and the success of *Minimus*, the Primary Latin Course (issues 23 and 25). Issue 8 ran a feature on 'Why Classics?', with readers explaining their often eye-opening reasons for choosing Classics as their subject. Here is Richard Wallace, our then Treasurer and the prime mover behind the CA's transformation in the late 1980s (again, see Chapter 5):

The school I attended (this was in the 1950s) was one of those which taught virtually no Classics. Potential university entrants were taught Latin up to O-Level (for the sake of Oxbridge entrance), and the Latin teacher was rewarded for this chore by being allowed to have a small A-Level group (three in my year). There was no Greek on the syllabus.

Given that my best subject (by a long way) at O-Level was Physics you might think that a decision to do Classics instead could only arise from sheer perversity. You would be right.

I *think* that my mental processes went something like this: 'They let them study Classics in posh places like Newcastle, but not us down here in South Shields. If they've got it, and don't want us to have it, it must be pretty good. So I'm having some.' Consequently I persuaded my bewildered parents and bullied my incredulous teachers into letting me take Latin at A-Level (plus some other things), and my long-suffering Latin teacher taught me a bit of Greek in the games periods.

I was, of course, absolutely right. Classics is a dangerous, and deeply subversive, subject. It tells you that things do not have to be like this, and that there are many other ways of organising society than the one we know, some of which have released stores of energy and creativity in ordinary people which have enabled them to create things which still astonish us. No wonder they wanted to keep it secret from the rebellious proletariat of South Tyneside!

If you like, you can think of studying Classics as my contribution to the class war.

It is also fun.

We have had plenty of feature-length articles on what might be called 'mainstream' classical topics, such as Alan Bowman on the Vindolanda Tablets (issue 3), two pieces on Aristophanes by Paul Cartledge (4) and Angus Bowie (9), Richard Hunter (5) and Stephen Harrison (22) on the ancient novel, Peter Wiseman on Roman myths (21), Elizabeth Moignard with two pieces on vase-paintings by Exekias (14 and 16), Roger Ling on mosaics of Roman Britain, and a whole (and still continuing) series on Medieval Latin by Peter Walsh from issue 9 onwards. But I have always particularly enjoyed publishing articles that explore more unexpected tributaries of Classics, such as B. W. Robinson on connections between Heracles and the Persian national hero Rustam (15), Kai Brodersen on the Carthaginian origin of King Kong (23), Sue Blundell on Amazons, ancient and modern (18), Stanley Ireland on sequels to Virgil's *Aeneid* (19 and 20), and Philip

Howard in 'Gotcha, Horace' on connections between modern journalism and ancient rhetorical advice (4) – such as the following:

. . . Turn to Cicero's *The Orator*: 'Your prologue should attract or arouse, your narrative should be succinct, clear, sensible. *Confirmatio* should prove, *refutatio* demolish. Conclusion should inflame or dampen emotions.' Cicero's advice could come straight from any newspaper's style-book. The intro *is* all-important in a literary form that has so tenuous a grip on its readers' attention. When Claud Cockburn applied to join *The Times* as a young man in the United States, the head of the Washington bureau invited him to write a 3000-word state-of-the-nation survey to show what he could do. Cockburn scribbled, and polished, and took it in, and waited while the owlish mandarin read through his piece with infuriating deliberation. Eventually, the *Times* man looked up, and said: 'Mr Cockburn, in our business you are competing with two cats for the attention of a little old lady in Eastbourne.' (Newspaper executives are notorious for their sexism.) 'On this occasion, I regret to have to tell you, the cats win.' And he tore Cockburn's masterpiece tidily into four quarters and let it fall into his wastepaper-basket. Cicero's remarks about succinctness and clarity are found word for word in the new style-book we are writing for *The Times*. His description of the tricks of *confirmatio* include the way that modern journalism uses adjectives to smuggle in coded messages: gorgeous, pouting = sexually promiscuous; soft-spoken = mousy; loyal = thick; high-minded = inept; hardworking = plodding; self-made = crooked; pragmatic = totally immoral; ashen-faced = that slogan of popular journalism, 'I name the guilty man.' . . . Although the world and the language have changed, professional writers are still at their old tricks, and you need to keep your eyes on the rascals while you read them.

I cannot resist adding some comic and wickedly accurate insights into tabloid journalism offered by William Eve in issue 11, with a few extracts from reports in the *Helios*:

Homicidal husband hacks hangers-on
When Mr Odysseus (49) returned home from a business trip abroad he found the house full of squatters, all trying to get a leg over lovely Penelope (39) the hot housewife, winner of the Miss Ithaca contest before her marriage to hunky hero Odysseus. 'Yes, they really made themselves at home', said Penelope. 'They emptied the cocktail cabinet, raided the deep freeze and dropped fag ash all over the Axminster.'

Telemachos (21): 'I told them to sod off, but they just would not listen to me, bleeding typical!'

Plucky Telemachos (21) set off to find his missing dad whom he hadn't seen for ten years. Is the Ithacan family under threat? Read Medea's hard-hitting article on the women's page.

When Mr Odysseus, known to his friends as Big 'O', technical advisor to Menelaus, the Achaean team manager, slipped into the party disguised as a dosser and joined in the game of darts 180, then things turned ugly. Big 'O' and Telemachos waded into the suitors with kitchen cleavers, yes, it was chop, chop and that's your lot! It was tomato ketchup all the way!

The Helios asks was Big 'O' O.T.T.? Ring us now with your opinion and get a free 'I slew a suitor' T-shirt . . .

That's one in the eye for Polyphemus

Mr Polyphemus (104), a visually-challenged anthropophage, was viciously attacked and blinded in his own home. A police spokesman says that they have reason to believe that they were Ithacan supporters on their way home from the big match. Mr Poseidon (4004), Polyphemus' father, says, 'There's too much of this sort of thing going on, I won't rest until the thugs who did this to my boy are brought to book.' Police wish to interview a bearded man with an Ithacan accent and possible seafaring connections.

Helios readers will be pleased to know that Mr Polyphemus is now getting around with the aid of a guide goat called Snuggles, and I'm sure we all wish Mr Polyphemus and Snuggles all the best . . .

I have also delighted in printing pieces on the sometimes unusual classical activities enjoyed by readers: with Anne Dicks we have learnt how to make a Roman mosaic (17) and to create a Roman garden (19); Peter Marshall has taught us how to make replica Roman inscriptions (19); H. J. P. Arnold has invited us to join his 'Roman' legion, Legio Secunda Augusta (19); Richard Wallace has introduced us to the strange world of the bodybuilders and their (unintentional) similarities to the Farnese Hercules (11). And articles uncovering links between Classics and modern art and literature have always spoken to my heart, emphasising as they do the ongoing vitality of our subject. We have had Richard Jenkyns on classical influences on the novel (14), Jean Mingay on Aristotle and Mr Darcy (15), Dennis Blandford on Caravaggio and the Classics (23), and Richard Wallace (again!) on 'Some unregarded aspects of the reception of Classics in the 20th century' – or the fantasy novels of Terry Pratchett (15). Here is Richard's encouraging conclusion:

Since Pratchett's work regularly makes the 'Best-Sellers', it seems reasonable to assume that his frame of reference gives us a reasonably accurate map of the shared culture of his readership (usually young and well-educated). By looking at the picture of the ancient world assumed in his books, we can learn something about modern perceptions.

Greece (under the name of Ephebe) features strongly. The picture given of Greece is almost embarrassingly rosy, and it is used as a sort of contrast to the forces of obscurantism and tyranny which rule elsewhere in the Discworld. In *Small Gods* Ephebe is 'a place where madmen have mad ideas'. It is a democracy, where everyone has a vote (except, obviously, anyone who is poor, foreign or disqualified by reason of being mad, frivolous or a woman). It seems to be populated entirely by squabbling philosophers who are totally mad (and we can recognise among them Plato, Heraclitus, Democritus, Zeno, Diogenes, Aristotle, Theophrastus, Archimedes, and several others); they are tolerated because although out of 100 of their ideas 99 are indisputably dotty, the 100th is a winner. Ephebe, then, is a kind of symbol of everything that is right about our own society: democracy, freedom of speech, disinterested pursuit of the truth, progress, and tolerance. It is on the side of the good guys in a view of the world which is also reflected in what Pratchett himself has said about his own work:

'Fantasy is like alcohol – too much is bad for you, a little bit makes the world a better place. Like an exercise bicycle it takes you nowhere, but it might just tone up the muscles that will. Daydreaming got us where we are today; early on in evolution we learned to let our minds wander so well that they started coming back with souvenirs.'

There is something reassuring about finding that where the classical world features in this map of contemporary culture, it is not on the side of hierarchy, stagnation, or tradition, but represents the daydreamers, the creators, the best side of the human race. Perhaps at last we have got something right.

A small group of *CAN* readers are interested in Latin (and sometimes Greek) verse composition, so to represent these, here is a Latin epitaph on a black cat called Micky, composed by Mary Mortimer, the mother of Mark Mortimer. Mark himself is the accomplished translator of many hymns, carols, poems and limericks which have appeared in our magazine over the years, but he would perhaps prefer to see this epitaph chosen for reprinting here, for he himself calls it perfect – which it is:

> Eius in tutela sit
>   noster felis,
> a quo nomen habuit,
>   Michaelis.
>
> Qui in equo candido
>   equitas,
> huic tamen nigerrimo
>   faveas.

An interest shared by a larger group of readers is translation of poetry into English, and in every issue I have printed at least one modern translation, usually several, with many of them making poetry in their own right. In issue 7 Mary Hodgson gave us a moving version of Simonides' epitaph for the Spartans who died at Thermopylae (literally 'Stranger, tell the Spartans that here we lie, obedient to their words'):

> Special task force to G. H. Q. Lacedaemon:
> anyone receiving please transmit.
> Mission accomplished. Over and out.

Here too is Mary's version of Hadrian's address to his soul (issue 10):

> Poor little, lost little, sweet little soul,
> My body's companion and friend,
> Where are you going to now, little soul –
> Pale little, stiff little, bare little soul –
> Now that the jokes have to end.

Tim Ades translated Silvina Ocampo's 'Palinurus Sleepless' (issue 7):

> *Nudus in ignota, Palinure, iacebis harena*
> Seawaves seaweeds and seawings
> snailwhorls seawrecked and sounding
> salt iodine and stormwind
> sparse dolphins and the chorus
>
> of sirens tired of singing:
> no match for lands of pleasure
> you roamed with silent footfall
> to keep the deep ships from you.
>
> Night sleeps not Palinurus
> to see you beached and seachanged:
> your face is sealed. Lie naked
>
> and die and die, and mindless
> as stone your nails and hair still
> shall grow among the ivy.

Here is Simon Raven, who writes (issue 6):

For years, as a lover of Arles, I have been trying to translate these nine lines of Paul Jean Toulet's. Inappropriate, you may think, for a journal of Classics? Well, the Alyscamps were a pagan cemetery long before they were a Christian one, and this rare and melancholy place is haunted by Roman ghosts.

> In Arles, along the Alyscamps
> Red shadows through the roses come,
>   Though day is bright:
>
> Beware the old sweet panic spell
> That makes heart leap with vain delight,
>   Heart thump and swell:
>
> Oh learn the quiet of the dove;
> Speak soft among the tombs, soft tell
>   Your tales of love.

And here is a translator's sensitive response to the work of another translator: Colin Sydenham on A. E. Housman and Horace (issue 26):

It is well known that Housman publicly declared Horace's *Diffugere nives* (*Odes* 4, 7) to be the most beautiful poem in Latin literature, and that he underlined this judgement by translating it into English verse. Naturally his version is an outstanding example in the huge anthology of such translations. What is less well known is a deeply revealing omission which it harbours.

Why was Housman so moved by this ode? Not, I suggest, merely because of the opening recital of the inevitable succession of the seasons, appealing as that no doubt was to his pastoral bent, but because of its haunting closure:

> *infernis neque enim tenebris Diana pudicum*
> *liberat Hippolytum,*
> *nec Lethaea valet Theseus abrumpere caro*
> *vincula Pirithoo.*

Horace has moved on to the finality of death: neither Diana nor Theseus can free their loves from that irrevocable parting. To Housman the thought was supremely poignant, for he had been irrevocably parted from his dear Oxford friend, his Pirithous, Moses Jackson. It was a shattering event, which shaped his life. The whole corpus of his poetry can be understood as an attempt to come to terms with this emotional catastrophe. This may sound fanciful, but consider the closing lines of the Latin poem addressed to '*Sodali meo M. I. Jackson harum litterarum contemptori*', with which Housman prefaced his great scholarly work, his edition of Manilius:

> *en cape: nos populo venit inlatura perempto*
> *ossa solo quae det dissoluenda dies,*
> *fataque sortitas non immortalia mentes*
> *et non aeterni vincla sodalicii.*

Our bodies and minds are destined for dissolution – along with the bonds of a companionship that did not last for ever. The reminiscence of Horace is unmistakable, but with that *non aeterni* it has become a heartfelt cry of pain and reproach.

So where does the translation fall short? Here is the rendering of the quatrain set out above:

> Night holds Hippolytus the pure of stain,
> Diana steads him nothing, he must stay;
> And Theseus leaves Pirithous in the chain
> The love of comrades cannot take away.

Fine, but what about *Lethaea*? Horace's bonds are bonds of oblivion; for all the love that was between them, Pirithous has forgotten Theseus. This word cannot have been overlooked by the Kennedy Professor of Latin, nor can it have been beyond the craftsmanship of the poet of *The Shropshire Lad*. But the pain of being forgotten was too much for both of them.

It is time to turn to the humorous side of *CAN*, for humour must have its place. Indeed, I see it as an essential part of any undertaking which aims to be serious without being solemn. Doug Lawrence has been producing brilliant classical cartoons from issue 6 onwards. Student howlers too have proved popular with very many readers, and when Doug has provided illustrations for some of these, there has been double the fun, such as his cartoon for the howler 'Dionysiac religion, a wild and grizzly practice . . .':

OK you guys, let's take it from the top ... one more time ...

"Dionysiac religion, a wild and grizzly practice ..."

Double the fun too when Doug illustrated some phrases from Miles Kington's 'Latin Tourist Phrase-book' in issue 27 – here are examples of both:

Post hoc propter hoc

Post hoc propter hoc: a little more white wine wouldn't hurt us
Ad hoc: wine not included
Exempli gratia: token tip
Carpe diem: fish frying tonight
Compos mentis: mint sauce

Curriculum: Indian restaurant
Infra dig: terrible accommodation
Post mortem: mail strike
Ex libris: dirty books
Ex cathedra: ruined church
Casus belli: gastro-enteritis
Tertium quid: 33p
Ars longa, vita brevis: unsuitable bathing costume
Quis custodiet custodes ipsos?: do you keep the Guardian?

Quis custodiet custodes ipsos?

Along similar lines to howlers was T. J. Leary's article 'Sootiness and the Arch of Tits' (issue 23) on the ways in which his computer spell-checker mangled the classical names in notes that he wrote for his GCSE pupils:

Emperors included Clouds, Dalmatian and Nerd, to say nothing of Tuberous. During the reign of Nerd there was a rebellion in Britain led by Queen Bodice. Earlier, resistance to the Roman invaders had been offered by Cataracts. The tribes of Britain included a branch of the Belgic Attributes. Other provinces in the Roman Empire were Aquatint and Judo. It was to mark the suppression of a revolt in Judo that the Arch of Tits was built.

As for writers: the biographer Sootiness aside, there were the historian Tactics, the comic dramatist Plaits and, under the patronage of Meanness, there were Hoarse and Virgule. Virgule wrote a work called *The Annalid* which featured Queen Diode. . . .

This prompted the following response by John Betts in the next issue:

> Eye halve a spelling chequer
> It came with My pea sea
> It plainly marques four My revue
> Miss steaks eye kin knot sea
>
> Eye strike a quay and type a word
> And weight four it two say
> Weather eye am wrong or write
> It shows me strait a weigh
>
> As soon as a mist ache is maid
> It knows bee fore two long
> And eye can put the error rite
> Its rare lea ever wrong
>
> Eye have run this poem threw it
> I am shore your pleased to no
> Its letter perfect awl the weigh
> My chequer tolled me sew

As for gentle humour on a larger scale, Niall Rudd's series of memoirs will long be remembered. Indeed, who could forget his portrait of M. M. Gillies in issue 24, or that of Fritz Heichelheim in issue 28 (forthcoming as I write)? Like so many of the pieces I print, these were of such quality that I deeply regretted I was not giving them a more permanent existence than the pages of an ephemeral newsletter. Here is Fritz Heichelheim, of the University of Toronto:

He had studied under some of the great continental scholars of the 1920s and 30s and had what could only be called a religious devotion to scholarship. Hounded out of Germany in 1937, he had spent a decade in England before emigrating to Canada, by which time he had published two large volumes on Ancient Economic History and over 400 articles. I was never quite sure what his classes made of him. For one thing, he had retained a strong German accent; so in his first lecture on Greek history bewilderment was relieved only when a student passed round a note saying 'Essence' = 'Athens'. Certainly his colleagues were constantly amazed. At coffee with the Principal, who had joined the College after a distinguished career in the Canadian Diplomatic Service, we were discussing the problem of St George Street, which ran straight through the campus between residences and academic buildings. As the University's numbers grew and the city's traffic increased, there were fears for the students' safety. Should there be a bridge across the road or an underpass? Or should the road itself be raised or sunk? Heichelheim proposed an original solution: 'The University's President should simply write to Paul Hellier, the Minister of Defence, asking him to explode an atomic bomb. Thereby will sufficient ground be moved.' The Principal's face was a study. Was the small round man with the large intense eyes a joker given to harmless fantasy (in which case he really ought to laugh), or . . .? The alternative was too dreadful to entertain.

On a later occasion the conversation turned to the various academic conferences that were held in American cities immediately after Christmas. At that time of year the snow made air travel unreliable and the railway system was slow and inadequate. According to Fritz, the problem would soon cease to exist: 'Each scholar will simply board a suitable rocket and whoosh! We are then arrived!'

More disconcerting was the fact that he conceived similar notions about the past. At some point he noticed a hitherto undetected likeness between a former Principal (Moffat St Andrew Woodside) and a bust of Cicero. From this he inferred that Woodside, whose ancestry was plainly Scottish, was a genetic descendant of the great statesman. 'But Fritz,' objected someone, 'Cicero was never in Britain.' 'No,' came the answer, 'but his brother was.' Q.E.D. His intellect seemed to operate without any reference to reality. A young American, Alan Samuel, who was also a Jew, told what we thought was a nice Jewish Story. It was about a Democratic politician in Connecticut, Abe Ribicoff, who had recently become so popular with the Goyim that his own people were asking, 'What was his name before it was Ribicoff?' All of us laughed except Heichelheim, who saw the question as a scholarly challenge. 'Well,' he mused, 'his name might have been Rubinsohn already, or perhaps Ben Reuben.'

Tea in College presented another kind of problem. For some reason I was in charge of the budget. Subscriptions went on provisions and on the services of the good Mrs Cliff, who set out the tea things and then washed up. By a tacit convention the biscuits, which were put on a large salver, were rationed to two, or at the most three, per person. By now Heich was almost spherical and had been put on a diet by his wife. He countered this campaign by eating large numbers of biscuits. In the main he escaped notice by somehow hoovering them up his sleeve, but he did not fool Mrs Cliff, who beckoned me aside and said, 'There's one guy here who's way out of line.' I let it ride for a couple of weeks. Then a complication occurred. The profound Hegelian, Professor Emil Fackenheim (now said to be a strong force on the right in Israeli politics) began to come in for tea, and Mrs Cliff somehow conflated the two: 'Gee, that fellah Fangelheim sure hits the cookies. I'll need more money; I'm fresh out of everything I bought last Monday.' All I could do was put an impersonal note on the tray; but it never did much good.

At these tea-sessions Heichelheim would keep us in touch with his research. *A History of the Roman People* was nearing completion, with the assistance of a scholar from another university whom he called Joe. 'Joe what?' asked someone. 'Why, just Joe, as in the old English joeman.' Joe's function, it transpired, was to translate Heich's prose into 'the English of the Hemingway period' (presumably along the lines of: 'So Brutus said "Let's do it quick and clean." And they did it quick and clean. And the bald man hit the floor . . .'). One more puzzle remained. Moving to his chair with half a dozen biscuits up his cuff, Heich said, 'So then, today comes news. Joe is now in jail.' 'What on *earth* is he doing in jail?' 'Why research of course. Jail has substantial grants for visiting scholars.'

Eventually *A History of the Roman People* by Heichelheim and Yeo appeared. The principal author sent a copy to Prime Minister John Diefenbaker, wishing, quite reasonably, to thank Canada for giving him and his wife the opportunities that Germany had taken away some thirty years before. It was an expensive volume, but out of affection I bought a copy and asked Heich to sign it. He was delighted, and took out a thick fountain pen, saying, 'Well here, then, is a small verse by a once quite famous but now in my opinion unjustly neglected German poet, Dehmel.' The first line was *Der*

Kritiker hat immer Recht (the critic is always right). It continued, 'exactly like the woodpecker. / The oak withstands the strongest storm. / The pecker espies therein the worm.' The inscription, in Heich's scholarly hand, rambled over most of the fly-leaf. He stood back, and then raised a finger. 'One moment please. We now correct the text.' With that, he viciously crossed out the word 'exactly', substituting 'infallible' (*unfehlbar*). After two more emendations the page was utterly defaced – and that was before he added his expansive signature.

At the beginning of every vacation Heichelheim would go over to the library to bring his enormous bibliography up to date. For this purpose he employed those rectangular sheets of cardboard that laundries use for packaging shirts. One afternoon, returning with a sheaf of notes under his arm, he collapsed on the steps of the University College and died instantly. That was, of course, a shock; but he could not have asked for a more fitting death.

A few months earlier he had been welcomed back and officially honoured by Giessen, his old university. It was a belated gesture of atonement, but only a man of saintly forbearance would have accepted it. Fritz Moritz Heichelheim had also one other quality not possessed by the rest of us. It was the heroic spirit of Browning's Grammarian:

> Let me know all! Prate not of most or least,
> Painful or easy!

The 'Letters to the Editor' column has grown longer and more diverse over the years, just as *CAN* itself has, and it too is a rich source of wit and irony. Here is just one example from many, printed in December 2000 (issue 23):

Dear Dr March,

While consulting an aged copy of a dictionary (*A Smaller Latin/English Dictionary*, Smith revised Lockwood, Third Edition) I came across the following definition:

> **destituo**, uere, ui, utum. to set aprat in a place.

Clearly this is a most useful verb. Perhaps it will prove very appropriate in the forthcoming election year:

> Yours sincerely,
> Clive Letchford

The wit and incisiveness of the many 'classihews' and 'classimericks' printed have always been a delight. Here is Ana Healey on Paulinus of Nola:

> Paulinus of Nola
> Always wore a bowler.
> He said, 'It befits the decorum
> Of a member of the Corpus Scriptorum Ecclesiasticorum Latinorum.'

And Chris Preddle on ancient Greek poets:

Ancient Greek poets
Conversed in epithets
Like Agamemnon the callous phallus
Or Helen with the rosy, fingered breasts.

An anonymous versifier offered a limerick on Oedipus:

Watch out for my eyes on the floor.
Small wonder I feel pretty sore!
    I murdered my *pater*,
    Then married my *mater*
And now Sigmund Freud's at the door.

And from George Engle (issue 10) came a limerick to accompany an illustration in *The Quiver* (Vol. XI, 1876; 'An Illustrated Magazine for Sunday and General Reading'):

A classical scholar is Freda,
Of myths an assiduous reader.
    One girl, she has heard
    Was seduced by a bird –
Now she's hoping to follow her Leda.

A story attaches to Martin West's limerick 'Guess Whodipus':

> The Thebans agreed, 'twas a sad do;
> but what could a well-meaning lad do?
>   He was doomed from first youth
>   by oracular sooth:
> 'They fuck you up, your mum and dad do.'

I had printed the dreaded f-word, and one CA member immediately resigned at the sight of it – though she later forgave me and rejoined, for the last line of the limerick is of course a slight adaptation of a famous line by Philip Larkin. So it turned out respectable after all.

ONE CAN'T BE TOO CAREFUL

The same cannot be said for the notorious Girl of Naupactus. The late Ian Martin wrote in issue 14:

The great Greek poet, George Seferis, was in the habit of writing limericks both in Greek and in English. One of his last ran as follows, but sadly the great man died before he could finish it:

> There was a young girl of Naupactus
> Who had an affair with a cactus . . .

Another well-known poet once offered a prize to anyone who might complete the limerick successfully, but as far as I know the prize was never claimed. I feel sure that one or more of your learned readers may be able to oblige!

And indeed they did! This generated more responses than any other item in *CAN*, before or since. Limericks flooded in by every post for some weeks, and I had great difficulty in selecting which to print. This is Jasper Griffin's limerick, together with its Latin version which came later:

> There was a young girl of Naupactus
> Who had an affair with a cactus.
>   Though she played many tricks
>   And endured many pricks,
> Still the cactus is virgo intactus.

> Habitabat puella Naupacti
> cruciata cupidine cacti,
>   dolis bene functa
>   spinis male puncta:
> cacto restat nomen intacti.

And here is Michael Parsons:

> There was a young girl of Naupactus
> Who had an affair with a cactus.
>   Her cries as she thrilled: 'O
>   spiniferous dildo!'
> Enlivened the air of Naupactus.

And Charles Low:

> There was a young girl of Naupactus
> Who had an affair with a cactus.
>   But she changed her mind quick
>   When she felt a small prick
> And escaped with her honour *intactus*.

Charles Low added: 'My wife thought this a little rude for a family publication, but I told her that classicists have broad shoulders (and minds).' Well, I always hope that's the case, for my trouble is that, imbued as I am with the delights of Aristophanes *et al.*, I don't always see what I print as risqué, let alone rude. In issue 15 I printed the following limerick from William M. Calder III, thinking nothing about it:

> There once was a lawyer named Rex
> with diminutive organs of sex
> > who, when charged with exposure,
> > replied with composure:
> 'de minimis non curat lex.'

He was delighted to see what he called his 'scurrilous' limerick in print, and told me that it had been refused publication in America. He then, however, sent me another limerick about Sappho, one that even I thought rude, so I refused it. *CAN* readers will be reassured that I do draw the line somewhere.

There are many more aspects of *CAN* that could be mentioned: the recurring 'Food and Drink' column, book reviews, drama reviews, the 'Classics in the Media' column, currently compiled by Philip Hooker, the 'Small Ads' (like Mary Passande's 'Call Clytemnestra for the bathroom to die for'), and many more. But space (just as it does in *CAN*) runs out. So let me end with one final (serious) topic: poetry. I have always had a particular fondness for the poems that I print, and it has been a difficult choice to single out from many just two or three to represent here the best in *CA News*. But in the end I have chosen, first, one of several poems on ancient works of art by 'Pedasos'. Here we have another pseudonym, and I shall be giving a little away when I say that, like Argus, Pedasos has been one of our Presidents. But this time I give no more clues. Here is Pedasos with 'Sarpedon, Son of Zeus' (issue 4), on the red-figure calyx-krater signed by Euphronios and now in the New York Metropolitan Museum:

Says Sleep 'Your wings are weak.'
Death does not speak.
Says Sleep 'You have no sword.'
From Death no word.
Says Sleep 'Sarpedon's dead.
I'll take the feet and you the head.'

They grip and heave.
Sarpedon's toes and fingers do not leave
the feet of Death and Sleep
but still their earthly contact keep.
Sleep's fingers lose their grip.
Death's do not slip.

Death and the God both look across and know
Sleep's knees and spirit are about to go.
Sleep is our chatty, comfortable friend
but Death it is who takes us in the end.
Strange that in all this scene of grief and grace
the only smile is on Sarpedon's face.

Next, here is a haunting and untitled poem by Antony Rowe (issue 25):

I wish I could sit in a field
On a green hill under a tree
Watching a golden morning
Cover the golden sea

Or watching a hollow river
Supine mirror the sky
Then borrow again its urgent clouds
To flood the daylight by

I wish I could watch the shepherd
Come over the broken stile
And drive his sheep from Backsey
To grass by Linden mile

Or listen to musical Pan
Piping under my tree
Goatfoot telling his naked nymphs
That loving and youth are free

When love has burnt out to ashes
And beauty has crumbled down
And youth is an empty bottle
And that green hill is brown

I'll find my fading field
Sit under its yellow tree

> And breathe the air that carried away
> Visions I'll never see

And to end, let us have Ursula Vaughan Williams' 'The Quarry' (issue 15) – not a specifically classical poem, but one on a subject close to the heart of all the ancient writers whom we read with pleasure, and expressing it to perfection (and thus ironically refuting its theme):

> Along the green banks by the waterside
> the fishers sit and idle summer through,
> gazing at silver floats that nod and ride
> above the gleaming cool where fishes slide
> elusive under sky-reflecting blue.
>
> Out on wide, frozen marshes speared with reeds
> 'til winter sunset the numbed fowlers lie
> masking net and trap with rush and weeds,
> waiting to lure some wanderer where it feeds
> weary from flight across the snow-brimmed sky.
>
> I'll sit a patient year to take a thought,
> listen and wait until the bait is taken
> and out of depth and height the creature's caught
> and closed inside the cage of words I brought.
> Then from this tranced wait and watch I waken,
>
> knowing that somewhere meaning goes astray.
> Once shut in language the essentials fade
> like the heaped silver catch that lay
> filling the angler's basket at the end of day
> or the limp spoils of the fowler's trade.
>
> Under the summer bank smooth water lies
> where fish are flickering between reed and stone.
> Brown winter sleeps beneath its icy skies
> and high as cloud or wind the migrant flies
> remote as thought whose words are still unknown.

I have tried in this chapter to capture something of the variety, the vitality, the exuberance of *CAN*, and no doubt the end result – like the spoils of fisherman and fowler – has lost the essential spark that gives it its unique life. So let me finally sum *CAN* up by saying that each varied issue is intended as a celebration of the myriad facets of Classics.

CAN has received many tributes over the years, and these must go, not to its Editor, but to its contributors, honouring as they do the wit, the erudition, the humanity of CA members. One of the most heartwarming tributes came from Dame Felicitas Corrigan, the biographer of Helen

Waddell: '*CA News* must be one of the few proofs of civilisation in our chaotic world. I love the wit, humour, sheer cleverness of so much of the production.' Long may CA members keep *CAN* flourishing!

(On p. 147 above, Jenny March regrets that she could not give Niall Rudd's articles 'a more permanent existence than the pages of an ephemeral newsletter'. The revised text of the articles, together with an additional piece, will be published in booklet form in 2003, under the original series title *It Seems Like Yesterday*.)

11

THE UPS AND DOWNS OF BRANCHES

By BARBARA FINNEY

The Classical Association's Branches are the enduring legacy of the third of the Association's founding triumvirate – Professor Robert Conway, who had moved from Cardiff to become Hulme Professor of Latin at Manchester in 1903. He was particularly conscious of the need for local organisations with local activities, especially in the major industrial centres with new universities, to form the basis of a strong Classical Association – and he made numerous proposals and motions to Council. In July 1904, Council resolved that a Local Organisation committee be established and that local branches should be established. They also agreed that, if the local branch collected CA subscriptions, they could retain 20 per cent for their own use – so the branches could be the principal means of recruiting new members.

In his paper delivered to Council on the occasion of the CA's Jubilee in 1953, Professor L. J. D. Richardson, the Joint Honorary Secretary, having opened his address by invoking 'Our beloved President' (not a term regularly used today), devoted some time to a survey of the Branches that had been established in those first fifty years 'as the earliest expression of our fourth object', namely 'To create opportunities for friendly intercourse among all lovers of classical learning in this country'. He remarked that 'With those vigorous personalities, Professor Conway and Professor Sonnenschein, both moving spirits in our early counsels, it was only a question whether the first Branch would be that of Manchester or that of Birmingham. Manchester, perhaps true to its traditional *praerogativa* ('What Manchester says today. . . .') was first, the Branch there being founded in November, 1904'.[1]

The first branch was indeed constituted in Manchester on 18 November 1904, with the Vice-Chancellor of Manchester University as Chairman, Prof. Augustus Wilkins as President, eight eminent worthies including the Bishop of Manchester, the Bishop of Salford, Canon

---

[1] *Proceedings*, 1954, 25.

Hicks of Manchester Cathedral (who later became Bishop of Lincoln) and three other leading clergy as vice-presidents and a committee of seven, chaired by Robert Conway. It set a subscription of 7s 6d for joint membership of the local and national associations (of which the branch would keep 3s 6d) and 2s 6d for 'associate membership' of just the local association – and soon claimed 84 full members, and 94 associate members, including a contingent from the *Manchester Guardian*. Its activities consisted of a series of lectures, usually four a year, one a public lecture (given, in 1909, by J. W. Mackail), an annual excursion, and a programme of 20 or so lectures to schools. In 1905, the branch raised £70 to finance the archaeological excavations in Melandra Castle, and later funded excavations at Ribchester. In 1906, it organised the first big CA conference, a major municipal enterprise described elsewhere, very different from the brief meetings at London, Oxford or Cambridge.

Eleven months later the Birmingham and Midlands Branch was established by Edward Sonnenschein. The Bishop of Birmingham was Chairman, and there were twelve Vice-Presidents (including nine leading clergy, many of whom were also headmasters). In 1908 Sonnenschein organised an even more spectacular conference than that held in Manchester – complete with the Prime Minister and a production of Gilbert Murray's *Hippolytus*. It organised four or five lectures a year, set up a Reading Circle, which met fortnightly in the winter months, and soon claimed nearly 100 members.

Next, in December 1907, came Liverpool (after 'a protracted and somewhat voluminous correspondence' concerning its title, as it was the first example of an existing organisation becoming affiliated to the main body). Dr Richard Caton, the Lord Mayor, was the first chairman. It soon claimed 32 full members, 52 associate members and was organising up to 8 lectures a year and an annual excursion. Nottingham followed in February 1909, with a Bishop as President and over 50 members. In 1912, the London branch was set up by Max Caspari (later Cary), with a most distinguished President (the Dean of Westminster) and set of Vice-Presidents (including Lords Asquith, Cromer, Curzon, Loreburn and Professors Kenyon, Mackail, Page, Platt and Flamstead Walters); it quickly became the largest branch with 145 members. Bristol was founded in March 1912; Northumberland and Durham was founded in February 1913 with 84 members, Cardiff became the second affiliated branch in January 1914 with 65 members, following a reorganisation of the Frogs Society which had been founded in 1898/9. The Leeds branch was founded in March 1914 by Prof. W. Rhys

Roberts, with a good number of clergy in support, and it claimed an impressive 100 full members and 44 associates in its first year. It went on to organise a lavish conference in 1917, publish *Falernian Grapes*, a collection of papers delivered to the branch, and appoint Capt. F. R. Dale of Leeds Grammar School as Honorary Secretary of Reading Circles and Schools Lectures.

These early Branches were learned societies with a heavy clerical presence in the positions of authority – Bishops, Deans and Archdeacons abound! Scholarly lectures and Reading Circles featured on the programmes, together with the amassing of collections of lantern slides, visits to sites of interest and fundraising for archaeological excavations. Indeed, the Manchester Branch raised £70 in its first year of existence to begin excavating at Melandra Castle and on September 10th 1915 oversaw the opening of the Ribchester Museum. In 1910 a private committee under the aegis of the Nottingham Branch undertook an excavation on the site of the Roman station of Magidunum on the Fosse Way. Some Branches also displayed a keen interest in work with schools by devising a syllabus of lectures available to schools; the Leeds Branch had appointed an Honorary Secretary for Reading Circles and School Lectures within its first year of existence.

During the 1914–1918 War Branch activities naturally were 'in a state of suspended animation', but the 1922 issue of *Proceedings* comments on the 'vigorous activity' of fifteen Branches, as Branches had by that time also been established in Aberystwyth, Sheffield, Kent, North Wales, Oxford and Sussex. Although the earliest Branches had been formed in the larger University cities, it is clear that smaller towns with academic communities (such as the University Colleges) were now keen to participate. Some of the success of setting up new branches was the result of the efforts of 'Local Correspondents' who came into being in the very first year of the Association's existence and numbered 62 by 1914, being responsible for fostering interest and maintaining links with the parent body. Consequently branches arose in the South West, Southampton, Bedfordshire and Northamptonshire, Hull, Swansea, Reading, Leicester, Taunton and West Somerset, and East Anglia. Some of these branches, not attached to a university in a major city, were quite small, but individual initiative could significantly increase the numbers. In 1923, Leeds claimed 191 members, followed by London with 145, Oxford with 139, Liverpool with 115, Manchester with 108, Birmingham almost 100. North Wales, based at Bangor, at one point recruited 100 full members, thanks to T. Hudson-Williams. Bristol had

52, Nottingham 25 (it had to be reorganised in 1929 and again in 1935), Aberystwyth just 14 – and most of the later branches had about 30–40 members. Southampton started with 23, one of whom always provided tea; meetings were 'pleasantly informal'.

Some were remarkably energetic and enterprising. The Kent branch, which met in a variety of venues, organised a collection of Roman coins to be circulated to schools, attempted the formation of Inter-School Classical Clubs in most of the towns of Kent, supplied copies of tunes to Horace's Odes to its members, contributed funds to the dig at Reculver; membership rose to 164 at one point – the prime organiser was Miss E. C. Gedge who went on to become Secretary and Treasurer of CA. The Cardiff branch, with a modest membership of 36 (plus 30 students), became most active from about 1927, with 11 meetings a year, presidential addresses from the likes of Robert Conway and John Sheppard, and regular productions of classical plays by University College. Its prime organiser was Prof. L. J. D. Richardson, later a legendary CA Secretary. Bedford, in 1930, held a Virgil Bimillenary Dinner, with an elaborate menu, each item being followed by an appropriate quotation from the poet or a contemporary; after dinner, at the bidding of the President, half a dozen members got up and gave extemporary addresses on some animal, possible or impossible, mentioned by Virgil. Manchester, in contrast, organised a Virgil Bimillenary Competition for schools, with prizes and certificates, which may have been the first reading competition.

From the earliest years the relationship between the parent body and the local branches was fraught with problems. Many branches operated two grades of membership – 'full' members who belonged to the central body as well as the local branch and 'associate' members who only paid a subscription to the local branch. Some branches also had a 'student' member category – to cause further confusion! Thus it was always difficult to ascertain a precise number for the membership and regular pleas appear in Council Minutes urging that recruitment campaigns be mounted to entice all branch members into a full commitment. Indeed, in the *Proceedings* of 1929 – in an attempt to impose regularity – this statement occurs: 'The Council has passed a Standing Order to the effect that no new Branch be recognised unless it be a rule of the Branch that the Secretaries and Treasurer be members of the Parent Association'. In general the agreed view is that branches are affiliated but independent organisations. The overseas branches that were established began with South Australia on 28 March 1908, followed rapidly by others in New South Wales (1909), Victoria (1912) and Queensland (1923), in India at Bombay (1910) and in South Africa (1928); they soon spread throughout the Commonwealth (and merit a separate chapter). Some of these overseas branches formally remained subject to the central body, but over time the majority were independent affiliated organisations. Communications are still received from Ceylon (*sic*) which was founded in 1935 and from one of the New Zealand branches, at Otago (1922).

In 1923, J. W. Mackail undertook an Australian tour. In 1929 serious consideration was given to the proposal to hold a CA Conference in South Africa, but it was eventually decided that too few CA members would be able to attend. Canada was affederated in 1946, Jamaica and the Gold Coast followed in 1952; Nigeria, thanks to some missionary work by Professor John Ferguson, became most active from 1957, when Rhodesia and Nyasaland also joined. Some of these overseas branches formally remained subject to the central body but over time the majority were independent affiliated organisations. In 1973, the Classical Association of Scotland, founded in 1902 and upstaged by the CA in 1903, became an Allied Association.

The outbreak of World War II caused almost total cancellation of all branch activities, as most schoolchildren in London and the larger cities were evacuated (sometimes more than once) and many members of both sexes joined the forces or were engaged in other war work – 'in fact, classical graduates seemed to have a special *flair* for certain hush-hush work' commented Professor Richardson.[2] Air raids and the black-out also militated against unnecessary meetings. Nevertheless a few lectures were held, notably in Manchester and Reading, with the cooperation of the Workers' Educational Association (at some point there was a formal affiliation).

However, one exciting venture emerged from the darkness of those years. In September 1943 a Classical Teachers' Conference took place at Cheltenham Ladies' College with the general aim of re-enthusing teachers for their subject. Among the suggestions put forward was the idea that the Classical Association should, by funding prizes, encourage its branches to organise Latin Reading Competitions among the schools of their districts. In the words of the Jubilee address, 'This was to be the genesis of a large movement.'[3] In the first year competitions were

---

[2] *Proceedings*, 1954, 36.
[3] *Proceedings*, 1954, 39.

organised by the Reading, Bristol, Newcastle (*sic*) and Durham, Sheffield and Oxford branches, who were seemingly happy with the financial arrangement that the parent body would contribute one guinea towards expenses, provided that one guinea was raised locally. Some branches were bold enough to introduce Greek too. By 1949 ten branches were involved, and a higher profile was allotted the venture by the publication of the names and schools of the prize winners in *Greece & Rome* and the commissioning of a specially designed bookplate to be presented with the prize books. The bookplate is still in use! The Horatian and Virgil Societies also awarded grants towards these prizes and the offer in 1957 from the Trustees of the Gilbert Murray 90th Birthday Fund of £25 per annum towards prizes for reading Greek aloud or recitation *memoriter* further boosted the enterprise. In 1958–9 twenty branches claimed sixty-two prizes at a total cost of £72.15s; in 2001 seventeen branches held competitions and £75 was the average grant per branch for prize money (some branches are willing and able to fund their own competitions). It is interesting to note that those branches that responded to the Reading Competition challenge in the early years still run such events.

Some of the more adventurous branches have attempted to broaden the appeal of these contests by introducing extra events in addition to the straight reading/recitation of a passage. For instance, the Southampton branch produces a handsome booklet containing the set passages with translations opposite – to encourage the attendance of the contestants' parents and friends and to ensure that they are able to follow what is being said! In some areas *Minimus* has made a frisky appearance as a set text in order to attract younger participants. Playlets and dialogues are now commonly offered so that a pair (or more) of pupils may give one another moral support. A handful of branches hold 'Ludi Scaenici' competitions in which school teams perform a five-minute play in Latin that has (ideally) been written by the pupils themselves – but some help and guidance from teachers is acceptable. A few branches include some project work (drawings, writing, models etc.) on a set theme such as 'Food in Roman Times' or 'The Problems of Ancient Transport'. The South West branch runs an annual 'Klassickle Kartoon Kompetishun' (*sic*) 'to provoke interest in classical themes among schoolchildren who were less likely to take part in the Association's traditional Reading Competitions because they lacked the confidence to read a strange language in public, or because their skills lay elsewhere', as one of last year's judges commented; some of these excellent cartoons have been published in CA News. This type of competition also allows the entry of topical allusions such as RyanAir cheap flights being on offer for Daedalus and Icarus and their sighting by plane-spotters in Greece! An indication of all these activities is provided in the list of branches which follows. In addition a number of branches are involved in setting up and running Day Schools for AS/A2 topics such as Epic and Latin set texts (at GCSE level too), as well as the more ambitious ventures of 'Hands On' archaeology and Classics for Adults.

Some branches were extraordinarily active. At Birmingham, in 1949, a new regime organised 6 lectures, a Presidential address, 2 Exhibitions, 3 excursions (including a Greek Play), a Social Meeting, a Conversazione, a Bulletin, a (Modern) Greek Song Recital by Arda Mandikian, an inter-school reading of *The Frogs*, a series of lectures to schools, and a summer tour of Roman France; later years were not quite so energetic, but they added an annual Dinner and conferences for schools, including a Bimillenary one on The Ides of March, featuring films of *Julius Caesar* and *Caesar and Cleopatra*. Membership more than doubled to 164 by 1961. Geoffrey Hooker went on to become Editor of *Greece & Rome*, Edna Hooker went on to become CA Treasurer; the lavish CA conference of 1979 was their parting shot. The London branch was also most active, raising membership to 243 by 1961. It formed an Inter-Schools Classical Club; in 1958 it arranged a conference on 'The Changing Face of Classical Studies' and a Debate with the Haldane Society, chaired by Cyril Hinshelwood, on the motion 'That the education of our future should be principally in the sciences rather than the humanities'; the audience were reported to be predominantly scientific, but their sympathies were overwhelmingly for the humanities. It also organised an Annual Wine Party with guests such as Viscount Hailsham, the Bishop of London, Robert Graves and Bernard Miles. By 1960, it was clear that the bulk of their efforts (and those of most other branches) were being directed at schools, with special lectures, conferences, and teaching discussions.

After the conclusion of World War II, branch activities gradually revived. In 1948, when *Proceedings* resumed reports of branch activity, there were 23 branches with 1400 members, about half of whom were 'full members'; ten were organising Latin Reading Competitions, six were organising School Lectures. London was the largest with 153 members, followed by Oxford with 145, Manchester with 121, Northumberland & Durham with 109, Liverpool with 85, Reading with 83, Birmingham with 80 and Leeds with 68. Several new branches were founded – in Shropshire in 1946, in North Staffordshire in 1950 (based at the University College of North Staffordshire, which subsequently became the University of Keele), in Northamptonshire in 1951 (a shortlived venture which was officially wound up in 1957) and in 1954 two branches – Worcestershire and Malvern and Teesside/Cleveland. Often these branches were started by a keen few – and declined once these pioneers retired, moved job or area or died. Occasionally members of an existing branch felt threatened by the proposal to found a new branch in the next county, as happened in 1965 when a flurry of letters emanated from the Southampton branch officers over the founding of the Salisbury and District branch (sometimes referred to as the Wiltshire branch) in the previous year; the main concerns were the potential loss of candidates for the Reading Competitions and possible clashes of programme. That particular conflict was resolved amicably – and both branches are still operational. During this period too JACT had come into being in 1962 (see Chapter 4 for details). Local JACT branches were founded in order to give support to school-teachers, many of whom were lone classicists in maintained schools. Often individuals were members of both CA and JACT local branches but over time these groups have tended to merge – with one or the other association retaining the formal title. Thus the Sussex CA branch now encompasses SACT, while in the East Midlands EMACT cooperates with both the Nottingham and the recently revived Leicestershire and Rutland CA branches in supporting and publicising each other's programmes.

The *Proceedings* of 1962 included (pp. 44–6) the text of a letter sent by the CA and the Society for the Promotion of Roman Studies to the Vice-Chancellors of the Universities of East Anglia and York and to the Chairmen of the Academic Planning Boards of the Universities of Essex, Kent, Lancaster and Warwick urging the inclusion of the classical subjects in these new establishments. Since there had traditionally been a link between university departments and CA branches, doubtless there was a hope that new branches would spring up together with new departments. This, however, did not generally occur, except in the North West where the Lancaster and Northwestern branch was inaugurated in 1967 (as a complement to the University Department) but was defunct by 1988.

1967 also witnessed the establishment of the Gloucestershire branch due to the enthusiasm of teachers in some of the local independent schools – and it still flourishes. The 1972 founding of a Lincoln branch proved less successful as it has lapsed, although there have been several attempts to revive it. The Guildford branch was established in 1975 and boasts a substantial membership (70+) and lively programmes, with entries from some seven schools (around seventy pupils) for the Reading Competition. Then, after an interval of twenty-one years, the baby of the family was set up as the Lampeter and Mid Wales branch in 1996; this aimed to provide a forum for interested people froma wide area of Wales, who were not catered for, especially since the demise of the Aberwystwyth branch.

Recent years have proved to be more difficult for the branches. The closure of University Classics Departments, the reduction of teaching of Latin in schools (as a result of the abolition of compulsory Latin for Oxbridge entrance and subsequently the straitjacket of the National Curriculum) and the general decrease in commitment to membership of all sorts of groups (well documented by sociologists) have all contributed. A typical branch now has 30 to 40 members; only the largest can claim 100. Some, with enthusiastic secretaries, such as Tim Ryder at Hull and Brian Sparkes at Southampton have done relatively well. (Indeed, it was a meeting at the Southampton branch which introduced Jenny March to the CA – later its Publicity Officer and now editor of *CA News*). Once, branch secretaries had a special lunch at Conferences at which they discussed matters of mutual interest with the CA officers – and the local branch hosted the reception which preceded the Annual Dinner. In 1989 an attempt was made to form a branches Group that would meet 'as often as it thinks necessary' for the purpose of advising the CA officers 'on all matters concerning the relationship of the Association with its branches'; at the Canterbury conference in April 1990 seven branch representatives (lured by the payment of travel expenses) met with the Branches Secretary and Treasurer and discussed a wide range of topics. But the Branches Group lapsed. In truth, few Branch Officers do attend the Annual Conference and even fewer people have time for extra meetings.

So – at the Centenary there are twenty-four active branches; some more vigorous than others. Some remain wedded to university departments and operate almost as departmental meetings, others coexist amicably with departments and others are almost entirely school-orientated. Branch activities vary considerably. Some branches still succeed in holding regular termly meetings with distinguished speakers delivering papers on a vast range of topics – a programme not unlike the early branch meetings, except that the proportion of clergy is likely to be much smaller. Other branches struggle to put together a programme of events in that the organisers are aware that the numbers who may attend may not justify the expense of travelling speakers. But there is considerable evidence of classical vigour even in adversity. For example, the Bangor branch was deprived of its University Classics Department in 1988 and has no local schools where any Latin is taught, but maintains an interesting and lively programme. A similar fate befell the University of Keele's Classics Department recently, but the North Staffordshire branch is now arranging talks, play readings and reading groups in mediaeval Latin and New Testament Greek, as well as annual trips to sites of interest – with a determination 'to keep the Classics to the fore in North Staffordshire', to quote from that branch's last annual return of information. Wine tastings, showings of films with a classical theme, *prandia* (in Southampton), dinners to celebrate particular milestones and achievements all feature in the life of branches.

It is abundantly clear that many branches have cause to give thanks for the devoted service that some members have given over a period of forty or fifty years. In recognition of this sort of dedication, the newly revived Leicestershire and Rutland branch has honoured the memory of its late Branch Secretary by establishing the Dorothy Buchan Memorial Lecture. An enormous amount of energy has to be expended by the officers of lively branches in order to maintain momentum. The CA Officers are well aware of the debt owed to all the branches and are committed to providing generous financial support for their activities, whenever it is requested. The Delphic Oracle would, no doubt, return an ambiguous answer to any request for reassurance regarding the future of branches, but there are plenty of members who are committed to their survival.

BRANCHES IN ORDER OF FOUNDATION
(* indicates that the branch is still active)

Abbreviations: RC – Reading Competition; LS – Ludi Scaenici; P – Project.

1904 *MANCHESTER AND DISTRICT: inaugural meeting held on October 15. RC.

1905 *BIRMINGHAM AND MIDLANDS: inaugural meeting held in October. RC.

1907 LIVERPOOL AND DISTRICT: inaugural meeting held in December.

1909 *NOTTINGHAM AND DISTRICT: involved with RC/P organised by EMACT.

1912 *LONDON: RC 7 LS.

*BRISTOL: RC.

*NORTHUMBERLAND AND DURHAM: RC/P.

1914 *CARDIFF AND DISTRICT: formally became a CA branch on January 23, having been originally founded as The Frogs (Classical) Society in 1898–9.

*LEEDS AND DISTRICT: inaugural meeting held on March 14. RC.

1919 (THE) ABERYSTWYTH AND DISTRICT: became defunct in 1995.

1920 *SHEFFIELD AND DISTRICT: inaugural meeting held on January 21.

KENT: became defunct before 1990; attempts made in 1990 and 1995 to revive the branch failed.

*BANGOR AND NORTH WALES: inaugural meeting held in October.

*OXFORD: RC.

1922 *SUSSEX: inaugural meeting held in April. Had a chequered history: the branch was officially wound up in 1951, but was revived in 1955 'after fourteen years in abeyance': RC in association with SACT.

*SOUTH WEST: inaugural meeting was held on November 25. RC and KKK!

1923 *SOUTHAMPTON: for the previous twelve months the branch had been called the Winchester and Southampton branch. RC.

BEDFORDSHIRE AND NORTHAMPTONSHIRE: inaugural meeting held in July. Subsequently known as BEDFORD BRANCH, BEDFORD SCHOOLS' CA and reincarnated in 2001 as *THE HARPUR CLASSICAL SOCIETY. RC.

1924 *CAMBRIDGE: affiliated as a CA branch, having been founded on May 9 1903 as the Cambridge and District Classical Society. RC/LS.

1928 *HULL AND DISTRICT: inaugural meeting held on November 16.

SWANSEA AND DISTRICT: inaugural meeting held in December. Defunct by 2000.

1929 *READING AND DISTRICT: RC.

1930 LEICESTER: reincarnated as *LEICESTERSHIRE AND RUTLAND in 2002.

TAUNTON AND WEST SOMERSET

1932   EAST ANGLIAN: inaugural meeting held on October 1. Defunct by 1989. (Records 1932–73 held at Norfolk Record Office, SO 214.)

1946   SHROPSHIRE: defunct by 1989.

1950   *NORTH STAFFORDSHIRE

1951   NORTHAMPTONSHIRE: officially wound up in 1957.

1954   WORCESTERSHIRE AND MALVERN: inaugural meeting held on January 16.

TEESSIDE / CLEVELAND: inaugural meeting held on January 22. Defunct by 1985.

1964   WILTSHIRE (later known as *SALISBURY AND DISTRICT): RC.

1967   *GLOUCESTERSHIRE: RC/LS.

LANCASTER AND NORTHWESTERN: defunct in 1988.

1972   LINCOLN

1975   *GUILDFORD: RC.

1996   *LAMPETER AND MID-WALES

12

THE CONFERENCES

By PHILIP HOOKER

At the Inaugural Meeting in December 1903, it was resolved that there should be a General Meeting each year at a university town. Dr D. B. Monro, Vice-Chancellor of Oxford University, spoke fondly of the Philologen-Versammlungen meetings in Germany at which excellent papers were given, scholars were brought together and 'there is a very considerable convivial element'. The first General Meeting, in Oxford, in May 1904, started on a Friday evening, with a conversazione in the Public Examination Schools (Schola Borealis), hosted by the Vice-Chancellor. Alongside were exhibits of Oxyrhynchus papyri, photographs and prints of ancient sites (from the Ashmolean Museum) and maps and plans of classical countries and sites. At 10 am on the Saturday, there was a formal welcome from the Vice-Chancellor, a reply from Sir Richard Henn Collins (Master of Rolls and CA President) and fraternal greetings from Professor Ramsay of the Classical Association of Scotland. J. W. Mackail then gave an address: 'On the Place of Greek and Latin in Human Life', which was followed by formal business. In the afternoon J. W. Headlam led a debate on 'The Reform of Classical Teaching in Schools', with twelve other recorded contributions.

There was extensive debate about the best timing for General Meetings; a plebiscite of members had revealed a strong preference for January (rather than September or July), though there were protests from headmasters who had three conferences of their own at that time. Full term was inconvenient for those working at universities (which, they thought, could explain the marked absence of Cambridge men from this meeting); Easter vacations were at different times. So the second meeting was in London in January 1905, starting on a Friday evening with a conversazione, alongside an exhibition of prints and books (the first CA meeting display from leading classical publishers) which was followed by two lectures – one describing the latest teaching technology: 'The Use of the Lantern for Archaeological Illustration' and one from Gilbert Murray (starting at 10.15 pm) on 'Some Points in teaching Greek Plays'. At 10.30 am on the Saturday, the formal business was dealt with and there then followed a series of debates, in full Parliamentary style, with proposers, seconders, proposed amendments to the wording, votes (all reported at length, in oratio obliqua, in the *Times* and in *Proceedings*) on the topics of pronunciation, utilitarian aspects of the study of Latin, the Army's plans to substitute science for classics for candidates to Sandhurst and Woolwich. Lord Halsbury, CA President, then gave a brief address; after lunch, there were more debates about working parties on how to keep teachers informed of recent discoveries and on how to lighten the curriculum and improve the means of instruction. The third meeting, in London in January 1906, started earlier, at 3 pm on a Friday afternoon, with two added plenary lectures – and there would have been a third, if Alfred Austin, the Poet Laureate, had not had to withdraw from his talk 'On the Practical Utility of a Classical Education' because of a bereavement.

The fourth meeting, in Manchester in October 1906, the first at a new university, was intended to be a spectacular civic occasion. It started still earlier, on 8.15 on a Thursday evening, with a reception hosted by the Vice-Chancellor at Whitworth Hall, with exhibits in the museum and library, and music. This was followed, at 10 pm, by a lecture from Professor Rhys Roberts of Leeds on 'Youth and Age in Homer'. Friday started with a visit to Manchester Museum to view the Finlay Collection at 10.45 am, a brief talk from Prof. J. P. Postgate on 'Horace as a Rustic' at 11.15, a visit to Chetham's Hospital and Library at noon. After lunch, members visited the Roman fort at Deansgate at 2.15, and the Rylands Library at 2.45 (collecting a special catalogue on its classical books), before attending a special Congregation at 4.30 at which Honorary Degrees were awarded to Sir Richard Henn Collins, Samuel Butcher, J. P. Postgate and Prof. W. Ridgeway, with tributes from the Lord Mayor of Manchester and Edward Hicks, Canon of Manchester Cathedral (Chairman of the new Manchester branch of the CA and subsequently Bishop of Lincoln and CA President in 1912). The next event should have been a Presidential Address from no less than Lord Curzon, who had recently stepped down as Viceroy of India – but the death of his wife obliged him to cancel all engagements a few weeks before the meeting, so Sir Richard Henn Collins and Mr Justice Kennedy had to step in with some remarks on the importance of a classical education for lawyers. (Manchester was also unlucky with its weather, as is often the case with CA Conferences; 'it is not normally like this', Canon Hicks insisted). At 9 pm, there was the first debate – on 'The Relative Functions of Classical and Modern Language Teaching in Secondary Education'. Saturday started at 9.30 with another plenary lecture from Prof. Robert Conway, the local leader, followed by the Business Meeting at 10.15 (at which 120 members were present). There was then a report from the Pronunciation Committee and another debate. In the afternoon, there was an excursion to Chester. In the Vote of Thanks, tribute was paid to all who had provided private hospitality; in those days, the new universities serviced local students, there were no halls of residence, so, when there was a conference, a committee of wives had to organise accommodation and meals for the guests in various homes.

This was the first conference which created a significant social event, with the first civic reception, the first excursions (both local and further afield), the first opportunity to see a new, flourishing, centre of classical activity and what should have been the first major Presidential address – all spread over three days. The next meeting, in Cambridge, in October 1907, was back to a Friday afternoon and a Saturday, with over 100 guests (who might have been stranded with their hosts if a threatened railway strike had taken place). It featured the first full Presidential Address, given by Samuel Butcher.

But the next meeting, in Birmingham in October 1908, was to prove to be the most spectacular event for many years. It started at 3 pm on a Thursday at the New University Buildings at Bournbrook, with two plenary lectures, followed by a Vice-Chancellor's Reception and Tea in the Great Hall, with visits to the new science departments or to a new hall of residence for women. At 8 pm, there was a Conversazione, hosted by the Lord Mayor in the Council House, attended by many leading Birmingham citizens. On Friday, there were three major events. At 11 am, in the Old University Buildings in the centre of Birmingham, Prof. Sonnenschein gave a lecture on 'The Unity of the Latin Subjunctive', which was followed by a vigorous debate on the report of the Pronunciation of Greek Committee. At 2.30 pm, in the Midland Institute, an audience of 850 saw a special production of *Hippolytus*, in the Gilbert Murray translation, given by Miss Horniman's newly formed Gaiety Theatre company from Manchester; Gilbert Murray had spent nine days supervising the rehearsals, special music had been composed by Granville Bantock. At 8.15 pm, in Birmingham Town Hall, an audience of 2000 came to the Presidential Address of Prime Minister Herbert Asquith; the Bishop of Birmingham led the Vote of

Thanks. At 9.45, Charles Waldstein (later Sir Charles Walston) gave a lantern lecture on Herculaneum. On Saturday, there was the Business Meeting and a debate on the report from the Curricula Committee. Due tribute was given to the Hospitality Committee led by Mrs Joseph Chamberlain and Mrs Sonnenschein, who coped with rushed breakfasts and dinners at 6 pm, instead of the usual 8 pm, and to the contributors to the Guarantee Fund, which underwrote the cost of the conference. The only misfortune was the late discovery that, because of one of Archbishop Laud's 1636 statutes, Oxford's Michaelmas Term started at an exceptionally early date (the Saturday in fact); many from Oxford were unable to attend.

In 1910, the CA was back in London, in January, with a day and a half of formal business, debates, a conversazione, the Presidential Address. This style of meeting alternated with provincial meetings, which had an extra day, with added civic receptions, excursions, entertainments, at Liverpool in 1911, Sheffield in 1913, Leeds in 1917, which most members found to be more interesting. They felt a bit like missionaries, supporting the pioneers who were upholding the position of classics in a new university, alongside the sciences, in an industrial centre up North – and they briefly became part of a different community.

These meetings were all in January, but, in 1919, they started to change. In 1919, it was a day and a half in Oxford in May. 1920 was very different. It was held in April, over four days, in Newcastle and Durham. It started on a Wednesday evening with a Lord Mayor's Reception at the Laing Art Gallery, Newcastle, followed by two lantern lectures on the excavations at Corbridge and the Roman Wall. Thursday was in Newcastle, with the Presidential Address and lectures by Prof. J. Wight Duff of Newcastle (on Martial) and Prof. A. H. Cruickshank of Durham (on Richard Bentley); there was then an excursion to the Black Stone Museum, a reception hosted by the Vice-Chancellor and a lecture from Prof. H. J. Rose of Aberystwyth. Friday was in Durham with a Debate on the Report on Latin in Advanced Courses in Schools in the morning followed by a visit to the Chapter Library and lunch in Durham Castle. The business meeting and tea with the Dean of Durham was followed by an evening performance of Euripides' *Electra* by the Armstrong College Dramatic Society in the Gilbert Murray translation. On Saturday, 21 members remained for a motor char-a-banc visit to Corbridge and the Roman Walls. 'Thus ended one of the best-attended and most enthusiastic meetings ever held'.

This is the first example of a meeting with most of the ingredients of a modern CA conference. It was out of town, it was run over four days in April, it had only a few plenary lectures, it had receptions, a Presidential address, an entertainment, excursions, an opportunity to see the local classical sites. And it was evidently most enjoyable.

1921, at Cambridge, was completely different. It was held in August, over five days, with lavish local hospitality and extensive overseas participation. It was a joint venture with the American Philological Association who provided three US lecturers, one of whom was present in person; other participants came from Scotland, Canada, Australia and France. Walter Leaf, banker and polymath, gave the Presidential Address. The Prime Minister's Committee on the Position of Classics in English Education had just published its (favourable) report which was extensively debated. One morning saw four plenary lectures, from Prof. A. E. Housman, Prof. R. S. Conway, Prof. G. N. Calhoun (of California) and F. M. Cornford, leading scholars of their age. It opened with a garden party in Emmanuel College on Tuesday evening and closed with John Sheppard's exposition of the *Oresteia* (with extracts from the recent film of the Cambridge Greek Play production) on the Saturday morning. In style and timing, this Conference antici- pated many of the features of the Triennial Conferences which started in 1942.

1922 was back in London, in January – Lord Milner, President, was only available at this time, before his tour of the Empire. 1923 was in Bristol, in April. And so two styles of meeting alternated, with the provincial meetings moving further afield – Bangor in 1925, Cardiff in 1929 (where the secretary was a young L. J. D. Richardson), Hull in 1930 (in which year there was also an extra London meeting in January), Reading in 1932, Nottingham in 1933, Southampton in 1935, Belfast in 1937. Hull was the last meeting at which tribute was paid to 'hosts and hostesses'; Reading was the first at which tribute was paid to wardens of halls of residence; in future, members would mostly reside in student accommodation. And Hull was the first to hold an Annual Dinner, with after-dinner speeches; this was immediately converted into a tradition; it was sometimes called an Informal Dinner, which presumably means that it was not black tie.

There was considerable wartime disruption – meetings were evac- uated to St Peter's Hall in Oxford in 1940 and to St Alban's High School for Girls in 1944 – and the question was raised with a 'high Government quarter' as to whether meetings should continue, given the disruption and general mobilisation ('classics graduates seemed to have a special flair for hush-hush work'). The answer was that 'it is patriotic and laudable for learned societies to continue holding meetings' and, although the organisers were concerned about the numbers who would be able to attend (were their railway journeys strictly necessary?), wartime conferences were, in fact, very well attended.

None more so than the first Joint Conference in 1942. The Hellenic and Roman Societies had held a joint conference in Leeds in summer 1937; in 1942, they held another one, in Oxford, in the summer, to which Classical Association members were also invited. Up to 100 were expected to attend – 450 turned up. This became the first Triennial Conference (though, as we have seen, there was a prototype in Cambridge in 1921). Triennials have since been held every three years, alternating between Oxford and Cambridge, occasionally skipping a year so as not coincide with the International Federation of Classical Studies, which meets every five years; the 20th Triennial will be in Cambridge in August 2005. They are sponsored by the CA, the Hellenic and Roman Societies, the British Schools at Athens and Rome and by JACT, they run over five days, they have a high proportion of international scholars in attendance and a good turn-out from Oxbridge; parties are organised for most evenings, there is also some sort of entertainment and an excursion. The excursion was once an all-day event, with a packed lunch, on a Sunday, but, now that Triennials are midweek, this is just for an afternoon. Attendance numbers in recent years have been similar to those of CA conferences.

After the war, enthusiasm was riding high; the CA regularly scheduled its annual meetings in April in provincial centres (some of which extended over five days) and also, from 1950, one-day meetings in January in London, starting with one on the theme of Ancient Theatre (complete with an afternoon performance of the *Mostellaria*). Members can still recall some of these conferences. Dennis Blandford, for example, was a student at Bristol at the time of its 1950 conference. 'I remember the wide spectrum of speakers, ranging from luminaries like Gilbert Murray and Hugh Last to fellow undergraduates such as George Boon. George enthused about the Roman villa he had discovered at King's Weston – he went on to become president of the Society of Antiquaries'.

Bristol provided a good example of what had become a formula for a successful CA conference. It started on a Wednesday at 5 pm with the first plenary lecture (there were six in all; oddly, one slot was usually reserved for the local organiser, on this occasion Norman Gulley, who

THE CLASSICAL ASSOCIATION visited the Roman villa at Kings-weston, yesterday, as part of their annual meeting. Here Mr George C. Boon points out something of interest.

(April)
1950

'Something of interest': a local excursion during an annual conference. George Boon, then a Bristol undergraduate, went on to become President of the Society of Antiquaries. (Photograph courtesy of Dennis Blandford.)

can hardly have had much spare time to prepare his paper). This was followed by a University reception. On the Thursday, there were two plenary lectures in the morning (at Bristol, these were from Gulley and Gilbert Murray), followed by a choice of two local excursions in the afternoon (at Bristol either a walking tour of the city or a visit to the Roman Villa at King's Weston), which usually led to the Lord Mayor's Parlour for a civic reception and tea. Then came the Presidential Address (Hugh Last at Bristol), which was usually followed by a Branch reception (sherry) and the Annual Dinner, which at Bristol attracted 'an unusually large attendance of 174'. On the Friday, there were two more plenary lectures (at Bristol, these were D. S. Colman on Classics at Shrewsbury and Prof. L. R. Palmer); after an early lunch, members divided between at least two longer excursions. There was usually a choice between an archaeological site (wet and windy) and a stately home (with an assured tea), sometimes also a power station or a steel factory; most members opted for the site; at Bristol members were evenly divided: 70 went to Bath, 70 to Wells and Cheddar. The next engagement was in the evening; at Bristol this was a special entertainment: '776 and All That', 'a veritable *lanx satura*', devised by Basil Cottle, performed by local schoolchildren; elsewhere, it could have been a production of an ancient play, or a film or a concert. On the Saturday, there was another plenary lecture (this time F. R. Dale), followed by 'Communications'; this was a feature devised by Prof. L. J. D. Richardson – a series of ten-minute papers offered by conference participants, at which they could outline some results of work in progress, an opportunity for the emerging scholar, or, as Richardson put it, 'a whole General Meeting in microcosm'. Communications started in 1947 and continued on and off until 1979. Finally, there was the Business Meeting, which went through a variety of formal reports on the finances, the journals, educational initiatives, reported deaths, officers for the coming year (including new Vice-Presidents), an announcement of next year's meeting – and wound up with a vote of thanks from a selected guest for the conference organiser and all who had supported them.

We can note some conference highlights. Sheffield, in 1948, was the first to provide a choice of long excursion (though it did omit the Dinner). Leeds, in 1953, was the first to attract Royalty – honorary degrees were awarded to Goodwin B. Beach, P. J. Enk and Viscount Samuel with HRH the Princess Royal, Chancellor of Leeds University, presiding over the Congregation. (Leeds did it again in 1962.) London, in 1954, celebrated the CA Jubilee, with delegations from many other

Conference dinner, Keele 1955: Standing: 2nd from left, Canon Armstrong (senior vice-president); 4th from left, L. J. D Richardson. Seated, third row from front: 3rd from left, T. W. Melluish; second from right, F. R Dale.

learned societies, at home and abroad. 1955 introduced members to Keele, a new university, with unusually diverse courses. 1957 saw the memorable Durham dinner at which John Spedan Lewis announced his annual endowment to the CA; chairman of Council Prof. W. S. Maguinness immediately, glass in hand, proposed an impromptu toast for his long life and happiness. 1960, at Southampton, saw the notable educational debate, opened by Prof. C. O. Brink, on the future of O-Level Latin if this was no longer a requirement for entrance to Cambridge (such debates had long ceased to be a regular feature of Conferences); there was also a memorable school production of Menander's recently recovered *Dyskolos*, translated by W. G. Arnott, directed by Brian Sparkes, and high attendance – 172 sat down to the Dinner.

The 1961 Birmingham meeting substantially followed the formula. It started at 5 pm on a Wednesday with a lecture from the two organisers which was followed by dinner and a University reception. On Thursday, there were two plenary lectures in the morning (O. E. Loewenstein on Greek Science, P. J. Enk on Plautus' *Truculentus*, 'his least popular play'), a choice of local excursion in the afternoon, leading to the Council House and a civic reception (afternoon tea), and then came the Presidential Address in the adjoining City Museum and Art Gallery – on this occasion, Lord Hailsham, with a fine address: '*Vos Exemplaria Graeca*', which was, in turn followed by the Annual Dinner for 112. On Friday there were two plenary lantern lectures in the morning (from R. P. Winnington-Ingram and C. M. Robertson) and, in the afternoon, a choice of long excursion, involving adjoining CA branches – one to Wroxeter and Shrewsbury, the other to Malvern Hills and Worcester. In the evening, members went to King Edward's School, where there was an exhibition and a production of the *Mostellaria* recently translated by two former pupils – M. D. Reeve and I. D. Mackenzie. On Saturday, there was a lecture from D. R. Dudley, the local professor – and the Business Meeting. Catherine Wolstenholme, then 'a raw undergraduate', had her first experience of a CA conference. 'I looked forward to meeting people with the same enthusiasm as myself for Classics; the reality was an almost complete absence of people of my own age group, a preponderance of teachers nice enough in their way but wrapped up in classical anecdotes, teaching methods and even, at that time, ways of survival, a younger set of university lecturers who I was told later regarded the conference as a kind of workseeker's market – a calumny I hope – and, most depressing of all, lectures which tended to examine obscure topics of interest to dedicated specialists. I was in fact so horrified by this lack of popular appeal that I wrote to the then secretary, pointing out my concerns; I was firmly put in my place by the reply I received'.

In fact, the conferences at this time appeared to be increasingly successful. Numbers at the dinner rose to 132 at Leeds in 1962 (a five-day event which also celebrated the tercentenary of Richard Bentley), 160 at Swansea in 1963, 150 at Leicester in 1964, 168 at Manchester in 1965, 187 at Cardiff in 1966, and 218 at Reading in 1967 (which claimed a record overall attendance of 312), 155 at Sheffield in 1968, 151 at Royal Holloway College in 1969, c.110 at Bangor in 1970, 129 at Canterbury in 1971 – and then *Proceedings* ceased to record the numbers.

Philip Howard, *Times* journalist, started his regular Conference attendance in 1965. He was advised that there were fences to mend. Hugh Noyes, normally the parliamentary correspondent, had visited Swansea, disregarded the Presidential Address and just focused on the lecture from Prof. L. R. Palmer, a notorious polemicist, presumably in the hope of something controversial. This was the time of *That Was The Week That Was*, and his report of Palmer's lecture was distinctly disrespectful, not to say satirical. (This is the version of events supported by contemporary documents; Philip Howard, in his own Presidential Address, tells a much funnier story, set in Leicester, involving Prof. E. R. Dodds and the crux of the axeheads – Dodds did, in fact, deliver the Presidential Address, a prescient review of the coming changes in classical education, which was properly reported in the *Times*, and whose daring suggestion that less time be devoted to Latin prose composition excited the *Times* correspondence columns for several weeks.)

He was also advised to maintain a proper distance and was obliged to spend a sad and lonely time at the Midland Hotel, well away from the delegates. He quickly went native – and has fond memories of these times.

Then it was a rather nostalgic tribal gathering of true but embattled believers. Nevertheless it was an endearing event. The excursions were more central than they have become. There was more spare time for tea and conversation – not the relentless modern rush of simultaneous panels. People made an effort to dress up in their best for the annual dinner – there were some remarkable Victorian buttons and bows (and bow ties) on display. There were magnificent characters. The son of one of the founders who always (sensibly) wore his pyjamas under his suit, from which the bottoms protruded, who was never well shaven (when shaven at all) and always wore white shoes, blancoed daily, leaving white footprints wherever he went. The family from Birmingham who always brought their three delightful children from the early age of about six – exemplary behaviour to sit through the lectures. The teacher from a choir prep school, painfully shy, who always wore his hat, and never normally spoke; I eventually got him to exchange more than 'Good morning' in the queue for porridge – but not much more. A magnificent Edinburgh Jean Brodie, a stout lady in vast tweeds, an avid tea drinker, a great teacher, who said that the CA meeting was the high point of her year.[1] A soldier scholar who survived the horrors of the Chindit campaign with an edition of Horace in his breast pocket; younger women had to be wary of him on excursions. The local Professor who went on far too long, at one point dropping his notes, collecting them in the wrong order, just like the Great Sermon Handicap, prompting Betty Radice to boom, *sotto voce*: 'that was, without exception the worst lecture that I have EVER listened to in my entire life'. The Professor at Hull who delivered his lecture wearing a purple suit, beads and a beard, carrying a handbag – a brilliant lecture and original scholarship. Ur CA was like the Roman Republic before the Empire. Smaller, less professional, a bit provincial. But it kept the flame alive. Without it, we would not be what we have become.

[1] This was Mary Arnold (1906–94) who is still fondly remembered in her home city of Edinburgh. A memoir by her pupil Elizabeth Jones was circulated at the CA meeting there in 2002. Miss Arnold was the illegitimate daughter of John Sampson ('The Rai'), librarian of the University of Liverpool and expert on gypsy lore: see Anthony Sampson, *The Scholar Gypsy: the Quest for a Family Secret* (London, 1997). (Ed.)

It is clear that the lectures – normally six of them, spread over four days – were just the pretext; the Conference had become primarily a social event, with afternoons and evenings devoted to excursions and entertainments, which attracted a small, but loyal, band of provincial teachers and university lecturers (Oxbridge people were normally too grand to attend, though they might agree to give a lecture), many of whom had been attending regularly for almost 20 years. In the 1970s, Conferences were starting to struggle, star lecturers were few and far between (more of the slots were being taken by local speakers), though Erich Segal did drop in on Liverpool in 1977 on one of his book tours. But, in 1978, there was the first joint meeting with the Classical Association of Scotland in Edinburgh, which drew a strong attendance (183, including supernumeraries) and then, in 1979, there was the most lavish conference ever, in Birmingham.

It was designed to celebrate the 75th anniversary of the CA and the centenary of the Hellenic Society and was combined with the Symposium of Byzantine Studies, a well-established Birmingham event. It ran over five days, each day starting with a plenary lecture from one of Professors George Kennedy, Eric Turner, Anthony Long, Douglas MacDowell and Dr Robert Bolgar, which was followed by two or three parallel sessions (including a revival of Communications). There was a stirring Presidential Address from Prof. Bryn Rees, a CA stalwart, entitled 'Strength in what remains'. There were two sets of excursions, local ones leading to a Civic Reception (and tea), the other set being a choice of four all-day Sunday excursions (on Triennial lines) – with alternative lectures and papers for the more studious. There were two professional entertainments – a production at the Birmingham Repertory Theatre and a musical entertainment – again with alternative colloquia or lectures. The Jubilee Dinner featured five courses and three wines. The all-in cost was about £50 – and it was a considerable financial success.

Attendance was good – 318 in all, including more than a hundred Byzantinists – but not up to the Triennial levels which had been hoped for – and it did have a severe effect on future conferences; after this one, ordinary conferences were bound to appear a bit disappointing. It was not long before a distinct fall in numbers and a need for action became apparent; at Reading in 1987, the long excursion and entertainment were cut (so the Conference was a day shorter), an experiment never repeated. Bristol made a valiant effort to restore standards in 1988 – with a strong set of speakers, including Niall Rudd, Peter Wiseman, Brian

Sparkes, a most inspiring Presidential Address from Tony Harrison, the first Civic Reception since 1979, excursions, an entertainment – but delegates were most likely to remember the catering, which provoked so many complaints that the organisers felt obliged to secure refunds all round.

Sheffield, in 1989, was dismal. The Classics and Ancient History department was being closed down. Attendance, at 101, was at an all-time low. Pat Easterling, the estimable President, could provide little help: 'The President has an awesome responsibility – to deliver an address which will dispense Olympian wisdom and offer guidance and inspiration. Not feeling equal to the task, I hope you will forgive me if what I have to say turns out to be more or less indistinguishable from a lecture'. And then there was snow.

But a new generation had just taken office, who appreciated that, if the Conference is the main annual achievement of the Classical Associ-ation (aside from the journals), then it did have to be radically reformed. The full story is told by Malcolm Schofield in Chapter 5, but the two main changes which have transformed matters are easily summarised. First, there are now no more than one or two plenary lectures (plus the Presidential Address) – instead there are dozens of short papers, now of 20 minutes duration, with 10 minutes allowed for questions, from a wide range of emerging scholars, both from the UK and overseas. Second, the CA now uses its charitable funds to provide bursaries to enable postgraduates (and, to a lesser extent, teachers) to attend the conference – so there are now dozens of young people about the place. In the first new-style conference, at Warwick, in 1991, there were 50 papers and 12 bursaries; in 2003, again at Warwick, there were about 170 papers, with seven parallel sessions and nearly 70 bursaries. Overall attendance numbers are now regularly in the 300–350 range and rising, close to overtaking the Triennials, to make the CA conferences the most successful (as well as the most enjoyable) classical events in the UK (and, probably, Europe).

Conference veterans, who remember the old days, might reasonably point out that most of the elements of a successful modern conference – the receptions, the limited number of plenary lectures, the opportunities for discussion and social contact, the Presidential Address, the entertain-ment, the choice of excursions, the Dinner, the venues, the timing (all this, in four days, creates considerable momentum) – were originally developed many years ago – and even the modern call for papers is, in fact, an improved and much enlarged version of the old Communications. But the improvements have been crucial; a good crowd is the making of a successful conference; attenders are now for the most part younger, more interested in intellectual stimulation, more likely to find talks related to their subjects of interest and people of their own age group. There is also more interest in the bars (an earlier generation looked for a cup of tea before retiring early) and there was the first disco at Royal Holloway in 1997, though members do seem to prefer ceilidhs. Conferences have, indeed, changed with the times, but they still retain their traditional spirit and enduring appeal. We will leave Philip Howard with the last words, taken from his 2002 Presidential Address:

The only fixed point in my random year comes at Easter. Then I know that I shall be staying in some university lodgings in England or Scotland. I shall be sleeping in a student's bedsitter. I shall be eating cooked breakfasts for the only time of the year. I shall be struggling to keep up with the learned lectures. I shall be enduring the blizzards, thunderstorms and Force 10 gales that are the traditional weather for the CA excursions. I shall visit some of the best universities and stately homes. And I will be among my friends. The best, cleverest, wittiest, funniest, wisest, dearest friends have been met at and through the Classical Association.

13

THE PRESIDENTS

By PHILIP HOOKER

'The testimony of leading men of affairs is of the greatest value to our cause. It sounds a note which appeals to the public and impresses that great body of practical men whom we desire to influence.' So said Sir Frederic Kenyon, Director of the British Museum and Chairman of the Association's Council for most of its formative years, in his own Presidential Address in 1914.

In those days, it could reasonably be assumed that the Great and the Good had all had a classical education and could all testify to its beneficial influence and importance. Sir Richard Henn Collins, the first President, was Master of the Rolls; Lord Halsbury, who succeeded him, was Lord Chancellor. Next came Lord Curzon, who had just retired as Viceroy of India, then, in 1908, the Prime Minister, Herbert Asquith. He was followed by Lord Cromer, the former Proconsul of Egypt, and the Bishop of Lincoln. In 1917, when Lord Bryce led a deputation to the Board of Education, they received a sympathetic reception from its President, his old friend Henry Fisher, previously a fellow of New College and then Vice-Chancellor of Sheffield University.

Initially, the Presidents did not give Addresses. Sir Richard Collins made an Opening Statement at the 1903 Inaugural Meeting, which he chaired, Lord Halsbury made a few brief remarks ahead of one of the debates in 1905. We might have heard more from Sir Richard Jebb who had accepted an invitation to be President in 1906, but sadly, he died before he could take it up. Lord Curzon took his place but, unfortunately, the death of his wife meant that he was unable to attend the meeting. Mr Justice Kennedy, at short notice, substituted a short talk on Classics and the Law – how lawyers benefit from classical studies. So it was Samuel Butcher, for many years Professor of Greek at Edinburgh University, successor to Jebb as MP for Cambridge University, the first Chairman of Council, who gave the first real Presidential Address in 1907. Herbert Asquith, in 1908, gave his Address to an audience of 2000 in Birmingham Town Hall; he had been one of the first Vice-

Presidents and had accepted the Presidency when he was still Chancellor of the Exchequer; he then became Prime Minister, but still maintained his engagement; the Bishop of Birmingham had been one of his best friends at Oxford. The actual Address appears now to be somewhat slight, a mixture of good wishes and topical references, but such support from the Prime Minister was doubtless much appreciated. Lord Cromer, in 1910, gave the first extended Presidential Address, on 'Ancient and Modern Imperialism', which later emerged as a book. Cromer was not a classics graduate, though he had been brought up in Ionia and read Anacreon in his youth; but he was the first of many Presidents who were not classical scholars, who had achieved distinction in another walk of life and who later compared and contrasted their own experiences with those of the ancient world.

There was then some wartime disruption, but, in his 1918 address, Professor Gilbert Murray could observe: 'It is the general custom of the Association to choose as its President alternately a Classical scholar and a man of wide eminence outside the classics', which was nearly right and has since become the established pattern. ('Man' was, for a long time, the operative word – the first woman President was Dorothy Tarrant in 1958). Gilbert Murray was already a celebrity – his translations of Greek drama were originally intended to enliven his lectures, but Bernard Shaw, a fellow vegetarian (who made Murray a character in *Major Barbara*), urged that they be published and they were successfully produced in the West End (prompting curtain calls of 'Author!' on opening night). He became Regius Professor of Greek at Oxford in 1908. His CA address 'Religio Grammatici', some profound thoughts on the nature of classical scholarship, still reads well today. He was President again in 1954, the Jubilee year, with 'Are Our Pearls Real?'

The next most spectacular Presidential Address was probably that of Stanley Baldwin, Prime Minister, at Middle Temple Hall, in January 1926. He did not have a classical education (he scraped a third in history at Cambridge before entering the family ironmaster business), but he was a founder member of CA and an enthusiast. Preparation of 'Classics and the Plain Man' had been 'a nightmare for the last fortnight' (in those days, Prime Ministers wrote their own), but its reception was most gratifying. 'The Classics will never perish out of the land so long as they are cherished by ordinary people. And it seems to me good that you should have a President occasionally who is not a scholar, who is not particularly distinguished, but who can speak for the common folk as an ordinary man. I wonder how many of you can remember your Eginhard? . . .' Baldwin recalled his first parliamentary election.

The candidate was expected to spend three evenings a week during the time of his probation in one or another of the public houses which jostled each other through the constituency listening to and vociferously applauding what, for want of a better name was called, on the *lucus a non lucendo* principle, comic or humorous song. After a time I felt the need of a moral purge and a literal sedative. It was the work of a moment to find what my soul needed. When I came home at night from these orgies I seldom went to bed without reading something of the *Odyssey*, the *Aeneid* or the *Odes* of Horace. By the date of the election, I had read all the last-named, and most of the others, not without labour in the dictionaries, not always with ease, but with care and increasing joy, with the desired result that, though defeated, I had passed through the fire and the smell of burning was not on my garments.

And classical texts also had contemporary relevance. 'A political leader should know his *Knights* by heart, for there is no profounder truth than that the sausage-seller lies ever on the flank of Cleon'. This address was published by John Murray (as part of the 'On England' collection of speeches), was well-reviewed and sold nearly 5,000 copies; it was also translated into French and German. 'It may be safely said that no statement of the claims of the Classics has ever carried more conviction to the General Public.'

The most notable subsequent address from a politician is probably that of Lord Hailsham in 1961: '*Vos Exemplaria Graeca*'. He was a distinguished Classics graduate who became a lawyer and then an MP and Minister, but, at the time of his address, he was, in fact, Minister of Science and Technology and he was called upon for comment on Yuri Gagarin's space flight, which had been launched on the previous day. 'Though I doubt whether the Romans would have made much of it, the Greeks would have revelled in space research. Indeed I seem to remember that Aristophanes more than once made it the subject of a play'. Other politician Presidents have been Leo Amery (1936), best known for his peroration 'In the name of God, go' in the 1940 House of Commons debate which led to the fall of Neville Chamberlain, who talked about his great love, the *Odyssey*, and Edward Boyle (1973) a former Minister of Education who had become Vice-Chancellor of Leeds University. Monty Woodhouse (1969) was MP for Oxford for many years, but he was better known for his wartime exploits in German-occupied Greece and his subsequent Philhellenism. There was also the Marquess of Crewe (1924), HM Ambassador in Paris, who had previously chaired the 1919 committee which had reviewed the position of Classics in education and Lord Soulbury (1949) a former President of the Board of Education who had then chaired the Burnham Committees.

Educational administrators have included J. W. Mackail (1923), who set up a new system of secondary education at the Board of Education (and was also Professor of Poetry at Oxford); Sir George Macdonald (1932), former Secretary of the Scottish Education Department; Sir James Mountford (1963), Vice-Chancellor of Liverpool University and later Chairman of the Leverhulme Research Awards Committee; and Lord Wolfenden (1980), successively Headmaster of Shrewsbury, Vice-Chancellor of Reading, Chairman of the University Grants Committee, Principal Librarian of the British Museum, who served on numerous government committees – and, when he eventually retired, lectured on Hellenic cruises. When at the British Museum, he was said to be rather slow to make decisions: 'When confronted by any problem, I always ask myself: what would the Greeks have done?' Sir John Hackett (1971) was a professional soldier who became Principal of King's College, London. Sir David Hunt (1982) was an Oxford don who became a soldier and then a diplomat, and achieved televisual fame as Mastermind of Masterminds in 1982.

Edward Hicks, Bishop of Lincoln (1912), was the first clerical President; he was a renowned epigraphist and had been President of the Manchester branch of the CA. William Temple (1930) was Archbishop of York (and later of Canterbury). W. R. Inge (1934) was Dean of St Paul's ('the gloomy Dean'), best known for his regular weekly articles in the *Evening Standard* from 1921 to 1946. Dom David Knowles (1975) was a monk who became Professor of Modern History at Cambridge; unfortunately, he died before his AGM. Robert Runcie (1992), who had just retired as Archbishop of Canterbury, gave one of the most memorable of recent addresses, 'Still Yearns My Heart', reprinted in this volume

From the arts world, the CA has had Sir William Richmond (1916), the artist who decorated St Paul's Cathedral, T. S. Eliot (1942), poet, publisher and dramatist, whose plays were based on classical themes, Tony Harrison (1988), another poet and dramatist, well-known for his version of the *Oresteia*, Lindsey Davis (1998) an English graduate who has achieved popular success with her historical crime novels featuring the private eye Didius Falco, and Emma Kirkby (2000), Oxford Classics graduate and classical music concert singer, who provided the first Presidential Recital in lieu of an Address. Sir Stephen Gaselee

(1940) was Librarian and Keeper of the Papers at the Foreign Office (and an anthologiser of mediaeval verse); Harold Nicolson (1951) was a noted author and journalist, with a regular column in the *Spectator*; Raymond Williams (1984) was Professor of Drama at Cambridge and 'a major Socialist thinker'; Philip Howard (2002) has been reporting AGMs and supporting the Association regularly in *The Times* since 1965; his witty address was replete with anecdote and real affection for the languages and for the Association. Dilys Powell (1967), film critic and Philhellene, produced one of the best-written addresses, 'The Mirror of the Present': 'When I was at Oxford, I wondered whether I should study classics. My brother said: 'Don't – the Classics are a terrible grind for a girl and you will be prematurely wrinkled'.

There have been two publishers. Sir Basil Blackwell (1965) inherited the family bookshop in Oxford and set up his own publishing imprint. He was awarded an honorary degree and, as the Public Orator pointed out, 'it is not only classical scholars who profit from the activities of this beneficent man. All over the world there are scholars in many different disciplines who, if they were honest, would admit that they owe him a great deal'. The other was Colin Haycraft (1994), who published a remarkable number of classical works at Duckworths and provided another of the most memorable recent addresses 'On Not Knowing Greek, or Latin either'. The first President from a less gentlemanly part of business or commerce was Walter Leaf (1921), who became a fellow at Trinity College, Cambridge before his father's illness obliged him to take charge of the family silk and ribbon business; this led to his becoming a director and later chairman of the London and Westminster Bank and an authority on banking and political economy. He was also a Homeric scholar and mountaineer, and on matters of mathematics, astronomy and botany was said to be 'the best-informed man in the room'. The President who made the greatest financial contribution to the CA was John Spedan Lewis (1957), who studied Classics at Westminster School (and later became a member of the Association) but did not go on to university; instead he joined the family business, which he later transformed into the John Lewis Partnership, in which all employees are partners. In his address 'Ancient Athens and Modern Private Enterprise' he explained that the problem with business was not (as most people suppose) how to make a profit, but, rather, how to distribute the profits equitably. He was an unexpected choice of President (and not everyone approved), but he was so gratified that he committed himself and his successor to a regular endowment for the

Association (which ran until 1971), which transformed the CA's otherwise precarious financial position. Subsequent Presidents from business and commerce have been Sir Nicholas Goodison (1986), then chairman of the London Stock Exchange, who seemed to be more interested in the fine arts than the market (and wrote the definitive monograph on barometers), Sir Jeremy Morse (1990), a distinguished banker, chairman of Lloyds Bank and subsequently Chancellor of Bristol University, and Sir Anthony Cleaver (1996), chairman of IBM UK and a director of numerous other boards and committees, who has also been a strong supporter of Friends of Classics.

In addition to the eminent lawyers who were so prominent in the early days of the Association, Lord Hewart of Bury (1926) was Lord Chief Justice who 'loved the classics and all good literature' and Lord Greene (1947) was Master of the Rolls, a fellow of All Souls before he went to the Inner Temple.

Several notable scientists have been President. Sir Archibald Geikie (1911) was a geologist, who had had a classical and literary training – he became secretary of the Royal Society. Sir William Osler (1919) was Regius Professor of Medicine at Oxford, where he was able to pursue his literary interests. D'Arcy Wentworth Thompson (1929) was the son of a Professor of Greek who became a zoologist – and produced glossaries of Greek birds and fishes. Sir Cyril Hinshelwood (1959) was Professor of Physical and Inorganic Chemistry at Oxford, who presided over the new Nuffield Laboratory which opened in 1941 and also served as President of the Royal Society from 1955–60; his catholic tastes included literature, music, cats, paintings, Dante's imagery and several languages. Susan Greenfield, Professor of Physiology at Oxford and Director of the Royal Institution, is President in 2004.

These Presidents have demonstrated the extraordinary variety of distinguished people in all manner of walks of life who have benefited from a classical training or who have derived inspiration from the achievements of classical civilisation – and who have been sufficiently emboldened to deliver an address to what they assume to be an audience of classical scholars.

Roughly half the Presidents have been classical scholars. They have typically supplied some anecdotage, some thoughts on the current state of classical education or the results of some recent research. They have usually been honoured because of their commitment to the effective promotion of the subject to the wider world.

In the early days, the few scholar Presidents tended to be the stalwarts of the Association, who had played a major role in its foundation or in its subsequent development. These included Samuel Butcher (1908), Frederic Kenyon (1914), John Mackail (1923), John Postgate (1925), and Robert Conway (1928). In more recent years, Bryn Rees (1979), George Kerferd (1991) and David West (1995) have been similarly honoured.

Subsequently, there was a tendency to invite the scholars who were arguably the best communicators. Cyril Bailey (1935) had been Oxford's Public Orator, a chairman of the annual 'Dons and Beaks' conference which promoted contacts with schools, and a notable actor in Greek plays. T. R. Glover (1938) had been Cambridge's Public Orator, an ever-entertaining historian, whose books 'were too readable to attract the approval of purists' and was wont to say 'it's a poor subject which cannot be brought into an ancient history lecture'. Sir Richard Livingstone (1941) was a strong promoter of the classics in government committees and elsewhere and an organiser of Oxford summer schools for colonial administrators; his address 'The Classics and National Life' was widely circulated to schools, librarians and educational associations, and was even sighted on railway bookstalls. John Sheppard (1943) was another Cambridge character, Provost of King's College, a dramatic lecturer, without notes, eager to speak to schools, a producer of eleven Cambridge Greek Plays. Maurice Bowra (1945) was an Oxford legend, successively Warden of Wadham, Professor of Poetry, Vice-Chancellor, the inspiration of many an anecdote. Frank Adcock (1948), one of the original editors of the Cambridge Ancient History, was known as 'the last of the studied wits'. William Beare (1962) was Public Orator (as well as Professor of Latin) at Bristol University for many years, where he was also Pro Vice-Chancellor.

In the 1950s, the Classical Association seems to have had a great respect for age. Presidents included William Calder (1952), aged 71, Lord Samuel (1953), age 83, Gilbert Murray (1954), aged 87 (but still, happily, on good form), Dr G. M. Young (1955), aged 73 (prevented by illness from attending, but whose paper was read on his behalf), Sir Harold Idris Bell (1956), aged 77, John Spedan Lewis (1957), aged 72, Dorothy Tarrant (1958), aged 73. In the 1960s, Presidents were mostly more youthful sixty-somethings.

Scholar Presidents have since included some of the finest writers – and some of the finest classical teachers – of their time in the UK. Eric Dodds, author of *The Greeks and the Irrational*, gave a prescient assessment of the future of classical education in 1964 and was followed by Keith Guthrie, author of the six-volume *History of Greek Philosophy*, in 1968, Frank Walbank in 1970, Patrick Wilkinson in 1972, Moses Finley in 1974 (the ancient historian who did much to help JACT, and served as its President in 1981–3), Kenneth Dover in 1976, Michael Grant (who retired from university work to write a series of popular books on the classical world) in 1978, Deryck Williams in 1981, and Ted Kenney in 1983.

Most recently the CA has looked, above all, for service to the Classics community and devotion to the wider cause of Classics – as well as academic distinction – when making its invitations. Few have fought as valiantly for Classics in their different ways as, for example, Pat Easterling (1989), Fergus Millar (1993), Oliver Taplin (1999), Peter Wiseman (2001) or Peter Jones (2003) – or, indeed, as Carol Handley (1997), former Headmistress of Camden School for Girls, the first schoolteacher to serve as President for many years – and the first to emulate a spouse (Eric Handley, 1985).

III

Presidential addresses

14

THE PRESIDENTIAL ADDRESSES

By MALCOLM SCHOFIELD

I The enemy

'The enemy', declaimed Gilbert Murray in the peroration to the first of his two Presidential Addresses (1918), 'has no definite name, though in a certain degree we all know him.'[1] So he etched a character:

> He who puts always the body before the spirit, the dead before the living, the ἀναγκαῖον before the καλόν; who makes things only in order to sell them; who has forgotten that there is such a thing as truth, and measures the world by advertisement or money; who daily defiles the beauty that surrounds him and makes vulgar the tragedy; whose innermost religion is the worship of the Lie in the Soul.
>
> (*Proceedings* 1918, p. 96)

Other Presidents were more prepared to name and shame. Dean Inge in 'Greeks and Barbarians' (1934) lambasted democratic populism on the American model, and spoke darkly of 'new dictatorships . . . far more tyrannical, more searching in their inquisitional terrorism, than the rule of any Tsar, Sultan, or Emperor'. More than a decade before *1984* he was fearing 'a completely mechanical society', 'a servile State in which all spiritual and intellectual life would be strangled'[2] (*Proceedings* 1934, p. 22). T. R. Glover (1938), the Baptist preacher and populariser of ancient history, saw many causes for gloom, including a prevalent scientific materialism and the rise of vocational training, but he too deplored 'democratic control' over educational policy, and the standard-isation (above all through obsession with examinations) and intimida-tion by common opinion which he thought came with it (*Proceedings* 1938, 9). Peter Wiseman's contemporary diagnosis is, as Aristotle might have said, in a way the same, in a way not the same. 'The totalising

---

[1] I have occasionally added a little biographical detail about Presidents mentioned in this narrative, but for the most part – as with Murray – refer the reader to Philip Hooker's chapter on Presidents and to the complete list of Presidential Addresses.

[2] Chris Stray notes a deliberate allusion to Hilaire Belloc's's tract *The Servile State* (London, 1912).

power of corporate culture and the business ethos' (*The Principal Thing*, p. 7) were a main preoccupation of his Presidential of 2001, as he documented their malign influence on the approach of modern government to the public services in general and higher education in particular.

Wiseman went on to remark:

> Our subject has always been in crisis. J. W. Mackail's address to this Association's very first General Meeting ninety-seven years ago referred to the defensive anxiety of classicists at that time; a much more serious challenge came in the fifties and sixties of the last century, and the way it was overcome has resulted in our present state, which I think can be described as vigorous, confident, and without illusions.[3]
>
> (*The Principal Thing*, 8)

That historical assessment had been anticipated by more than one of his predecessors, including Bryn Rees, formerly Secretary to the Association's Council and then its Chairman, who developed the military metaphor in 'Strength in what remains' (1979, the year of the 75th anniversary):

> From the time of its foundation this Association, supported by its allies in the field, was continuously on the defensive, resisting attacks from all sides, consolidating its entrenched and embattled positions, extending its lines of communication by building up a network of branches, establishing new journals, holding regular conferences, maintaining and improving its contacts with schools, and engaging in many other activities which were essential to the survival of Classics in the face of popular prejudice and changing educational trends – and without which we would certainly not be here today. (*Proceedings* 1979, 10)

But *what* was the Association defending? Bryn Rees suggested that 'so much time and energy had to be devoted to ensuring that the message could be got across that there was little left for considering whether that message was still the right one for the times and for our needs in the long term' (ibid.). He called on the Association to be encouraging of new developments, 'not burying our heads in some remote corners like ostriches and pretending that this alone is scholarship, treating our precious discoveries as so much esoteric knowledge, "consciously designed *not* to be read outside the small circle of mandarins", as Moses Finley once wrote – and who better to act as a model for young scholars to copy?' (*Proceedings* 1979, pp. 20–1). Much of his Address reviewed and endorsed the changes he had seen and helped to

---

[3] Wiseman's sentence concludes (as does the quotation above from 'the gloomy Dean') with what one might call the Presidential tricolon: second nature to Classicists brought up on a diet of Ciceronian rhetoric, but a tricky trope to bring off successfully in contemporary English. There will be further examples.

foster in the course of his career: the teaching of classical civilisation, a broader view of ancient history, new ways of teaching the languages.

Rees was not, of course, the first President to raise the question of the identity of Classics. Lord Hailsham (1961), for example, had taken a firmly traditionalist view. 'There is no point', he argued, 'in keeping Greek and Latin studies alive at all unless it is intended to preserve them at a high level. Indeed I would claim that it is impossible to do so even if it were desirable. You cannot preserve the tradition in translation.' (*Proceedings* 1961, 14). Yet fifty years previously, long before the JACT Greek Course or degree programmes in Classical Studies were ever dreamed of, the thoughts of the Bishop of Lincoln were beginning to move along different lines:

Perhaps fewer of our schoolboys can write good Iambics, or steer safely at sight through a passage even of Lucian or Xenophon; possibly fewer boys are adepts in Homer or Euripides: but the excavation of ancient sites, the newly created science of archaeology, the fresh interest in Hellenic art, and above all, the vastly increased opportunities for travel, have combined to make us feel far more than before what the Greek meant by beauty of line and form, and what was the life of the old Greek peoples.

(Proceedings 1912, 75)

Family disagreements, internal debates within Classics about what we should be fighting for, are one of the constants of the history of the Presidential Address. Sir Frederic Kenyon (1914) thought the introduction of the reformed Latin pronunciation in the schools an especially significant triumph for the Association, with resistance – in Oxford, although not in Cambridge, Scotland or the newer Universities – resting 'either upon indolence or upon an irrational preference for the old mumpsimus' (*Proceedings* 1914, 51). The Prime Minister Stanley Baldwin (1926), on the other hand, confessed that he continued to 'pronounce Latin as it was taught to me fifty years ago':

I have lived for many years in a backwater, and the flood of culture has swept forward far away from me. I speak not as the man in the street even, but as a man in a field-path, a much simpler person, steeped in tradition and impervious to new ideas. To pronounce Latin as our Association has decreed may be to Professor Postgate the breaking of an adhesion; to me it is to convert it into a foreign language.[4]   *(Proceedings* 1926, 28)

---

[4] Baldwin had launched his Presidential with a studied exercise in the faux-naïf, teasing his audience with his homely political image. E.g.: 'The Classics will never perish out of the land so long as they are cherished by ordinary people. And so it seems to me good that you should have a President occasionally who is not a scholar, who is not particularly distinguished, but who can speak for the common folk as an ordinary man.' In case anyone was by now inclining to take him *au pied de la lettre*, he began his next paragraph: 'I wonder how many of you remember your Eginhard?' (*Proceedings* 1926, 27)

Sir Idris Bell gave his 1956 Address the title: 'A Specialist's *Apologia*' (though as we shall see his scope proved to extend far wider than that might suggest). But T. R. Glover had anticipated Moses Finley in thinking that Classics was getting too specialised: 'Too much of our Classical work is open to the reproach that we sacrifice ends to means, and that, in our colleges, forgetful of man and citizen, oblivious of life, we devote ourselves to training specialists, who restore texts and pursue minutiae, and forget to read the great literature' (*Proceedings* 1938, 17). Sir Frederic Kenyon spotted a different danger:

There is a certain tendency, as it seems to me, among some of our most interesting and stimulating leaders, to divert attention from the central products of the Greek genius to the fringes and background of the subject, and to dwell on just those parts of Greek thought which are least peculiar to the race and in which it is most akin to other peoples. Anthropology and mythology are great and mysterious goddesses, who have a fascination of their own, even if it be sometimes akin to the fascination of a nightmare; but I confess the Greek interests me least when he is nearest to the level of the blackfellow or the Hottentot.[5]   (*Proceedings* 1914, 66)

For David West in 1995 the enemy within was theory (Colin Haycraft (1994) hadn't had a good word for 'theory', either). Gilbert Murray would probably have seen an inevitability in operation here. 'An ancient work', he had said back in 1918, 'may, or indeed must, gather about itself new special environments and points of relevance', although he was insistent on the need to escape enslavement by theories and imprisonment in 'the mere Present' (*Proceedings* 1918, 79, 83).

II Autobiography and empire

The politician Lord Hailsham concluded his personal declaration of devotion to the Classics with the antiphon:

In the middle of the Suez crisis I found it the most comforting thing in the world to translate Catullus; the tedium of a railway journey I have often used to render an epigram from the Greek anthology.   (*Proceedings* 1961, 10)

Twenty years later Sir David Hunt rounded off his Presidential (1982) with this disclosure, designed to underline his stress on the importance in diplomacy – his own profession – of keeping one's word:

---

[5] Kenyon's dig was presumably aimed at the 'Cambridge ritualists', principally Gilbert Murray and Jane Harrison.

I think I have been influenced as much as anything by one aspect of the character of Julius Caesar. . . . I have frequently repeated to myself in the course of various problems in Africa and elsewhere the words of what appears to be the only surviving fragment of his speech *pro Bithynis*: 'neque clientes sine summa iniuria deseri possunt'.[6]

(*Proceedings* 1982, 19)

These are characteristic Presidential moments: when the great and the good confess the strength they have found in the Classics as they reflect on what it was like helping to conduct the affairs of a modern (post-)imperial state. 'My lifetime', said the international banker Sir Jeremy Morse a few years later still (1990), 'has coincided with a prolonged retreat by Britain from political and economic empire.' And in terms rather different from Hunt's he ended the autobiographical section of his Address with an apposite lesson he had drawn from Greek history (and with a witty tricolon):

Thucydides tells us how the Spartans, in trouble at Pylos, decided that they must abandon one of their fundamental principles (for ever enshrined in Simonides' epigram about Thermopylae), and let their people surrender rather than die fighting. Such, I thought when I first read it, are the hardest choices that may have to be faced in retreat. . . . I played a small part in the dismantling of the sterling era, and I have helped to conduct other lesser retreats, some tactical and temporary, some strategic and secular. In all of them one has often had to abandon minor baggage, occasionally major belongings, very occasionally principles. (*Proceedings* 1990, 9)

Something more private and sensuous and nostalgic was offered by the publisher Colin Haycraft, who told those assembled in Exeter in 1994:

I was lucky to spend my formative years before school on the Riviera, at the foot of the Ligurian Alps in Italy and France, at Alassio and Menton (Mentone), where my mother settled for a time after my father's death.[7] It is to this period of my childhood that I owe my love of the Classics.

My earliest memories are of Mediterranean vegetation (some of it of course post-classical) – mimosa, figs, artichokes, olives, vines, cypress trees, lemon groves, fields of narcissus – and the noon-day heat when

> The lizard, with his shadow on the stone
> Rests like a shadow, and the cicada sleeps.

---

[6] 'You can't abandon those who depend on you without terrible moral damage.'

[7] 'Since my father was a professional soldier, I was put down for a school with a strong military tradition, Wellington College in Berkshire. Sadly, my father was killed when I was two months old. My elder brother and I were therefore entered on the Foundation. We were technically 'Heroum Filii', the sons of heroes – what the school was for. A *herois filius*, one step down from *Divi Filius*, was educated free.' (*Proceedings* 1994, 20)

I quote from the first edition of *Oenone* (1833), before the poet was told that grass-hoppers tend to get livelier, not sleepier, the hotter it becomes, and changed the second line to

Rests like a shadow, and the winds are dead.

The lizard comes from Theocritus:

ἀνίκα δὴ καὶ σαῦρος ἐν αἱμασίαισι καθεύδει

'When even the lizard slumbers in the crannies of the wall.' (*Proceedings* 1994, 24)

After tangling with the editors of Theocritus, and following a learned passage on the Greek and Latin for 'artichoke', Haycraft continued:

I have often thought that people are drawn to the ancient languages either by an interest in solving puzzles, regarding them as a kind of algebra, in which the complicated grammar takes the place of mathematical symbols, or by a desire to evoke through beautiful language an old Mediterranean world. Both pleasures can be indulged, but for me the second has always predominated.

I am grateful to my mother for this early Mediterranean experience. As I never knew my father, she was my only living parent. According to Virgil, Aeneas carried Anchises on his shoulder through the flames of Troy so that he would have the benefit of his father's advice during his long voyage to Italy to found Rome. The modern *philosophe* J. P. Sartre boasted complacently that he did not 'carry Anchises on his back'. Nor sadly did I, but at least, like the younger Aristippus, I was μητροδίδακτος, mother-taught.[8] (Ibid., 26)

Sometimes Presidents have recalled the giants of their youth. Here are the Scottish – or perhaps more precisely Morningside – accents of D'Arcy Thompson in 1929:[9]

I can just remember that great scholar Veitch, who was a very old man when I was a boy in Edinburgh. In his early youth he had been frail of body and even threatened in mind. A wise physician bade him find a task which should give him occupation without solicitude, and above all should have no visible end, no prospect of completion. Veitch had a slender patrimony, enough to provide books and oatmeal; and he sat down, after much searching of heart for a congenial occupation, to study *aorists* throughout all the vast and endless literature of Greece. He grew hale and hearty and learned and old; after many years his *Greek Verbs, Irregular and Defective* made him famous in all the world of scholars. He climbed hills when he was as old as Nestor, told stories and fished the Tweed; and all his health and happiness and fame and wisdom came of reading Greek, and making a truce with Time, and following the advice of an astute physician. (*Proceedings* 1929, 19–20)

---

[8] This led on in due course to a mini-disquisition on mothers in antiquity, which culminated with the remark: 'Many of you no doubt have been racking your brains to think of the Greek for "political correctness"' (ibid., 28).

[9] He had been brought up by an aunt in Edinburgh from the age of 3.

A greater scholar still was the subject of the exordium of Sir Idris Bell's rather more earnest 1956 Address. He is describing a visit in 1930 to a post-imperial Berlin:

The high-light of the celebrations was a meeting in (if I remember rightly) the *aula* of the University, at which the numerous delegates presented the greetings and complimentary addresses which they had brought with them. There were many academic robes and hoods to be seen; the Papal nuncio was prominent in his purple; but apart from the unobtrusive uniform worn by the head of the Reichswehr, military pomp was missing, and the Chair was taken by the Kultusminister of a Social-Democratic government.

It was not, however, at the chairman or at any of the notables around him that I looked most often, but at a figure seated on the very edge of the platform, the figure of Ulrich von Wilamowitz-Moellendorf. He was now in his eighty-fourth year, and he had aged since I had seen him last, though he was still easily recognizable. His hair was quite white, his aristocratic features, always finely moulded, were thinner and more refined than ever, his form, spare even of old, seemed shrunken; and as he sat there, in a drooping and rather dejected posture, he looked strangely out of place in this new democratic Germany; an aristocrat to his finger-tips, he was like a wraith from the old Imperial days revisiting a world which had grown alien and uncongenial.

Yet the sight of him brought vividly back to me the memory of his lectures on the Age of Pericles to which, with hundreds of other students, I had listened spell-bound in the winter semester of 1901–2. I have always thought of him as the greatest orator I have ever heard, and I have never forgotten, indeed shall never forget while my memory of anything lasts, the eloquence which, when he spoke about the death of Pericles or the fall of Athens, reduced many of his audience to tears.

The time came for his address, and he rose, came to the front of the platform, and began to speak. His voice was at first so low that I had to lean forward and strain my utmost to hear what he was saying, but as he proceeded, it grew stronger; and soon, while he spoke to us of the charm of the Muses, the wonder and beauty of Classical studies and all the 'glory that was Greece', he held the breathless attention of everybody present. I saw before me once again the Wilamowitz-Moellendorf of twenty-nine years earlier.[10]

(*Proceedings* 1956, 11–12)

I end this section with an anti–imperial voice. The poet and play-wright Tony Harrison gave a riveting Presidential Address of marathon proportions in Bristol in 1988, and I quote an extended autobiograph-ical passage about 'problems with my Classics teachers':

It's easy to deny the colloquial roots of a dead language. The upshot of what seemed to me like a conspiracy was to pretend that the language had never been alive or spoken at all. I wish I could remember the piece of Latin that I was translating, but I think it was a piece of a Plautus play, and there was some official or other moving a group of people on in a crowded street. My translation went something like: 'Move along there!', true to

---

[10] This is one of the few occasions when a Presidential allows us a glimpse of a world of classical scholarship that extends beyond Britain. (Wilamowitz was in fact 82 at this point.)

constabulary vernacular. I do remember that this was crossed out with a heavy red pen and the alternative I was offered in the margin was: 'Vacate the thoroughfare!' I'm sure that such terrible things don't happen today even if the National Curriculum permitted the possibility of translating Plautus.

I gave expression in another poem which I'll read to you to some of the frustrations I had as a working class boy with a Leeds accent translating upper class English into Patrician Latin and vice versa. It's a poem called *Classics Society* (Leeds Grammar School 1552–1952). The grammar schools were founded in the belief that poor old English hadn't the benefit of being a dead language, and the poem begins with a quotation from 1552, the year of my school's foundation, from one who felt humbly cowed by the gracious eloquence of Ciceronian rhetoric:

Classics Society

(Leeds Grammar School 1552–1952)

The grace of Tullies eloquence doth excel
any Englishmens tongue . . . my barbarous stile . . .
The tongue our leaders use to cast their spell
was once denounced as 'rude', 'gross', 'base' and 'vile'.

How fortunate we are who've come so far!

We boys can take old Hansards and translate
The British Empire into SPQR
but nothing demotic or too up-to-date,
and not the English that I speak at home,
not Hansard standards, and if Antoninus
spoke like delinquent Latin back in Rome
he'd probably get gamma double minus.

So the lad who gets the alphas works
the hardest in his class at his translation
and finds good Ciceronian for Burke's
a dreadful schism in the British nation.

That dreadful schism still regrettably exists in the British nation, and an awareness of it has helped to make me the kind of poet I am and the kind of translator I have become when I approach the Classics. The tensions in that schism made me into the kind of poet who uses an immensely formal prosody against colloquial diction and against working class speech of Leeds and even the language of street aggro and graffiti, as in my much-reviled (and I'm glad to say much-championed!) poem 'v.', where the language of the Beeston graveyard ranges from Latin and Biblical to obscene graffiti and four-letter words. And the same tension between my background and my education, between my awareness of the inarticulate on the one hand, and being presented with the models of eloquence from the ancient world on the other, at a time of my maximum need to discover utterance, also made me into the kind of translator that I am.

My earliest experience among people I loved who felt hugely inadequate when it came to using language made me value the word above all, even though there seemed to be a 'retreat' from it under the Medusa-like gaze of the Fifth Age of mankind, and the pressure of other media. My feeling was then, and still is, although I have every poet's despair at times, that language could take on anything and everything, the worst things perhaps above all, and this lesson I learned at that impressionable period of my life in Greek tragedy. However galling it could be at the time, the fact is that I learned ancient Greek, and the sad thing about the new National Curriculum is that no one from my background especially, with my kind of hunger and appetite for language, will have the chance to make his own way to those founding models of European eloquence.[11]

(*Proceedings* 1988, 14–15)

III The body

'The Scholar's special duty', said Murray, 'is to turn the written signs in which old poetry or philosophy is now enshrined back into living thought or feeling' (*Proceedings* 1918, 82). Yet what has often got Presidents going is not mind or emotion but the body. At least as interesting as Dean Inge's views on democracy are his comments on the Greek ideal of the athletic body:

Even the older men took their gymnastic exercises, and kept their figures. Sixty, not fifty, was the age of exemption from military service. The flabby bodies of the barbarians were noticed with displeasure. This bodily perfection was perhaps helped by their habit of exposing the body to the air. The most perfectly formed men I have ever seen were two Zulus in Barnum's show, who danced on the stage almost naked. Sir Francis Galton told me that the English athletes whom he had seen unclothed were all imperfectly formed about the legs, and I have noticed the same in cricket changing rooms at Cambridge.

(*Proceedings* 1934, 13)

General Sir John Hackett's 'Reflections upon Epic Warfare' (1971) found him recalling, perhaps a bit more discreetly than his audience would have liked:

Those of us whose soldiering has spanned the middle of this century have moved from one age into another. In our own military upbringing the use of hand weapons was important. It is not so important now. I could myself be among the very last to have used a sword from a horse in mounted attack. That was in 1938 in Palestine but though there were casualties enough that day in killed and wounded my sword was in the event the cause of none. Its only victim suffered more from injured dignity than grievous bodily harm in an incident which was possibly not very creditable at the time and is certainly irrelevant now.

(*Proceedings* 1971, 25)

Lord Wolfenden's 'true story of the origins of the Trojan War' was whimsical rather than coy. The nub of the explanation was that Helen

---

[11] The National Curriculum was promulgated in the year Tony Harrison gave his Address.

was not (as usually supposed) a woman, but a horse with 'white "stockings" (as horse-folk call them) on her fore-legs':

You see how it all fits. Why should the whole might of Hellas be immobilised for ten mortal years hundreds of miles from home and wives and other comforts just for the sake of one worthless adulteress – as commonplace then as now? A serious threat to a country's trade is a very different story. Why does Achilles say, in his row with Agamemnon, 'It wasn't *my* horses the Trojans stole'? Why should Helen be labelled throughout the *Iliad* as λευκώλενος? What is distinctively odd about a Greek woman being white-armed?   (*Proceedings* 1980, 18)

The Roman body has been less in evidence. The best I can offer is something on farming. D'Arcy Thompson, the authority on ancient Greek birds and fish, was full of information about Virgil's subject matter in the *Georgics*. Here he is on the line *rursus in obliquum verso perrumpit aratro/terga*:

Surely no Latin could be simpler – but few are they who know its meaning. You will find it explained in a forgotten book on the *Husbandry of the Ancients*, by Mr Adam Dickson, who was Parish Minister of Whittinghame (Lord Balfour's parish) a hundred and fifty years ago. He farmed his own glebe, and knew as much about ploughing as any farmer in East Lothian; Virgil knew no more, and Mr Conington knew infinitely less. The minister understood both the old-fashioned plough and the modern one which was then superseding it; and he well knew that the two are totally different things. For the old wooden plough did little more than cut straight into the soil, while the other has its mouldboard, to lift the clod and cast or shear it to one side. With the little ancient plough it is something like cutting cheese, where it takes two cuts to remove a portion. You begin by ploughing with the plough held upright; then you come back *along the same furrow* holding it aslant (or *vice versa*). By so doing you shear and turn the clod, and obtain with double labour much the same result as ours. There is no easier line in Latin: *aratro in obliquum verso*, 'with your plough leaning over on the slant', you retrace the furrow and break up the clod.   (*Proceedings* 1929, 22–23)

I cannot resist the temptation – after all, Presidents never pass up the opportunity for a digression – to quote more of D'Arcy Thompson, although the themes of school and Mediterranean geography might have fitted better into the previous section. He went on as follows:

As Dyer[12] loved his *Martyn's Georgics*, so I also had a favourite lesson-book at school. It was a little Classical Geography, now long obsolete and forgotten, by James Pillans, Sellar's predecessor in the Edinburgh Chair of Humanity, and formerly Rector of the

---

[12] Sir William Thistelton-Dyer, 'the acknowledged head of English botany' and Director of Kew, who had died a few weeks before D'Arcy Thompson's Address was due to be delivered: 'As botanist and gardener his influence went out into all lands, to the benefit of mankind, from the garden where he had the happiness to dwell. And all the while he was a true scholar – a Hellenist, acute, fastidious and profound.' (*Proceedings* 1929, 20) A less flattering assessment of Thistelton-Dyer's scholarship is offered in J. E. Raven, *Plants and Plant Lore in Ancient Greece* (Oxford, 2000), 5–10.

High School (Walter Scott's school) in succession to Adam. I mean that famous Adam, that very great schoolmaster, whose beautiful face Raeburn has immortalised and whose dying words have escaped oblivion – 'Boys, it is growing dark; we have done enough for today.'

This geography of the classics, of the region to which our classical and Biblical training had accustomed us, was almost all the geography we ever learned at school. When Dr Johnson said that 'The great object of travel is to see the shores of the Mediterranean', he was thinking of the same romantic and half-imaginary world. (ibid, 23)

I return to the body, and end this section like the last with a long quotation from Tony Harrison, who brings an incomparable blend of knowledge and speculation to interpretation of the mask in the Greek tragic theatre:

I'd like us to think about masks for a while because I have the sense that when you scholars consider masks, if and when you do consider them, it only occurs to you as a rather embarrassing afterthought, and it's been my contention that masks are central to understanding the style and *language* of ancient drama. Although, as I have said, I am not of the opinion that masks are obligatory gear in modern productions, I have to maintain that we cannot understand the action or verbal style of Greek theatre without continually reminding ourselves that it was a theatre of masks. Perhaps you leave masks out of your dramatic considerations because you have never had the opportunity, as I have, of experimenting with masks and actors. Some of you may recall Jocelyn Herbert's beautiful masks for the NT *Oresteia*. They were the result of much experiment and workshops with actors which were to find out, as much as anything, what kind of language would be spoken by masks in this theatrical situation of 'obvious reciprocity' in a shared space and a shared light. . . .

The reason that Peter Hall and Jocelyn Herbert and I had to spend so much time in workshops on masks for our *Oresteia* was that there really is nowhere to turn for help. Even when some practical work has been done there exists a general stylistic confusion between Noh Drama and *commedia del arte* and the full Greek tragic mask. There is no help either in what little writing there is on masks. When Susan Harris Smith in her recent book *Masks in Modern Drama* (University of California Press, 1986) writes about masks, even though she has the NT Furies on the cover of her book, she gets it almost a hundred percent wrong when she writes:

The mask challenges the primacy of language that is undisputed in realistic and naturalistic drama.

This is absolutely the wrong way round, as the mask actually reinforces the primacy of language, at least in the theatre of ancient Greece. The mask reinforces that primacy by continuing to speak in situations that 'normally' or in realistic or naturalistic drama would render a person speechless. It is exactly the primacy of language that allows us to gaze in terror and not be turned to stone. Adrian Poole in another recent book, *Tragedy: Shakespeare and the Greek Example* (Basil Blackwell, 1987) gets it wrong in a related way when he writes that 'tragedy represents the critical moment at which words fail'. Words might fail you or me at such critical moments when we see the city burned to the ground, our children slaughtered, devastation and horror in all their worst forms, but words do not fail the mask. It is designed with an open mouth. To go on speaking even at 'critical moments'.

Let's juxtapose the naked human face that you and I have with a tragic mask and ask three questions to get a feel of the difference between life and theatre.

1. What does a human face do, what do we tend to do, when we're presented with real or very realistically filmed versions of blood, death, violence and terror? We tend to close our eyes in psychic self-preservation. The psychiatrist Anthony Clare wrote in *The Listener* not long ago that 'the portrayal of Ulster violence has only numbed viewers into anaesthetised silent voyeurs'. They've looked into terror and been turned to stone. The Medusa-like countenance of the Fifth Age has petrified them. Silent voyeurs!

2. What does the human face do, what do we do, when we gaze on such terrors? We become silent. We are speechless with anguish or grief. We have no words to describe them. 'There can be no poetry after Auschwitz', the familiar and utterly dispiriting adage of Adorno. *Das Wort ist tot.* The word is dead. For my new piece for the Delphi stadium in July 1988 I have been reading papyri and studying their fragments and I found one the other day which is an appeal to a Roman general to come and save the inhabitants of Egyptian Thebes from a barbarian tribe thought to be the Blemyres, of whom the pleader writes:

   οὐ μία τις βιότοιο γὰρ ἔμφασις, οὐ χορὸς αὐτοῖς,
   οὐχ Ἑλικὼν, οὐ Μοῦσα

   'For such people life has no emphasis, no significance. They have no dance, no Helicon, no Muse.' The mask, facing up to the Muses, refuses to surrender *emphasis*.

3. What does the head tend to do when it suffers or witnesses suffering?
   It tends to bow down.

And now we should imagine the Greek mask in the same three situations. If a mask gazes on the same horrors, the same terrors, it goes on gazing. It is created with open eyes. It *has* to keep on looking. It faces up to the Muses. What does a mask do when it suffers or witnesses suffering through these continually open eyes? Words never fail it. It goes on speaking. It's created with an open mouth. To go on speaking. It has faith in the word. The chorus in *Agamemnon* might say:

τὰ δ᾽ ἔνθεν οὔτ᾽ εἶδον οὔτ᾽ ἐννέπω

but what they *have* seen they will tell you about and in such spell-binding language that you have to listen. The open eyes and the open mouth of the mask come together very powerfully in the figure of Cassandra in the same play of Aeschylus. For almost three hundred lines of the *Agamemnon* she stands gazing silently into the terrors she has already witnessed in the destruction of Troy and gazing into the terror she sees in the future, her own bloody death and Agamemnon's. Her silence establishes the seeing, and the seeing prepares the way for her bursting into speech. The open-eyed silence is full of seeing. The mask creates that expectancy. If the human head bows down when it suffers, the mask keeps its head upright. It is created to stay upright. It's created to present itself. In this theatre of 'obvious reciprocity' the mask is created to see, to speak, and to present itself so it can be seen. Even Oedipus has to present his bloody sockets to be seen. When he enters blinded, the messenger intoduces him as a *theama*, something to be seen in the *theatron*. . . . Words have not failed the mask of Oedipus. The head stays unbowed for us to see the terrible sockets and also to register the carriage of survival.

(Proceedings 1988, 18–21)

IV Religio Grammatici

Murray's 1918 Address was entitled 'Religio Grammatici'. It took someone of Murray's genius to find the words, but they capture in their succinctness and simplicity something true of virtually all Presidentials. The Presidential Address is a form of religious literature. The religion is Classics. Its sacred texts and monuments are the texts and monuments of classical antiquity, the heroes and torch-bearers of its faith the teachers and scholars who have instructed and inspired their pupils over the years or discovered new ways of communicating the message to new audiences in changing times. The Address is at once a confession and a sermon, testifying to the speaker's own commitment and fortifying that of the Church Militant, by whatever medley of reminiscence, information, exhortation, congratulation, humour and rebuke the preacher judges or hopes will hit the spot.

When this volume was in its planning stage, the first idea was to have it consist entirely of Presidential Addresses – we thought perhaps about a dozen.[13] Second thoughts suggested that like any volume of sermons such a collection might well prove repetitious and indigestible, not least because nothing dates so fast as the transcript of an occasional talk (even if – a real 'if' – it hit the right note when originally delivered). In the end we decided on a parsimonious sample of three complete Presidentials, prefaced with an introduction presenting extracts from a wider range. The choice had in the end to be personal, although not one person's alone, and makes not the least claim to be representative (its unrepre-

---

[13] Jenny March made a selection of 21 Addresses delivered prior to the resumption of the practice of publication as self-standing pamphlets in 1995, and I have drawn almost exclusively on these in the extracts included in the present chapter. My thanks to her, as also to Philip Hooker and Philip Howard for general advice, and to Mary Beard and Chris Stray for encouraging comments on my draft. Mary Beard put some searching questions about what kind of history of twentieth-century Classics in Britain a study of the Presidential Addresses might or might not be able to sustain. In this final version I have picked up some of the issues she raised – although seldom very explicitly. Perhaps the snack served up here will tempt someone to prepare a proper meal.

sentativeness is so multi-dimensional as to need no further comment). One of the three pieces selected is by a practitioner of the subject, and communicates a vivid sense of what it was like teaching and fighting for Classics in 'our time', i.e. the second half of the twentieth century. Another offers the reflections of an Archbishop, one of the 'great and good' who have so often been elected to the Presidency of the Association, on the common ground shared by Classics and a Christianity which looks for no support from fundamentalist certainties. The third is pure reminiscence from a celebrated film critic who was never – as she laments – a classicist herself, but wrote two masterpieces, *Affair of the Heart* and *The Villa Ariadne*, about Greece and classical archaeologists between the wars.

We hope readers will find these Addresses as compelling as we do. I end this introduction, however, with an extract from what may be the most sustained and impassioned statement of the faith of a classicist ever delivered by a CA President. It is taken from a single paragraph near the end of the 76-year-old Idris Bell's Presidential, and begins at the point where he is concluding a sparkling survey of the very varied material available for study by his own specialist discipline, papyrology. Section I above noted the unstraightforwardness of the question: 'What *is* Classics?' Not everyone would define it as Bell does. For example, in his 1993 Address Fergus Millar suggested: 'Classics is the study of the culture, in the widest sense, of any population using Greek and Latin, from the beginning to (say) the Islamic invasions of the seventh century AD' (*Proceedings* 1993, 12). Bell for his part stakes his case without any hint of embarrassment on the 'canon'.

Here I interject a reminiscence of my own. When in 1999–2000 I was chairing a group of reluctant and initially suspicious classicists charged by the Quality Assurance Agency for Higher Education with drawing up a 'benchmark statement' for the teaching and assessment of the subject in universities, we fought shy initially of making any appeal to the notion of the canon in our own attempts at definition. After a bit, and prodded as I recall by Charles Martindale, we concluded that there was no way of making sense of why and how 'Classics' has the shape it does in our schools and universities without invoking that much-contested notion. And if you consult the document that finally emerged (on the QAA website at http://www.qaa.ac.uk/crntwork/benchmark/classics_textonly.html), you will find at 2.1.5 a full-blooded restatement of the idea, complete with reference to 'the finest examples of epic, drama and love poetry in world literature' and 'the perennial importance for philosophy' of the 'questions, methods and teachings' of the Greeks. Although no more full-blooded than this:[14]

Papyrology is an enrichment of our knowledge; it helps to make our acquaintance with the ancient world more precise in detail, to correct by concrete examples any touch of that vague idealization to which we are sometimes tempted; but it is no more than a branch of knowledge, like any other. It is not for the sake of such knowledge, it is indeed hardly for mere knowledge at all *as* knowledge, that we advocate Classical studies or regard their virtual disappearance from the educational curriculum of many people as a disaster to modern civilization. It is the glories of Classical literature and art which justify our claims. It is such things as Hector's farewell to Andromache when he goes out to meet Achilles and to die for his people; it is Priam and Achilles, reconciled at last, weeping together, the one for Hector slayer of men, the other for Patroclus, dead before his time; it is Nausicaa marvelling at the strength and beauty of Odysseus and asking him not to forget her when he is back in his own country, or the grim slaughter of the suitors at the end of the *Odyssey*, a scene not to be matched again till the Icelandic sagaman related the death of Burnt Njal. It is Sappho, singing with a restrained but quivering passion which was hardly to find a parallel in literature till, at the end of the eighteenth century, a Welsh Methodist girl of twenty-two wrote her little sheaf of immortal hymns, of Anactoria who 'shines out among the Lydian women, as, when the sun is gone down, the rosy-fingered moon outshines all the stars, and her light is shed alike on the salt seas and on the many-flowered acres, and the lovely dew is poured out and the roses bloom and the slender chervil and the flowery clover', or the temple with its 'lovely apple grove and altars smoking with frankincense', where 'cold water murmurs between apple boughs and all the place is shaded with roses, and through the quivering leaves sleep flows down', or declaring that, though some think that a host of horsemen and some of footmen and some of ships is the fairest sight on the black earth, to her the most beautiful is the thing she loves. It is Pindar hymning the golden lyre of Apollo, at whose music the eagle of Zeus sinks to sleep and Ares forgets the lust of battle, and the minds of gods are soothed, or, in the dithyramb we owe to a papyrus, the wild, ecstatic music of Dionysus, with its drums and castanets, which stirs into movement the thunderbolt breathing fire and the sword of Ares and sets the aegis of Pallas Athene hissing with a myriad snakes. It is Agamemnon, beguiled by his wife's flattery, going into his palace to be murdered by her and Aegisthus, and Cassandra seeing in her trance the shame of the blood-stained house of Atreus, and Antigone led to her death because she sets the eternal laws of heaven above any man-made ordinance, and Alcestis giving her own life to save her husband, and Pentheus, crazed by Dionysus, setting out, garlanded and holding his thyrsus, to meet his ghastly doom, and the inspired nonsense of Cloudcuckootown in the *Birds* of Aristophanes. It is Herodotus when, after conducting his readers round the whole of the known world, he begins to quicken the tempo and tighten the stress of his narrative as he goes on to relate the epoch-making struggles at Marathon, at

---

[14] Perhaps intoned with a Welsh lilt? Bell was Welsh on his mother's side, 'a determining factor in his life' (C. H. Roberts, in *Dictionary of National Biography 1961–70*, 91), and had spent his school holidays in Llanfairfechan. His translations from Welsh poetry exhibited 'a life-long devotion to poetry (especially for that in the tradition of Swinburne) joined with a no less deep and lasting enthusiasm for Welsh language and literature' (ibid., 92). Bell was admitted to the Gorsedd as a druid in 1949. The 'Welsh Methodist girl' was presumably Ann Griffiths (1776–1805).

Thermopylae, at Salamis and Plataea which saved Hellas and European civilization, and Thucydides narrating with a restrained objectivity more moving than pages of rhetoric the Athenian tragedy at Syracuse, and Xenophon telling how, at the news of Aegospotami, 'lamentation spread from the Piraeus through the Long Walls to the city, so that that night nobody slept; for they mourned not only for the fallen but yet much more for themselves; reflecting that they would suffer what they themselves had inflicted on the Melians . . . and the Histiaeans and the Scionians and the Toronaeans and Aeginetans and many others of the Greeks', and Socrates discussing the nature of love or trying in long discussion to define what justice is, in the individual and in the state. It is Catullus, 'tenderest of Roman poets nineteen hundred years ago', lamenting that suns indeed can die and return again but that for us, when our brief light is extinguished, nothing is left but one perpetual night of sleep, and Virgil, 'majestic in (his) sadness at the doubtful doom of human kind', perpetually enchanting us with unforgettable lines, from the idyllic loveliness of his early

> saepibus in nostris parvam te roscida mala
> (dux ego vester eram) vidi cum matre legentem

through the ripe art of the *Georgics*, with such splendid lines as '*fluminaque antiquos subterlabentia muros*', to the splendours of the *Aeneid*, and pictures like that of the vestibule of Hades or the

> locos laetos et amoena virecta
> fortunatorum nemorum sedesque beatos,

and the vignettes of Italian scenery in the seventh book of the *Aeneid* and the Cyclopes at their forge making the thunderbolt. It is the *curiosa felicitas* of Horace's odes and the mellow worldly wisdom of his epistles, and Lucretius beginning with his noble invocation of Venus the very poem in which he sets out to banish from men's minds the spectre of religion, yes, and Tacitus as, with a truly diabolical ingenuity, by suggestion and innuendo and indirect hints, he blackens the character of his *bête noire*, Tiberius. These and many other things like them are the imperishable glories of Classical literature; and at their side we must set the works of art which time and decay and the vicissitudes of history have left us, the sculptures of the Parthenon, the Hermes of Praxiteles, the great vase paintings, the terracottas, the coins, and such relics of Greek architecture as we still possess.   (*Proceedings* 1956, 22–24)

15

THINGS THAT MATTER

By CAROL HANDLEY

We all make mistakes. Two years ago, induced by the subtle and honeyed words of our secretary, Dr Malcolm Schofield, I made a serious mistake when I agreed to let my name go forward for consideration as President of this association and committed myself to giving an address today. Today I – and you – are paying the price of that mistake.

There were several reasons why I agreed. The first, and most obvious, is the tremendous honour of being invited to become President of the Classical Association for the year. The Association is, I think, a remarkable phenomenon, a splendid mix of professionals and amateurs in the Classics which has managed in the 93 years of its existence to adapt most successfully to the changing needs and interests of its members. It has always emphasised its dual nature by its policy of inviting a distinguished layman to be president one year followed by a professional academic in the next year. This year however the Council decided that they wished to recognise the school-teaching side of the profession and I feel doubly honoured to have been invited to represent all the workers at the chalk face who have done so much to keep the study of Classics alive by kindling the first spark of interest in their pupils.

A further reason is the fact that the meeting is being held here at Royal Holloway, a place that all those of us who were fortunate enough to know her will always associate with Norma Miller, who contributed so much to the Classics and who was President of this association in 1987. It is a place that is also close to my heart because I was a member of the Council here for nineteen years and watched it grow through a very difficult period during its three incarnations as Royal Holloway College, Royal Holloway and Bedford New College and now Royal Holloway London. In particular, I think Norma would be delighted to see the way in which the Classics Department flourishes today, whether its members are teaching elementary Greek in Englefield Green or excavating Greek cities on the Black Sea coast (Phanagoria) or looking after the Classical

Association with such kind attention. Finally, it was irresistibly tempting to follow once again in my husband's footsteps. He was President of the Classical Association in 1985.

All of us here are deeply concerned about the future of Classics teaching in this country. And though a meeting such as the present one with its wealth of speakers on such a diversity of topics is evidence of the strength of classical scholarship in this country at the present time, the immediate future presents a much more disturbing prospect. We must all be aware that the base of the pyramid is growing dangerously small in schools (the numbers taking AL Latin have shrunk by half from 3117 in 1975 to 1625 in 1996 while the numbers taking AL Greek have shrunk correspondingly from 583 in 1975 to 283 in 1996). The universities have adapted and are adapting their courses successfully and imaginatively to accommodate late starters, but, if Latin teaching becomes too rare in schools, how many pupils will ever discover that they would like to learn about any aspect of the classical world at university? Would this matter? I believe it would matter most seriously. And I hope that you will allow me to reflect a little further on this theme in the light of my own personal experience. I hope very much that I can draw some useful lessons from the recent past, or at least provide a little comfort for those at present in the forefront of the battle, through the realisation that the Classics have appeared to be in crisis before, but have survived, reshaped, and sometimes better equipped to face the future.

The Classical Association was founded in 1903 to combat the then perceived decline in Classical Teaching. In 1954 it celebrated its half century with a Presidential Address (his second) from Professor Gilbert Murray entitled 'Are our Pearls Real?' (His first had been in 1918 entitled 'Religio Grammatici'). With eloquent charm he proved that our pearls are indeed real, and with exquisite courtesy he refrained from considering the nature of the swine. I was there, a young teacher attending my first Classical Association meeting. It was a most moving occasion. We were all aware that we were embarking on a new era, when education and society itself were changing fast. We were listening to a man who had done perhaps more than anyone else to bring Greek poetry to a wider audience through his translations of Greek plays, and his passionate belief in the need to be 'working not so much to make new discoveries in obscure places, as to keep the great things really alive'. He clearly feared that all his work for Classics, like his work for the League of Nations, might prove to be in vain, that the barbarians might really be coming. Yet he retained his belief and his faith in both

Classics and international relations as a bulwark against barbarism. Opinions of course differ sharply now about the merit of his translations and even of his scholarship. When I first read his *Antigone*, at the age of sixteen, I was bowled over, and I read all the others I could find in the school library. His translations persuaded me that it was Classics, and not English that I wanted to read at university. Not everyone likes the rich Swinburnian style then or now. Sir Maurice Bowra unkindly pointed out that the translation of the line (or gasp) ἒ ἒ, ἆ ἆ as 'Death and a cold, white thing within the house'[1] was perhaps a little excessive. Nevertheless, despite changing tastes, Murray's translations still live on, and still charm us with 'the apple trees the singing and the gold'. It may not be *your* idea of Euripides, or *your* idea of poetry, but it still has power to move. In every age Classical literature needs its inspired translators if it is to continue to sustain and appeal to a wider audience than professional linguists. Fortunately there is no lack of them today – but more of that later.

It is perhaps hardly surprising that I ended up as a teacher of classics. Both my parents were. My father got there by the conventional route of scholarships to Westminster and to Christ Church, where his career on the cricket field was more distinguished than his academic career – he was opening bat for the university and the first freshman ever to score a century in the varsity match, while his tutor said to him 'your essays, my dear boy are always so good and clear, but then you know so very little'. I got the strong impression, that while he was a very able classicist, none of his teachers at school or at university had inspired him with any strong enthusiasm for what he was doing. He enjoyed much of Latin and Greek literature, but his real passion was for English Literature and for music. My mother was at the University of Glasgow. English was her main interest, backed up by Latin and a little Greek. Not many wives of professional men did jobs in the thirties, but she always managed to find some teaching to do, and continued to do so until the end of her life.

So I was brought up in an environment where it seemed perfectly natural to learn Latin, and perhaps Greek also, and to think in terms of aiming for university. I began Latin in the most traditional way at the age of ten at the prep school to Gordonstoun, but I had no chance to learn Greek until I went to St Paul's Girls' School at the age of sixteen. Thus, like so many today, I had to learn my Greek in a hurry and have never been as secure in basic Greek grammar as in Latin. I was, however,

---

[1] Quoted by Duncan Wilson in *Gilbert Murray OM 1866–1957* (Oxford, 1987), 198.

supremely lucky to be taught by the High Mistress, Miss Strudwick, all on my own because I was the only person taking Greek that year. She was a superlative scholar, who loved all the nuances and subtleties of language. Prose Composition with her was inspiring. And it was she who supported me against the rest of the Classics staff when I said that I did not wish to go to Oxford. Miss Strudwick recommended University College London, and she was so right. I found once again some remarkable teachers, notably Professor T. B. L. Webster (President in 1961) who had just arrived from Manchester. The London syllabus at that time allowed one to read pretty much what one liked, and so I did just that. It was hardly a balanced introduction to Greek and Latin Literature, but I had a marvellous time and was offered the opportunity to go on to do research on Greek Tragedy. In the event, I decided to go straight into schoolteaching, and I think I was right to do so. Researchers need a burning desire to find things out and track things down, and a formidable persistence in reading books about books. I lack these qualities. The thing that I find exciting and endlessly rewarding is to rediscover a piece of literature with someone who has not encountered it before and to share its impact with them.

Once again, I was fortunate to start on my teaching career in the fifties. There was a tremendous sense of excitement. More and more pupils were staying on into the sixth form so more subjects could be added to the curriculum; new schools were being built, new courses planned. By the sixties the Robbins expansion of the universities brought new opportunities and new ideas. Money was not a problem. Today that seems a golden age indeed, as resources are reduced year by year so that the state schools struggle and the universities have to spend more and more of their time in fund-raising. No economist has yet explained to me why there was so much money to spend on education then and so little now. Is it is just a change of fashion or is it a loss of faith in the value of education? Why did politicians then believe that the road to economic success lay through giving everyone free access to all levels of education, whereas now, worldwide, they worship at the shrine of market forces and reduced public expenditure? At all events, I am glad that I lived through that brief time of hope, for it is hard to be optimistic today.

But even in the sixties amid all the expansion there were grave anxieties for classicists. The movement towards comprehensive schools, mixed-ability teaching and 'relevant subjects' seriously threatened the position of Latin and Greek in state schools. Even some independent schools felt that it would do wonders for their image if they were seen to throw out Latin and introduce Russian or Business Studies. At this point the Nuffield Foundation came to the rescue. They had already been responsible for revolutionising science and Maths teaching with the highly prestigious Nuffield Science and Nuffield Maths Courses. Now they proposed Nuffield Latin. I remember going to a meeting in what was then Nuffield Lodge, one of the Regent's Park Villas, where some of the plans were discussed. I came away immensely excited. At a stroke the image of Latin as an outdated, elitist and useless subject was being transformed into a modern forward-looking, even experimental one. Soon afterwards, Camden School was asked to be one of the test schools for what later became the Cambridge Latin Course. Of course many traditionalists criticised it for not providing the solid basis of grammatical knowledge that came from Ritchie or Hillard and Botting. It was based on a different theory of language learning. Instead of parrot-learning of accidence, verbal drills and endless practice with short sentences, it assumed that pupils would acquire the patterns of language by reading and manipulation exercises. In practice this proved to be rather over-optimistic and many teachers reverted to more traditional methods of teaching grammar. But the text for reading was set in a genuine cultural context which interested even the most linguistically challenged.

Those of us who taught it and observed the keenness of our pupils and the amazed reaction of parents to their childrens' enthusiasm had no doubts. It was suitable for any kind of school and for less able pupils as well. Parents and children wept all over North London when at the end of Unit 1 Vesuvius erupted and killed the family they had got to know. And today, with hindsight, I have still no doubt that without this brilliantly innovative course book, whatever its faults, there would be far less Latin available in schools than there is now.

Thus Latin had won a reprieve and continued as a popular subject in schools against the gloomy predictions of many, even when it had ceased to be a requirement for Oxbridge entrance. But what of Greek? The JACT Council set up a committee of which I was a member, to look into this, under the chairmanship of Malcolm Willcock. Our first thought was naturally to try to raise funds to set up a Greek Project akin to the Cambridge Latin Project, and we invited a professional fund raiser to come and advise us. A very smooth gentleman assured us that we should be wasting our time unless we could secure a very large donation to start the fund off. This was bad news. Various members of the committee had various contacts which they thought they could pursue, but it was clear that nothing very much could happen immediately, and in the meantime the situation about Greek was critical. So we decided to set up a summer school, where people could study Greek intensively for two weeks to give them a flying start for Greek in the sixth form or even for university Greek.

Bedford College Classics Department lent us their rooms in their Regent's Park home, David Raeburn acted as Director and Maurice Balme as Director of Studies and some thirty students came. Next year Christopher Turner provided residential accommodation at Dean Close School at Cheltenham and many more came. Thus was born the JACT Greek Summer School and later its related summer schools (including the Classical Association's Summer Workshop now at Lampeter). These summer schools have done so much to endorse the enthusiasm of students of Classics and make the continued study of Greek possible in this country. Anyone who has taught on one of these summer schools knows what an exhilarating experience it is, to find so many young (and not so young) people thrilled by the experience of learning Greek (or Latin or Classical Civilization). Nowadays the six summer schools cater for nearly 700 students between them each year, and there is no doubt that their existence has made it easier for universities to accept entrants with little or no knowledge of Greek or Latin.

But in 1967 a new course was still needed and still we had no major donor. Eventually we decided to set up an appeal and see what happened. What happened was proof of the value that astonishing numbers of ordinary people placed upon the classics that they had learned at school or university. Small donations poured in accompanied frequently by touching letters. The amount subscribed by small donors eventually attracted the larger donors. We had done it – or Greek had done it – in the way which was said to be impossible. So, in the early seventies the JACT Greek Project was set up, with Peter Jones as its Director and in 1978, after severe testing in schools and at successive Greek summer schools, *Reading Greek* was published by C.U.P. It was deliberately aimed at older school students, undergraduates and adult learners and it has entirely fulfilled its aims and it is used all over the world. At the same time universities were rethinking their courses and Classical Studies courses were being developed at all levels from primary school to university. By the end of the seventies it seemed that much had been achieved and that Classics in all its varied forms was no longer regarded as a badge of outmoded Victorian elitism, but as a worthwhile and even exciting option.

Then came the eighties with relentless cuts in resources for schools and universities which were dependent on the state for their funding. In the early seventies at Camden School (as a reasonably well-funded grammar school) we were able to offer pupils the chance to learn French and Latin and to add either Greek, German, Spanish or Russian, if they wished. By the end of the eighties (when as a comprehensive school it had to cater for a far wider range of intellectual needs with ever more limited funds) that choice had been reduced by necessity (and Government action) to French, some Latin, and Greek only in the dinner hour. By 1985 it was clear to me that something like this must happen, and I was glad to secure early retirement. I was fortunate to be able to escape. Colleagues tougher or less fortunate than I have stayed and fought and improvised and preserved some Classics teaching, even in the maintained schools, and we owe them an incalculable debt. But how long can they keep up the struggle? Even in some of the former strongholds of Classics in the independent schools classicists are facing formidable pressures. People say that you cannot solve a problem by throwing money at it. I'm not sure about that. Money can often help. But the converse is certainly true and there is no doubt at all that you can create a major problem any day by cutting the money off.

So where are we now in the nineties, and where shall we be in the next millennium? The imposition of the National Curriculum on state schools together with the squeeze on their resources has made it very difficult for them to continue to offer 'minority subjects'. Even the Dearing amendments have provided little relief, for even if there is *time* to teach more languages, there is no *money* to pay the teachers. On the plus side, children in primary schools now learn about the Greeks at Key Stage 2 and want to learn more. There is no longer the hostility, born of inverted snobbery, that there once was to the study of Classics, and many parents are eager for their children to have the opportunity to do so.

And one thing is indisputable: the boundless enthusiasm of our pupils, whatever their age, for Classics. After one summer school a student wrote me a thank-you letter. In it he said 'The course proved to me just how 'alive' Classics still is, and in my opinion embodies the 'spirit' and enthusiasm for Classics which I've never known exist for any other subject'. It is quite a tribute, and he is not alone. In the twelve years since I left Camden School, I have encountered students of Greek of all ages, school and university students who come to the JACT Greek summer school, adults in retirement or mid-career who come to learn Greek at weekend courses at Madingley Hall, Cambridge undergraduates starting out on a Classics degree and Cambridge dons, experts in a wide range of subjects who simply want to learn Greek. The variety of people attracted to learn Greek is endless, their enthusiasm is the same. This year the Open University is offering a Greek Language module. They thought that, with luck a hundred people might be interested. In fact five hundred applied. The same is true of Latin, as the massive response to Q. E. D., Peter Jones' Instant Latin Course, has proved. So what is it that fuels this desire to learn a 'dead' language? And does it have real value for the individual? Perhaps before we try to answer this, we could go even further 'back to basics' and ask ourselves about the nature and purpose of education, why do we enjoy the process of learning, what do we get out of it, or hope to achieve?

I once heard Sir Peter Newsam say (when he was Education Officer in Inner London), that education is about filling pots or kindling flames. A certain amount of pot-filling is essential. Certain facts have to be transmitted and explained by the teacher if the student is to be able to function at all. It can be a satisfying process for both parties if all goes well. It is satisfying for the teacher to feel that information has been clearly imparted and that the student has grasped it and digested it. It is satisfying for the student to feel that he/she is now equipped with new information which is understood, and the result will be increased confidence in gaining and handling new information and an increased appetite for learning. If, however, things do not go well, the results can be most unhappy. If the teacher expects too much, or does not present the material clearly, or fails to see where the student is at a loss, the student will become increasingly confused and eventually lose all confidence in his/her ability to cope, and, in all probability, will switch off and either sink into an apathetic trance or turn to active disruption. This, I suspect is what happens to many students at some stage in Maths lessons when the gradient is too steep, and I know that it is what used frequently to happen to them in the traditional kind of Latin teaching. It is for this reason that I am deeply suspicious of so much talk about *stretching* and *rigour*. The ablest put plenty of pressure on themselves, and too much external pressure can undermine their confidence disastrously. The less able will simply become alienated, confirmed in their view that there is nothing in this for them. Teachers should open the door to a new world, but should not try to kick their pupils through it.

But pot-filling, however essential, and however skilfully performed can never be enough. Kindling a flame is what really counts. A flame that is a light in the darkness and brings new illumination to the mind. It is not easy to talk about this without sounding embarrassingly evangelical, but I am sure that we can all think of some passage of literature, a piece of music or a picture which has been an illumination for us personally, which seems to have widened our understanding and allowed us an insight into things we had only glimpsed before. One of the most important functions of a teacher is to try to arrange for his/her students to encounter such moments and to create an atmosphere in which they can be experienced. Teachers of Classics are fortunate, for so much of what they read with their pupils deals with the great issues of life and death and deals with them in words which have power, even in translation, to captivate the mind and stir the soul. The fact that this same literature has influenced the artists, writers and musicians of the western world is of course an important and added bonus, as is the fact that we are dealing with literature in the context of its culture, of the history, philosophy and art of its time. Given all this, it is not surprising that so many young people are drawn strongly to the study of various aspects of the Classical World, if only they can discover in the course of their schooling that it exists.

And then, of course, there is the burning question of 'learning to tell right from wrong'. This is not quite such a simple matter as politicians appear to think. Society is still struggling to make its mind up about some major issues of morality, such as abortion and euthanasia, quite apart from lesser issues such as the degree of sleaze which is acceptable in public life. But even if we can decide what is right we are still left with the problem that Phaedra posed: 'We know what is right and recognise it, but we do not do it'. There are few children who do not know right from wrong in simple issues. They know they should not bully other children, or steal or tell lies, but some children get a kick out of doing all these things. One of the best ways that children can learn how to judge the consequences of their actions and how to choose to behave is to listen to stories and discuss them. Once again we have a rich source of material in Classics. For younger children mythology, and stories from Homer will provoke plenty of thought and discussion, as well as feeding the imagination. For older ones there is tragedy, history and philosophy, all full of questions to which we still seek the answers, and ideas which underlie our culture.

From our education, then, we seek three things in particular – information, understanding and insight. Information about the world around us, understanding of how the ideas of the past have shaped our present and may shape our future, and insight into what it is all about. The study of Classics provides illumination on all three, and without it much of our inheritance is lost.

It is not easy to convince those in Government or those in charge of administrative decisions in the education world that teaching Classics is still immensely valuable in our schools today. That must be our task – unremittingly – for the millennium. Even if we are to be judged by the most utilitarian standards we have the testament of several of our former Presidents, including our last year's President Sir Anthony Cleaver, that the study of Classics can be a useful foundation for a distinguished career in the business world. But it has a much more valuable function even than that. We must also continue, as Gilbert Murray said, 'to strive to keep the great things really alive', and, much more difficult, strive to convince the unconvinced that we *do* have access to 'the great things' and that we *can* share them with many others.

And how can we share them? In translation, or in the original? A stupid question. It must be both. Not everyone has the time or inclination to learn a difficult language, whatever the promised reward. But in every generation there must be some who can learn the language well enough to translate the original anew into the idiom of the time, or else the freshness will be lost and the immediacy may not be perceived.

> For last year's words belong to last year's language
> And next year's words become another voice.[2]

Good translation, like good criticism, can legitimately be regarded as a creative art, if only a minor one, and many poets have exercised it. Of course something is lost, but sometimes something is added too. Something of the original writer is lost but something of the translator is added, a new element which may highlight a particular theme or characteristic of the original, as a portrait photographer uses the fall of light to enhance some particular feature. Think of Tony Harrison's translation of the *Oresteia*. The Anglo-Saxon monosyllables are far from the polysyllabic compounds of Aeschylus, but they produce a similarly striking effect and suggest a particular style which reflects an archaic diction. And it is wonderful to listen to! Certainly the astonishing number of productions of Greek tragedy in London in recent years suggests that translation does not prevent a very high degree of appreciation of great plays.

But even the greatest translations need replacing, though we may still

---

[2] T. S. Eliot, 'Little Gidding', from *Four Quartets*, (London, 1944).

go back to them for interest or for comparison. I notice that today it has become fashionable to refer people to Pope's translations of Homer. In the *Oxford Book of Classical Verse in Translation* Chapman is several times set next to Robert Fitzgerald. I am not sure I would choose either, but they certainly illustrate the force of fashion as it affects translation. Of course translation is never easy, as we all know, even the simplest phrases can cause awful problems, particularly if one is trying to use everyday language and not to archaize. Let us look at one example:

In *Odyssey* IX the blinded Cyclops sits outside his cave feeling the backs of his sheep as they come out of the cave, but failing to discover that Odysseus' men are tied beneath them. Last of all comes the great ram, bearing Odysseus 'with his teeming brain'. The tension is prolonged while the Cyclops speaks to his ram, wondering why he is not at the head of the flock as usual. It is the one moment of pathos when we feel a touch of sympathy for Polyphemus, but it ends with bitter irony when he suggests that the ram is last, in sympathy for his master's blinding, when in fact we know the ram is last because he is bearing the perpetrator to freedom. All sympathy is finally banished when the Cyclops longs for his ram to speak so that he can tell him where Odysseus is hiding, so that he can smash him to pieces.

In Homer the Cyclops speaks to his ram as κριὲ πέπον. No problem, you think, to translate, but it is perhaps not so easy to get it right in the context. Let us see what five translators in this century have done with it.

Richmond Lattimore in 1965	'My dear old ram . . .' (too much the clubman?)
Robert Fitzgerald in 1961	'Sweet cousin ram . . .' (shades of Shakespeare?)
T. E. Lawrence in 1932	'Beloved ram . . .' (O. K., I suppose)
Walter Shewring in 1980	'You that I love best . . .' (Why this far from the Greek?)
E. V. Rieu in 1946	'Sweet ram . . .' (O. K., but is this Polyphemus?)

Is this really how you talk to a sheep, even in Homer? I think I would prefer 'Ram, my beauty . . .', less poetic, but more practical. But everyone, fortunately, will have their own view of what is appropriate.

Translations, of a sort, can surface in strange places. Classic FM have a mid-morning feature called *Henry's High Flyer* which gives tips for the afternoon's racing. When Spring and the Newmarket Stakes came round again 'Henry' was moved to quote:

Eheu fugaces, Postume, Postume,
Where have the years gone,
Lost to me, lost to me?

And as an illustration of the effect of the choice of language on the reader, how about George Orwell's translation into institutionalese of a passage of Ecclesiastes taken from the King James' Bible ?

I returned and saw under the sun, that the race is not to the swift, nor the battle to the strong, neither yet bread to the wise, nor yet riches to men of understanding, nor yet favour to men of skill; but time and chance happeneth to them all.

Objective consideration of contemporary phenomena compels the conclusion that success or failure in competitive activities exhibits no tendency to be commensurate with innate capacity, but that a considerable element of the unpredictable must invariably be taken into account.[3]

Then there are some translations which have been accepted as poems in their own right, like Cory's translation of Callimachus, 'They told me Heraclitus, they told me you were dead', or Shelley's translation of Plato *Anthologia Palatina*, vii. 670:

ἀστὴρ πρὶν μὲν ἔλαμπες ἐνὶ ζωοῖσιν ἑῷος,
νῦν δὲ θανὼν λάμπεις ἕσπερος ἐν φθιμένοις

Thou wert the morning star among the living
Ere thy fair light had fled.
Now, having died, thou art as Hesperus, giving
New splendour to the dead.

Nearly as successful as the Shelley, though in quite a different mood, is R. C. Trevelyan's translation of the poem in which the great courtesan Lais dedicates her mirror to Aphrodite:

ἡ σοβαρὸν γελάσασα καθ' Ἑλλάδος, ἡ τὸν ἐραστῶν
ἑσμὸν ἐπὶ προθύροις Λαΐς ἔχουσα νέων
τῇ Παφίῃ τὸ κάτοπτρον· ἐπεὶ τοίη μὲν ὁρᾶσθαι
οὐκ ἐθέλω, οἵη δ' ἦν πάρος οὐ δύναμαι.

I, that Lais, who over Hellas flung her triumphant laughter forth,
Who held that swarm of youthful lovers ever round her doors,
Here to the Paphian dedicate my mirror, since on what I am
I will not look, and cannot upon that which once I was.[4]

And, last of all, three very different translations of Catullus 51 *ad Lesbiam* (itself a translation of Sappho).[5] I am indebted to the authors of

[3] Quoted by Stephen Pinker in *The Language Instinct* (Harmondsworth, 1994).
[4] From R. C. Trevelyan, *Translations from Greek Poetry* (London, 1950).
[5] For the Sappho and Catullus texts and all three translations, see pp. 223–5.

The Oxford Book of Classical Verse in Translation[6] for the first two. The first is by George Gordon, Lord Byron, written in 1806. The next was published in 1861 by William Ewart Gladstone. And finally a translation by which appeared in the September 1996 issue of *Omnibus*. It is by Matthew McClelland, a pupil at Repton School. I do not think that any of these three English translations is a great poem in its own right. They are interesting because they are translations, because we have the original, and because they so strongly reflect the period in which they were written. It is noteworthy that only the virtuous Gladstone translates Catullus' addendum to Sappho. It seems to suit the sombre Victorian sense of responsibility, where it would spoil the Byronic froth or the twentieth century egocentricity. The poems also remind us how carefully we must choose our translations if we are not to give a completely false impression to those who cannot read the original.

Let me read you Byron's version:

> Equal to Jove, that youth must be,
> Greater than Jove, he seems to me,
> Who, free from Jealousy's alarms,
> Securely, views thy matchless charms;
> That cheek, which ever dimpling glows,
> That mouth, from which such music flows,
> To him, alike, are always known,
> Reserved for him, and him alone.
> Ah! Lesbia! though 'tis death to me,
> I cannot choose but look on thee;
> But, at the sight, my senses fly,
> I needs must gaze, but gazing die;
> Whilst trembling with a thousand fears,
> Parch'd to the throat, my tongue adheres,
> My pulse beats quick, my breath heaves short,
> My limbs deny their slight support;
> Cold dews my pallid face o'erspread,
> With deadly langour droops my head,
> My ears with tingling echoes ring,
> And life itself is on the wing;
> My eyes refuse the cheering light,
> Their orbs are veiled in starless night;
> Such pangs my nature sinks beneath,
> And feels a temporary death.

But you can say it more briefly than that:

[6] *The Oxford Book of Classical Verse in Translation*, ed. Adrian Poole and Jeremy Maule (Oxford, 1995).

```
man
nearing you
hearing you
seeing you
equal god
above god
Oh god
thing that
freezes that
numbs that
burns that
rings that
blinds that's
love.
```

Two words in every line except the first and last. Three lines end with 'you', three with 'god', six with 'that', and one with 'that's'. The first and last line are monosyllabic and the only capital letter comes in the ambiguous transition 'Oh god . . .' Love it or loathe it, it is totally assured and brilliantly competent.

While our schools are producing talent like this there *will* be translators for the future who will continue to open the door for those who have no time or no opportunity to read Greek and Latin literature for themselves. We must, however ensure that in every generation it is still possible for at least a few to learn Latin and Greek well so that they can keep alive for everyone the things that matter, and without which the world will be the poorer. The only way to do this is to keep thinking about how we teach and what we teach. The past fifty years have shown how successfully we have adapted our courses and our methods to changing circumstances. As long as we can continue to do this and as long as we can continue to persuade the powers that be that there is value in the study of Classics for the individual and so ultimately for society, then

> . . . all shall be well and
> all manner of thing shall be well[7]

and we shall have discharged our responsibilities to the past as well as to the future.

---

[7] T. S. Eliot, 'Little Gidding' from *Four Quartets* (London, 1944), quoting Dame Julian of Norwich.

Sappho 199 LGS / 31L-P

Φαίνεταί μοι κῆνος ἴσος θέοισιν
ἔμμεν᾿ ὤνηρ, ὄττις ἐνάντιός τοι
ἰσδάνει καὶ πλάσιον ἆδυ φωνεί-
σας ὐπακούει

καὶ γελαίσας ἰμέροεν, τό μ᾿ ἦ μὰν
καρδίαν ἐν στήθεσιν ἐπτόαισεν,
ὠς γὰρ ἔς σ᾿ ἴδω βρόχε᾿ ὤς με φώναισ᾿
οὐδ᾿ ἔν ἔτ᾿ εἴκει,

ἀλλ᾿ ἄκαν μὲν γλῶσσα πέπαγε λέπτον δ᾿
αὔτικα χρῷ πῦρ ὐπαδεδρόμηκεν,
ὀππάτεσσι δ᾿ οὐδ᾿ ἔν ὄρημμ᾿ ἐπιρρόμ-
βεισι δ᾿ ἄκουαι,

κὰδ δέ μ᾿ ἴδρως κακχέεται, τρόμος δὲ
παῖσαν ἄγρει, χλωροτέρα δὲ ποίας
ἔμμι, τεθνάκην δ᾿ ὀλίγω 'πιδεύης
φαίνομ᾿ ἔμ᾿ αὔται·

ἀλλὰ πὰν τόλματον ἐπεὶ καὶ πένητα

Catullus 51

Ille mi par esse deo videtur,
ille, si fas est, superare divos,
qui sedens adversus identidem te
    spectat et audit

dulce ridentem, misero quod omnis
eripit sensus mihi: nam simul te,
Lesbia, aspexi, nihil est super mi
    vocis in ore.

lingua sed torpet, tenuis sub artus
flamma demanat, sonitu suopte
tintinnant aures, gemina teguntur
    lumina nocte.

otium, Catulle, tibi molestum est:
otio exsultas nimiumque gestis:
otium et reges prius et beatas
    perdidit urbes.

Translation from Catullus: Ad Lesbiam

Equal to Jove, that youth must be,
Greater than Jove, he seems to me,
Who, free from Jealousy's alarms,
Securely, views thy matchless charms;
That cheek, which ever dimpling glows,
That mouth, from which such music flows,
To him, alike, are always known,
Reserved for him, and him alone.
Ah! Lesbia! though 'tis death to me,
I cannot choose but look on thee;
But, at the sight, my senses fly,
I needs must gaze, but gazing die;
Whilst trembling with a thousand fears,
Parch'd to the throat, my tongue adheres,
My pulse beats quick, my breath heaves short,
My limbs deny their slight support;
Cold dews my pallid face o'erspread,
With deadly langour droops my head,
My ears with tingling echoes ring,
And life itself is on the wing;
My eyes refuse the cheering light,
Their orbs are veiled in starless night;
Such pangs my nature sinks beneath,
And feels a temporary death.

George Gordon, Lord Byron 1806

Catullus to Lesbia

Him rival to the gods I place,
    Him loftier yet, if loftier be,
Who, Lesbia, sits before thy face,
    Who listens and who looks on thee;

Thee smiling soft. Yet this delight
    Doth all my sense consign to death;
For when thou dawnest on my sight,
    Ah wretched! flits my labouring breath.

My tongue is palsied. Subtly hid
    Fire creeps me through from limb to limb:
My loud ears tingle all unbid:
    Twin clouds of night mine eyes bedim.

Ease is my plague: ease makes thee void,
    Catullus, with these vacant hours,
And wanton: ease that hath destroyed
    Great kings, and states with all their powers.

W. E. Gladstone 1861

Catullus 51

man
nearing you
hearing you
seeing you
equal god
above god
Oh god
thing that
freezes that
numbs that
burns that
rings that
blinds that's
love.

Matthew McClelland
Omnibus 32
September 1996

16

STILL YEARNS MY HEART

By ROBERT RUNCIE

> The awful intelligence of your election has just reached me . . . I have not
> heart to say more than that I adjure you by your reverence for your great
> predecessor, your sense of the sacredness of your office... .to lay aside every
> thought for the present except that of repairing your deficiencies . . . my
> main fears are for your sermons being dull, and your Latin prose – and
> compositions generally – rather weak.

These are not my tutors at this university on my appointment as your
President in succession to such a distinguished scholar as Professor
Kerferd, but the future Dean Stanley to the future Archbishop of
Canterbury, Tait, on his appointment as Headmaster of Rugby on Dr
Arnold's death 150 years ago.

It is customary for those called to this office to plead 'non sum
dignus'. I am no exception. Would that I could call in aid those who
were my mentors in this place – the scholarly accuracy and exaggerated
courtesy of Marcus Niebuhr Tod, or the style of Ronald Syme, whose
Tacitean prose would most nearly fit the definition advanced by
Thomas Sprat: 'the means whereby men deliver so many things in
almost an equal number of words' or the excitement of Sir John Myres
interpreting Herodotus through his beard from his own experience of
gun-boat daring along the Turkish coast. I am short on such qualities
and there is another anxiety which I politely voice with some hesitation.
Let me put it in the form of a reminiscence. During my undergraduate
days an intelligent theologian called Kathleen Bliss came to deliver a
lecture to philosophers and classicists here. She felt it was not well
received. Shortly afterwards she met T. S. Eliot who asked her how her
lecture had gone. 'Badly', she said. To comfort her he produced the
memorable sentence 'Do not forget, my dear, that those to whom you
were speaking reserve for religion a degree of inattention which they
would accord to no other mental discipline.'

Evidence suggests that times have changed, and that we are in a more
open world, to our real advantage. The disciplined study of Greek and
Roman religion, for instance, has, if I understand it, shifted perceptions.

We now approach the religion of the ancients as something embedded in Greek and Roman life: less to be adjudged in terms of later Christian apologetic and rather as a field of human thought and conduct to be understood and appreciated on its own terms. However here I am brought back again to my own sense of diffidence. The Regius Professor of Greek in this University[1] in his inaugural lecture made the point that in our generation we have at our immediate command more knowledge of the ancient world than any previous generation, and any such reappraisals as I have just touched upon will come out of these new appreciations. If Trevelyan could say to Namier 'Your knowledge of history is microscopic', where in all this am I?

Where do I stand, indeed, as your president? Gratitude to those who laboured to instruct me at school and here in Oxford, leaves me unable to claim that happy freedom of the speculative amateur - happy, but dangerous too, for you will remember surely the egregious Terpiades in Odyssey 22, 347–8:

αὐτοδίδακτος δ' εἰμί, θεὸς δέ μοι ἐν φρεσὶν οἴμας
παντοίας ἐνέφυσεν.

One step more, in other words, and the amateur is claiming divine inspiration. I recall no such promise offered to me when I accepted your invitation.

The subject I have chosen is neither the details of ancient religion, nor the less tameable terrain of Christian theology. It will be an attempt to register the debt of gratitude which the Church owes to the classical culture in which it grew up. It will enable me to express the affection which my teachers planted in my heart and soul (ἐν φρεσὶν) for the Classics and perhaps make up for the years when I was held under other claims upon me and the great Masters looked down on me from the bookshelves with sad and accusing eyes. The opening lines of a sonnet composed by John Henry Newman on board ship off the shores of a Mediterranean island exactly match my mood.

> Why wedded to the Lord, still yearns my heart
> Towards these scenes of ancient heathen fame?

It is a question as old as Christianity itself.

When Tertullian launched his attack on classical learning, 'What has Athens to do with Jerusalem? What has the Academy to do with the Church?' he wrote in elegant Latin. He was one of the prose stylists of

---

[1] Oxford.

his era, the product of the best classical education that Roman North Africa could provide. Elsewhere he spoke of 'Seneca, saepe noster' (Seneca often speaks like one of us). In all this he was not unique. So many who spoke disparagingly about the classical inheritance were unable to extract themselves from it. It is impossible to understand Augustine without either some awareness of the Platonic tradition he took for granted, or knowledge of the Cicero and Virgil he knew by heart. Aristotle, the Stoa, and Epicurus have all played their part in influencing the faith they never knew.

In the ninth century it was left to a scholar with the improbable name of Ermenrich of Ellwangen to produce the most striking answer to Newman's question. Defending his many quotations from Virgil in the course of a grammatical treatise, he said 'since even as dung spread upon the field enriches it to a good harvest, so the filthy writings of pagan poets are a mighty aid to Divine eloquence'. Strangely enough there is an echo of this in which Newman was involved in the nineteenth century. An ultramontane, Abbé Jean Gaume, had written to him advocating the prohibition of all classical literature from schools to be replaced by a study of patristic writing. Newman could not agree. He wrote back: 'I do not see how Greek and Latin can be taught without the Classics. The Classics seem to me to do so very much in forming a correct taste'. The matter of taste is characteristic of Newman and perhaps congenial to those of us who are upset by some of the barbarisms of modern Christian literature and liturgy.

If we are looking for a Bishop who was formed by classical taste we could not do better than Synesius of Cyrene. Gibbon dismisses this fourth-century character as a kind of Vicar of Bray. However he has recently become fashionable. He might be a patron saint for Centres of Hellenic Studies. He was a remarkable combination of all eras of classical antiquity. A descendant of Hercules, he wrote in classical Greek. He was a neoplatonic philosopher initiated into Hellenistic mysteries. He was a Roman provincial from Africa who was able to speak eloquently before the Emperor. He was a Bishop, hostile only to fanatics, whether Jews, Christians, Honks or pagan philosophers. He said he was prepared to utter myths in Church provided he could be a philosopher in his study. (One is reminded of the logical positivist, R. B. Braithwaite, who on being baptised in King's College chapel, Cambridge in the late forties is alleged to have made a pact with the Bishop that he might preface his credal promises with (*sotto voce*), 'I agree to act as if . . .'.)

When it comes to taste I have little doubt most in this company would prefer Synesius to his contemporary stalwart for the full faith, Epiphanius of Cyprus, who I once heard described as having that mixture of rectitude and stupidity which sometimes passes for Orthodoxy. Now this regard for taste I believe to be neither antiquarian nor superficial. It takes us deep into our own times. In his address on 'The Pursuit of the Ideal,' Isaiah Berlin reviewed those ideologies that have proved so disastrous in the present century. He included religious bigotry, with the comment 'interestingly enough no one amongst the most perceptive social thinkers of the nineteenth century had ever predicted this'; and he has a powerful sentence: 'To force people into the neat uniforms demanded by dogmatically believed-in schemes is almost always the road to inhumanity.' It is my belief that the study of the classics with their endless variety, insight and inspiration, their restless curiosity, their pathos and irony will forever resist attempts to force people into the neat uniforms demanded by religious or any other dogmatists.

There are two strands in classical scholarship, the relationship between which illustrates for me something essential for interpreting our humanity. They are pathos and humour. We all have our favourite examples of pathos in classical literature, most of them, I suspect, culled from Homer or Virgil - perhaps Hector's parting from Andromache at the Scaean Gate, or Aeneas' grief and anger at the death of Pallas. It comes as something of a surprise to the solemn to find how much humour and irreverence the Greeks mixed in with their religion. If, like Thetis in Auden's 'Shield of Achilles' we 'look over their shoulder for ritual pieties', we often find 'quite another scene'. For in the *Iliad* the light relief comes from Olympus and the bickering of the gods, and only from the battlefield when deities like Aphrodite unwisely venture there. Few of the gods escape Aristophanes' mirth. Predictably the Romans – with the notable exception of Clodius – had a greater sense of religious decorum, and Virgil's gods, for all their quarrelling, managed to keep their dignity. But deification is another matter and moved even the worthy Seneca to a string of schoolboy cracks at Claudius' expense – though we probably find Vespasian's dying chuckle more amusing: 'vae' inquit 'puto deus fio'.

This combination of pathos and humour is a reflection, for me, of a religious truth. There is no laughter at the heart of faith where the incongruities, absurdities and tragedies of life are dealt with by a cross, but laughter on the outskirts of faith is the best safeguard against fantastic nonsense. People without a sense of humour lack proportion and should not be put in charge of anything.

These are personal generalities. I want now to be more systematic in arguing for a classical education as a defence against what has become known since the nineteenth century as religious fundamentalism. Christians, like Jews and Muslims, call themselves the people of the Book. Their faith is conveyed to them in revelation, and the story of that revelation is recorded in a corpus of writings which very early on acquired a special status. Collectively, these writings are remarkably cautious about the claims they make for themselves. In fact, there is only one biblical text which makes an absolute claim for scriptural authority – 'All scripture is inspired by God and profitable for teaching . . .'. This is in the Second Epistle to Timothy, which incidentally is one of the youngest writings of all contained in the Bible's covers. Out of this text comes the fundamentalist belief that the words of the Bible cannot be faulty or in error.

The Church has repeatedly rescued itself from scriptural fundamentalism or the absolute claims of its own authority, and has renewed and strengthened its life and thought – with the help of the classics. For it was not Christians who began commenting on texts in order to find their divine message and to apply it. It was the world of Greece and Rome which faced up to the puzzles of how to use a respected written text, and how to gauge its authority. The first great literary text to be treated in this way was that of Homer, as Greek commentators sought to draw out truths about human existence hidden beneath the surface of its stories. Superficially, they seemed to be tales of violence, trickery and murder which could do nothing to advance human happiness or encourage right behaviour. The solution was to allegorize: in other words, to look for the greater truths which were being conveyed by symbols in the stories.

Then Jews, much influenced by Greek culture, began borrowing the allegorical method, and applying it to their own sacred writings, for the same reasons. They found them embarrassing and unedifying. What sophisticated person living in a great university city like Alexandria would feel happy with the idea that the human race started with a woman being taken from Adam's rib? Who could take seriously a God who haggled like a market trader with Abraham, one of his own creatures, over the fate of the citizens of Sodom? So Philo, the Jew, a scholar who was a rather older Egyptian contemporary of Jesus Christ, made the Greek allegorical method his own as he wrote on the Hebrew scripture. And once there was a flourishing Christian community in Alexandria, Christian biblical scholars took to the same method with enthusiasm, to explain the difficulties in their enlarged collection of sacred books.

Of course, there are pitfalls in allegorical interpretation. There is a grave danger of the text being detached from its original moorings altogether – the modern phrase would be deconstruction, I suppose. How does one control the allegory and stop it running wild? There is no good solution to that problem, as deconstructionists will no doubt discover in due course.

Allegory is now out of fashion; which reminds us that different parts of the classical legacy may appeal to different ages. Another classical notion has more contemporary resonance in curbing fundamentalism – the consciousness that texts have a history. They demand an analysis which treats them with respect, but which sees them as products of their age. Such an attitude is dependent on a realisation which, for a classicist, is axiomatic: so much so, that we may forget what an effort of imagination it involves. This is the insight that societies change radically over time: that their customs and assumptions may be entirely different from ours, and may need detailed investigation in order to be recaptured. Moreover, this insight is coupled with one of the most exciting and enduring features of the Graeco-Roman legacy to the Western world – a restless curiosity about those who are different.

This was not an invariable feature of the Greek outlook – after all, the Greeks could apply the blanket label 'barbaroi' indifferently to Persian kings and hairy tribesmen from the Crimea; but curiosity emerged crucially at certain stages in classical civilisation, to illuminate great events. Herodotus was fascinated by differences in societies around the Mediterranean. Thucydides made clear the difficulties of comparing sources about the past: as he said rather wearily, 'different eye-witnesses give different accounts of the same events, speaking out of partiality for one side or the other, or else from imperfect memories.' It took one of the periodic rediscoveries of this classical world to trigger off a new approach to history and to the reading of texts. The humanists of the fourteenth and fifteenth centuries had a fresh sense of excitement about Greece and Rome. What was most exciting for them as they explored ancient texts, was the vision of a world so different from their own: a difference which they could analyse and explore for the benefit of their own society.

During the seventeenth century Christian scholars began applying humanist historical methods to problems of conflicting interpretations in the biblical text. Few of these problems were fresh discoveries. What was new was the application of the humanist criticism of text which saw these as historical questions rather than clues to some mystic pattern. Now biblical commentators could see the Bible as a library whose books contain many layers, some whose purposes could be guessed at, some of whose sources could be compared with other literatures. As other avenues of ancient history were opened up, and especially as archaeology became a science rather than a gentleman's entertainment, the sacred writings that had once stood in magnificent isolation took their place within a newly detailed and infinitely richer panorama of the ancient world.

Another of the fascinations of classical culture is that it expressed itself in two contrasting languages; strikingly different in their character and in their strengths. Greek was the language of subtle philosophical distinction, a vehicle of abstract thought; Latin, the language for lawyers and bureaucrats. Yet the distinction was not absolute. Each produced its own poetry and drama, speculative and imaginative prose. Neither language sought to drive the other from the stage; their role was complementary, and most educated people up to the fourth century of the Common Era would do their best to show familiarity with both. To translate from one language to the other required an awareness of all the problems of meaning. It taught the lesson that in the end all translation falls short of being exact. The Church learnt this the hard way, as in its theological debates, the Latin-speaking West struggled to make sense of what Greek-speaking theologians were saying. Very often, it must be admitted that the effort to resolve the difficulty generated more heat than light.

As long as the classics kept alive a constant sense of the problem of translation, no-one could oversimplify the task of communicating between human beings, let alone the task of communication between the human and the divine. How can one talk of verbal inerrancy in a text, when the nature of a word in language is to slip away from meaning all the time – when all communication is a constant approximation?

Moreover when we read the New Testament, the record of the earthly life and teaching of the Lord, we read virtually all his words in a translation into Greek; hardly more than a few phrases remain from the Aramaic which he actually spoke. The Christian message is contained in a translation, and we struggle through all time to understand what the pattern of these translated words might mean, using all our resources of historical and literary scholarship. We rely on human language and human knowledge, with all their imperfections, to see through a glass darkly.

Perhaps it was an awareness of the fleeting character of our human relationships, as they struggle to express themselves in language, which encouraged as part of classical culture the profound and increasing sense of helplessness and tragedy. Rightly, we find and enjoy in Greek civilisation a celebration of human achievement, a delight in human capacity for improvement. But already in Plato we also find a sense of the hollowness of all that we do: 'men and women are puppets chiefly, having in them only a small portion of reality'. Classical creativity was increasingly accompanied by a world denying strain, as much for Romans as for Greeks. For many first-century Romans the fall of the Republic and the triumph of the cynical political fictions which constructed the Julio-Claudian Empire were a sad betrayal of the past; upper-class Roman disillusion can be heard in the writings of Livy and Tacitus. By the Antonine era, the sadness seems more pervasive. In the writings of Marcus Aurelius, all human achievement is 'smoke and nothingness' – if precious in its evanescence – human reward 'a bird flying past, vanished before we can grasp it'.

Christianity is always in danger of exploiting this sense for its own purposes. It used to be argued that the depravity to which Sallust, Juvenal and Tacitus bore witness was the creation of this emptiness. In the words of Jowett: 'Christianity stopped the moral rot of the empire.' It would be difficult to prove there was much more vice in the world before or after the arrival of the Christian Gospel, which is about Love, Forgiveness and Promise – and not in its essence a moral code.

The deep contribution of the classics to religion lies in the ancient perception of the tragic dimension, pointing in its very completion and its beauty to human limits. It is part of our humanity to let the appeal of that be recognised – protested against sometimes as in Thucydides or Job – but the classics truly seen and speaking for themselves hold us to that reality. The Church lives by promise, not by fulfilment. We inhabit no island of the blessed anchored in the midst of time. Faith has always a *nondum* about it and Augustine knew this *desiderium* as part of a mature faith. More than any of the Christian fathers because he knew his own precariousness and the precariousness of his world – the classical world threatened by the barbarism that would engulf it. He knows what the cry of longing meant:

Da amantem, et sentit quod dico. Da desiderantem, da esurientem, da in ista solitudine peregrinantem atque sitientem, et fontem aeternae patriae suspirantem: da talem, et scit quid dicam.[2]

[2] Tractatus XXVI, on John 6, 41–59.

Augustine the master of words knew their limitation. 'Man can say nothing of what he is incapable of feeling, but he can feel what he is incapable of putting into words.' This too is part of the classical heritage. Augustine was persuaded by Plato's thesis that between music and the soul there is a hidden affinity: 'occulta familiaritas'. Music, like art or sculpture, can sometimes express the inexpressible because it does not have to pack its message into the capsules of ideas.

Over the last few years, with startling suddenness, we have seen the collapse in Eastern Europe of one of the most powerful modern fits of Utopian longing – Stalinist socialism. I am told that in the old German Democratic Republic, a most remarkable sight was the long queue whenever a church advertised an organ recital, particularly for the works of Bach. I do not suppose that this reflected a general enthusiasm for the Christian message, or even very often, a specialist love of baroque keyboard music. Rather, I suspect, it was a seeking of reassurance in the face of a political fundamentalism. Against one absolute creed which sought to control every aspect of people's lives in the name of earthly perfection, the clear, intricate, self-contained musical rules of Bach's genius showed that human beings were capable of producing a different sort of ideal: one which did not seek to dominate, simply to present truth and beauty to those who wished to contemplate it.

Benjamin Whichcote in seventeenth-century Cambridge was much admired for his own gentle fusion of Christianity and Plato's thoughts. 'Truth is the self-same thing materially, only called by several denominations: as the sea which is one and the same, is one-where called the Mediterranean, in another place, the German ocean.' His words carry the consequence that we must hunt for truth below its varied superficial forms and names. Such a hunt involves hard labour. It entails the rigour which classical scholarship has always demanded of its students: all the attention to texts, to their context, their interpretation and problems of meaning, to the detailed difference and glorious diversity of human experience. There is a nostalgia *for* the classics which is a false nostalgia. It is for a small manageable world in which the Church was able to see the answer to all the questions that it posed. There is a genuine nostalgia within the classical world that the Church, with all its assurances, must take into its own self-understanding.

> Why, wedded to my Lord, still yearns my heart
> Towards these scenes of ancient heathen fame?

The question has the author's answer in a later couplet.

'Tis but that sympathy with Adams race
Which in each brother's history reads its own

The sexist language is deplorable. The sentiments are sound.

I have two points to make to the Classical Association before I bring these sprawling remarks to an end. One is of envy, the other of warning. First to jealousy; if any of you have come across general knowledge crosswords or listened to the less vacuous quiz shows you will notice that the questions about the classical world are still there but their biblical counterparts are fading. Furthermore, the young know the classical answers better than those from the Bible. I realise that I am in company unlikely to be impressed by an ability to subtract the number of muses from the number of wounds counted on the corpse of Julius Caesar; but you should be. You are fortunate that ancient civilisation courses are now bringing a taste of the classics to people unlikely otherwise ever to rub shoulders with a declension. I know some of you fear that this is a Trojan horse, replete with shoddy compromise about to lay waste Ilium with poisoned barbs of falling standards.

This, I think, is a false anxiety. It is the path which religion has already taken. My warning is that you can learn from our mistakes. Few school children now are taught 'Religious Knowledge' in the way we were. Comparative religion courses bring questions about faith and a world larger than the individual to many children who would recoil from the prospect of lessons in Christian apologetics. These courses work when they draw children towards wanting to find out more. They only fail when they reduce belief to a meaningless telephone directory of interesting facts, where myth, history, faith and folly are all presented as quaint half-truths.

Religion and the classics ought to be allies against a one-dimensional world of religious bigotry or educational utilitarianism. So let me offer an eirenic appendix. The fathers of the Christian Church met for the Council of Nicaea in 325 AD. The record of voting figures has been made available to us by modern scholarly research. We are therefore able to judge the attendance at different sessions. It does not take the modern science of psephology to discover that the only session which was attended by all the bishops was the banquet given by the Emperor Constantine. This approval for the marriage of conviviality with conviction should never be entirely forgotten when classics and religion meet together.

That remarkable society the Dilettanti, formed in 1734, which introduced people of taste to the antiquities of Greece and to whom archaeologists, artists, tourists and interpreters owe a considerable debt had a motto: *seria ludo*. In such a spirit we should pass from this address in which I have tried to put before you serious thoughts without too much *gravitas* and enjoy together the conviviality of the Conference dinner.

17

THE MIRROR OF THE PRESENT

By DILYS POWELL

When I first received an intimation that I might be invited to address this learned assembly, my reaction was a mixture of extreme gratification and fright. I was flattered, you might say I was bowled over; but I wondered if I really had the audacity to accept. I am bound to say that a second thought then entered my mind. For a moment I wondered if your Council had been overtaken by a phenomenon not, I believe, unknown in the most reputable bodies. Was it possible, I asked myself, that the Classical Association was the victim of a case of collective hysteria? For I could see – I still can see – no qualification that I possess for the honour of being your President. If I look far enough back into the past, I can, it is true, recall acquiring a smattering of those noble ancient languages which to all of you here come so easily. I remember learning by heart a fragment or two of Horace; struggling with a book or two of the *Aeneid*; being with ill-concealed impatience taught to construe a line or two from the more genteel areas of Ovid. I will not conceal from you that these modest attainments came in extremely handy in later life, when as a young journalist I was required to write short, light-hearted leaders, known in the office by the title of 'the comic strip'. During some months there was a ruling that each of these exercises should contain a Latin quotation; my limited choice of tags came in for some pretty ribald comments from colleagues better equipped, but at least I lasted out the ordeal.

Small Latin, you see; and, goodness knows, less Greek. Of course, in the years of my formal education we tried. We had a shot – need I say? – at Xenophon. Laboriously, and doubtless erroneously, we translated: 'It seemed good to us to march nine parasangs'; I am afraid it all seemed a tremendous joke. Have no fear; I am not going to quote either Greek or Latin – though I see that the 'amateurs', so-called, who have preceded me, scholars to a man, have been impressively ready with their classics, with Lucretius, Ovid, Virgil; by their own record they have found relief from political crisis in translating Catullus or rendering epigrams from the Greek anthology, and their committee meetings have been enlivened by the exchange of Tacitean notes. As a matter of fact, for a brief spell there was a suggestion that when I went to Oxford I should read the great ancient tongues. But my brother, who in those days was a pretty good classical scholar, had other ideas on feminine upbringing. Hastily he wrote home: 'Don't,' he said; 'the classics are a terrible grind for a girl, and you will be prematurely wrinkled.' I fancy that I was swayed by indolence rather than by faith in this false, and indeed frivolous, warning: anyhow I took his advice. And today, as I stand here, I do indeed realize that the decision has robbed me of deep and solid pleasures. I envy all of you. I know what I have missed. And yet – through no laudable effort on my own part, simply by the accidents of my life – I have been lucky enough to find some compensation. Without the devoted work which all of you have given to the study of the ancient past I have been allowed a simple personal view; and that is what I should like to tell you about now.

I will ask you, then, to imagine, years ago, a young woman who has never travelled further than to northern France or the chillier reaches of Switzerland but who on her marriage is suddenly transported to Greece: to Athens. As a result of the embryonic classical education which I described a moment ago she can just spell out the names of the streets: Plutarch Street, she reads; Homer Street; Pindar Street. But the names mean very little to her. The month is January. The anemones have not yet blossomed on the hills, for that year it is cold. The city seems not at all Mediterranean; and that disconcerts her. For the sake of convenience she picks up a few phrases in modern Greek: 'To Constitution Square', she says to the tram-conductor, or to the taxi-driver: 'Turn right here'; she addresses everybody with the familiar 'thou', for the use of the second person plural involves complexities of conjugation quite beyond her. She makes no real attempt to learn, for as yet she has no inkling of the way in which her life will be bound up with Greece. Indeed there are times when she shrinks from some enormous purity in the air, in the landscape; the country seems to ask of her something she is not yet ready to give. Later that spring she has a chance of a week or two in Egypt, and there she feels more at ease – paradoxically, because Egypt is so remote from her experience that it cannot possibly make any demands on her (and perhaps just a little because it is not so cold). As for Rome, that seems almost manageable. It is heroic, it is magnificent, but even to her unaccustomed eyes it is half-familiar. The cinema has seen to that with versions of *Ben-Hur* and *Quo Vadis* with gladiators and legionaries, not to mention Vestal Virgins by the score. The Colosseum itself seems friendlier to her than the Hecatompedon.

And yet, when she is back in England, it is the memory of Greece which follows her; she never quite shakes it off. She finds herself recalling fragments of her visit. There was that moment on the Acrocorinth when she stood by a spring with water almost invisible, it was so clear. There was the spectacle of the waves sweeping up the channel between Delos and Rheneia and breaking on the rocks. There was a January day spent clambering about on the Acropolis of Mycenae and looking down on a plain with the corn already green and the mountains clear in the distance beyond. But she does not yet connect these fragments of experience with anything except a feeling of inexplicable delight. She is told that the clear spring is called Peirene; she is uninterested. Delos is simply an island where you can be held up for three or four days by a storm, a place where the wind blows so hard that you can put your weight on it, a place where a party of hospitable French archaeologists have been good enough to share their dwindling rations of eggs and beans with the stormbound visitors. It is the landscape that she cannot forget: the mountains, and the sea carving deep gulfs out of the shore. But why? Is it really distinct from other landscapes? Would not parts of New Zealand, for instance, look much the same? The Greek mountains are certainly higher than the mountains of Wales – but are their shapes so very different? One thing does indeed make her reflect: the image of the Argive plain. For, as she stood looking south towards Nauplion, she had imagined Agamemnon, back from Troy, driving furiously along the road from the sea, hurrying back to Mycenae and to his death. After all even this unclassical traveller has heard of Agamemnon; and perhaps with that tiny flash of imagination she has begun to connect the simple immediate sensation with a larger world of experience.

At any rate she is lucky. She goes to Greece again, and not once but many times. One must be grateful, as I say, for the benevolent accidents of life. For those accidents and that feeling for the landscape work together so that the surrender to the spell of the country becomes complete and irrevocable.

My first return – perhaps by now I can drop the third-person narrative – was in the summer. The sun blazed, everything trembled in the heat; this, I thought, is the most intense season, the season when, to me at any rate, Greece is at its most Greek. There were long walks that year: through Arcadia, up and down terrible mountain tracks, across plains so high that even in the heat they were emerald green and the frogs croaked beatifically in the swamps. I was supremely happy: sweating, exhausted, longing for sundown and a bed, even if it was only a sleeping-bag in a field, with a party from the nearest village amiably watching one's preparations for the night-but happy. And now indeed I began to connect – erratically at first, and not strictly with the terrain in which I was travelling. While we struggled over some rocky pass I would think of James Elroy Flecker's vision of Hellas in England:

> When I go down the Gloucester lanes
> My friends are deaf and blind:
> Fast as they turn their foolish eyes
> The Maenads leap behind.

One breathless afternoon at Olympia quite another association came into my mind. The Alpheus was half-dry now in the heart, its channels of water winding between shallow banks and the reeds scarcely stirring; this time it was a phrase of music I heard – the opening phrase of Debussy's 'L'Après-Midi d'un Faune'. Yet I think I was learning. At any rate I was listening to what I was told. Our path took us towards Mount Pholo – and the forest we went through was transformed for me. It was not merely a forest of oak-trees. It was the home of Centaurs; its life was rooted in a measureless past. Little by little the faint intimations which I had received of something beyond the rocks, the flowers, the plains, the villages lost in an enormous landscape grew into a recognition of continuity. Erymanthus was no longer a series of killing ascents and back-breaking declivities. The Scironian Cliffs were no longer a line of precipices threatening the road and the railway between Megara and the Corinth Canal. Heracles still hunted the boar, Theseus still slew the brigand. Or, to move from legend to history, the huge, irregular shape which came in sight as one swung over the low pass at Daphni and down the fine new road to Eleusis was not just an island called Salamis. It was the sound of victory.

Nowhere, I suppose, is this sense of continuity more deeply impressed on the learner than during an archaeological excavation. I shall never cease to be thankful that the experience was mine in Greece. I have enjoyed it elsewhere too: in Egypt. Friends were exploring the site of Abydos on the west bank of the Nile; there was the narrow strip of fertile ground, on each side there was the hostile, parching sand. I was excited by the place, by the monuments, by the spectacle of the work going on under what seemed to me the threat of the desert. But I was conscious of no connexion between the relics of the past and the life of the present. The monuments and the life they represented belonged, as I said just now, to a world outside any experience I could imagine. The Nile – that immortal fact – was the only link between that unimaginable world and the people, the Egyptians, whom I watched digging and hauling and carrying. Yet in Greece – on the mainland, in the islands, in Crete – I have the sense that everything belongs together, everything continues: and continues in more ways than one.

To begin with, there is the archaeological continuity. During the excavations which I watched at the Heraion of Perachora, on the promontory which separates the Halcyonic Gulf from the Bay of Corinth, it became necessary to move a tiny chapel of St. John – no more than a stone shack really, a shrine religiously visited perhaps once a year but for the rest of the time a tethering-place for goats or a storehouse for fishermen's gear. With all due rites the stones were moved, the chapel was rebuilt a little way up the hill; and beneath its original foundations were the foundations of an apsidal-ended temple – a Geometric-age temple; the walls belonged to the ninth century B.C. Farther up the hill, beyond the rebuilt chapel, there were the foundations of another temple: an eighth-century temple. Farther down the hill, near the sea, there were the remains of yet a third temple: this time, sixth-century. Close by, the remains of a stoa, an agora, an altar, all assigned to the late fifth or early fourth century. If you turned once again and climbed the hill you came to the foundations of a Hellenistic house with stone dining-couches still in position. And across the ruins of the Agora there lay the ruins of a Roman building of the second century A.D. The persistence of habitation, the persistence of a shrine – it is common enough, I know; you find it in a thousand places. But I had never been conscious of it as I was made conscious by the presence of the humble neglected chapel, built as it were on the bones of the past in that beautiful and remote spot (and in those days it really was remote; today, I know, it is easily accessible).

I am talking, I am afraid, as if I myself had been able to give a date to a fragment of a cornice or a tangle of broken walls. Of course I could have done nothing of the sort; I was the most uninstructed of observers. And the most uninstructed of listeners. All around me people were talking about classical history and classical literature, arguing about sites and references, about Livy, Plutarch, Strabo, Pausanias. This headland on which we camped – was it the temenos of Hera Acraea to which, according to Euripides, Medea brought the bodies of her children for burial? Apparently not: I listened, I struggled to learn, regretting now that I had not learned earlier, jealous of the ease with which my companions cited names and battles and campaigns. For even this far corner of Greece had not been left untouched by war; I was to hear much discussion of the episode in which the Spartan Agesilaus marched from the Isthmus of Corinth and what is now Loutraki and overcame the Corinthian defenders of the Heraion. And every day we looked out across the windy waters of the Gulf of Sicyon, or to Corinth, where the ruins of a great Roman city overlaid the Greek foundations, or north-west to where Delphi perched on a shelf of Parnassus. The names echoed in my mind. The past began to come alive.

One day among the treasures of bronze and ivory which were found a little bronze statuette of a bull came to light. It bore an inscription:

$$\text{Ναύμαχός με ἀνέθηκε τᾶι Ἥραι τᾶι Λιμενίας}$$
Naumachus dedicated me to Hera of the harbour.

If you go into any church in any Greek village, you are pretty certain to find today's equivalent in the offerings suspended round the icon – the miniature hands or feet or arms or legs of thin flat silver offered in anxiety, in hope, in prayer. It is true that the Virgin, instead of Hera, may receive these votive offerings; but the intention is the same. And now I began to see another kind of continuity: a link between the people whose altars and temples we were uncovering, the names of whose heroes we exchanged across the table or the camp-fire, and the Greeks I met every day.

Some historians, I know, will say that the inhabitants of modern Greece are a mixed race, that the centuries of invasion and occupation, Roman, Frankish, Venetian, Turkish, have contaminated the purity of blood. All right, then, the blood is mixed. The people of Perachora village, where the workmen on the dig came from, are Albanian in origin, and, when I first knew them, the elder members often spoke Albanian amongst themselves. Nevertheless their names are Greek; a particular friend of mine was called Aspasia. Here, no less than in any other district, they think as Greeks. They identify themselves with the past of the country. The workmen were passionately interested in the results of the exploration. The walls and the foundations which were uncovered belonged to their own history. There was something proud in their sense of possession – and something touching in the genuine reverence with which men, women and children looked on the relics of an ancient civilization. And as I came to know them better and to live more at ease in their country, I found myself thinking of them as indistinguishable from the common people of that ancient Greece which was the background of the excavation. When a party of wives and mothers came down from the village five or six miles away to embrace me and talk to me (an occasion which, I can assure you, greatly hastened my acquisition of a little rustic, conversational Greek), I accepted them as a flutter of country-women from two and a half millennia ago. When two men from the lighthouse on the headland set off in their boat to fetch water from the spring half-way to Loutraki, I thought of the storms which can blow up even in the enclosed Gulf of Corinth; I thought of the enormity of the sea and the audacity with which the men of classical and pre-classical Greece had defied it. For a moment the boat with the two men unfurling the sail – or, if for once there was a calm day, painfully rowing – was an image from Herodotus.

Perhaps you will say that there is at any rate one place in Greece which gives the lie to this belief of mine in the unity of past and present: Athens itself. Ever since I have been going to Greece, people have been complaining about Athens. I remember it first as a charming, rather quiet little capital into which the internal combustion engine in the shape of the taxi-cab was only beginning to make inroads. In winter the wind whistled up the hilly streets round the Acropolis; in summer the outdoor cafés were sweet with jasmine – and the visitors complained of the irregularity of the paving-stones and the inadequacies of the plumbing. Today the city booms with life. The boulevards radiate into vast suburbs, the cosmopolitan hotels multiply, the night-clubs pullulate, and, if you want to find a quiet beach for a swim, you have to drive the best part of forty miles. Now the visitors complain of the noise, the traffic, the radios, the neon signs, the photographers round the Parthenon and the tourists: in fact, of themselves. Everybody complains, the Athenians as well as the foreigners; especially they complain about the architecture. The buildings, they say, are too high, so that in summer they trap the heat in the streets – and ugly too; rectangular blocks of concrete. I will not deny that a more imaginative style of architecture might possibly be devised to suit the climate. But to me the bronze and purple shadows cast by the tall, undecorated buildings are beautiful; and I deplore the idea that Athens ought to be marmoreally classical. An Athens which stood still would be the antithesis of the Athens of the past. It would be a mausoleum, not the city which fought the Persians – nor, come to that, the city where centuries later, at the time of St. Paul, the people 'spent their time in nothing else, but either to tell or to hear some new thing'.

Even that ancient marble, the scarcity of which in the modern capital so deeply disappoints the purist, was not always as Parsifal-like as it has sometimes been imagined. Look at the sculptures in the Acropolis Museum, and you see that the eyes, the hair and the folds of the dress still bear traces of blue and red and gold; great Athens was a city which enjoyed colour. I am of course open to correction from this learned audience, but it will take a great deal of correction to persuade me that the Athenians of the age of Themistocles, of Pericles, of Socrates and Plato spent their entire lives speculating on justice, goodness and the nature of truth. Indeed I am bound to say that the subjects depicted in the vase-painting of the sixth, the fifth and the fourth centuries B.C. suggest that the citizens often had other and less spiritual matters on their minds. Come to that, Aristophanes strikes me as reflecting a frame of mind considerably less lofty than the academic traveller has been known to expect of today's Athenians.

But I am wandering into fields of knowledge where I have no right. What I am trying to say is this: that for all the traffic lights and cinemas and bars, in spite of *son et lumière* on the Acropolis, in spite of the funicular which carries you up to dine at the top of Lycabettus and look out on a city brilliant with emerald, crimson and golden lights, I fancy modern Athens has a great deal in common with ancient Athens. The same spirit of enquiry, the same tendency to scepticism, the same gifts for analysis – I learned long ago never to cross swords with a sophisticated Athenian; I would as soon disagree with Socrates himself. Perhaps the Pnyx and the Theatre of Dionysus are no longer the scene of political assembly. But political discussion goes on unceasingly – and at a great variety of levels. Last summer I had to deliver a package to an Athenian whom I did not know. I asked where I could find him; he might, I was told, be at a certain café some time during the morning: I could leave my parcel there for him. I found the cafe, I went in, I made my way to the counter. At every table there sat a group of men, young, old, middle-aged, all arguing; as I passed, a wave of surprise and watchfulness followed me; there was a momentary silence. When I got out, embarrassed by what I felt had been an intrusion on my part, I asked someone to explain. 'Oh, that! That is one of the cafés where journalists sit all morning talking about politics. Women don't go there.' I felt as if I had interrupted a session of the Areopagites.

Living in Athens as I once did, visiting it on occasion as I now do, one can still, I believe, hear faint echoes of the ancient home of political faction. One can even recognise, in the stubborn individualism of one's own friends, the characteristics of the people who got so sick of hearing Aristides called 'the Just'. But if it is the heroic quality of the past for which you are searching, if you feel the need to revive the sense of awe which is the other side of the nature of ancient Greece, that is still easier. A couple of years ago a Greek friend of mine, walking with me through the National Museum, suddenly exploded into rage: 'Have they no respect?' she hissed. She was looking at a party of foreigners, boys and girls, who were rambling vaguely through one of the sculpture galleries; they were all wearing shorts. For a moment I was startled; then I understood. We all feel that the monuments of Greece's great past should be approached with circumspection. I fancy, though, that her emotions were more complex. The splendid Poseidon – or, as some say, Zeus – drawn up, you remember, by fishermen's nets; the noble bronze and marble figures discovered only a few years ago by workmen at Piraeus – she was judging them, certainly, as superlative works of art; and a work of art requires silence and surrender. But I believe she felt, perhaps without recognising it, that she was in the presence of religious symbols. The link with the beliefs of the past may appear to have been broken for centuries. Nevertheless there are times when you are aware of the ancient reverence returning. Look at the command in the gesture of the Apollo from the Olympia pediment, and you may yield to it yourself for a fraction of a moment.

I am drawn several ways when I am in Athens. There are times when I find acute pleasure in the new gaieties of the city: the crowded bathing beaches; the cafés with the bouzouki players; the taverns with the singers moving from table to table with sentimental modern songs; especially the incessant murmur of life at night, the footsteps, the voices, the snatches of music from the radio; and then I wonder whether, taking into account the advances in communication and in the capacity for noise – and the fact that in classical times as a woman I should have found my own share severely restricted – the Athenians have changed so very much in the last 2,400 years. Again, I think of an evening spent in the theatre at Piraeus, watching the folk-dancers who come from districts all over Greece: the ancient theatre, the traditional dances and songs of the villages – setting and performance seem perfectly matched, the continuity of life seems unbroken. Or there are the times when I join an audience of Greeks as well as foreigners like myself to sit in the theatre of Herodes Atticus and listen to a performance of a classical play, and strain my ears to follow the cadences of the Greek; the rumour of traffic is muffled in the distance, and the summer sky of Attica encloses theatre and audience and players; the Athens of today fades, the contrast between the heroic figures of tragedy and the watchers perched on thin cushions on relentless stone seats dissolves, and I am half-way to the past.

But when I go to the National Museum – I am ashamed to think that, because at one time or another I have spent so many hours there, I am inclined to leave it to the last day of my visit – the translation is more startling. Why, I say to myself, why do I do anything else while I am in Athens? Why not give all my days to this? Why not spend a whole morning with the finds from Piraeus? But of course I know I shall never do it; and perhaps in the long run it is right not to do it. For this experience of repose and surrender I believe to be only one half of a satisfying response to Greece: the Greece of today – and the Greece of the ancients. And I am quite sure that without my liking for the noisy, restless, questioning Athens of today I should not have found so deep a feeling for the composed, serene monuments of antiquity. I learned the one from the other.

And in the same way I learned a relationship with the legendary past of the mountains and the plains through an acquaintance with people in village and small towns. No doubt it was at the great sanctuaries that my apprenticeship began. I assimilated scraps of mythology from the conversation of my archaeological companions, I loitered round the museums of Delphi and Olympia with a guide-book in my hand. But the time came when I travelled by myself and then, sitting at rickety iron tables in village eating-houses, bumping over mountain passes in local buses, I talked with anyone who offered to talk. And I began exploring on my own. In Ithaca, searching for the Homeric sites, I prevailed on someone to take me to the Raven's Rock. I doubt if I should have found it by myself; indeed it was not easy to get hold of a guide, for nowadays only the old people remember the remote paths. However, an old man agreed to lead me, and together we made our way down the straggling pebbly track towards the sea and the high rock-wall. His name, he said, was Dionio: short for Dionysios; as he trudged down the hillside, a compact, tough old figure, he looked as if he came straight out of the *Odyssey*. And for the first time the homecoming to Ithaca meant something to me: the sea, the rocky island, the cliffs, the scrub, the scent of thyme.

Or there was one evening towards sunset in Paros when I was shown the quarries – no longer worked, I am sorry to say, though the pavements in the town are edged with marble; as I scrambled down into the grotto of Pan, so-called, to look at the relief on the wall, the sense of history, the years, the centuries passing, was suddenly over-whelming. In Crete, which I came to enjoy rather later than the mainland or the other islands, it was the persistence of myth which I recognized: on Mount Dicte, for example, where a local guide supported me with a firm hand down the steep slope into the Cave and indicated a niche in the rock: the cradle of Zeus, he said, with all the certainty a Londoner might display in pointing out the Nelson Column. Of course, to anybody who will take the trouble to go about the country, all Greece is alive with both myth and history. Amphissa, Thebes, Epidaurus, Ithome, Aegina, Tiryns – every name on the map calls up ghosts, friendly, noble, sometimes awe-inspiring. And now I recall the time when a muleteer took me most of the way up Olympus; as we rode through fir-woods, he told stories of the andartes, the guerrillas who had hidden in these precipitous valleys during the last war. But the final naked crests, he said, had remained solitary; and when the official mountain guide dragged me up the last few hundred feet, the rock-scramble to the summit, I could see why. I watched the eagles circling overhead, I looked down into terrifying abysses, and I could understand why to the ancient world this was the home of the gods.

But there is no need to keep to the famous sites and the majestic mountains in order to experience the extraordinary spell. A year or two ago I went up Parnassus; slept in a shepherd's hut; and saw the sunrise from the crest. On the way down, recovering my breath and rubbing the cold out of my bones, I got above myself and began talking of going up Helicon next day. I had as my guide a charming Greek from the village of Arachova; he had decided that he must be not only my guide but my defender and counsellor too, and it soon became clear that he thought the Helicon project far too ambitious for his English charge. However, he was ready to settle for the Valley of the Muses; and at a village where we found lodgings for the night we discovered an old man who undertook to show us the way. Early next morning we set off on donkeys, prepared, or so I thought, for a long excursion. Not a bit of it. A few miles, and our new guide led us into a pine-wood between gentle hills. Far in the distance Helicon raised its dark head; at our feet lay a few crumbling blocks of limestone. This, he said, was what he called the Valley of the Muses, and now he would gather some bracken and some pine-branches and make a couch and we would all have lunch. It was very hot. Suddenly I felt a sharp disinclination to argue and a strong desire to dismount, sit in the shade and eat and drink. As for my friend from Arachova, he did not know the Valley of the Muses from the Bay of Marathon; it was not until evening, when we were on our way to Livadia for me to catch a bus back to Athens, that he began to suspect something. 'The old man deceived us,' he said. But he was wrong; the old man meant what he said: to him that really was the Valley of the Muses. And, when I look back now, I see the hot, aromatic pine-wood and the half-buried foundations as a place haunted – not, perhaps, by the Muses, but by the shade of some ancient legend. The old peasant recognized the omnipresence of myth, and I am still grateful to him for reminding me that it is not only the celebrated sites which hold the memory of gods and heroes. There are a thousand mountain paths, a thousand tracks through forests in Greece where the silence makes you hesitate to disturb the tutelary spirits.

The distinguished scholars who have presided over this Association have spoken eloquently for the preservation and extension of classical learning: eloquently and, goodness knows, rightly. I should like in all modesty to add my voice. I hope this will not seem an impertinence from someone so humbly equipped in the classics. In a way I believe I am an advocate as well-justified as even the most scholarly of my predecessors; for I am a living example of the handicaps of a classical education cut short too soon. I am thankful for what I had: I can scarcely imagine my life without it. But I still wish I had learned more at an age when learning is second nature. When I undertook to address this meeting of scholars, I made myself a promise: I would speak only of matters which lay strictly within my personal experience. That is why I have confined myself to Greece and to what I have discovered with my own eyes and ears in Greece. When, armed with that experience, I have travelled elsewhere, I have found my pleasure intensified – in Sicily, for instance: but then in Sicily I was inevitably drawn to what is Greek: to that huge shell at Segesta and the splendid tumble of ruins at Selinunte, to the Doric temples at Agrigento and the theatre at Syracuse – and to those terrible Syracusan quarries, softened now by shady trees, where the remains of the Athenian expeditionary force starved and died. I confess that my interest was diverted when I visited the magnificent Roman mosaics at Piazza Armerina. But then, a few miles away, I was back with my Greek associations, with

> that fair field
> Of Enna where Proserpin gathering flowers,
> Herself a fairer flower, by gloomy Dis
> Was gathered, which cost Ceres all that pain
> To seek her through the world . . .

Even when, after crossing to the mainland, I came to Cumae, it was of the flight of Daedalus from Crete I thought before I remembered my Virgil and the visit of Aeneas to consult the Sibyl. I have tried, you see, to be honest. I have not thought it proper for me to stray into the affairs of Rome. In fact, what I have been saying has somehow turned into an apology not, perhaps, for my life but certainly for part of it. And the conclusion is that everything would have been better if I had acquired in youth a fuller knowledge of the literature and the history which it is your business to cherish and to impart.

But I have one consolation. When I had thought of what I wanted to say, and when I had begun to write it down, I received a copy of a book of essays – *On the Greek Style* – by the poet and Nobel prize-winner George Seferis; and reading it I found that Seferis had this to say about the Greek cultural heritage:

There are times when this heritage is in the hands of the most famous men in the history of the world, and there are other times when it goes into hiding among the nameless, waiting for the reappearance of the great names. . . . Our folk song can, in the sensitivity of one and the same person, throw fresh light on Homer and fill in the meaning of Aeschylus.

I have had to begin with the folk song and try to work back. What Seferis says encourages me in that it is an argument for the continuity of Greek culture. For to me the real Greece is all one, her literature and her history, her past and her present indivisible: Sophocles and the voice of today's herdsman singing on the far side of the valley; Spartan Helen and the woman spinning in a doorway in Scyros; Hesiod's country and the olive-groves where the cicadas will screech in this year's heat. The land is still cruel; the mountains are still terrible; and the myths which by giving a name and a shape to terrors and cruelties made them more comprehensible and more bearable are still alive. Everything I know I have seen in the mirror of the present. What I see is no more than a dim reflection of what you can see. But I see it.

IV

Appendices

Appendix 1

THE CLASSICAL ASSOCIATION OF SCOTLAND: THE FIRST HUNDRED YEARS

By RONALD KNOX

The Classical Association of Scotland: what exactly does that conjure up to any of us? The answer will vary according to our own experience of it, to how long we have known it, to how we relate to it, and so I could not, even if I wanted to, produce a historical survey which is free from my own perspective. So this is not going to be an account according to the Tacitean ideal of *sine ira et studio*. There is certainly going to be *studium*, in the sense of partiality for the Association, and perhaps even some *ira* from time to time; nor can I make the Thucydidean profession that I have lived through all the history of CAS, giving it my mature attention, for my memory of it only goes back forty years, which is less than half. And some of you who have known it for a good while longer than I have will wonder what a mere stripling is doing holding forth on its history at all – it is to you above all that I look to for correction and amplification on matters below. Still, let me begin by going back my own forty years, because the Association as I encountered it then, in November 1962, is the one which I think of as the canonical later twentieth-century version. That is when many of us came in, give or take a decade or two, and a look at it in 2002 will give us something against which to set the Association of our Edwardian founding fathers.

In 1962, as for many years after, we met twice a year, on a Saturday in May and a Saturday in November, and we proceeded round the four universities, as they were then, in an order which was as fixed as the seasons. Edinburgh and Glasgow were visited in the winter months, and Aberdeen and St Andrews in the summer, Edinburgh going in the same year as Aberdeen and Glasgow in the same year as St Andrews. (I later came to see that this was an arrangement which subtly favoured the two big cities in the central belt, since the Edinburghers and Glaswegians had thereby less far to travel in the winter than the St Andreans and Aberdonians, but, this apart, equality ruled, which has long been one of the major virtues of the Association). The meetings nearly always consisted of two lectures on academic subjects, one before and one after lunch, except in Glasgow where until 1972 everything was got over in the morning with a coffee break; the reason for this was in my early Glasgow years variously given as being to let Dr Borthwick (now President) away to a football match in the afternoon and to allow those of us in Glasgow to say 'you'll not be wanting lunch', a sort of variation on the assumption 'you'll have had your tea', which Glaswegians like to ascribe to their rivals in the east. Although the meetings were attended mostly by university staff, interested schoolteachers and others were not lacking, and it was not simply a meeting of the departments of the four universities. My own first meeting, which I attended along with my fellow Edinburgh student Ian Moxon, was held in the Humanity Classroom at Glasgow and was a revelation. At that date, well brought up young people from Edinburgh did not visit Glasgow, which was well known to be a drunken and dangerous place, and I had only been there once as a schoolboy, to visit Lewis's emporium in order to ride on the escalator there, because in the 1950s the only escalator in Scotland was in Lewis's on Argyle Street. So to encounter instead the rich Victorian woodwork in the Humanity Classroom and find that there was indeed culture in Glasgow was salutary. The actual lectures were by Professor Ian Campbell, our own Professor of Humanity in Edinburgh, on Thomas Dempster and the Etruscans, a characteristically urbane and polished address, and a more rumbustious piece of flyting by Douglas Young, called 'The rescue of Homer from the Milman Parryites'. Both were well worth hearing, though I don't remember the details now, but what made even more impression on us as young students was the affability of our mentors over coffee in the Fore Hall, when Professor Beattie and David Robinson told us about how they had recently been marched up a hill near Amphilochian Argos by the Greek police and interrogated as suspected spies, mainly because David was wearing a red shirt. I mention this last personal detail because it is a reminder that the informal contacts which we enjoy at the meetings over the years have been a valuable feature alongside the formal.

Well, if that was how the Association was in the 1960s, had it always been thus? How different was it for the founding fathers in 1902, and why did they found it? Would they recognise our endeavours now as their own, or would they say sadly with Prufrock 'That is not what we meant at all! That is not it at all!'? Tantalisingly, our principal Minute Book, the most precious of our records, begins with the *second* meeting, held in the Grand Hotel, Aberdeen on Saturday, 14th March 1903. At the front of the Minute Book is an infuriating note, which reads 'minutes of previous meetings are to be found in another volume, kept by the Hon. Secretary Mr Coutts.' This volume must have contained notes of the preliminary meeting about forming the Association, held in the Royal High School, Edinburgh, in March 1902, and the actual first meeting, held in Edinburgh in November 1902. Mr Coutts himself died in December 1903, and his volume seems to have gone to the grave with him.

However, we are not left entirely in the dark about the aims of the founders, because the Association issued *Proceedings* in its early years and we have the first volume, for 1902–3, which contains the inaugural address of our first President, Professor George Gilbert Ramsay, and we have the rules of the Association, printed in the *Proceedings* from 1903–4 onwards. We can also see some of the things they were aiming to do from what they actually did.

But before we look at these, one question which immediately occurs to one is whether our foundation here in 1902 has any significant relation to the founding of the Classical Association south of the border in 1903. We have long been proud of our priority, but – for it's our Lenaea and there are no strangers present – can I between friends ask the insidious question whether the movement north and south of the border was all one movement really and we just happened to get in first because our smaller size allowed greater speed? However, there are some signs that we really were independent in our actions. In his tribute to Mr Coutts, Professor Ramsay described him as 'the practical originator of the Association' who 'had the idea in view for many years'. Although both Associations were concerned about developments in the schools which called for vigilance, the developments were different ones in the two different countries, and there is no sign that the founders of our own Association were concerting action with our friends in the south. Such influence as there was indeed the other way. On the 28th May 1904 Ramsay attended the first meeting of the English and Welsh Association in Oxford, presented the congratulations and good wishes of CAS, and reported to the latter in November on (I quote from the *Proceedings*) 'the notable fact that England, the ancient and secure home of classical learning and classical education, has paid Scotland the rare compliment of following her example in founding a Classical Association for England and Wales on lines almost identical with our own.' And at a meeting in 1924 Professor John Burnet was to refer to the younger

Association not even just as our sister (a frequent image) but as our daughter – which makes us, conceivably, grandmother of all the Classical Associations in the British Empire.

The aims of our founding fathers emerge clearly from the second article of the original Rules: 'The objects of the Association are to bring together for practical conference all persons interested in Classical Study and Education; to promote communication and comparison of views between Universities and Schools; to discuss subjects and methods of Teaching and Examination, and any other questions of interest to Classical Scholars that may from time to time arise.' Ramsay's remarks at the second meeting add some flesh to this succinct statement of aims. 'The President in the course of some introductory remarks said the Classical Association had been formed at the right time when the question of higher education was before the country, and the claims of Classics were being canvassed in a more general way than he had ever known. It was the business of the Association to show why Classics had been put where they were in a liberal education, and as the work of the educator was to deal with the mass of the people the aim must be to see that the basis of education was kept broad and liberal and that the Classics should be so taught as to become an instrument for training the mind and heart and character of the average man.' That seems to me admirably democratic and far-seeing and as long as 'man' is clarified as 'human being' (which is certainly as Ramsay would have meant it) it is an aim that would do us not badly for the next century also. If there are heroes in this talk of mine, Ramsay is definitely one of them. He was President for the first six years and contributed numerous addresses. He was both a classicist and an educationalist to the core, and had held his Chair since 1863. And among his virtues, may I remind you that he was a pioneer of commentaries on translations? I don't know how many of you like me when reading Tacitus in your youth were referred to Furneaux's commentary, and found it fairly useless for the purposes of the historical evaluation of Tacitus as a source. Then I discovered Ramsay's Tacitus lurking neglected in the library and found his commentary on the translation full of pith and sense.

However, Ramsay did not work unaided, and it is time to look at who gave the talks in the early days and what they discussed. For this purpose one finds that the period from 1902 to 1914 forms a unit. The Association fast settled down to a pattern of meetings and subjects which worked, and all four universities were contributing. In retrospect, as one reads the Minutes, it seems to have been one of our finest periods, although those who lived through it, as so often, felt they were fighting a rearguard action against the tendencies of the times.

Several conclusions can be drawn from a perusal of the lists of office-bearers, meetings and lectures. First, we see that the members met twice a year, in spring and autumn, and that they made sure that they visited each university in succession. At first nearly every talk and discussion seems to concentrate on the teaching of classical languages and this was obviously well designed to find common ground between school and university concerns. However, there was surely a limit to how much flesh and blood could stand in discussing the admirable uses to which unseens and prose composition could be put (or is my reaction anachronistic? Perhaps it is). At any rate one notices that from the beginning members welcomed the allurements of archaeology, with a talk on visual aids in teaching at the first meeting and another in November 1905 by Professor Baldwin Brown on classical costume, which was engagingly said to be illustrated with photographs of the living model. On this occasion they met in the Natural Philosophy class room (Natural Philosophy is of course the correct Scottish term for Physics) so that they could use the class lantern for the slides. (Incidentally Baldwin Brown was the Professor of Fine Art at Edinburgh and a keen supporter of the Association as well. He held his chair for an amazing fifty-one years, from 1880 to 1931.) After his talk in 1905 we find that archaeological topics appear fairly regularly in the afternoons in this first period – ten of them between 1905 and 1912 – and the lantern is duly mentioned on these occasions, except in November 1906 when Dr (later Sir) George Macdonald produced what are called 'limelight views'. Now although in my more cynical moments, from experience of CAS meetings in the afternoon, I might think that the lantern lectures were very well designed to make it easy for the members to take a little nap, it is I think, speaking more seriously, to the credit of the early members that they did appreciate the importance of archaeology. And it wasn't all Roman Britain either. They had Sir William Ramsay on Asia Minor in 1907, R. C. Bosanquet on Sparta in 1908, Gilbert Davies on Lycia in 1910 and most far-reaching of all, I suspect, Professor John Myres in 1909 on 'The place of Classical Geography in a classical curriculum: a plea for correlation of studies' – a subject which we have, I fear, largely neglected since.

So of archaeology they had plenty. Ancient history on the other hand was, I am sorry to say, almost totally neglected. A straight historical topic only appears once in the first twelve years, in the shape of a talk on 'The teaching of Ancient History' in 1908. It is significant that it was given by Professor Richard Lodge, who held the History chair at Edinburgh, not by anyone in a classical post. The positive side of this is the cooperation with scholars in other fields: we have already seen Baldwin Brown and Lodge, and can add Professor Saintsbury of the Chair of Rhetoric and English Literature at Edinburgh in 1904. Linguistic and paedagogic concerns predominated, however, and the members clearly enjoyed them, with wide participation in the discussions, and in effect more than one paper in the morning on them, because the first three Presidents often gave addresses prior to a morning talk by someone else.

Although members often stressed the need for precision and proper linguistic discipline, as one would expect, they showed a refreshing breadth of outlook as well. Harrower in 1903 argued that two different curricula in Greek were needed all through school and university, one aimed at enhancing general culture, the other at producing specialists; Butcher in the same year thought that in both Greek and Latin there was 'much useless lumber which might be discarded'; Phillimore in 1907 commended unseens as 'a loophole upon literature', arguing that they should be used to facilitate the study of a broader repertoire of authors, in the interests of students who wanted to work with history or the Romance languages; in 1912 Dr Heard of Fettes, the third President, deplored the examination system, 'with its hurry and cram, and false tests of efficiency, as tending to kill the vitalizing personality of the Teacher, and to suffer the finer breath of literature to expire'. Ramsay himself at the very beginning warned of the dangers of too much narrow research which would interfere with the more important aims of education.

Among the valuable achievements of this educational concern was a report on the pronunciation of Latin produced in 1905 by a committee of the association headed by Professor Hardie of the Edinburgh Humanity chair (he is the Hardie of *Latin Prose Composition* and *Res Metrica*). The report was accepted by the Scottish Education Department and has formed the basis of reformed pronunciation of Latin in Scottish schools ever since. A similar exercise was carried through in England by CA. When it came to Greek, to which CAS turned its attention in 1907, things seem to have languished a little more, and by 1910 CAS simply accepted the CA's proposals, with which it had no evident disagreements. And it may be too that members had their minds on other distractions. The Minutes amply show year after year a good deal of alarm at developments regarding the Leaving Certificates (which were the ancestors of Highers) and the Intermediate Certificates: the regulations of the Education Department were too uniform and cramped the freedom of the teacher to adapt classwork to suit particular pupils; the time allowed to science and drawing was excessive; the university bursary competitions were actually equalising marks given for French and German with those given for Greek. The numbers studying Greek in the grant-earning schools were found to have diminished by 40 per cent in five years, and in 1912 Professor Harrower went so far as to draw up a map of Greekless areas of the country. (It would be an interesting sight; perhaps we should send a delegation to Aberdeen to look for it.) Many resolutions were passed, and in the end a delegation of the Association 'waited upon Sir John Struthers' as the phrase in the Minutes has it, and received at least some satisfaction. (Sir John was Secretary of the Scottish Education Department.)

As a footnote to this, may I say that I was at first baffled by some cogitation which members gave to 'Hidden Quantities'. In 1912 Professor Hardie presented a motion from Council to the effect that 'the time is not yet ripe to insist on 'Hidden Quantities', and no more has been heard of them in CAS from that day to this. What on earth would they have been? (One answer is in the *Proceedings* for 1904–5, p. 21: when a syllable is long by position, the natural length of the vowel may be considered hidden.)

One rather different question of importance which came up was how close the relationship with the larger but younger southern association was to be. We have seen Ramsay attending its first meeting, and cooperation in reforming the pronunciation of Latin and Greek. Then in January 1911 Dr Heard, Professor Davies and Professor Hardie attended by invitation a meeting of CA at Liverpool at which a federation of the Scottish, Irish, and English and Welsh Associations was discussed. But when the delegates came back they had declined to barter away our independence, and moved the following motion, which was accepted by the general meeting in November 1911: 'The Classical Association of Scotland desires to acknowledge with full sympathy and appreciation the proposal to unite the various Classical Associations in closer relationships: but, while more than willing to cooperate to the utmost in all common interests, [it] believes that it would be scarcely expedient to formulate any definite scheme of federation.' I may say about this (and here is the *studium* of which I warned you) that this seems to be exactly the right sort of response: yes to friendship and cooperation but no to self-obliteration. And whenever this question comes up, as it has done at least three times through the century, I think we can regard the response as a litmus test of the health and self-respect of Scottish classicism.

I have said nothing so far of the size of the Association. By the end of 1903, there were 168 annual members and 28 life members; by 1908 we hear of '30 ladies and 271 gentlemen' (the only time the two are differentiated) and by 1912 the total was 274 ordinary members and 50 life members. Naturally numbers at the meetings were smaller, since it was difficult to get to meetings from some parts of the country, and some members must have paid their subscriptions just in order to receive the *Proceedings* and to demonstrate loyalty to the cause. We have some attendance figures, which vary a good deal: 40 for Burnet on 'Form and Matter in Classical Teaching' in 1904, 60 for Hardie on Pronunciation, and generally about 25 for the morning meetings in Aberdeen and St Andrews as against about 50 in Edinburgh and Glasgow.

But *labuntur anni,* and inexorably one arrives at 1914, and sure enough there is a grim lacuna: no meetings of Council were held beween 1914 and 1922 and no general meetings between November 1914 and May 1919, apart from a sole general meeting in December 1916, when Professor Burnet took over the Presidency and his address showed how much the war was on their minds:

Professor Burnet laid before the meeting his conception of the task which the Association was called upon to perform. That task lay in making the spirit of Humanism more operative in our national life than it had been before and in labouring to bring about a new Humanist Renaissance. He first of all dealt with the delusion that the success of German industry was due to the amount of science teaching in the schools and showed that in Germany specialization in science came only after a long training in the Humanities. To the French mind the Great War was a conflict between Graeco-Latin civilization and Germanic barbarism and the imperative need of Europe in the coming years was not primarily economic reconstruction, but the revival of *humanitas* or better still of *philanthropia*. History showed that modern science itself was the outcome of the rediscovery of Greek, just as its continued progress was conditioned by constant contact with the Greek mind. But science would not rebuild our shattered European civilization: only the re-fashioning of the human soul could do that and the studies that deal with the things of the spirit were alone capable of helping us here.

If my first hero in this talk was Ramsay, the second is Burnet, not only in this context because he kept the Association together at a difficult time, but because he did so much to illuminate the Greeks. I am thinking not just of his work on philosophy and his excellent commentaries on Plato, which have in some respects never been bettered, but of his sterling elementary Greek book called *Greek Rudiments,* to which so many Scots have owed their Greek.

When the war was over, the Association seems to have taken time to get itself together, and when it did the pattern of meetings seems thin by comparison with pre-war days. Although two meetings a year were held from 1919 to 1921, three of those six are described as having very small attendances, and the other three were held jointly with the English Association, perhaps to bolster the numbers. The Secretary, Dr King Gillies (some of you will have been brought up on Gillies' and Shepherd's *Latin Grammar*) stopped numbering the Association's meetings in the minute book after 1916, and the traditional numbering was not resumed until 1928, and even then on a basis that one could now dispute, so that I am by no means sure now that we celebrated our hundredth meeting at the right time! No meeting was held in 1922 and from 1923 to 1934 there was never more than one a year. Indeed in 1931 and 1932 there were no meetings at all for reasons unexplained. Furthermore, between 1920 and 1935 there were no meetings in St Andrews and between 1919 and 1935 there was only one in Aberdeen, in 1930, and that was only because the then President, Dr Peter Giles, Master of Emmanuel College, Cambridge, had an Aberdeen connection. The limiting of meetings to one a year was in fact a deliberate decision of the Council in 1922, and the original idea was that the annual meeting would be held in Perth, presumably as a central point, but the idea of Perth was too much for the long-suffering members, particularly those from Edinburgh and Glasgow, and it is no surprise to anyone who knows the strength of those two cities in Scottish affairs that they now secured nearly all the meetings. There was also a major change in the pattern of office-bearers, which you will see if you turn to the first page of the list below (p. 273). Before the First War, Presidents had held office for a few years at a time, but from 1923 it was decided that there should be a President chosen every year, and that this should be some non-professional scholar, distinguished in public life, a practice that Burnet said had proved advantageous in our sister association in England. There would also be a Chairman of Council, whose term of office after a time settled down at two years.

How well did this work? If you look at the list of Presidents between the wars, you will see that they did indeed find some distinguished men, the greatest celebrity being the Earl of Oxford in 1926; and if you can't remember who the Earl of Oxford was, you are no worse than I was, for I had to look him up, having forgotten that this was the title bestowed on the former Liberal Prime Minister H. H. Asquith. Very impressively, he did not talk safely on some very general subject but chose to speak on the Renaissance humanist Scaliger, and he drew an audience of 700 when there had only been about 35 for poor Professor Gilbert Davies on the morning of the same day. Is this not a familiar pitfall? The big names will bring in the big numbers but they melt away again for the routine meetings. It is also fairly clear from the Minutes that the big names were difficult to catch when they knew that they would have to give an address. The Council was prone to aiming too high: for 1927 the Chairman tried to get in succession the Duchess of Atholl, Sir Robert Horne and Earl Balfour, but ended up with the former Principal of Aberdeen Sir George Adam Smith, a fellow academic, albeit a hugely distinguished one; similarly for 1928 they decided on Earl Balfour, failing whom Viscount Haldane, failing whom Professor Harrower of Aberdeen, and it was Professor Harrower whom they got. But, in fairness, the distinguished scholars whom they did attract were excellent men and well worth having: apart from the two I have already mentioned, look down the list and you will see J. W. Mackail in 1925, Gilbert Murray in 1929 and the great classically minded Professor of Natural History at St Andrews, D'Arcy Wentworth Thompson, best known to classicists as the author of those two volumes on Greek birds and Greek fishes, in 1935. (He must have been an accomplished linguist, because in her biography of him his daughter recounts how on one occasion he recognised in his class a student who was a classicist and gave the rest of his lecture in Latin.)

The afternoons were reserved for the great men (the reverse of what we do now); so what did they do in the mornings? In the list of lecture titles for the 1920s and 1930s, the same sort of linguistic and educational subjects appear as before the war, with participation by teachers in schools just as much as by their university colleagues, and with good opportunities to deplore the backsliding of the times. Here for example is some of the Minute of the 20th March 1926: see if you can recognise any of your own views in it.

Professor Davies of Glasgow [this is the G. A. Davies of the Pitt Press edition of Demosthenes' *Philippics*] then read a short paper on 'Illiteracy in the universities'. He stated that for some time he had had an uneasy feeling that the students in his own department were writing less pure and less intelligible English than when he first came to Scotland. His opinion had been confirmed by an external examiner in Classics who declared that the English written in the degree examinations was decidedly discreditable.

Professor Davies thought that it was futile to teach literature as such to children of twelve. What could be done at that stage, however, was to plant in the mind of the child the seeds of accurate thinking and expression and for this purpose Latin was beyond question better fitted than English. Mr Ritchie Girvan, lecturer in English, Glasgow University, agreed with Professor Davies that modern teaching had gone off on a false scent – the teaching of literature. He thought that the emphasis should be laid on language and proceeded to illustrate the sordid ignorance on the part of university students of the meanings of quite ordinary words.

A valuable and interesting discussion followed in which [various names follow] took part, and among the suggestions made in explanation of the prevailing illiteracy were the popularity of things scientific and mechanical, the tendency to bring secondary education down to a lower social level, and the iniquitous examination system which prevailed in the country.

A good time was clearly being had by all, but it is difficult not to feel that, with meetings confined to one a year, and the mornings almost completely confined to pedagogical and linguistic topics, and the Presidents' addresses sometimes very general, there were areas of Classics that were less well covered than by the Edwardians. Surprisingly, there were no archaeological lectures between Sir George Macdonald on the Traprain Treasure in 1920 and Stuart Miller on the Romans in South-west Scotland in 1948 (a sad comedown from the pattern before 1914) and ancient history continued to be notably neglected. It was left to a thoughtful schoolmaster, Mr John Clarke of Hutcheson's Grammar School, to lament in 1929 that in all the school classical examinations in Scotland it was possible for pupils to succeed by linguistic ability alone, and that as a result the history, life and thought of the Greeks and Romans were almost totally neglected. His plea for the importance of these was supported in the debate by Gilbert Murray (who was present as President that year) and A. W. Pickard-Cambridge, who was filling in the Edinburgh Greek Chair for a year between Mair and Calder, but there was no change in the pattern of the Association's lectures, and it was not till 1938 that there was any lecture in these years on what I would call Greek History, when Dr W. W. Tarn, as he then was, lectured upon the Greek Empire in India.

However, there is an important aspect to the situation of CAS between the wars which I have not yet mentioned, which is competition from its own branches, or local Centres as they were soon called. St Andrews was first off the mark, its local association being recognised by CAS in November 1920, and Professor Phillimore saw to it that one followed in Glasgow during 1921. I can remember the redoubtable Miss

McCulloch, a splendid lady whom some of you will recall for her large brown hats, telling Professor MacDowell and me how 'the Professor' (i.e. Phillimore) sent a message to Hutchie Girls, where she was teaching in 1921, with an urgent request to go and see him at Gilmorehill. When she got there, she was told that she was to found a Glasgow Centre and be the first Secretary. The great man spake, and it was done, and she remained Secretary from 1921 to 1945. That was how professors were obeyed in those days. By November of 1921 Phillimore was pressing those in Edinburgh to found their own Centre. In Aberdeen a local association had formed independently of CAS by 1923, and that was duly invited to affiliate. And Phillimore seems to have hoped also that Centres would be founded in Inverness and Elgin.

The mention of Elgin shows, does it not, just how much the classical scene has changed over the century. To be personal again for a minute, when my father was a schoolboy at Elgin Academy in the 1920s, there was a strong classical department, which produced Frederick Fyvie Bruce, later Professor of Biblical Criticism in Manchester; in the previous century, Elgin Academy had educated H. A. J. Munro, the editor of Lucretius, and Principal Geddes of Aberdeen, whose edition of the *Phaedo* was the first commentary on a Platonic text to be written in Scotland and is still worth consulting: it contains a more useful note on the suicide passage than any of the later commentaries. I mention Elgin not because it was highly unusual, but because it was this sort of strong local classical tradition on which the universities and CAS could build; now there has not been a classical teacher in Elgin for a generation, and classics in the northeast as a whole has all but disappeared.

The growth of the local Centres is a sign of health which arguably should be seen as a corrective to some of the picture which I have outlined about the parent body between the wars. After all, why meet so often, and why rotate north of the Forth, if there were active local Centres in the four universities? Arguably too the local Centres had a broader programme, giving proper weight to ancient history and archaeology, for example. The Aberdeen and St Andrews Centres are no more, but thanks to Dr Panayotakis I have had a look at the Minute book for the Glasgow Centre for the 1920s. It was holding on average five lectures a year, as well as running two attractive-sounding Reading Circles. But if members joined the local Centres, they did not necessarily join the parent body or support it financially, though some of them helped to swell the numbers at what were now joint meetings of parent and Centre in Edinburgh and Glasgow. (This account is not about the local Centres, but they are part of the fuller story. I am conscious that the history of Classics in Scotland in the twentieth century owes an enormous amount to them, and that we really ought to hear their history from someone else on a future occasion.)

But relations with a Centre could turn sour, as is illustrated strikingly by the Council Minutes for 10th January 1931:

The chairman explained that the present meeting had been summoned in consequence of a communication from the Secretary of the Edinburgh Centre expressing dissatisfaction with the parent body and intimating the possibility of the Edinburgh and S.E. Centre members resigning from the said parent body.

Mr Mylne, the Secretary of the Edinburgh Centre spoke at considerable length. What was objected to was not the policy of the parent body but a lack of business-like method in carrying out that policy. With regard to the book of Proceedings, could annual publication not be resumed, and could nothing be done by the parent body to make it more worth publishing? Why did the names of no St Andrews representatives appear in the last volume; and why were the accounts of the Association not audited?

The answers duly given were that annual publication would be too expensive, there were no St Andrews representatives because that Centre had temporarily lapsed, and auditing would be considered. It is interesting that there were then no meetings of the parent body at all that year and the next, and that when they resumed in 1933 the Secretary and Treasurer both resigned. (Who were they, you ask? They were James Paterson of Paterson and MacNaughton's *Approach to Latin* and H. D. F. Kitto. They were succeeded by W. K. Smith, who was to serve twenty years, longer than any other Secretary, and A. S. Kelly. Not that Paterson and Kitto had not given years of conscientious service, but one suspects they had fallen victim to the ennui that all too easily comes on officials of any society after a certain period of years.)

Under the new administration the Association decided wisely to increase its meetings to two again, and in the later 1930s it ventured back to St Andrews and Aberdeen. Indeed plans were in hand in 1939 and 1940 to meet in Inverness, a development welcomed by the head of the IRA – which is, of course, in a Scottish context, Inverness Royal Academy. Audiences for the Presidential Addresses kept up well, with 90 for Principal Hamilton Fyfe (the editor of Longinus), in 1937, and 90 for Lord Normand, the Lord President of the Court of Session, the next year. The latter gave one of the few lectures on Thucydides, arguing that the study of the Peloponnesian War had a wholesome cathartic power, a rather curious view to take in 1938.

Sadly, as in the First War, the effects on the Association when the

Second War did come were disruption and demoralisation. The disruption is clear. Apart from a meeting in Glasgow in May 1940, when the Treasurer is already noted as away on government service, there were no general meetings between early 1939 and December 1946: this time it was C. J. Fordyce as Chairman of Council who seems to have kept affairs ticking over, as Burnet had done in the First War. As for demoralisation, that is how I would read the sad state of affairs when at the first post-war meeting a motion was put forward to seek amalgamation with the Classical Association in the south. The matter was controversial and the motion to appoint a committee to negotiate, which was proposed by Professor Calder of the Edinburgh Greek Chair, was opposed by W. L. Lorimer. A vote was taken (one of the only two occasions recorded at a general meeting) and the motion was carried by 15 to 10. Irritatingly, the Minutes give no inkling of the arguments on either side. Lorimer's opposition is what one would expect of his lifelong cultural patriotism: this is the man who devoted so many years to translating the New Testament into Scots and was vigilant in preserving what he saw as the characteristic features of the Scottish tradition – for which he has to be my third hero. But what are we to make of Professor Calder, a man born in Edinkillie by the banks of the Divie, and educated at Gordon's College in Aberdeen? Did his motion stem from the wish to swim in a bigger pond, or the hope that English gold would come of amalgamation, or weariness at the thought of reviving the Association? Or was it a more positive and outgoing impulse, the product of the terrible years of struggle, in which what bound us to our English friends in a British patriotism seemed more important than what divided us from them? The record is silent, and, unless oral testimony can help us, it will remain so.

Fortunately for our present existence as an association, the Committee's endeavours petered out, again for reasons unstated in the Minute Book. In 1948, we hear that negotiations are still being continued, but then no more. At the Edinburgh conference last April, I asked Dr Chris Stray, who is editing a volume on the history of CA, whether he could shed light on this from the English side, and he said it looked to him from what he had seen as if in the end our forebears just drew back from the finality of surrendering independence.

And to do them justice, the men of the late 1940s did a good job in reviving the Association, although what I have called the canonical post-war pattern took time to establish itself. From 1948, there were again usually two meetings a year, although from 1946 to 1950, there were hardly any speakers from furth of Scotland. In three years during the 1950s there was only one meeting in the year, and no meetings were held in Aberdeen between 1939 and 1954, or in St Andrews between 1938 and 1949. But from 1954 a not quite regular rotation around the four universities was re-established, and this reached in 1959 the form in which it was to remain till 1991, with Aberdeen and St Andrews in alternate years in the summer and Edinburgh and Glasgow similarly alternating in the winter.

One necessary casualty of the early post-war years was the *Proceedings*, which in twenty volumes from 1902 to 1937 had carried texts of papers, office-bearers' reports, lists of members' names and addresses and occasionally an account of an annual dinner. Yet Minutes of Council Meetings are curiously silent about the *Proceedings* most of the time, and I presume that their compilation was left to the long-suffering Secretary of the day. It is after the Second War that financing of them surfaces as a serious issue. In 1951 an application was made to the Carnegie Trust for help, but without success. In May 1953, the Chairman proposed to a general meeting to raise the subscription from 5 shillings to 10 shillings, then a considerable amount of money, to finance the *Proceedings* but the motion did not even find a seconder! So the *Proceedings* lapsed, though in May 1955 Council was wondering about starting a Scottish Classical Journal. The then Secretary, John Bishop, was to investigate, but again no more is heard.

One post-war development in which the Association played an honourable part was the foundation of the International Federation of Societies of Classical Studies, the FIEC, of which we were founder members. A. W. Gomme went to Paris on our behalf for the preparatory meeting in 1948 and to Naples in 1953, C. J. Fordyce went to the meetings from 1949 to 1951, and W. K. Smith appears to have been at the Copenhagen meeting in 1954. But enthusiasm waned as membership became more expensive compared with any benefit received, and in 1966 Council decided to pull out, a decision which Alex Garvie once told me led to indignant Gallic reproaches during his treasurership in the late 1960s.

Another sign that the Association was in good heart by the 1950s was the Jubilee celebrations of 1952. An extended two-day meeting was held in Edinburgh on 2nd and 3rd May, with four lectures culminating in a Presidential lecture by Principal Taylor of Aberdeen on Thucydides, attended by 100 people. Representatives were present from CA and from the Klassiek Verbond of the Netherlands. In fact it had originally been hoped to invite CA to hold a joint meeting in Scotland for the

Jubilee, just as we did for the Centenary, but CA was tied to a previous engagement with Reading.

But, the Jubilee over, we enter the long Elizabethan peace, and what is there to say about that? Well I promise to say less than I have already said, but some features of our second half-century are worth noting. The first, more in sorrow than in anger, is our loss of any substantial school-teaching connection. No school-teacher addressed the Association after James Paterson in 1954, and the last talk to have school education as a main theme was that by Hugh McArdle of Moray House in 1956. Some individual serving and retired school-teachers have supported us in recent decades, and very welcome they have been and are, but they have been few in comparison with the first half-century. Was the disappearance of school subjects from our programme cause or symptom of our school teaching colleagues' widespread disappearance? I am inclined to think that it was mainly symptom. Although the Minutes say nothing directly about it, we would surely have kept up school subjects had there been a demand. To some extent, it may have been felt that teaching subjects were catered for elsewhere, either in the local Centres, or in the Associations of Teachers of Classics in Edinburgh and Glasgow or in the Tayside Classical Association, but this splintering and divorce between education at school and university would certainly have distressed Ramsay and the other founding fathers.

At intervals we have gone searching for our lost colleagues, like the Ents searching for their wives in Tolkien, but it has been to little avail. Most recently, in 1998, we sent members to give talks to schools in Aberdeen and used part of the profits of the 1995 conference with CA to provide book grants to schools which applied. We also circulated all the schools in Scotland presenting candidates for Highers in classical subjects, but the attempt to remind our colleagues that we are the only body devoted to speaking for Classics nationally in Scotland fell largely on deaf ears. Some of this is inevitable, given that a much smaller proportion of our students have studied classical subjects in Scottish schools, and that a smaller proportion of those who have see it as their patriotic duty to support their national universities. But we have lost something all the same, when we no longer find a school-teacher from Keith or Portree or Dumfries able and willing and invited to address this Association.

The second thing which I would note about the last fifty years is that we can draw a line somewhere about the end of the 1970s, after which the challenges for Scottish Classics become altogether steeper. Is it just nostalgia on my part which makes me regard the 1950s to the 1970s as the Indian summer of traditional Classics in Scotland? Certainly in the Minutes of this Association for those years there is a sense of a Mendelssohnian calm sea and prosperous voyage. From 1966 to 1971 Council never even met, though there is the rumour that the then Secretary, Ron McCail, just forgot to call a meeting, and it seems that poor Professor A. H. Campbell had to serve twenty years as President because nobody remembered any longer that the post was not held for more than two years! And when in the 1970s Roy Pinkerton was Secretary and I was Treasurer, Council met at moderate intervals and had no crises to deal with. The hundredth meeting was duly celebrated in 1972 with a special lunch, and in 1973 Roy Pinkerton expanded the Notice of Meeting into the first Newsletter. The future looked relatively assured.

Even the finances were relatively untroubled. Our subscription was five shillings in 1902, and apart from 1904–6, when it was briefly seven shillings and sixpence, it remained at five shillings till 1969 when it was raised again to seven and six; at decimalisation in 1971 we were one of the few organisations to round our subscription down, to thirty-seven pence, though the figure proved unpopular with members, and it was raised to fifty pence in 1976. (One scandal unreported at the time which it may now be time to confess is that the Treasurer in the 1970s on one occasion used the society's funds to pay his domestic milk bill. Mistaking the Association's cheque book for his own when torn from sleep one Saturday morning by an importunate milk boy ringing his bell, he used one of our official cheques to pay his bill, and was then puzzled to discover on doing the annual accounts that a cheque for £1.82 had been paid to Wiseman's dairy. To replace the missing sum by making a prompt donation of £1.82 was easy, but how was the original payment to be entered in the official account book? The advantages of a classical education are many and Gibbon's 'decent obscurity of a learned language' allowed me – for I was the guilty man – to enter the discreet word 'galactodaneisma' in the account book, where I dare say it still remains.)

The 1980s were altogether grimmer, as for Scotland as a whole. In the Minutes we find members of Council at each anxious meeting comparing notes about staffing gaps and, in some cases, falling student numbers; this was the time when south of the border there were disappearances of departments and amalgamations, and Council was commendably anxious to avoid the loss of one of our own four departments, all with venerable and valuable traditions. It was the worst blow to university Classics in Scotland in four centuries, when, owing to a fatal combination of an unsympathetic Principal in Aberdeen and a spineless University Grants Committee report, which showed no emotional or intellectual understanding of the historic role of Aberdeen in the northeast, the department in Aberdeen was closed in 1990; our meetings there on a regular basis duly stopped as from 1991. For myself, especially on a good Saturday in May, I still miss the sun sparkling off the granite on the walk to King's, I want to look again at the clean lines and douce mass of the professors' manses and the civilised late Gothic of King's Chapel, and to meet again the welcome of classical friends there. (As footnote to that, I'd just like to pay tribute to Patrick Edwards and Thomas Pearce and Morton Gauld, who have been teaching beginners languages, paid by the hour, as at least a *susurrus* of the classical spirit.) The loss of Aberdeen required us to revise our pattern of meetings. For a time St Andrews generously had us to visit every summer in place of the alternation, but in 1999 we settled into a new three-way rotation, and this is still serving us well.

However, let us pass from the shadow to the light. It is time to sum up the positive features of the past fifty years, and there are indeed plenty of them. First, in our regular meetings, we can credit ourselves with having provided a steady and rich stream of speakers on all aspects of classical studies. If you look at the lists, you will see I think an extremely impressive coverage over the last half century, and, long before research seminars became fashionable in each separate institution, we have been inviting speakers to present their work in an intelligible form to audiences of sympathetic fellow-classicists. During the secretaryship of David West, the number of speakers from furth of Scotland, which had been small since the war, was increased, to make sure that we were open to ideas from elsewhere, while home speakers allowed us all to know the calibre and strength of mind of our colleagues in our own universities; and this has been the pattern since.

Our second achievement has been to preserve the respect and friendship which colleagues in our departments have for each other. I do not pretend that all have contributed equally to this. There have always been some people who, sadly, never come to meetings outside their own university and even inside only come if the meeting suits their research interest. But there has always been in each university a sufficient number of collegially minded members who are glad to travel and see their friends, and are equally glad to welcome the visitor. It is these who have, in the words of Ecclesiasticus, made our inheritance. Examples are dangerous, but nobody will feel *phthonos* if I pay tribute here to our present President, whom I think I have never seen miss a meeting, and who has been an example to us all, and I will also just recall with appreciation the warmth of the greetings which those of us from the south always met from Professors Cormack and Watt and their colleagues in Aberdeen, and, before the Swallowgate was available for tea close by, the generous and unfailing hospitality of the Smiths, the Kidds and the Hines in St Andrews.

I emphasise this *concordia universitatum* because I think it is something that the late twentieth century made at once a little more difficult and even more worth striving for. The 1990s have ushered in the RAEs and similar wicked devices, which tend to foster rivalry between departments and universities where there should be cooperation, distrust where there should be trust, and self-interest where there should be friendship. This Association is particularly precious because it was founded on the opposite ideal, that of the friendship and similarity of interests of all Scottish Classicists, and the equality of the classical universities in Scotland.

Thirdly, I would mention a number of initiatives where we have moved forward. Preeminent is the cooperation with the Classical Association in the south, entered into while Douglas MacDowell was Chairman and Roy Pinkerton Secretary, which has brought us four conferences since 1978. These have shown a wider world the strength of our classical traditions here while bringing us fresh air, new ideas, and valuable contacts with our southern friends. They have also brought us income, which we have tried to use in an enlightened way, by supporting our local Centres, which themselves keep up a more constant flow of meetings, and by giving grants to help specific local initiatives like the Prose and Verse Speaking competitions for schools at one end of the learning spectrum and postgraduate attendance at conferences at the other. It is right for me to mention also in this connection a generous bequest in 1989 from Miss J. T. Mitchell of Castle Douglas.

In 1993 we updated our Constitution when I drafted one on the mistaken assumption we then shared that, if there was an original one, it was lost – not realising that the forgotten 'Rules of the Association' had been the constitution. But the updating has I hope been useful. In 1999 we broke new ground by devoting an afternoon session to hearing talks by young researchers, an experiment which might be worth repeating. Another innovation has been the introduction, thanks to Graham Whitaker, of our own website, which sets out our activities with admirable clarity. Finally, what gave me most satisfaction on a national front was that we recently persuaded the Scottish Teaching Council to drop the outdated rule that only those who had studied the Greek or Latin language at university could teach Classical Studies. This had disqualified nearly all our excellent Classical Civilisation graduates from entering teacher training, exacerbating the shortage of classical teachers. Our initiative has removed the log-jam and there are now several graduates training in Jordanhill.

But I am beginning to sound alarmingly like a headmaster reporting at prize-giving. Enough of the recent past. And the future? Well, I have always been better at the past than the future, but I hope I have shown that we still have worthwhile work to do. We are still the body best fitted to speak for Classics in Scotland, with among our members the knowledge and the talent and the experience. There are even innovations worth considering. I am such a Luddite that it will seem absurd coming from me, but I do wonder in these days of electronic journals whether a revised *Proceedings* which would serve in some form as a Journal or Forum for Scottish Classics is worth mooting.

My other suggestion is more of a plea, and that is that we do not forget our specifically Scottish cultural inheritance. When I look at the lecture lists, I realise how few lectures we have had that illuminate the classical tradition in Scotland, in literature, art, history or whatever, and how few scholars are using their classical expertise in this area. We can take pride, of course, in what great men no longer with us have done: Professor Lorimer with his Scots New Testament, Dr David Murison on the *Scottish National Dictionary*; and there are scholars trained in Scottish classical departments who have gone into Scottish studies (I am thinking of Mairi Robinson and the *Concise Scots Dictionary*, of Professor R. D. Jack in Edinburgh, or for that matter the fact that Professor Robert Crawford here in St Andrews, poet and critic, took the Ordinary Greek class while he was an English Literature student at Glasgow, and of course gained a prize). But these cases are now few. If the Scottish classical tradition is to be understood and illuminated, we should perhaps give some more thought to it in the new century of the Association. However, I claimed just now to be a man of the past, not the future, and so it is time that I stopped talking and sat down. Let us go and, in lieu of a libation or a prayer, at least take a dish of tea in honour of the Association's next century.

OFFICE-BEARERS OF THE
CLASSICAL ASSOCIATION OF SCOTLAND

1902–22

Presidents
Prof. G. G. Ramsay (1902–8)
Prof. J. Harrower (1908–11)
Rev. Dr W. Heard (1911–16)
Prof. J. Burnet (1916–22)

Secretaries
Mr William Coutts (1902–3)
Mr W. Lobban (1903–8)
Mr R. G. Nisbet (1908–11)
Mr W. King Gillies (1911–20)

Treasurers
Mr W. Lobban (1902–3)
Mr H. Manners (1903–20)
Mr P. McGlynn (1920–5)

1923–47

Presidents
Viscount Finlay (1923–4)
Dr J. W. Mackail (1925)
The Earl of Oxford (1926)
Very Rev. Sir G. A. Smith (1927)
Prof. J. Harrower (1928)
Prof. Gilbert Murray (1929)
Dr Peter Giles (1930–2)
Sir John Simon (1933)
Dr G. S. Gordon (1934)
Prof. D'Arcy Thompson (1935)
Sir George Macdonald (1936)
Principal W. Hamilton Fyfe (1937)
Lord Normand (1938)
Sir Philip Macdonnell (1939)
Dr W. G. S. Adams (1940–7)

Secretaries
Mr G. T. Pringle (1920–27)
Mr James Paterson (1927–33)
Mr W. K. Smith (1933–53)

Chairmen of Council
Prof. J. Burnet (1923)
Mr A. Gemmell (1924–5)
Prof. O. L. Richmond (1926–7)
Dr. J. M. Wattie (1928–9)
Prof. W. Rennie (1930–2)
Prof. W. M. Calder (1933–4)
Dr W. King Gillies (1935–6)
Mr J. D. McPetrie (1937–8)
Prof. C. J. Fordyce (1939–46)

Treasurers
Mr P. McGlynn (1920–5)
Mr H. D. F. Kitto (1925–33)
Mr A. S. Kelly (1933–8)
Mr M. Mackay (1938–40)
Mr J. A. H. Way (1940–53)

1948–2002

Presidents
Prof. W. Rennie (1948–9)
Prof. J. Dover Wilson (1950)
Principal T. M. Taylor (1951–2)
Prof. H. J. Paton (1953–4)
Prof. H. J. Rose (1955–6)
Prof. A. W. Gomme (1957–8)
Lord Cameron (1959)
Sir John Spencer Muirhead (1960–2)
Prof. A. H. Campbell (1963–83)
Prof. W. S. Watt (1983–8)
Sir Kenneth Dover (1988–93)
Prof. P. G. Walsh (1993–8)
Prof. E. K. Borthwick (1998–)

Chairmen of Council
Mr W. M. Smail (1948–9)
Mr W. L. Lorimer (1950–1)
Mr John Clarke (1953–4)
Prof. A. W. Gomme (1955–6)
Mr W. McL. Dewar (1957–9)
Mr G. D. Gray (1960–8)
Prof. C. J. Fordyce (1969–74)
Prof. J. Cormack (1975)
Prof. K. J. Dover (1975–6)
Prof. D. M. MacDowell (1976–81)
Prof. P. G. Walsh (1982–7)
Prof. E. K. Borthwick (1987–92)
Prof. H. M. Hine (1993–8)
Prof. R. P. H. Green (1998–)

Secretaries
Mr W. K. Smith (1933–53)
Mr J. H. Bishop (1953–9)
Mr D. A. West (1960–6)
Dr R. C. McCail (1966–71)
Mr R. M. Pinkerton (1971–80)
Mr T. E. V. Pearce (1980–8)
Dr C. Carey (1988–91)
Dr L. M. Whitby (1991–5)
Dr R. A. Knox (1995–2002)

Treasurers
Mr J. A. H. Way (1940–53)
Mr A. Treloar (1953–5)
Mr T. E. Kinsey (1955–66)
Mr A. F. Garvie (1966–71)
Dr R. A. Knox (1971–81)
Dr M. H. B. Marshall (1981–95)
Dr K. E. Stears (1995–2000)
Mr A. B. E. Hood (2000–)

This appendix began as a centenary lecture to the Classical Association of Scotland in October, 2002. I am extremely grateful to Dr Stray and the Council of the CA for finding space for it here, to Professors Roger Green and Douglas MacDowell for comment on an earlier version, and to them and many office bearers and members of CAS for helpful information. They are none of them responsible for any heresies that remain!

Appendix 2

ANNUAL GENERAL MEETINGS, PRESIDENTS AND ADDRESSES

By PHILIP HOOKER

Years are based on dates of Meetings, not the commencement of a term of office. Positions of Presidents are those held at the time of their address.

1903 Saturday 19 December, Botanical Theatre, University of London
Inaugural Meeting

1904 27–28 May, Oxford
Rt. Hon. Sir Richard Henn Collins
(1842–1911; Master of the Rolls)

1905 6–7 January, University College, London

1906 5–6 January, King's College, London
Rt. Hon. Earl of Halsbury
(1823–1921; Lord Chancellor)

1906 11–13 October, Manchester
Lord Curzon of Kedleston
(1859–1925; formerly Viceroy of India. Unable to attend, following the death of his wife. Hon. Mr Justice Kennedy gave an address on 'Classics and the Law in his place).

1907 18–19 October, Cambridge
Prof. Samuel Butcher – 'Greek and the Classical Renaissance of Today'.
(1850–1910; Professor of Greek at Edinburgh 1882–1904, MP for University of Cambridge 1906–10.) Butcher replaced Sir Richard Jebb, d. December 1905, a founder of the Classical Association and Chairman of Council.

1908 8–10 October, Birmingham
Rt. Hon. Herbert Asquith – 'The Function of a Classical Association'.
(1852–1928; Prime Minister).

1910 10–11 January, London
Rt. Hon. Earl of Cromer – 'Ancient and Modern Imperialism'.
(1841–1917; formerly Proconsul of Egypt)

1911 5–7 January, Liverpool
Sir Archibald Geikie – 'Love of Nature among the Romans'.
(1835–1924; geologist, President of the Royal Society)

1912 8–9 January, King's College, London
Rt. Rev. Edward Lee Hicks – 'Hellenism as a Force in History'.
(1843–1919; Lord Bishop of Lincoln)

1913 3–4 January, Sheffield
Rev. Henry Montagu Butler – 'On Writing Greek and Latin Verses and the
Value of Translations'.
(1833–1918; Master of Trinity College, Cambridge)

1914 12–13 January, Bedford College, London
Sir Frederick George Kenyon – 'The Classics as an Element in Life'.
(1863–1952; Director of the British Museum, Chairman of Council)

1915 8 January, Merchant Taylors' Company, London
Prof. William Ridgeway – 'The Classics in Wartime'.
(1853–1926; Disney Professor of Archaeology, Cambridge)
This brief business meeting replaced the meeting previously scheduled in
Newcastle, where the buildings had been requisitioned for military purposes.

1916 7 January, University College, London
Sir William Blake Richmond
(1842–1921; artist. Shortly before the meeting, which was scheduled at the
Royal Academy, Lady Richmond was tragically killed in a street accident and
Sir William was unable to organise the meeting and prepare an address).

1917 4–6 January, Leeds
Rt. Hon. Viscount Bryce – 'The Worth of Ancient Literature in the Modern
World'.
(1838–1922; jurist, historian, politician) The first full meeting since 1914.

1918 7–8 January, King's College, London
Prof. Gilbert Murray – 'Religio Grammatici'.
(1866–1957; Regius Professor of Greek, Oxford)

1919 16–17 May, Oxford
Sir William Osler – 'The Old Humanities and the New Science'.
(1849–1919; Regius Professor of Medicine, Oxford)

1920 14–16 April, Newcastle and Durham
William Warde Fowler – 'The Imagination of the Romans'.
(1847–1921; Fellow of Lincoln College Oxford, historian) Because of illness,
the paper was read on his behalf by Professor R. S. Conway.

1921 2–6 August, Cambridge
Walter Leaf – 'The Classics and Reality'.
(1852–1927; Chairman of London and Westminster Bank)

1922 5–7 January, City of London School, London
Rt. Hon. Viscount Milner – 'A Liberal Education'.
(1854–1925; statesman)

1923 10–12 April, Bristol
J. W. Mackail – 'The Classics'.
(1859–1945; classical scholar, civil servant, literary critic, poet)

1924 3–5 January, Westminster School, London
HE The Marquess of Crewe – 'The Classics in France'.
(1858–1945; HM Ambassador in Paris, previously chairman of the Prime
Minister's Committee on the position of Classics in education)

1925 15–18 April, Bangor
Prof. John Postgate – 'Classics Today'.
(1853–1926; Professor of Latin, Liverpool (retired) and founder of the CA).

1926 7–9 January, Merchant Taylors Hall, London
Rt. Hon. Stanley Baldwin – 'Classics and the Plain Man'.
(1867–1947; Prime Minister)

1927 7–9 October, Manchester
Rt. Hon. Lord Hewart of Bury – 'The Classics'.
(1870–1943; Lord Chief Justice)

1928 9–11 January, St Paul's Girls School, London
Prof. Robert Seymour Conway – 'Poetry and Government'.
(1864–1933; Professor of Latin, Manchester, a founder of the CA)

1929 8–11 April, Cardiff
Prof. D'Arcy Wentworth Thompson – 'Science and the Classics'.
(1860–1948; zoologist and classical scholar)

1930 8–11 April, Hull
Rt. Hon. and Most Rev. William Temple – 'The Distinctive Excellences of
Greek and Latin'.
(1881–1944; Archbishop of York, later Archbishop of Canterbury)

1931 5–8 January, Bedford College, London
Prof. Albert Clark – 'Petrarch and the Renaissance'.
(1859–1937; Corpus Christi Professor of Latin, Oxford)

1932 11–14 April, Reading
Sir George Macdonald – 'Agricola in Britain'.
(1862–1940; numismatist, classical scholar, archaeologist and civil servant)

1933 5–8 April, Nottingham
Sir Willam Ross – 'The Problem of Socrates'.
(1877–1971; Provost of Oriel College, Oxford)

1934 3–5 January, St Paul's School, London
The Very Rev. William Ralph Inge – 'Greeks and Barbarians'.
(1860–1954; Dean of St Paul's)

1935 8–11 April, Southampton
Cyril Bailey – 'Fate, Men and Gods'.
(1871–1957; Fellow of Balliol College, Oxford)

1936 2–4 January, London
Rt. Hon. Leo Amery – 'The Odyssey'.
(1873–1955; politician and journalist)

1937 7–10 April, Belfast
Prof. Robert Mitchell Henry – 'The Roman Tradition'.
(1873–1950; Professor of Latin, Belfast)

1938 5–8 January, University College, London
T. R. Glover – 'Purpose in Classical Studies'.
(1869–1943; Fellow of St John's College, Cambridge)

1939 12–15 April, Royal Holloway College
Arthur Pickard-Cambridge – 'The Value of some Ancient Greek Scientific Ideas'.
(1872–1952; formerly Vice-Chancellor, Sheffield University)

1940 10–13 April, St Peter's Hall, Oxford
Sir Stephen Gaselee – 'An Intelligence Service for the Classics'.
(1882–1943; Librarian and Keeper of the Papers, Foreign Office)

1941 21–23 April, St Hilda's College, Oxford
Sir Richard Livingstone – 'The Classics and National Life'.
(1880–1960; President of Corpus Christi College, Oxford)

1942 14–16 April, St John's College, Cambridge
T. S. Eliot – 'The Classics and the Man of Letters'.
(1888–1965; poet and playwright)

1943 13–15 April, Cambridge
John Sheppard – 'The Relevance of Greek Poetry'.
(1887–1968; Provost of King's College, Cambridge)

1944 11–14 April, St Albans High School For Girls
Sir Walter Moberly – 'Plato's Conception of Education and its Meaning for Today'.
(1881–1974; Chairman of University Grants Committee)

1945 3–5 April, Oxford
Maurice Bowra – 'A Classical Education'.
(1898–1971; Warden of Wadham College, Oxford)

1946 8–11 April, Exeter
Sir Frank Fletcher – 'Our Debt to the Classics: a Retrospect'.
(1870–1954; formerly Headmaster of Charterhouse)

1947 15–18 April, Royal Insitute of British Architects, London
Rt. Hon. Lord Greene – 'Classics and the Social Revolution of Our Time'.
(1883–1952; Master of the Rolls)

1948 31 March–3 April, Sheffield
Sir Frank Adcock – 'The Cleverness of the Greeks'.
(1886–1968; Professor of Ancient History, Cambridge)

1949 19–23 April, Manchester
Rt. Hon. Lord Soulbury – 'Classics and Politics'.
(1887–1971; politician, chairman of Burnham Committees)

1950 12–15 April, Bristol
Prof. Hugh Last – 'Ancient History and Modern Education'.
(1894–1957; Principal of Brasenose College, Oxford)

1951 3–7 April, Liverpool
Hon. Harold Nicolson – 'Nature in Greek Poetry'.
(1886–1968; author and critic)

1952 16–19 April, Reading
Prof. William Calder – 'On Getting to Know the Greeks'.
(1881–1960; formerly Professor of Greek, Edinburgh)

1953 8–11 April, Leeds
Rt. Hon. Viscount Samuel – 'The Classical Age and Our Own'.
(1870–1963; Liberal politician, administrator and philosopher)

1954 7–10 April, University College, London
Prof. Gilbert Murray – 'Are Our Pearls Real?'
(1866–1957; formerly Regius Professor of Greek, Oxford. Previously President
in 1917/8)

1955 13–16 April, Keele
Dr George Young – 'Cephalus, or the Fancies of a Dilettante'. (Illness
prevented him from delivering this in person, so it was read on his behalf.)
(1882–1959; historian, author of 'Early Victorian England)

1956 11–14 April, Bangor
Sir Harold Idris Bell – 'A Specialist's Apologia'.
(1879–1967; formerly Keeper of the Manuscripts, British Museum

1957 9–13 April, Newcastle and Durham
John Spedan Lewis – 'Ancient Athens and Modern Private Enterprise'.
(1885–1963; founder of the John Lewis Partnership)

1958 16–19 April, Nottingham
Prof. Dorothy Tarrant – 'The Long Line of Torchbearers'.
(1885–1973; formerly professor of Greek, Bedford College, London)

1959 8–11 April, Hull
Prof. Sir Cyril Hinshelwood – 'Classics among the Intellectual Disciplines'.
(1897–1967; physical chemist and biochemist, President of the Royal Society).

1960 11–14 April, Southampton
Prof. T. B. L. Webster – 'First Things First'.
(1905–1974; Professor of Greek, University College London)

1961 12–15 April, Birmingham
Viscount Hailsham – 'Vos Exemplaria Graeca'.
(1907–2001; Minister of Science and Technology)

1962 9–13 April, Leeds (Tercentenary of birth of Richard Bentley near Leeds)
Prof. William Beare – 'Scholars and Scientists'.
(1900–1963; Professor of Latin, Bristol)

1963 16–19 April 1963, Swansea
Sir James Mountford – 'Investment in the Classics'.
(1897–1979; Vice Chancellor of Liverpool University)

1964 7–10 April, Leicester
Prof. E. R. Dodds – 'Classical Teaching in an Altered Climate'.
(1893–1979; formerly Regius Professor of Greek, Oxford)

1965 12–15 April, Manchester
Sir Basil Blackwell – 'The Retreat from Grammar'.
(1889–1954; publisher and bookseller)

1966 12–15 April, Cardiff
Prof. Sir Roger Mynors – 'Classics Pure and Applied'.
(1903–1989; Corpus Christi Professor of Latin Language and Literature, Oxford)

1967 4–7 April, Reading
Dilys Powell – 'The Mirror of the Present'.
(1901–1995; film critic and philhellene)

1968 16–19 April, Sheffield
Prof. W. K. C. Guthrie – 'The First Humanists'.
(1906–81; Laurence Professor of Ancient Philosophy and Master of Downing College, Cambridge)

1969 8–11 April, Royal Holloway College
Hon. Montague Woodhouse – 'The Modern Environment of Classical Studies'.
(1917–2001; diplomat and politician)

1970 7–10 April, Bangor
Prof. Frank Walbank – 'An Experiment in Greek Union'.
(1909– ; Rathbone Professor of Ancient History and Classical Archaeology, Liverpool)

1971 13–16 April, Canterbury
Sir John Hackett – 'Reflections upon Epic Warfare'.
(1910–1997; soldier, Principal of King's College, London)

1972 4–7 April, Bristol
Patrick Wilkinson – 'Ancient Literature and Modern Literary Criticism'.
(1907–1985; Fellow of King's College, Cambridge)

1973 16–19 April, Lancaster
Lord Boyle of Handsworth – 'A Classical Education Revisited'.
(1923–1981; politician, Vice-Chancellor of Leeds University)

1974 26–20 April, Newcastle
Prof. Moses Finley – 'The World of Odysseus Revisited'.
(1912–1986; Professor of Ancient History, Cambridge)

1975 8–11 April, Keele
Dom David Knowles. (1896–1974; monk and monastic historian)
(Sadly, he died before the AGM, so there was no Presidential address.)

1976 12–15 April, Aberystwyth
Prof. Kenneth Dover – 'On Writing for the General Reader'.
(1920– ; Professor of Greek, St Andrews University, later President of Corpus Christi College, Oxford and Chancellor of St Andrews)

1977 12–15 April, Liverpool
Prof. David Daube – 'The Duty of Procreation'.
(1909–1999; Professor at the School of Law, Berkeley, California, previously
Regius Professor of Civil Law, Oxford)

1978 28–31 March, Edinburgh
Dr Michael Grant – 'A View of the Etruscans'.
(1914- ; author, previously Vice-Chancellor of Belfast and Khartoum and
Professor of Humanity at Edinburgh)

1979 6–10 April, Birmingham
Prof. Bryn Rees – 'Strength in What Remains'.
(1919– ; Principal, University College Lampeter, previously Professor of Greek
at Birmingham, CA Hon. Secretary and CA Chairman of Council)

1980 8–11 April, Hull
Lord Wolfenden – 'I Speak as a Fool'.
(1906–1985; Headmaster, Vice-Chancellor of Reading, Chairman of University
Grants Committee, Director and Principal Librarian at the British Museum)

1981 7–10 April, Exeter
Prof. R. D. Williams – 'Virgil's Aeneid – the First 2000 Years'.
(1917–86; Professor of Latin, Reading)

1982 14–17 April, University College, London
Sir David Hunt – 'Lessons in Diplomacy from Classical Antiquity'.
(1913–1998; Diplomat, Chairman of Commonwealth Institute).

1983 12–15 April, Nottingham
Prof. E. J. Kenney – 'The Key and the Cabinet : Ends and Means in Classical
Studies'.
(1924- ; Fellow of Peterhouse, formerly Kennedy Professor of Latin,
Cambridge)

1984 9–12 April, Cardiff
Prof. Raymond Williams – 'Writing Speech and the 'Classical''.
(1921–1988; formerly Professor of Drama, Cambridge)

1985 9–12 April, Bangor
Prof. Eric Handley – 'Aristophanes and the Real World'.
(1926– ; Regius Professor of Greek, Cambridge)

1986 1–4 April, Glasgow
Sir Nicholas Goodison – 'Education and Business'.
(1934– ; Chairman of the London Stock Exchange)

1987 8–10 April, Reading
Norma Miller – 'Talking about Tacitus'.
(1925–88; Emeritus Professor of Classics, Royal Holloway College)

1988 11–14 April, Bristol
Tony Harrison – 'Facing up to the Muses'.
(1937– ; poet and dramatist)

1989 3–6 April, Sheffield
Prof. Pat Easterling – 'City Settings in Greek Poetry'.
(1934– ; Professor of Greek, University College London)

1990 9–12 April, Canterbury
Sir Jeremy Morse – 'The Usefulness of Classics'.
(1928– ; Chairman, Lloyds Bank)

1991 8–11 April, Warwick
Prof. George Kerferd – 'Wider Yet the Challenge'.
(1915–1998; formerly Professor of Greek, Manchester, Chairman of Council 1977–90)

1992 6–9 April, Oxford
Lord Runcie – 'Still Yearns my Heart'.
(1921–2002; formerly Archbishop of Canterbury)

1993 5–8 April 1993, Durham
Prof. Fergus Millar – 'Taking the Measure of the Ancient World'.
(1935– ; Camden Professor of Ancient History, Oxford)

1994 4–7 April 1994, Exeter
Colin Haycraft – 'On not Knowing Greek, or Latin either'.
(1929–1994; publisher)

1995 1–4 April, St Andrew's
Prof. David West – 'Cast out Theory: Horace Odes 1.4 and 4.7'.
(1926 – ; Professor of Latin, Newcastle)

1996 11–14 April, Nottingham
Sir Anthony Cleaver – 'From Homer to Harwell'.
(1938– ; formerly chairman of IBM UK and of the Atomic Energy Authority)

1997 12–15 April, Royal Holloway College
Carol Handley – 'Things that Matter'.
(1929– ; Senior Member, Wolfson College, Cambridge, previously Headmistress of Camden School for Girls)

1998 7–10 April, Lampeter
Lindsey Davis – 'The Descent to Avernus – with ticket office'.
(1949– ; author)

1999 8–11 April, Liverpool
Prof. Oliver Taplin – 'Greek with Consequence'.
(1943– ; Professor of Classical Languages and Literature, Oxford)

2000 17–20 April, Bristol
Emma Kirkby – Presidential Recital – 'Orpheus and Corinna'.
(1949– ; singer)

2001 18–21 April, Manchester
Prof. Peter Wiseman – 'The Principal Thing'.
(1940– ; Professor of Classics, Exeter)

2002 4–7 April, Edinburgh
      Philip Howard – 'Tempora Mutantur'.
      (1933– ; journalist, 'The Times)

2003 11–14 April, Warwick
      Peter Jones – 'Fac et Spera'.
      (1942– ; writer and journalist, founder of Friends of Classics, formerly Senior
      Lecturer in Classics, Newcastle)

2004 1–4 April, Leeds
      Baroness Susan Greenfield
      (1950– ; Director of the Royal Institution, Professor of Physiology, Oxford)

Appendix 3

OFFICERS OF THE CA

By PHILIP HOOKER

Vice-Presidents

This list does not include those who had previously served as President who are listed elsewhere nor does it include Presidents of Allied Associations, who were briefly Vice-presidents, ex-officio. Titles and positions are those held at time of appointment. Where no institution is specified, reference to the CA is implied.

1903	Rt. Hon. H. H. Asquith	MP, later Prime Minister; President 1908
	Prof. Sir Richard Jebb	MP, Regius Professor of Greek, Cambridge
	Hon. Mr Justice Kennedy	Judge, Court of Appeal
	Dr D. B. Monro	Vice-Chancellor, Oxford
	Hon. Mr Justice Phillimore	Judge, King's Bench
	Sir Edward Maunde Thompson	Director and Principal Librarian, British Museum
	Rev. E. Warre	Headmaster of Eton College
1904	Rt. Hon. Sir Robert Finlay	Attorney-General, later Lord Chancellor
1905	Sir Archibald Geikie	President, Royal Society; President 1911
	Sir Edward Poynter	President, Royal Academy
	Rt. Rev. Dr C. Gore	Bishop of Birmingham; President of the Birmingham Branch
1906	Prof. R. Ellis	Professor of Latin, Oxford
	Prof. J. P. Postgate	Founder; Hon. Secretary 1903–06; President 1925
	Prof. R. S. Conway	Founder, Manchester Branch; President 1928
1907	Rev. Canon E. L. Hicks	Canon of Manchester Cathedral; Founder of Manchester Branch; President 1912
	Rev. E. S. Roberts	Master of Gonville & Caius College, Cambridge
	Prof. W. G. Hale	Professor of Latin, University of Chicago
	Prof. H. Jackson	Regius Professor of Greek, Cambridge
	Prof. J. W. Mackail	Assistant secretary, Board of Education; President 1923
1908	Dr H. Warren	Vice-Chancellor, President of Magdalen College, Oxford
	Dr F. G. Kenyon	Director, British Museum; President 1914

1910 Prof. G. G. A. Murray   Regius Professor of Greek, Oxford;
                                      President 1918, 1954
1911 Prof. E. A. Sonnenschein   Founder; Hon. Secretary 1903–11
1912 Rt. Hon. Lord Loreburn   Lord Chancellor
      Rt. Hon. Lord Morley   Lord Privy Seal; Chancellor, Manchester
                                      University
1913 Rt. Hon. & Most Rev. C. Lang   Archbishop of York
1914 Prof. F. Haverfield   Camden Professor of Ancient History,
                                      Oxford
1915 Prof. W. R. Roberts   Professor of Greek, Leeds; founder of Leeds
                                      Branch
1920 Dr R. W. Macan   President of University College, Oxford
      Prof. J. W. Duff   Professor of Classics, Newcastle, 1893–1933
1921 Dr P. Giles   Vice-Chancellor, Cambridge University
      Sir John Sandys   Fellow of St John's College, Cambridge
      Prof. J. S. Reid   Professor of Ancient History, Cambridge
1923 Prof. J. F. Dobson   Professor of Greek, Bristol; founder of
                                      Bristol Branch; Chairman of Council 1934-
1925 Prof. A. F. West   Dean of Arts, Princeton University
      Prof. E. V. Arnold   Professor of Latin, Bangor 1884–1924;
                                      Editor of CQ 1911–26
1926 Prof. A. C. Pearson   Regius Professor of Greek, Cambridge;
                                      Secretary 1920–23
      Rt. Rev. W. Temple   Bishop of Manchester, later Archbishop of
                                      York and of Canterbury; President 1930
1929 Prof. H. A. Ormerod   Treasurer 1921–26, Chairman of Council
                                      1929–34
      Rev. Dr G. C. Richards   Secretary 1920–26
1930 Dr D. M. Brock   Headmistress, Mary Datchelor School,
                                      Camberwell
      Prof. E. K. Rand   Professor of Classics, Harvard University
1933 Dr A. W. Pickard-Cambridge   Vice-Chancellor, Sheffield University;
                                      President 1939
      Mr H. Stewart   Principal, Nottingham University
1940 Miss J. Bacon   Principal, Royal Holloway College
      Rt. Hon. H. Ramsbotham   President, Board of Education; President
                                      1949
1943 Rt. Hon. Lord Caldecote   Lord Chief Justice
      Dr E. H. Alton   Provost, Trinity College Dublin
1944 Miss N. Jolliffe   Secretary 1936–40
      Mr A. L. Irvine   Schools Secretary 1938–48
      Mr C. F. Taylor   Housemaster, Clifton College (rtd)
1945 Miss E. Archibald   Headmistress, High School, St Albans;
                                      Chairman of Council 1948–51
      Mr H. H. Hardy   Headmaster, Shrewsbury School
      Prof. B. D. Merritt   Professor of Classics, Princeton University
1946 Dr J. Murray   Principal, Exeter University

1947	Miss E. C. Gedge	Secretary 1927–34, Treasurer 1935–47
1948	Mr J. J. R. Bridge	Secretary 1938–48
1949	Prof. H. E. Butler	Professor of Latin, University College London 1911–43
	Prof. P. N. Ure	Professor of Classics, Reading, 1911–36; Secretary 1918–20
	Prof. T. B. L. Webster	Professor of Greek, University College London 1948–68; founder of Institute of Classical Studies; Secretary 1934–8, Chairman of Council 1951–56, President 1960
1951	Sir Harold Idris Bell	Keeper of MSS, British Museum 1903–44; President 1956
	Rev. Canon C. B. Armstrong	Canon of Worcester; Chairman of Council 1964–69
1952	Mr R. H. Barrow	HM Inspector of Schools, founder of *Greece & Rome*
1954	Mr J. T. Christie	Principal of Jesus College, Oxford
	Prof. G. C. Field	Professor of Philosophy, Bristol, 1926–52
1955	Rev. Dr J. A. Nairn	Headmaster, Merchant Taylor's School (rtd)
	Prof. P. J. Enk	Professor of Latin, University of Groningen
1956	Prof. W. S. Maguinness	Professor of Latin, King's College London, Chairman of Council 1956–64
1957	Prof. E. R. Dodds	Regius Professor of Greek, Oxford, President 1964
	Prof. D. S. Robertson	Regius Professor of Greek, Cambridge, 1928–50
1958	Prof. H. J. Rose	Professor of Greek, St Andrews, 1927–53
	Mr J. Shields	Treasurer 1947–57
1962	Dr G. B. Beech	Trinity College, Hartford, Connecticut
1963	Mr F. R. Dale	Headmaster, City of London School (rtd)
1966	Prof. R. G. Austin	Journals Board 1947–68 ; Professor of Latin, Liverpool
	Mr C. W. Baty	Hon. Secretary-General of JACT; previously HM Inspector of Schools
1968	Mr T. W. Melluish	Secretary 1948–68
1969	Prof. B. R. Rees	Secretary 1963–69, Chairman of Council 1969–77, President 1979
1970	Mr B. W. Forrest	Jubilee Fund Treasurer; Headmaster, Southgate County Grammar School; a founder of JACT
1972	Prof. H. C. Baldry	Professor of Classics, Southampton
	Prof. L. A. Moritz	Treasurer 1963–72
1973	Mr L. W. de Silva	Barrister; Editor of Ceylon CA Bulletin
1977	Prof. G. B. Kerferd	Chairman of Council, 1977–90, President 1991
1979	Dr E. Hooker	Treasurer 1957–63

	Mr G. T. W. Hooker	Editor, *Greece & Rome*, 1953–64
	Prof. C. Collard	Secretary 1972–79
1984	Mrs B. Radice	Editor, Penguin Classics
1985	Prof. G. B. Townend	Chairman of *Greece & Rome* Board 1973–85; Professor of Latin, Durham
	Mr R. Watson	Treasurer 1972–85
1989	Prof. J. Percival	Secretary 1979–89, Chairman of Council 1990–95
1991	Prof. P. Walcot	Editor of *Greece & Rome*, 1969–2002
1992	Prof. D. A. West	Chairman of *Greece & Rome* Board 1985–92; Professor of Latin, Newcastle; President 1995
1995	Dr J. Ellis-Jones	Organiser of Bangor branch since 1963
1999	Prof. R. Wallace	Treasurer 1985–99
2002	Ms N. Curtis	Head of Humanities Journals, Oxford University Press
	Mr I. McAuslan	Editor of *Greece & Rome* 1977-
	Prof. C. Rowe	Chair of Council 1995–2002; Professor of Greek, Durham
2003	Prof. M. Schofield	Professor of Ancient Philosophy, Cambridge
	Mr J. Betts	Formerly Senior Lecturer in Classics, Bristol; founder of Bristol Classical Press

Chairmen of Council*

1903–05	Sir Richard Henn Collins
1905–10	Prof. S. H. Butcher
1910–23	Dr F. G. Kenyon
1922–29	Prof. J. W. Mackail
1929–34	Prof. H. A. Ormerod
1934-	Prof. J. F. Dobson
	(in some of the wartime years, the Council elected the President as its Chairman)
1944–47	Sir John Sheppard
1948–51	Miss E. Archibald
1951–56	Prof. T. B. L. Webster
1956–64	Prof. W. S. Maguinness
1964–69	Canon C. B. Armstrong
1969–77	Prof. B. R. Rees
1977–90	Prof. G. Kerferd
1990–95	Prof. J. Percival
1995–2002	Prof. C. Rowe
2002–	Prof. R. L. Fowler

* In 1997 the title was changed to 'Chair'.

Honorary Secretaries

1903–06	Prof. J. P. Postgate	Trinity College, Cambridge
1903–11	Prof. E. A. Sonnenschein	Birmingham University

1906–08	Mr E. A. Harrison	Trinity College, Cambridge
1908–13	Mr J. H. Sleeman	Sidney Sussex College, Cambridge; later Sheffield
1911–15	Mr M. O. B. Caspari (later Cary)	Birmingham, later University College London
1913–18	Mr W. H. Duke	Jesus College, Cambridge
1915–20	Prof. D. A. Slater	Bedford College, London
1918–20	Prof. P. N. Ure	Reading University
1920–26	Rev. G. C. Richards	Oriel College, Oxford
1920–23	Prof. A. C. Pearson	Liverpool University, later Cambridge
1923–25	Mr M. P. Charlesworth	Jesus College, Cambridge
1925–27	Mr C. T. Seltman	Queens' College, Cambridge
1926–30	Mr E. N. Gardiner	Epsom College
1927–34	Miss E. C. Gedge	Westfield College, London
1930–36	Mr R. M. Rattenbury	Trinity College, Cambridge
1934–38	Miss N. Jolliffe	Royal Holloway College, later Girton College, Cambridge
1938–48	Mr J. J. R. Bridge	HM Inspector of Schools (rtd)
1940–41	Miss D. H. F. Gray	St Hugh's College, Oxford
1941–43	Mr W. S. Barrett	Keble College, Oxford
1943–63	Prof. L. J. D. Richardson	(C) Cardiff University
1948–68	Mr T. W. Melluish	(B) Bec School, London
1963–69	Prof. B. R. Rees	(C) Cardiff University
1968–71	Mr M. R. F Gunningham	(B) London
1969–72	Dr John Landels	(C) Reading University
1971–75	Miss E. Tucker	(B) Christ's Hospital School, Hertford
1972–79	Mr C. Collard	(C) University of Kent, later University College Swansea
1976–83	Mrs E. Varney	(B) Lincoln
1979–89	Dr J. Percival	(C) Cardiff University
1983–90	Miss H. M. Jones	(B) Pinner
1989–2003	Prof. M. Schofield	(C) St John's College, Cambridge
1989–92	Mrs M. Baldock	(B) Haberdasher Aske's School for Girls
1992–97	Mrs A. M. Hunt	(B) London
1997–	Mrs B. Finney	(B) Bolton
2003–	Dr D. Cairns	(C) Glasgow University

(C) = Secretary to Council (B) = Branches Secretary

Executive Secretary

| 1999- | Ms C. Roberts |

Honorary Treasurers

1903–04	Mr J. W. Mackail (pro tem)	Board of Education
1904–06	Dr F. G. Kenyon	British Museum
1906–11	Prof. W. C. Flamstead Walters	King's College, London
1911–15	Mr R. C. Seaton	Reigate

1915–18	Mr H. Williamson	Manchester
1918–21	Mr E. N. Gardiner	Epsom College
1921–26	Dr H. A. Ormerod	Liverpool University, later Leeds
1926–27	Prof. M. T. Smiley	University College, London
1927–32	Mr H. F. Hose	Dulwich College
1932–35	Mr F. C. G. Langford	Dulwich College
1935–47	Miss E. C. Gedge	Westfield College, London
1947–57	Mr J. Shields	Queen Mary's School, Basingstoke
1957–63	Mrs E. Hooker	Birmingham University
1963–72	Prof. L. A. Moritz	Cardiff University
1972–85	Dr G. R. Watson	Nottingham University
1985–99	Prof. R. Wallace	Keele University
1999	Mr K. Rix	Accountant, London
2000–	Mr P. Hooker	Hoare Govett, London

Editors of Journals

Classical Review

1887–93	Prof. J. B. Mayor	King's College, London
1894–97	Mr G. E . Marindin	Farnham
1898–07	Prof. J. P. Postgate	Trinity College, Cambridge
1907–20	Dr W. H. D. Rouse	Perse School, Cambridge
1911–20	Mr A. D. Godley	Magdalen College, Oxford
1921–22	Mr J. T. Sheppard	Kings College, Cambridge
1921–22	Mr R. W. Livingstone	Corpus Christi College, Oxford
1923–43	Mr E. A. Harrison	Trinity College, Cambridge
1923–34	Prof. W. M. Calder	Manchester University, later Edinburgh
1935	Mr M. Bowra	Wadham College, Oxford
1935–74	Prof. C. J. Fordyce	Glasgow University
1943–60	Mr R. M. Rattenbury	Trinity College, Cambridge
1961–67	Prof. H. Tredennick	Royal Holloway College
1968–76	Mr J. S. Morrison	University (now Wolfson) College, Cambridge
1975–87	Mr L. D. Reynolds	Brasenose College, Oxford
1976–87	Mr N. G. Wilson	Lincoln College, Oxford
1987–93	Dr A. F. Garvie	Glasgow University
1987–93	Prof. H. Hine	St Andrews University
1993–97	Prof. C. Carey	Royal Holloway, London
1993–2002	Prof. R. G. Mayer	King's College, London
1997–2001	Prof. M. Whitby	Warwick University
2001-	Prof. J. G. F. Powell	Royal Holloway, London
2002-	Prof. D. Scourfield	National University of Ireland, Maynooth

Classical Quarterly

1907–10	Prof. J. P. Postgate	Trinity College, Cambridge, later Liverpool
1911–26	Prof. E. V. Arnold	University College of North Wales, Bangor
1911–30	Mr F. W. Hall	St John's College, Oxford
1927–34	Mr R. L. Hackforth	Sidney Sussex College, Cambridge
1931–35	Mr J. D. Denniston	Hertford College, Oxford
1935–39	Mr B. L. Hallward	Peterhouse, Cambridge
1936–47	Mr M. Platnauer	Brasenose College, Oxford
1939–46	Mr W. K. C. Guthrie	Peterhouse, Cambridge
1947	Mr W. Hamilton	Trinity College, Cambridge
1947–53	Mr D. L. Page	Christ Church, Oxford, later Trinity College, Cambridge
1947–52	Mr G. T. Griffith	Gonville & Caius College, Cambridge
1952–56	Dr G. F. Chilver	Queen's College, Oxford
1953–59	Mr D. W. Lucas	King's College, Cambridge
1956–62	Mr A. R. Harrison	Merton College, Oxford
1959–65	Dr E. J. Kenney	Peterhouse, Cambridge
1962–68	Prof. K. J. Dover	St Andrews University
1965–70	Mr D. A. Russell	St John's College, Oxford
1968–75	Prof. J. P. A. Gould	University College Swansea
1970–77	Dr M. Winterbottom	Worcester College, Oxford
1975–81	Prof. A. A. Long	Liverpool University
1977–81	Prof. R. M. Ogilvie	St Andrews University
1981–86	Prof. M. D. Reeve	Exeter College, Oxford, later Pembroke College, Cambridge
1982–87	Dr T. Cornell	University College London
1986–92	Dr D. Sedley	Christ's College, Cambridge
1987–93	Dr A. Hollis	Keble College, Oxford
1992–97	Dr P. C. Millett	Downing College, Cambridge
1993–98	Dr S. Heyworth	Wadham College, Oxford
1997–02	Prof. C. Collard	University of Wales Swansea (rtd)
1998–00	Prof. J. S. Richardson	Edinburgh University
2000–	Prof. R. Maltby	Leeds University
2002–	Dr M. Griffin	Somerville College, Oxford (rtd)

The Year's Work In Classical Studies

1906–10	Dr W. H. D. Rouse	Perse School, Cambridge
1911–12	Mr L. Whibley	Pembroke College, Cambridge
1913–15	Mr C. Bailey	Balliol College, Oxford
1916–17	Mr S. Gaselee	Magdalene College, Cambridge
1918–22	Mr W. H. S. Jones	St Catharine's College, Cambridge
1923–26	Prof. D. S. Robertson	Trinity College, Cambridge
1926–39	Dr S. G. Owen	Christ Church, Oxford (rtd)
1939–45	Prof. G. B. A. Fletcher	King's College, Newcastle
1945–47	Mr M. Platnauer	Brasenose College, Oxford

Greece & Rome

1931–53	Rev. C. J. Ellingham	City of London School
1931–46	Mr A. G. Russell	St Olave's School, London, later Holt School, Liverpool
1946–71	Mr E. R. A. Sewter	Newbury Grammar School
1953–64	Mr G. T. W. Hooker	Birmingham University
1964–70	Mr J. Muir	King's College, London
1970–01	Prof. P. Walcot	Cardiff University
1971–77	Mr A. C. F. Verity	Bristol Grammar School
1977–	Mr I. McAuslan	King Edward VI School, Southampton, later Eton College
2001–	Dr K. Clarke	St Hilda's College, Oxford
2001–	Dr C. Burnand	Abingdon School

CA News

1989–	Dr J. March	Institute of Classical Studies

Appendix 4

THE CA ARCHIVE

By CHRISTOPHER STRAY

The archive has in the past been held by one of the Secretaries, and as a result has been moved on several occasions. Some files have been held by individual office holders (e.g. secretaries of committees), and this probably accounts for some losses and currently unlocated files. The CA now has a permanent base in the Institute of Classical Studies, and from the end of 2003, the archive will be held there. It is hoped that it will then be properly catalogued. A rough listing is given below.

Council: minutes 1904–6, 1908–12, 1912–21, 1921–6, 1926–30, 1931–41, 1941–7, 1947–53, 1955–8, 1963–9, 1969–72, 1972–8. Index 1903–14.

AGM: minutes 1903–14, 1963–70. Index 1904–14.

Correspondence (mostly secretary's): 1936–48 (3 files), 1957–68 (box file), 1972–7, 1979–84, 1984–8.

Correspondence with branches 1960–8; correspondence with JACT, 1980s; new schemes, 1980s.

Pamphlets, circulars, presidential addresses.

Propaganda and the press: *Discovery*, *The Place of Classics*, *The Listener* (cuttings), letters to newspapers (mid 60s), *Classics in the School Curriculum*.

Finance and external relations: Doherty Trust, J. Spedan Lewis, John Benjamins, F.I.E.C.

Classical Journals Board: minutes 1908–60 (2 vols.), 1987-date. Correspondence files 1965–8, 1969, 1982–7, late 80s. Minutes of the Board of Management of *Greece & Rome* (from foundation in 1931 till its merger with the Classical Journals Board in 2000).

Proceedings (1904–88).

INDEX

Note: the various aspects of the CA's organisation, history and activities are distributed throughout this index. For an alphabetical list of these entries, see the entry on 'Classical Association'.